NEW PERSPECTIVES ON
Microsoft® PowerPoint® 2010

INTRODUCTORY

Beverly B. Zimmerman
Brigham Young University

S. Scott Zimmerman
Brigham Young University

Katherine T. Pinard

COURSE TECHNOLOGY
CENGAGE Learning·

Australia • Brazil • Japan • Korea • Mexico • Singapore • Spain • United Kingdom • United States

COURSE TECHNOLOGY
CENGAGE Learning™

New Perspectives on Microsoft PowerPoint 2010, Introductory

Vice President, Publisher: Nicole Jones Pinard

Executive Editor: Marie L. Lee

Associate Acquisitions Editor: Brandi Shailer

Senior Product Manager: Kathy Finnegan

Product Manager: Leigh Hefferon

Associate Product Manager: Julia Leroux-Lindsey

Editorial Assistant: Jacqueline Lacaire

Director of Marketing: Cheryl Costantini

Senior Marketing Manager: Ryan DeGrote

Marketing Coordinator: Kristen Panciocco

Developmental Editor: Kim T. M. Crowley

Senior Content Project Manager: Jill Braiewa

Composition: GEX Publishing Services

Art Director: Marissa Falco

Text Designer: Althea Chen

Cover Designer: Roycroft Design

Cover Art: © Veer Incorporated

Copyeditor: Michael Beckett

Proofreader: Kathy Orrino

Indexer: Alexandra Nickerson

For product information and technology assistance, contact us at
Cengage Learning Customer & Sales Support, 1-800-354-9706

For permission to use material from this text or product, submit all requests online at **www.cengage.com/permissions**
Further permissions questions can be emailed to
permissionrequest@cengage.com

Some of the product names and company names used in this book have been used for identification purposes only and may be trademarks or registered trademarks of their respective manufacturers and sellers.

Microsoft and the Office logo are either registered trademarks or trademarks of Microsoft Corporation in the United States and/or other countries. Course Technology, Cengage Learning is an independent entity from the Microsoft Corporation, and not affiliated with Microsoft in any manner.

Disclaimer: Any fictional data related to persons or companies or URLs used throughout this book is intended for instructional purposes only. At the time this book was printed, any such data was fictional and not belonging to any real persons or companies.

Library of Congress Control Number: 2010931789

ISBN-13: 978-0-538-75373-9

ISBN-10: 0-538-75373-0

Course Technology
20 Channel Center Street
Boston, MA 02210
USA

Cengage Learning is a leading provider of customized learning solutions with office locations around the globe, including Singapore, the United Kingdom, Australia, Mexico, Brazil, and Japan. Locate your local office at:
international.cengage.com/global

Cengage Learning products are represented in Canada by Nelson Education, Ltd.

To learn more about Course Technology, visit **www.cengage.com/course technology**

To learn more about Cengage Learning, visit **www.cengage.com**

Purchase any of our products at your local college store or at our preferred online store **www.cengagebrain.com**

Printed in the United States of America
2 3 4 5 6 7 16 15 14 13 12 11

Preface

The New Perspectives Series' critical-thinking, problem-solving approach is the ideal way to prepare students to transcend point-and-click skills and take advantage of all that Microsoft Office 2010 has to offer.

In developing the New Perspectives Series, our goal was to create books that give students the software concepts and practical skills they need to succeed beyond the classroom. We've updated our proven case-based pedagogy with more practical content to make learning skills more meaningful to students.

With the New Perspectives Series, students understand *why* they are learning *what* they are learning, and are fully prepared to apply their skills to real-life situations.

"The new Visual Overviews give students valuable insight into what they will learn in each tutorial session. Clearly seeing what's ahead will engage students from the start."

—Diane Shingledecker
Portland Community
College

About This Book

This book provides thorough coverage of PowerPoint 2010, and includes the following:

- The framework in which students can create well-designed presentations using the fundamental features of PowerPoint 2010, including slide layouts, placeholders, themes, transitions, animations, sounds, colors, and backgrounds
- Coverage of the most important PowerPoint skills—planning and creating a presentation, inserting and modifying text and graphics, adding media and charts, and collaborating with others
- Exploration of new features, including working in Backstage view, using the Broadcast feature to present a slide show over the Internet, formatting and trimming video clips, and saving a presentation to SkyDrive

New for this edition!

- Each session begins with a Visual Overview, a new two-page spread that includes colorful, enlarged screenshots with numerous callouts and key term definitions, giving students a comprehensive preview of the topics covered in the session, as well as a handy study guide.
- New ProSkills boxes provide guidance for how to use the software in real-world, professional situations, and related ProSkills exercises integrate the technology skills students learn with one or more of the following soft skills: decision making, problem solving, teamwork, verbal communication, and written communication.
- Important steps are now highlighted in yellow with attached margin notes to help students pay close attention to completing the steps correctly and avoid time-consuming rework.

System Requirements

This book assumes a typical installation of Microsoft PowerPoint 2010 and Microsoft Windows 7 Ultimate using an Aero theme. (You can also complete the material in this text using another version of Windows 7, such as Home Premium, or earlier versions of the Windows operating system. You will see only minor differences in how some windows look.) The browser used for any steps that require a browser is Internet Explorer 8.

www.cengage.com/ct/newperspectives

The New Perspectives Approach

Context

Each tutorial begins with a problem presented in a "real-world" case that is meaningful to students. The case sets the scene to help students understand what they will do in the tutorial.

Hands-on Approach

Each tutorial is divided into manageable sessions that combine reading and hands-on, step-by-step work. Colorful screenshots help guide students through the steps. **Trouble?** tips anticipate common mistakes or problems to help students stay on track and continue with the tutorial.

VISUAL OVERVIEW

Visual Overviews

New for this edition! Each session begins with a Visual Overview, a new two-page spread that includes colorful, enlarged screenshots with numerous callouts and key term definitions, giving students a comprehensive preview of the topics covered in the session, as well as a handy study guide.

PROSKILLS

ProSkills Boxes and Exercises

New for this edition! ProSkills boxes provide guidance for how to use the software in real-world, professional situations, and related ProSkills exercises integrate the technology skills students learn with one or more of the following soft skills: decision making, problem solving, teamwork, verbal communication, and written communication.

KEY STEP

Key Steps

New for this edition! Important steps are highlighted in yellow with attached margin notes to help students pay close attention to completing the steps correctly and avoid time-consuming rework.

INSIGHT

InSight Boxes

InSight boxes offer expert advice and best practices to help students achieve a deeper understanding of the concepts behind the software features and skills.

TIP

Margin Tips

Margin Tips provide helpful hints and shortcuts for more efficient use of the software. The Tips appear in the margin at key points throughout each tutorial, giving students extra information when and where they need it.

REVIEW

APPLY

Assessment

Retention is a key component to learning. At the end of each session, a series of Quick Check questions helps students test their understanding of the material before moving on. Engaging end-of-tutorial Review Assignments and Case Problems have always been a hallmark feature of the New Perspectives Series. Colorful bars and brief descriptions accompany the exercises, making it easy to understand both the goal and level of challenge a particular assignment holds.

REFERENCE

TASK REFERENCE

GLOSSARY/INDEX

Reference

Within each tutorial, Reference boxes appear before a set of steps to provide a succinct summary and preview of how to perform a task. In addition, a complete Task Reference at the back of the book provides quick access to information on how to carry out common tasks. Finally, each book includes a combination Glossary/Index to promote easy reference of material.

Our Complete System of Instruction

Coverage To Meet Your Needs

Whether you're looking for just a small amount of coverage or enough to fill a semester-long class, we can provide you with a textbook that meets your needs.

- Brief books typically cover the essential skills in just 2 to 4 tutorials.
- Introductory books build and expand on those skills and contain an average of 5 to 8 tutorials.
- Comprehensive books are great for a full-semester class, and contain 9 to 12+ tutorials.

So if the book you're holding does not provide the right amount of coverage for you, there's probably another offering available. Go to our Web site or contact your Course Technology sales representative to find out what else we offer.

CourseCasts – Learning on the Go. Always available…always relevant.

Want to keep up with the latest technology trends relevant to you? Visit our site to find a library of podcasts, CourseCasts, featuring a "CourseCast of the Week," and download them to your mp3 player at http://coursecasts.course.com.

Our fast-paced world is driven by technology. You know because you're an active participant—always on the go, always keeping up with technological trends, and always learning new ways to embrace technology to power your life.

Ken Baldauf, host of CourseCasts, is a faculty member of the Florida State University Computer Science Department where he is responsible for teaching technology classes to thousands of FSU students each year. Ken is an expert in the latest technology trends; he gathers and sorts through the most pertinent news and information for CourseCasts so your students can spend their time enjoying technology, rather than trying to figure it out. Open or close your lecture with a discussion based on the latest CourseCast.

Visit us at http://coursecasts.course.com to learn on the go!

Instructor Resources

We offer more than just a book. We have all the tools you need to enhance your lectures, check students' work, and generate exams in a new, easier-to-use and completely revised package. This book's Instructor's Manual, ExamView testbank, PowerPoint presentations, data files, solution files, figure files, and a sample syllabus are all available on a single CD-ROM or for downloading at http://www.cengage.com/coursetechnology.

Content for Online Learning

Course Technology has partnered with the leading distance learning solution providers and class-management platforms today. To access this material, visit www.cengage.com/webtutor and search for your title. Instructor resources include the following: additional case projects, sample syllabi, PowerPoint presentations, and more. For students to access this material, they must have purchased a WebTutor PIN-code specific to this title and your campus platform. The resources for students might include (based on instructor preferences): topic reviews, review questions, practice tests, and more. For additional information, please contact your sales representative.

SAM: Skills Assessment Manager

SAM is designed to help bring students from the classroom to the real world. It allows students to train and test on important computer skills in an active, hands-on environment.

SAM's easy-to-use system includes powerful interactive exams, training, and projects on the most commonly used Microsoft Office applications. SAM simulates the Office application environment, allowing students to demonstrate their knowledge and think through the skills by performing real-world tasks, such as bolding text or setting up slide transitions. Add in live-in-the-application projects, and students are on their way to truly learning and applying skills to business-centric documents.

Designed to be used with the New Perspectives Series, SAM includes handy page references, so students can print helpful study guides that match the New Perspectives textbooks used in class. For instructors, SAM also includes robust scheduling and reporting features.

Acknowledgments

The authors would like to thank the following reviewers for their valuable feedback on this book: Douglas Albert, Finger Lakes Community College; Sylvia Amito'elau, Coastline Community College; Sherrie Geitgey, Northwest State Community College; Kristen Hockman, University of Missouri–Columbia; Ahmed Kamel, Concordia College; Fred Manley, Northeast Wisconsin Technical College; Kelly Swain, Humber College; Barbara Tollinger, Sinclair Community College; Karen Toreson, Shoreline Community College; Raymond Yu, Douglas College; and Violet Zhang, George Brown College. We also would like to thank the always hard-working editorial and production teams at Course Technology, including Marie Lee, Executive Editor; Brandi Shailer, Associate Acquisitions Editor; Leigh Hefferon, Product Manager; Julia Leroux-Lindsey, Associate Product Manager; Jacqueline Lacaire, Editorial Assistant; Jill Braiewa, Senior Content Product Manager; Christian Kunciw, Manuscript Quality Assurance Supervisor; and MQA Testers Serge Palladino, Susan Pedicini, Danielle Shaw, and Marianne Snow. Special thanks to Kathy Finnegan, Senior Product Manager, whose leadership on the New Perspectives Series results in such beautiful, high-quality books, and to Kim Crowley, Developmental Editor, whose thoroughness and commitment to quality and accuracy were invaluable. Finally, I would like to thank Scott and Beverly Zimmerman for the opportunity to work on this book. Their friendship over the years has been important to me, and I have learned a tremendous amount working with them. Their commitment to excellence is an inspiration.
–Katherine T. Pinard

We would like to thank our co-author, Katherine Pinard, for her diligent and expert work. She has been a joy to work with these past 20 years. We also express our deep-felt thanks to all the editors, marketers, managers, and other workers at Course Technology. It was our honor to author the first book published by Course Technology back in 1990. We have loved working with such a vibrant company and have enjoyed seeing its spectacular growth since then. Thanks to all of you.

We dedicate this book to the memory of our daughter, Sheri Lynne Zimmerman Klein (1977-2009).
–Scott and Beverly Zimmerman

TABLE OF CONTENTS

POWERPOINT LEVEL II TUTORIALS

OBJECTIVES

- Explore the programs in Microsoft Office
- Start programs and switch between them
- Explore common window elements
- Minimize, maximize, and restore windows
- Use the Ribbon, tabs, and buttons
- Use the contextual tabs, the Mini toolbar, and shortcut menus
- Save, close, and open a file
- Learn how to share files using SkyDrive
- Use the Help system
- Preview and print a file
- Exit programs

Getting Started with Microsoft Office 2010

Preparing a Meeting Agenda

Case | *Recycled Palette*

Recycled Palette, a company in Oregon founded by Ean Nogella in 2006, sells 100 percent recycled latex paint to both individuals and businesses in the area. The high-quality recycled paint is filtered to industry standards and tested for performance and environmental safety. The paint is available in both 1 gallon cans and 5 gallon pails, and comes in colors ranging from white to shades of brown, blue, green, and red. The demand for affordable recycled paint has been growing each year. Ean and all his employees use Microsoft Office 2010, which provides everyone in the company with the power and flexibility to store a variety of information, create consistent files, and share data. In this tutorial, you'll review how the company's employees use Microsoft Office 2010.

STARTING DATA FILES

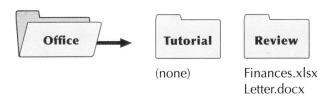

Office → Tutorial — (none)

Review — Finances.xlsx — Letter.docx

VISUAL OVERVIEW

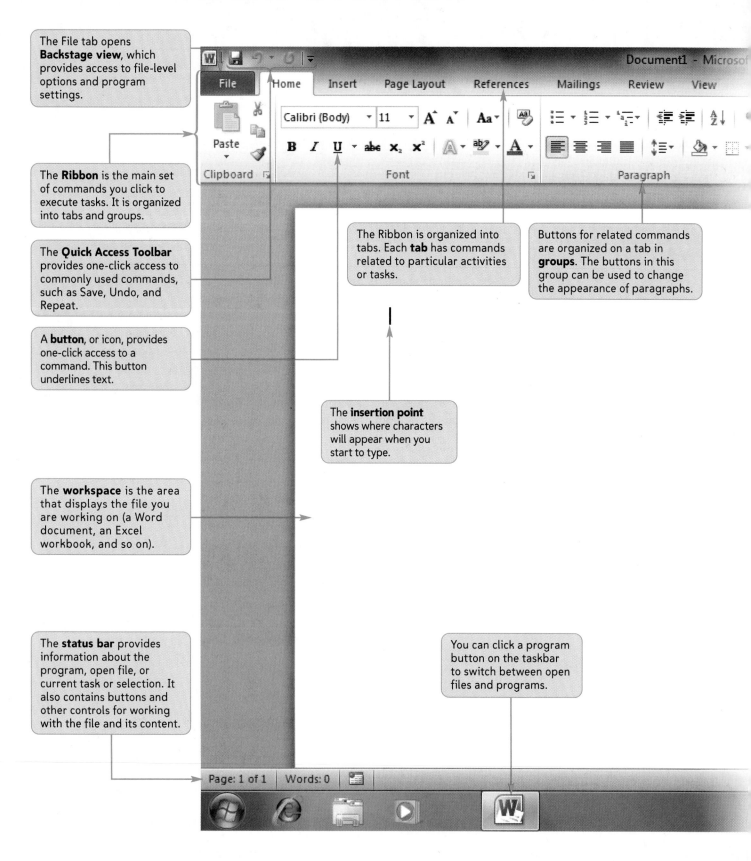

The File tab opens **Backstage view**, which provides access to file-level options and program settings.

The **Ribbon** is the main set of commands you click to execute tasks. It is organized into tabs and groups.

The **Quick Access Toolbar** provides one-click access to commonly used commands, such as Save, Undo, and Repeat.

A **button**, or icon, provides one-click access to a command. This button underlines text.

The **workspace** is the area that displays the file you are working on (a Word document, an Excel workbook, and so on).

The **status bar** provides information about the program, open file, or current task or selection. It also contains buttons and other controls for working with the file and its content.

The Ribbon is organized into tabs. Each **tab** has commands related to particular activities or tasks.

Buttons for related commands are organized on a tab in **groups**. The buttons in this group can be used to change the appearance of paragraphs.

The **insertion point** shows where characters will appear when you start to type.

You can click a program button on the taskbar to switch between open files and programs.

COMMON WINDOW ELEMENTS

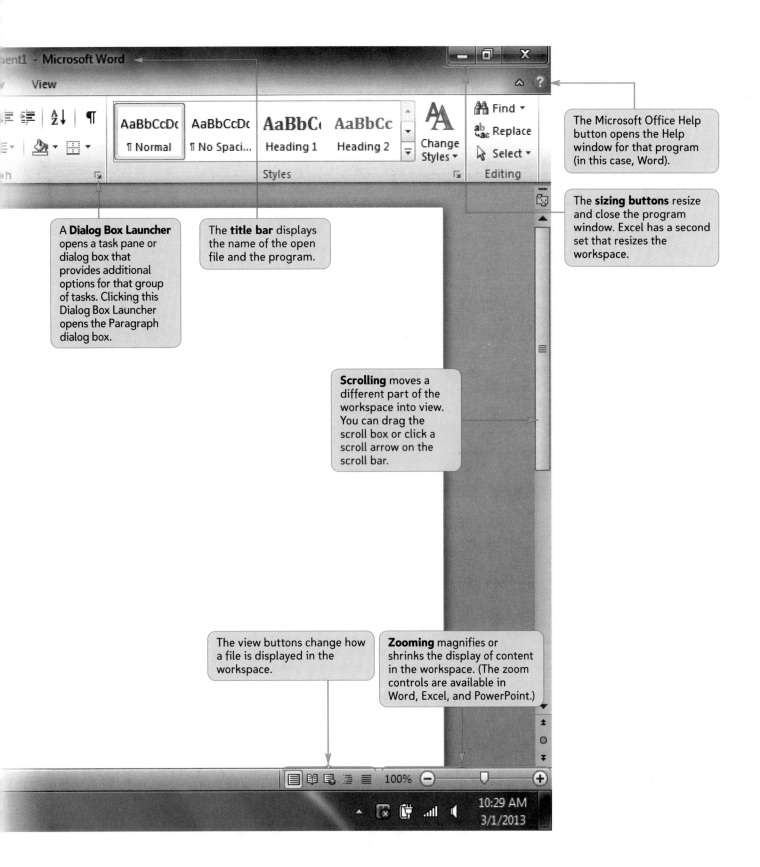

A **Dialog Box Launcher** opens a task pane or dialog box that provides additional options for that group of tasks. Clicking this Dialog Box Launcher opens the Paragraph dialog box.

The **title bar** displays the name of the open file and the program.

The Microsoft Office Help button opens the Help window for that program (in this case, Word).

The **sizing buttons** resize and close the program window. Excel has a second set that resizes the workspace.

Scrolling moves a different part of the workspace into view. You can drag the scroll box or click a scroll arrow on the scroll bar.

The view buttons change how a file is displayed in the workspace.

Zooming magnifies or shrinks the display of content in the workspace. (The zoom controls are available in Word, Excel, and PowerPoint.)

Exploring Microsoft Office 2010

TIP

For additional information about the available suites, go to the Microsoft Web site.

Microsoft Office 2010, or **Office**, is a collection of Microsoft programs. Office is available in many suites, each of which contains a different combination of these programs. For example, the Professional suite includes Word, Excel, PowerPoint, Access, Outlook, Publisher, and OneNote. Other suites are available and can include more or fewer programs. Each Office program contains valuable tools to help you accomplish many tasks, such as composing reports, analyzing data, preparing presentations, compiling information, sending email, planning schedules, and compiling notes.

Microsoft Word 2010, or **Word**, is a computer program you use to enter, edit, and format text. The files you create in Word are called **documents**, although many people use the term *document* to refer to any file created on a computer. Word, often called a word-processing program, offers many special features that help you compose and update all types of documents, ranging from letters and newsletters to reports, brochures, faxes, and even books, in attractive and readable formats. You can also use Word to create, insert, and position figures, tables, and other graphics to enhance the look of your documents. For example, the Recycled Palette employees create business letters using Word.

Microsoft Excel 2010, or **Excel**, is a computer program you use to enter, calculate, analyze, and present numerical data. You can do some of this in Word with tables, but Excel provides many more tools for recording and formatting numbers as well as performing calculations. The graphics capabilities in Excel also enable you to display data visually. You might, for example, generate a pie chart or a bar chart to help people quickly see the significance of and the connections between information. The files you create in Excel are called **workbooks** (commonly referred to as spreadsheets), and Excel is often called a spreadsheet program. The Recycled Palette accounting department uses a line chart in an Excel workbook to visually track the company's financial performance.

Microsoft Access 2010, or **Access**, is a computer program used to enter, maintain, and retrieve related information (or data) in a format known as a database. The files you create in Access are called **databases**, and Access is often referred to as a database or relational database program. With Access, you can create forms to make data entry easier, and you can create professional reports to improve the readability of your data. The Recycled Palette operations department tracks the company's inventory in an Access database.

Microsoft PowerPoint 2010, or **PowerPoint**, is a computer program you use to create a collection of slides that can contain text, charts, pictures, sound, movies, multimedia, and so on. The files you create in PowerPoint are called **presentations**, and PowerPoint is often called a presentation graphics program. You can show these presentations on your computer monitor, project them onto a screen as a slide show, print them, share them over the Internet, or display them on the Web. You can also use PowerPoint to generate presentation-related documents such as audience handouts, outlines, and speakers' notes. The Recycled Palette marketing department uses a PowerPoint slide presentation to promote its paints.

Microsoft Outlook 2010, or **Outlook**, is a computer program you use to send, receive, and organize email; plan your schedule; arrange meetings; organize contacts; create a to-do list; and record notes. You can also use Outlook to print schedules, task lists, phone directories, and other documents. Outlook is often referred to as an information management program. The Recycled Palette staff members use Outlook to send and receive email, plan their schedules, and create to-do lists.

Although each Office program individually is a strong tool, their potential is even greater when used together.

Teamwork: Integrating Office Programs

One of the main advantages of Office is **integration**, the ability to share information between programs. Integration ensures consistency and accuracy, and it saves time because you don't have to reenter the same information in several Office programs. It also means that team members can effortlessly share Office files. Team members can create files based on their skills and information that can be used by others as needed. The staff at Recycled Palette uses the integration features of Office every day, as described in the following examples:

- The accounting department created an Excel bar chart on fourth-quarter results for the previous two years, and inserted it into the quarterly financial report created in Word. The Word report includes a hyperlink that employees can click to open the Excel workbook and view the original data.
- The operations department included an Excel pie chart of sales percentages by paint colors on a PowerPoint slide, which is part of a presentation to stockholders.
- The marketing department produced a mailing to promote its recycled paints to local contractors and designers by combining a form letter created in Word with an Access database that stores the names and addresses of these potential customers.
- A sales representative merged the upcoming promotion letter that the marketing department created in Word with an Outlook contact list containing the names and addresses of prospective customers.

   Even these few examples of how information from one Office program can be integrated with another illustrate how integration can save time and effort. Each team member can focus on creating files in the program best suited to convey the information he or she is responsible for. Yet, everyone can share the files, using them as needed for their specific purpose.

Starting Office Programs

You can start any Office program from the Start menu on the taskbar. As soon as the program starts, you can immediately begin to create new files or work with existing ones.

Starting an Office Program

- On the taskbar, click the Start button.
- On the Start menu, click All Programs, click Microsoft Office, and then click the name of the program to start.

or

- Click the name of the program to start in the left pane of the Start menu.

You'll start Word using the Start button.

To start Word and open a new, blank document:

1. Make sure your computer is on and the Windows desktop appears on your screen.

   Trouble? If your screen varies slightly from those shown in the figures, your computer might be set up differently. The figures in this book were created while running Windows 7 with the Aero feature turned on, but how your screen looks depends on the version of Windows you are using, the resolution of your screen, and other settings.

2. On the taskbar, click the **Start** button 🔵, and then click **All Programs** to display the All Programs list.

3. Click **Microsoft Office**, and then point to **Microsoft Word 2010**. Depending on how your computer is set up, your desktop and menu might contain different icons and commands. See Figure 1.

Figure 1	Start menu with All Programs list displayed

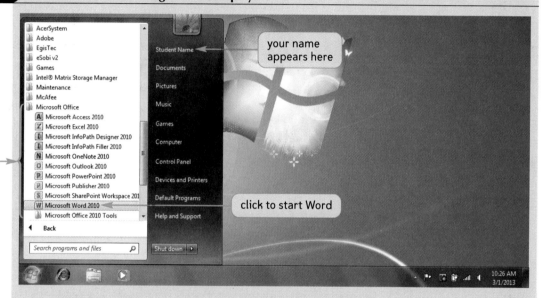

Trouble? If you don't see Microsoft Office on the All Programs list, point to Microsoft Word 2010 on the All Programs menu. If you still don't see Microsoft Word 2010, ask your instructor or technical support person for help.

4. Click **Microsoft Word 2010**. Word starts and a new, blank document opens. Refer to the Visual Overview to review the common program window elements.

   Trouble? If the Word window doesn't fill your entire screen as shown in the Visual Overview, the window is not maximized, or expanded to its full size. You'll maximize the window shortly.

You can have more than one Office program open at once. You'll use this same method to start Excel and open a new, blank workbook.

To start Excel and open a new, blank workbook:

▶ 1. On the taskbar, click the **Start** button 🔵, click **All Programs** to display the All Programs list, and then click **Microsoft Office**.

Trouble? If you don't see Microsoft Office on the All Programs list, point to Microsoft Excel 2010 on the All Programs list. If you still don't see Microsoft Excel 2010, ask your instructor or technical support person for help.

▶ 2. Click **Microsoft Excel 2010**. Excel starts and a new, blank workbook opens. See Figure 2.

| Figure 2 | New, blank Excel workbook |

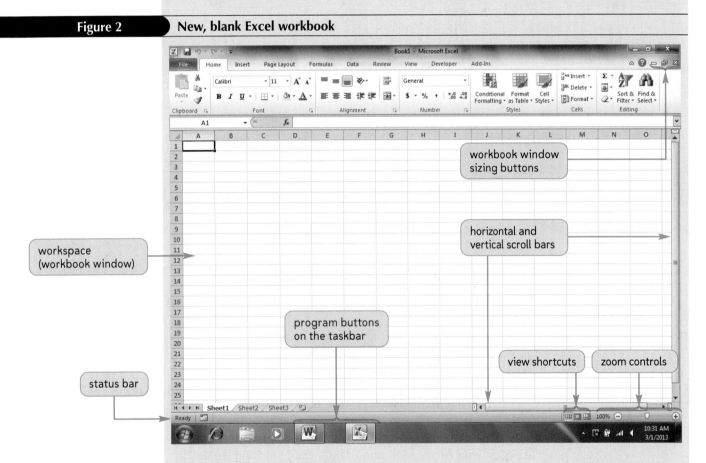

Trouble? If the Excel window doesn't fill your entire screen, the window is not maximized, or expanded to its full size. You'll maximize the window shortly.

Switching Between Open Programs and Files

Two programs are running at the same time—Word and Excel. The taskbar contains buttons for both programs. When you have two or more programs running or two files within the same program open, you can click the program buttons on the taskbar to switch from one program or file to another. When you point to a program button, a thumbnail (or small picture) of each open file in that program is displayed. You can then click the thumbnail of the file you want to make active. The employees at Recycled Palette often work in several programs and files at once.

To switch between the open Word and Excel files:

1. On the taskbar, point to the **Microsoft Word** program button [W]. A thumbnail of the open Word document appears. See Figure 3.

Figure 3   Thumbnail of the open Word document

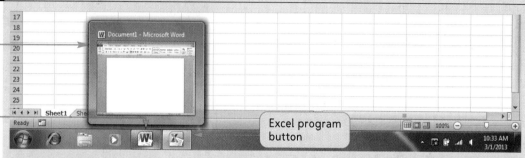

click the thumbnail that appears to make the file active

point to the Word program button

Excel program button

---

2. Click the **Document1 - Microsoft Word** thumbnail. The active program switches from Excel to Word.

Exploring Common Window Elements

As you can see, many elements in both the Word and Excel program windows are the same. In fact, most Office programs have these same elements. Because these elements are the same in each program, after you've learned one program, it's easy to learn the others.

Resizing the Program Window and Workspace

TIP

Excel has two sets of sizing buttons. The top set controls the program window and the bottom set controls the workspace.

There are three different sizing buttons that appear on the right side of a program window's title bar. The Minimize button [—], which is the left button, hides a window so that only its program button is visible on the taskbar. The middle button changes name and function depending on the status of the window—the Maximize button [□] expands the window to the full screen size or to the program window size, and the Restore Down button [▣] returns the window to a predefined size. The Close button [X], on the right, exits the program or closes the file.

The sizing buttons give you the flexibility to arrange the program and file windows to best fit your needs. Most often, you'll want to maximize the program window and workspace to take advantage of the full screen size you have available. If you have several files open, you might want to restore down their windows so that you can see more than one window at a time, or you might want to minimize programs or files you are not working on at the moment.

To resize the windows and workspaces:

1. On the Word title bar, click the **Minimize** button [—]. The Word program window is reduced to a taskbar button. The Excel program window is visible again.

2. On the Excel title bar, click the **Maximize** button [□] to expand the Excel program window to fill the screen, if necessary.

3. In the bottom set of Excel sizing buttons, click the **Restore Window** button 🗗. The workspace is resized smaller than the full program window. See Figure 4.

Figure 4	Resized Excel window and workspace

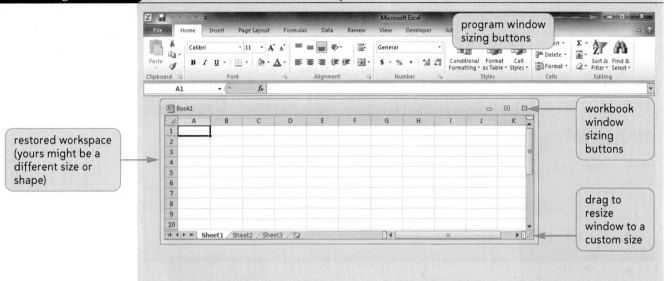

restored workspace (yours might be a different size or shape)

program window sizing buttons

workbook window sizing buttons

drag to resize window to a custom size

---

4. On the workbook window, click the **Maximize** button 🔲. The workspace expands to fill the program window.

5. On the taskbar, click the **Microsoft Word** 📄 program button. The Word program window returns to its previous size.

6. On the Word title bar, click the **Maximize** button 🔲 if necessary to expand the Word program to fill the screen.

Switching Views

Each program has a variety of views, or ways to display the file in the workspace. For example, Word has five views: Print Layout, Full Screen Reading, Web Layout, Outline, and Draft. The content of the file doesn't change from view to view, although the presentation of the content does. In Word, for example, Print Layout view shows how the document would appear as a printed page, whereas Web Layout view shows how the document would appear as a Web page. You'll change views in later tutorials.

Zooming and Scrolling

You can zoom in to get a closer look at the content of an open document, worksheet, slide, or database report. Likewise, you can zoom out to see more of the content at a smaller size. You can select a specific percentage or size based on your file. The zoom percentage can range from 10 percent to 400 percent (Excel and PowerPoint) or 500 percent (Word). The figures shown in these tutorials show the workspace zoomed in to enhance readability. Zooming can shift part of the workspace out of view. To change which area of the workspace is visible in the program window, you can use the scroll bars. A scroll bar has arrow buttons that you can click to shift the workspace a small amount in the specified direction and a scroll box that you can drag to shift the workspace a larger amount in the direction you drag. Depending on the program and zoom level, you might see a vertical scroll bar, a horizontal scroll bar, or both.

To zoom and scroll in Word and Excel:

1. On the Word status bar, drag the **Zoom slider** to the left until the percentage is **10%**. The document is reduced to its smallest size, which makes the entire page visible but unreadable. See Figure 5.

Figure 5 | Word zoom level set to 10%

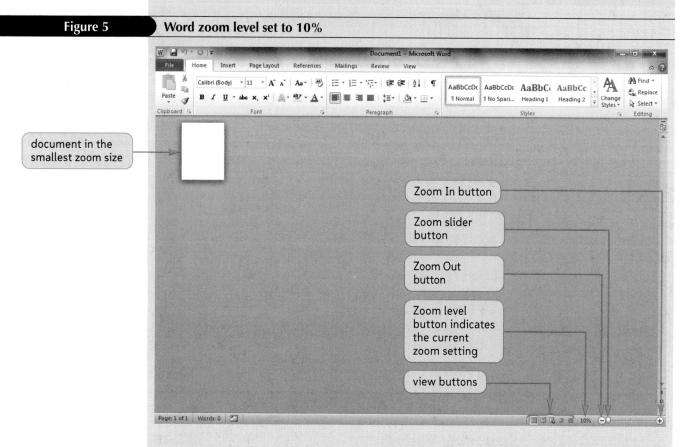

document in the smallest zoom size

Zoom In button

Zoom slider button

Zoom Out button

Zoom level button indicates the current zoom setting

view buttons

2. On the Word status bar, click the **Zoom level** button 10%. The Zoom dialog box opens. See Figure 6.

Figure 6 | Zoom dialog box

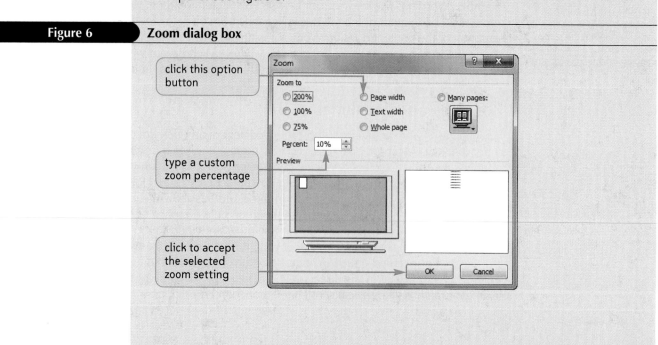

click this option button

type a custom zoom percentage

click to accept the selected zoom setting

3. Click the **Page width** option button, and then click the **OK** button. The Word document is magnified to its page width, which matches how the Word figures appear in the tutorials.

4. On the taskbar, click the **Microsoft Excel** program button. The Excel program window is displayed.

5. On the status bar, click the **Zoom In** button ⊕ twice. The worksheet is magnified to 120%, which is the zoom level that matches the Excel figures shown in the tutorials.

6. On the horizontal scroll bar, click the **right arrow** button ▶ twice. The worksheet shifts two columns to the right. Columns A and B (labeled by letter at the top of the columns) shift out of view and two other columns shift into view.

7. On the horizontal scroll bar, drag the **scroll box** all the way to the left. The worksheet shifts left to display columns A and B again.

8. On the taskbar, click the **Microsoft Word** program button. The Word program window is displayed.

Using the Ribbon

Although the tabs on the Ribbon differ from program to program, each program has two tabs in common. The first tab on the Ribbon, the File tab, opens Backstage view. Backstage view provides access to file-level features, such as creating new files, opening existing files, saving files, printing files, and closing files, as well as the most common program options. The second tab in each program—called the Home tab—contains the commands for the most frequently performed activities, including cutting and pasting, changing fonts, and using editing tools. In addition, the Insert, Review, and View tabs appear on the Ribbon in all Office programs except Access, although the commands they include might differ from program to program. Other tabs are program specific, such as the Design tab in PowerPoint and the Datasheet Tools tab in Access.

To use the Ribbon tabs:

1. In Word, point to the **Insert** tab on the Ribbon. The Insert tab is highlighted, though the Home tab with the options for using the Clipboard and formatting text remains visible.

2. Click the **Insert** tab. The Insert tab is displayed on the Ribbon. This tab provides access to all the options for adding objects such as shapes, pages, tables, illustrations, text, and symbols to a document. See Figure 7.

| Figure 7 | Insert tab on the Ribbon in Word |

Insert tab selected

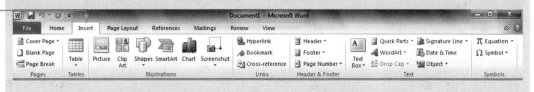

3. Click the **Home** tab. The Home tab options appear on the Ribbon.

Clicking Buttons

For the most part, when you click a button, something happens in the file. For example, the Clipboard group on the Home tab includes the Cut, Copy, Paste, and Format Painter buttons, which you can click to move or copy text, objects, and formatting.

Buttons can be **toggles**: one click turns the feature on and the next click turns the feature off. While the feature is on, the button remains colored or highlighted. For example, on the Home tab in Word, the Show/Hide ¶ button in the Paragraph group displays the nonprinting characters when toggled on and hides them when toggled off.

Some buttons have two parts: a button that accesses a command, and an arrow that opens a menu of all the commands or options available for that task. For example, the Paste button in the Clipboard group on the Home tab includes the Paste command and an arrow to access all the Paste commands and options. To select one of these commands or options, you click the button arrow and then click the command or option.

INSIGHT

How Buttons and Groups Appear on the Ribbon

The buttons and groups on the Ribbon change based on your monitor size, your screen resolution, and the size of the program window. With smaller monitors, lower screen resolutions, and reduced program windows, buttons can appear as icons without labels and a group can be condensed into a button that you click to display the group options. The figures in these tutorials were created using a screen resolution of 1024 × 768 and, unless otherwise specified, the program and workspace windows are maximized. If you are using a different screen resolution or window size, the buttons on the Ribbon might show more or fewer button names, and some groups might be reduced to a button.

You'll type text in the Word document, and then use the buttons on the Ribbon.

To use buttons on the Ribbon:

1. Type **Meeting Agenda** and then press the **Enter** key. The text appears in the first line of the document and the insertion point moves to the second line.

   Trouble? If you make a typing error, press the Backspace key to delete the incorrect letters, and then retype the text.

2. In the Paragraph group on the Home tab, click the **Show/Hide ¶** button . The nonprinting characters appear in the document, and the Show/Hide ¶ button remains toggled on. See Figure 8.

Figure 8   **Button toggled on**

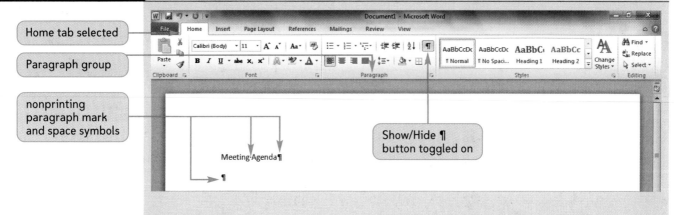

Home tab selected

Paragraph group

nonprinting paragraph mark and space symbols

Meeting·Agenda¶

Show/Hide ¶ button toggled on

Trouble? If the nonprinting characters disappear from your screen, the Show/ Hide ¶ button was already on. Repeat Step 2 to show nonprinting characters.

▶ **3.** Position the insertion point to the left of the word "Meeting," press and hold the left mouse button, drag the pointer across the text of the first line but not the paragraph mark to highlight the text, and then release the mouse button. All the text in the first line of the document (but not the paragraph mark ¶) is selected.

▶ **4.** In the Clipboard group on the Home tab, click the **Copy** button 📋. The selected text is copied to the Clipboard.

▶ **5.** Press the ↓ key. The text is deselected (no longer highlighted), and the insertion point moves to the second line in the document.

▶ **6.** In the Clipboard group on the Home tab, point to the top part of the **Paste** button 📋. Both parts of the Paste button are outlined in yellow, but the icon at the top is highlighted to indicate that it will be selected if you click the mouse button.

▶ **7.** Point to the **Paste button arrow**. The button is outlined and the button arrow is highlighted.

▶ **8.** Click the **Paste button arrow**. The paste commands and options are displayed. See Figure 9.

| Figure 9 | Two-part Paste button |

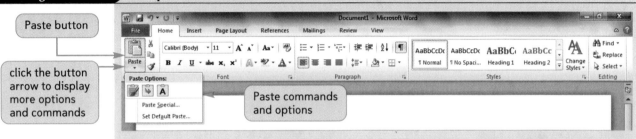

Paste button

click the button arrow to display more options and commands

Paste commands and options

▶ **9.** On the Paste Options menu, click the **Keep Text Only** button Ⓐ. The menu closes, and the text is duplicated in the second line of the document. The Paste Options button 📋(Ctrl)▾ appears below the duplicated text, providing access to the same paste commands and options.

Using Keyboard Shortcuts and Key Tips

Keyboard shortcuts can help you work faster and more efficiently. A **keyboard shortcut** is a key or combination of keys you press to access a feature or perform a command. You can use these shortcuts to access options on the Ribbon, on the Quick Access Toolbar, and in Backstage view without removing your hands from the keyboard. To access the options on the Ribbon, press the Alt key. A label, called a Key Tip, appears over each tab. To select a tab, press the corresponding key. The tab is displayed on the Ribbon and Key Tips appear over each available button or option on that tab. Press the appropriate key or keys to select a button.

You can also press combinations of keys to perform specific commands. For example, Ctrl+S is the keyboard shortcut for the Save command (you press and hold the Ctrl key while you press the S key). This type of keyboard shortcut appears in ScreenTips next to the command's name. Not all commands have this type of keyboard shortcut. Identical commands in each Office program use the same keyboard shortcut.

Using Galleries and Live Preview

Galleries and Live Preview let you quickly see how your file will be affected by a selection. A **gallery** is a menu or grid that shows a visual representation of the options available for a button. For example, the Bullet Library gallery in Word shows an icon of each bullet style you can select. Some galleries include a More button ⬝ that you click to expand the gallery to see all the options it contains. When you point to an option in a gallery, **Live Preview** shows the results that would occur in your file if you clicked that option. To continue the bullets example, when you point to a bullet style in the Bullet Library gallery, the selected text or the paragraph in which the insertion point is located appears with that bullet style. By moving the pointer from option to option, you can quickly see the text set with different bullet styles; you can then click the style you want.

To use the Bullet Library gallery and Live Preview:

➤ **1.** In the Paragraph group on the Home tab, click the **Bullets button arrow** ⬝≣ ▾. The Bullet Library gallery opens.

➤ **2.** Point to the **check mark bullet** style ✓. Live Preview shows the selected bullet style in your document. See Figure 10.

Figure 10   Live Preview of bullet icon

click the Bullets button arrow to open a gallery of bullet styles

Bullet Library gallery

Live Preview of the bullet style highlighted in the gallery

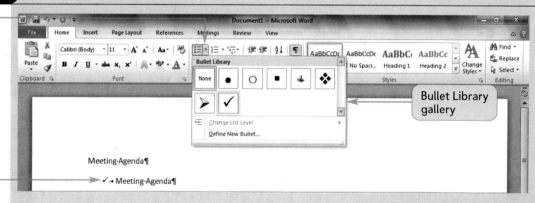

➤ **3.** Place the pointer over each of the remaining bullet styles and preview them in your document.

➤ **4.** Click the **check mark bullet** style ✓. The Bullet Library gallery closes, and the check mark bullet is added to the line, which is indented. The Bullets button remains toggled on when the insertion point is in the line with the bullet.

➤ **5.** On the second line, next to the check mark bullet, select **Meeting Agenda**. The two words are highlighted to indicate they are selected.

➤ **6.** Type **Brainstorm names for the new paint colors.** to replace the selected text with an agenda item.

➤ **7.** Press the **Enter** key twice to end the bulleted list.

Opening Dialog Boxes and Task Panes

The button to the right of some group names is the Dialog Box Launcher ⬝, which opens a task pane or dialog box related to that group of tasks. A **task pane** is a window that helps you navigate through a complex task or feature. For example, you can use the Clipboard task pane to paste some or all of the items that were cut or copied from any Office program during the current work session. A **dialog box** is a window from which you enter or choose settings for how you want to perform a task. For example, the Page Setup dialog box in Word contains options to change how the document looks. Some dialog boxes organize related information into tabs, and related options and settings are organized into groups, just as they are on the Ribbon. You select settings in a dialog box using option buttons, check boxes, text boxes, and lists to specify how you want to perform a task. In Excel, you'll use the Dialog Box Launcher to open the Page Setup dialog box.

To open the Page Setup dialog box using the Dialog Box Launcher:

▶ **1.** On the taskbar, click the **Microsoft Excel** program button 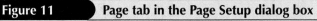 to switch from Word to Excel.

▶ **2.** On the Ribbon, click the **Page Layout** tab. The page layout options appear on the Ribbon.

▶ **3.** In the Page Setup group, click the **Dialog Box Launcher**. The Page Setup dialog box opens with the Page tab displayed. See Figure 11.

Figure 11   Page tab in the Page Setup dialog box

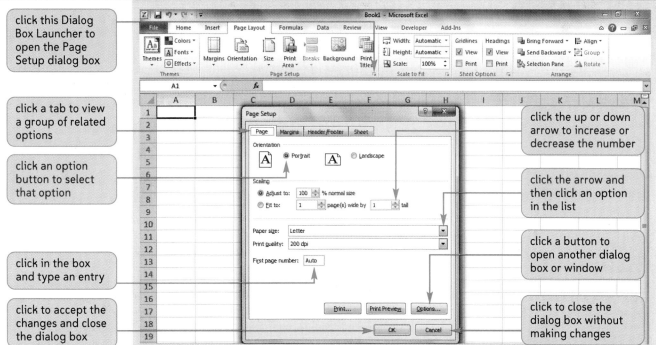

- click this Dialog Box Launcher to open the Page Setup dialog box
- click a tab to view a group of related options
- click an option button to select that option
- click in the box and type an entry
- click to accept the changes and close the dialog box
- click the up or down arrow to increase or decrease the number
- click the arrow and then click an option in the list
- click a button to open another dialog box or window
- click to close the dialog box without making changes

▶ **4.** Click the **Landscape** option button. The workbook's page orientation changes to a page wider than it is long.

▶ **5.** Click the **Sheet** tab. The dialog box displays options related to the worksheet. You can click a check box to turn an option on (checked) or off (unchecked).

▶ **6.** In the Print section of the dialog box, click the **Gridlines** check box and the **Row and column headings** check box. Check marks appear in both check boxes, indicating that these options are selected.

▶ **7.** Click the **Cancel** button. The dialog box closes without making any changes to the page setup.

TIP

You can check more than one check box in a group, but you can select only one option button in a group.

Using Contextual Tools

Some tabs, toolbars, and menus come into view as you work. Because these tools become available only as you might need them, the workspace remains less cluttered. However, tools that appear and disappear as you work can take some getting used to.

Displaying Contextual Tabs

Any object that you can select in a file has a related contextual tab. An **object** is anything that appears on your screen that can be selected and manipulated, such as a table, a picture, a shape, a chart, or an equation. A **contextual tab** is a Ribbon tab that contains commands related to the selected object so you can manipulate, edit, and format that object. Contextual tabs appear to the right of the standard Ribbon tabs just below a title label. For example, Figure 12 shows the Table Tools contextual tabs that appear when you select a table in a Word document. Although contextual tabs appear only when you select an object, they function in the same way as standard tabs on the Ribbon. Contextual tabs disappear when you click elsewhere on the screen, deselecting the object. Contextual tabs can also appear as you switch views. You'll use contextual tabs in later tutorials.

Figure 12	Table Tools contextual tabs

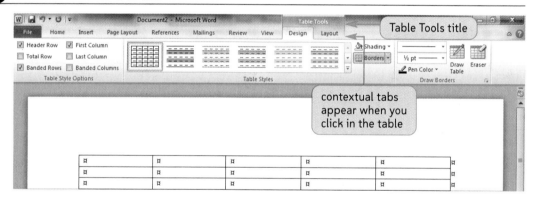

Accessing the Mini Toolbar

The **Mini toolbar**, which appears next to the pointer whenever you select text, contains buttons for the most commonly used formatting commands, such as font, font size, styles, color, alignment, and indents. The Mini toolbar buttons differ in each program. A transparent version of the Mini toolbar appears immediately after you select text. When you move the pointer over the Mini toolbar, it comes into full view so you can click the appropriate formatting button or buttons. The Mini toolbar disappears if you move the pointer away from the toolbar, press a key, or click in the workspace. The Mini toolbar can help you format your text faster, but initially you might find that the toolbar disappears unexpectedly. All the commands on the Mini toolbar are also available on the Ribbon. Note that Live Preview does not work with the Mini toolbar.

You'll use the Mini toolbar to format text you enter in the workbook.

To use the Mini toolbar to format text:

▶ **1.** If necessary, click cell **A1** (the rectangle in the upper-left corner of the worksheet).

▶ **2.** Type **Budget**. The text appears in the cell.

3. Press the **Enter** key. The text is entered in cell A1 and cell A2 is selected.

4. Type **2013** and then press the **Enter** key. The year is entered in cell A2 and cell A3 is selected.

5. Double-click cell **A1** to place the insertion point in the cell. Now you can select the text you typed.

6. Double-click **Budget** in cell A1. The selected text appears white with a black background, and the transparent Mini toolbar appears directly above the selected text. See Figure 13.

Figure 13	Transparent Mini toolbar

Mini toolbar is transparent at first

select text to display the transparent Mini toolbar

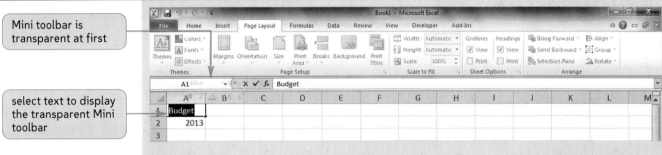

Keep the pointer directly over the Mini toolbar; otherwise, it will disappear.

7. Move the pointer over the Mini toolbar. The Mini toolbar is now completely visible, and you can click buttons.

   Trouble? If the Mini toolbar disappears, you probably moved the pointer to another area of the worksheet. To redisplay the Mini toolbar, repeat Steps 6 and 7, being careful to move the pointer directly over the Mini toolbar in Step 7.

8. On the Mini toolbar, click the **Bold** button **B**. The text in cell A1 is bold. The Mini toolbar remains visible so you can continue formatting the selected text. See Figure 14.

Figure 14	Mini toolbar with the Bold button selected

Mini toolbar remains open for additional formatting

Bold button toggled on

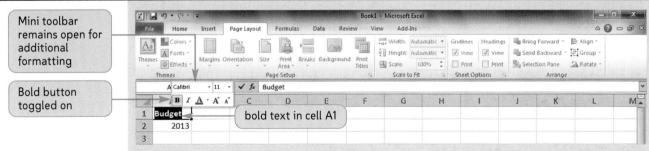

bold text in cell A1

9. Press the **Enter** key. The Mini toolbar disappears, and cell A2 is selected.

Opening Shortcut Menus

A **shortcut menu** is a list of commands related to a selection that opens when you click the right mouse button. Shortcut menus enable you to quickly access commands that you're most likely to need in the context of the task you're performing without using the tabs on the Ribbon. The shortcut menu includes commands that perform actions, commands that open dialog boxes, and galleries of options that provide Live Preview. The Mini toolbar also opens when you right-click. If you click a button on the Mini toolbar, the rest of the shortcut menu closes while the Mini toolbar remains open so you can continue formatting the selection. For example, you can right-click selected text to open a shortcut menu with a Mini toolbar; the menu will contain text-related commands such as Cut, Copy, and Paste, as well as other program-specific commands.

You'll use a shortcut menu to delete the content you entered in cell A1.

To use a shortcut menu to delete content:

1. Right-click cell **A1**. A shortcut menu opens, listing commands related to common tasks you'd perform in a cell, along with the Mini toolbar. See Figure 15.

Figure 15	Shortcut menu with Mini toolbar

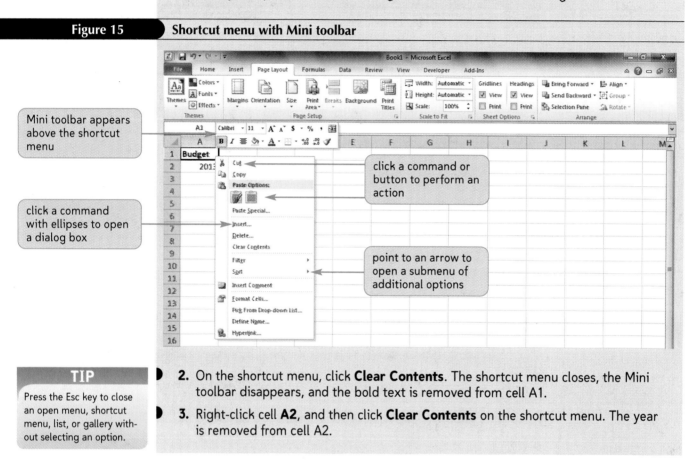

Mini toolbar appears above the shortcut menu

click a command with ellipses to open a dialog box

click a command or button to perform an action

point to an arrow to open a submenu of additional options

2. On the shortcut menu, click **Clear Contents**. The shortcut menu closes, the Mini toolbar disappears, and the bold text is removed from cell A1.

3. Right-click cell **A2**, and then click **Clear Contents** on the shortcut menu. The year is removed from cell A2.

Working with Files

The most common tasks you perform in any Office program are to create, open, save, and close files. All of these tasks can be done from Backstage view, and the processes for these tasks are basically the same in all Office programs. To begin working in a program, you need to create a new file or open an existing file. When you start Word, Excel, or PowerPoint, the program opens along with a blank file—ready for you to begin working on a new document, workbook, or presentation. When you start Access, the New tab in Backstage view opens, displaying options for creating a new database or opening an existing one.

Saving a File

As you create and modify an Office file, your work is stored only in the computer's temporary memory, not on a hard drive. If you were to exit the program without saving, turn off your computer, or experience a power failure, your work would be lost. To prevent losing work, save your file frequently—at least every 10 minutes. You can save files to the hard drive located inside your computer, an external hard drive, a network storage drive, or a portable storage drive such as a USB flash drive.

To save a file, you can click either the Save button on the Quick Access Toolbar or the Save command in Backstage view. If it is the first time you are saving a file, the Save As dialog box will open so that you can specify save options. You can also click the Save As command in Backstage view to open the Save As dialog box, in which you can name the file you are saving and specify a location to save it.

TIP

Office 2003 and earlier files use the extensions .doc (Word), .xls (Excel), .mdb (Access), and .ppt (PowerPoint). To save in an earlier format, click the Save as type button in the Save As dialog box and click the 97-2003 format. When you open an earlier version file in Office 2010, you can save it in the same format or the Office 2010 format.

The first time you save a file, you need to name it. This **filename** includes a title you specify and a file extension assigned by Office to indicate the file type. You should specify a descriptive title that accurately reflects the content of the document, workbook, presentation, or database, such as "Shipping Options Letter" or "Fourth Quarter Financial Analysis." Your descriptive title can include uppercase and lowercase letters, numbers, hyphens, and spaces in any combination, but not the special characters ? " / \ < > * | and :. Each filename ends with a **file extension**, which is a period followed by several characters that Office adds to your descriptive title to identify the program in which that file was created. The default file extensions for Office 2010 are .docx for Word, .xlsx for Excel, .pptx for PowerPoint, and .accdb for Access. Filenames (the descriptive title and extension) can include a maximum of 255 characters. You might see file extensions depending on how Windows is set up on your computer. The figures in these tutorials do not show file extensions.

You also need to decide where to save the file—on which drive and in what folder. A **folder** is a container for your files. Just as you organize paper documents within folders stored in a filing cabinet, you can organize your files within folders stored on your computer's hard drive or on a removable drive such as a USB flash drive. Store each file in a logical location that you will remember whenever you want to use the file again. The default storage location for Office files is the Documents folder; you can create additional storage folders within that folder or navigate to a new location.

REFERENCE

Saving a File

To save a file the first time or with a new name or location:
- Click the File tab to open Backstage view, and then click the Save As command in the navigation bar (for an unnamed file, click the Save command or click the Save button on the Quick Access Toolbar).
- In the Save As dialog box, navigate to the location where you want to save the file.
- Type a descriptive title in the File name box, and then click the Save button.

To resave a named file to the same location with the same name:
- On the Quick Access Toolbar, click the Save button.

The text you typed in the Word window needs to be saved.

To save a file for the first time:

▶ 1. On the taskbar, click the **Microsoft Word** program button ![W]. Word becomes the active program.

▶ 2. On the Ribbon, click the **File** tab. Backstage view opens with commands and tabs for creating new files, opening existing files, and saving, printing, and closing files. See Figure 16.

| Figure 16 | Backstage view |

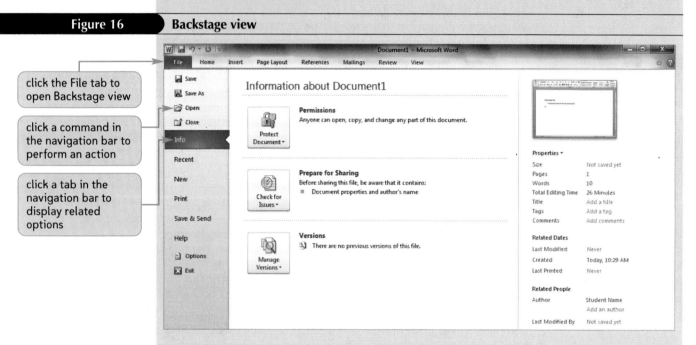

click the File tab to open Backstage view

click a command in the navigation bar to perform an action

click a tab in the navigation bar to display related options

▶ 3. In the navigation bar, click the **Save As** command. The Save As dialog box opens because you have not yet saved the file and need to specify a storage location and filename. The default location is set to the Documents folder, and the first few words of the first line appear in the File name box as a suggested title.

▶ 4. In the Navigation pane along the left side of the dialog box, click the link for the location that contains your Data Files, if necessary.

Trouble? If you don't have the starting Data Files, you need to get them before you can proceed. Your instructor will either give you the Data Files or ask you to obtain them from a specified location (such as a network drive). In either case, make a backup copy of the Data Files before you start so that you will have the original files available in case you need to start over. If you have any questions about the Data Files, see your instructor or technical support person for assistance.

▶ 5. In the file list, double-click the **Office** folder, and then double-click the **Tutorial** folder. This is the location where you want to save the document.

▶ 6. Type **Agenda** in the File name box. This descriptive filename will help you more easily identify the file. See Figure 17 (your file path may differ).

Figure 17   Completed Save As dialog box

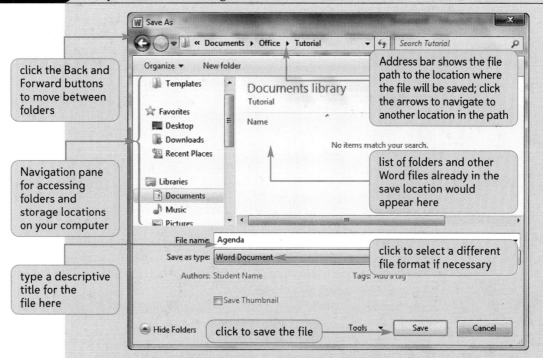

click the Back and Forward buttons to move between folders

Navigation pane for accessing folders and storage locations on your computer

type a descriptive title for the file here

Address bar shows the file path to the location where the file will be saved; click the arrows to navigate to another location in the path

list of folders and other Word files already in the save location would appear here

click to select a different file format if necessary

click to save the file

Trouble? If the .docx extension appears after the filename, your computer is configured to show file extensions. Continue with Step 7.

7. Click the **Save** button. The Save As dialog box closes, and the name of your file appears in the Word window title bar.

The saved file includes everything in the document at the time you last saved it. Any new edits or additions you make to the document exist only in the computer's memory and are not saved in the file on the drive. As you work, remember to save frequently so that the file is updated to reflect the latest content.

Because you already named the document and selected a storage location, you don't need to use the Save As dialog box unless you want to save a copy of the file with a different filename or to a different location. If you do, the previous version of the file remains on your drive as well.

You need to add your name to the agenda. Then, you'll save your changes.

To modify and save the Agenda document:

1. Type your name, and then press the **Enter** key. The text you typed appears on the next line.

2. On the Quick Access Toolbar, click the **Save** button. The changes you made to the document are saved in the file stored on the drive.

INSIGHT

Saving Files Before Closing

As a standard practice, you should save files before closing them. However, Office has an added safeguard: if you attempt to close a file without saving your changes, a dialog box opens, asking whether you want to save the file. Click the Save button to save the changes to the file before closing the file and program. Click the Don't Save button to close the file and program without saving changes. Click the Cancel button to return to the program window without saving changes or closing the file and program. This feature helps to ensure that you always save the most current version of any file.

Closing a File

Although you can keep multiple files open at one time, you should close any file you are no longer working on to conserve system resources as well as to ensure that you don't inadvertently make changes to the file. You can close a file by clicking the Close command in Backstage view. If that's the only file open for the program, the program window remains open and no file appears in the window. You can also close a file by clicking the Close button in the upper-right corner of the title bar. If that's the only file open for the program, the program also closes.

You'll add the date to the agenda. Then, you'll attempt to close it without saving.

To modify and close the Agenda document:

1. Type today's date, and then press the **Enter** key. The text you typed appears below your name in the document.

2. On the Ribbon, click the **File** tab to open Backstage view, and then click the **Close** command in the navigation bar. A dialog box opens, asking whether you want to save the changes you made to the document.

3. Click the **Save** button. The current version of the document is saved to the file, and then the document closes. Word is still open, so you can create additional new files in the open program or you can open previously created and saved files.

Opening a File

When you want to open a blank document, workbook, presentation, or database, you create a new file. When you want to work on a previously created file, you must first open it. Opening a file transfers a copy of the file from the storage location (either a hard drive or a portable drive) to the computer's memory and displays it on your screen. The file is then in your computer's memory and on the drive.

REFERENCE

Opening an Existing File

- Click the File tab to open Backstage view, and then click the Open command in the navigation bar.
- In the Open dialog box, navigate to the storage location of the file you want to open.
- Click the filename of the file you want to open.
- Click the Open button.
- If necessary, click the Enable Editing button in the Information Bar.

or

- Click the File tab, and then click the Recent tab in the navigation bar.
- Click a filename in the Recent list.

Any file you open that was downloaded from the Internet, accessed from a shared network, or received as an email attachment might open in a read-only format, called **Protected View**. In Protected View, you can see the file contents, but you cannot edit, save, or print them until you enable editing. To do so, click the Enable Editing button on the Information Bar, as shown in Figure 18.

Figure 18   **Protected View warning**

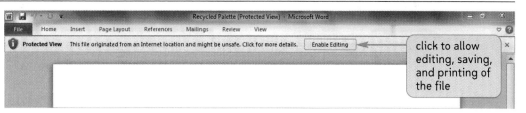

You need to print the meeting agenda you typed for Ean. To do that, you'll reopen the Agenda document.

To open the Agenda document:

1. On the Ribbon, click the **File** tab to display Backstage view.

2. In the navigation bar, click the **Open** command. The Open dialog box, which works similarly to the Save As dialog box, opens.

3. In the Open dialog box, use the Navigation pane or the Address bar to navigate to the **Office\Tutorial** folder included with your Data Files. This is the location where you saved the Agenda document.

4. In the file list, click **Agenda**. See Figure 19.

Figure 19   **Open dialog box**

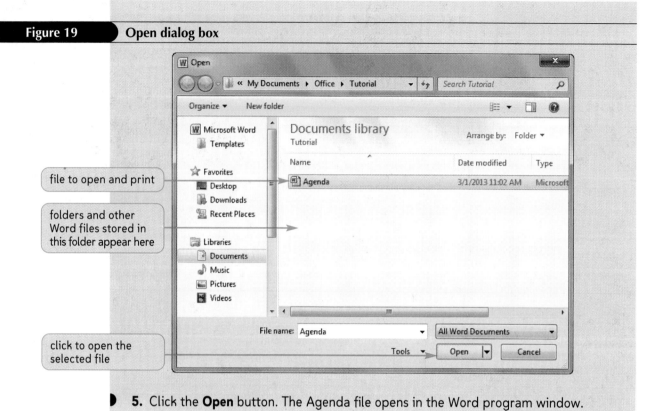

file to open and print

folders and other Word files stored in this folder appear here

click to open the selected file

5. Click the **Open** button. The Agenda file opens in the Word program window.

Sharing Files Using Windows Live SkyDrive

Often the purpose of creating a file is to share it with other people—sending it attached to an email message for someone else to read or use, collaborating with others on the same document, or posting it as a blog for others to review. You can do all of these things in Backstage view from the Save & Send tab.

When you send a file using email, you can attach a copy of the file, send a link to the file, or attach a copy of the file in a PDF or another file format. You can also save to online workspaces where you can make the file available to others for review and collaboration. The Save to Web option on the Save & Send tab in Backstage view gives you access to **Windows Live SkyDrive**, which is an online workspace provided by Microsoft; your personal workspace comes with a Public folder for saving files to share as well as a My Documents folder for saving files you want to keep private. (SkyDrive is not available for Access.) Figure 20 shows the Save to Web options on the Save & Send tab in Backstage view of Word. SharePoint is an online workspace set up by an organization, such as a school, business, or nonprofit group.

Files saved to an online workspace can be worked on by more than one person at the same time. The changes are recorded in the files with each author's name and the date of the change. A Web browser is used to access and edit the files. You choose who can have access to the files.

TIP

To use SkyDrive, you need a Windows Live ID, which you can sign up for at no cost. After you sign in, you can create new folders and save files into the folders.

| Figure 20 | Save to Web options on the Save & Send tab |

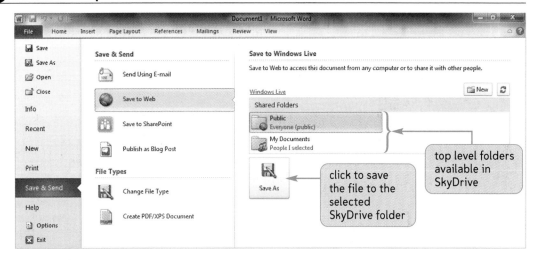

Saving a File to SkyDrive

- Click the File tab to open Backstage view, and then click the Save & Send tab in the navigation bar.
- In the center pane, click Save to Web.
- In the right pane, click the Sign In button, and then use your Windows Live ID to log on to your Windows Live SkyDrive account.

Getting Help

If you don't know how to perform a task or want more information about a feature, you can turn to Office itself for information on how to use it. This information is referred to simply as **Help**. You can get Help in ScreenTips and from the Help window.

Viewing ScreenTips

ScreenTips are a fast and simple method you can use to get information about objects you see on the screen. A **ScreenTip** is a box with descriptive text about an object or button. Just point to a button or object to display its ScreenTip. In addition to the button's name, a ScreenTip might include the button's keyboard shortcut if it has one, a description of the command's function, and, in some cases, a link to more information so that you can press the F1 key while the ScreenTip is displayed to open the Help window with the relevant topic displayed.

To view ScreenTips:

1. Point to the **Microsoft Office Word Help** button ⑦. The ScreenTip shows the button's name, its keyboard shortcut, and a brief description. See Figure 21.

Figure 21   ScreenTip for the Help button

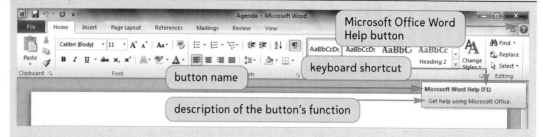

2. Point to other buttons on the Ribbon to display their ScreenTips.

Using the Help Window

For more detailed information, you can use the **Help window** to access all the Help topics, templates, and training installed on your computer with Office and available on Office.com. **Office.com** is a Web site maintained by Microsoft that provides access to the latest information and additional Help resources. For example, you can access current Help topics and training for Office. To connect to Office.com, you need to be able to access the Internet from your computer. Otherwise, you see only topics that are stored on your computer.

Each program has its own Help window from which you can find information about all of the Office commands and features as well as step-by-step instructions for using them. There are two ways to find Help topics—the search function and a topic list.

The Type words to search for box enables you to search the Help system for a task or a topic you need help with. You can click a link to open a Help topic with explanations and step-by-step instructions for a specific procedure. The Table of Contents pane displays the Help system content organized by subjects and topics, similar to a book's table of contents. You click main subject links to display related topic links. You click a topic link to display that Help topic in the Help window.

REFERENCE

Getting Help

- Click the Microsoft Office Help button (the button name depends on the Office program).
- Type a keyword or phrase in the Type words to search for box, click the Search button, and then click a Help topic in the search results list.
  or
  In the Table of Contents pane, click a "book," and then click a Help topic.
- Read the information in the Help window and then click other topics or links.
- On the Help window title bar, click the Close button.

You'll use Help to get information about printing a document in Word.

To search Help for information about printing:

1. Click the **Microsoft Office Word Help** button [?]. The Word Help window opens.

▶ **2.** If the Table of Contents pane is not open on the left side of the Help window, click the **Show Table of Contents** button ▨ on the toolbar to display the pane.

▶ **3.** Click the **Type words to search for** box, if necessary, and then type **print document**. You can specify where you want to search.

▶ **4.** Click the **Search button arrow**. The Search menu shows the online and local content available.

▶ **5.** If your computer is connected to the Internet, click **All Word** in the Content from Office.com list. If your computer is not connected to the Internet, click **Word Help** in the Content from this computer list.

▶ **6.** Click the **Search** button. The Help window displays a list of topics related to the keywords "print document" in the left pane. See Figure 22.

| Figure 22 | Search results displaying Help topics |

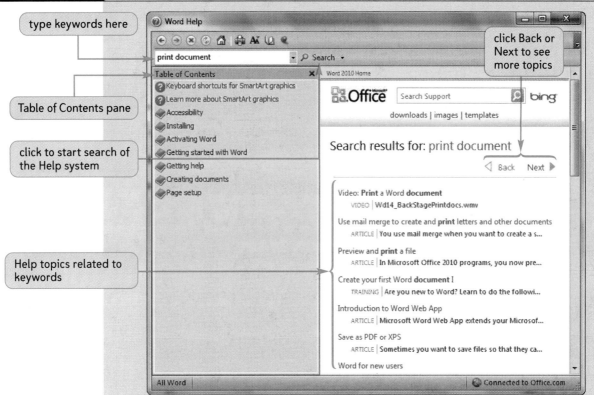

Trouble? If your search results list differs from the one shown in Figure 22, your computer is not connected to the Internet or Microsoft has updated the list of available Help topics since this book was published. Continue with Step 7.

▶ **7.** Scroll through the list to review the Help topics.

▶ **8.** Click **Preview and print a file**. The topic content is displayed in the Help window so you can learn more about how to print a document. See Figure 23.

Figure 23 Preview and print a file Help topic

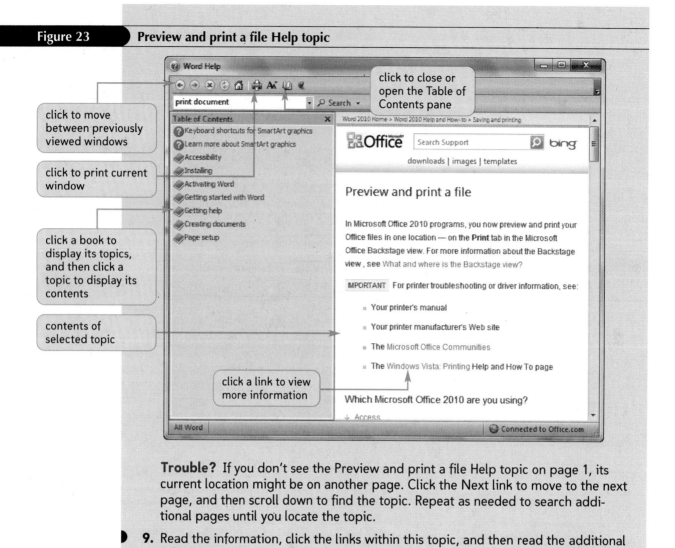

Trouble? If you don't see the Preview and print a file Help topic on page 1, its current location might be on another page. Click the Next link to move to the next page, and then scroll down to find the topic. Repeat as needed to search additional pages until you locate the topic.

9. Read the information, click the links within this topic, and then read the additional information.

10. On the Help window title bar, click the **Close** button ▬✗▬ to close the window.

Printing a File

At times, you'll want a paper copy of Office files. Whenever you print, you should review and adjust the printing settings as needed. You can select the number of copies to print, the printer, the portion of the file to print, and so forth; the printing settings vary slightly from program to program. You should also check the file's print preview to ensure that the file will print as you intended. This simple review will help you to avoid reprinting, which requires additional paper, ink, and energy resources.

Printing a File

- On the Ribbon, click the File tab to open Backstage view.
- In the navigation bar, click the Print tab.
- Verify the print settings and review the print preview.
- Click the Print button.

You will print the agenda for Ean.

To print the Agenda document:

1. Make sure your printer is turned on and contains paper.

2. On the Ribbon, click the **File** tab to open Backstage view.

3. In the navigation bar, click the **Print** tab. The print settings and preview appear. See Figure 24.

Figure 24   **Print tab in Backstage view**

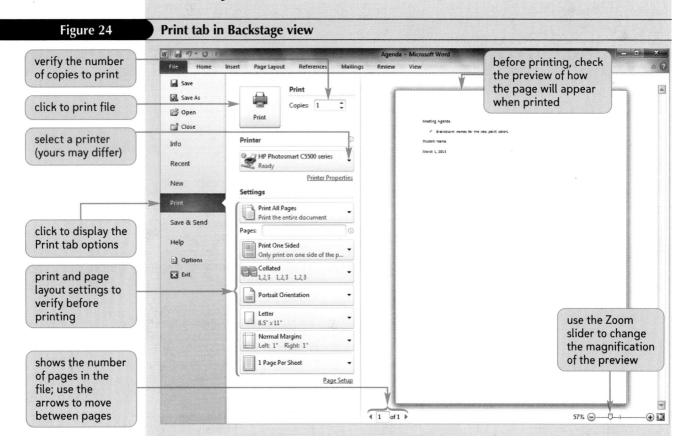

verify the number of copies to print

click to print file

select a printer (yours may differ)

click to display the Print tab options

print and page layout settings to verify before printing

shows the number of pages in the file; use the arrows to move between pages

before printing, check the preview of how the page will appear when printed

use the Zoom slider to change the magnification of the preview

4. Verify that **1** appears in the Copies box.

5. Verify that the correct printer appears on the Printer button. If it doesn't, click the **Printer** button, and then click the correct printer from the list of available printers.

6. Click the **Print** button to print the document.

Trouble? If the document does not print, see your instructor or technical support person for help.

Exiting Programs

When you finish working with a program, you should exit it. As with many other aspects of Office, you can exit programs with a button or a command. You'll use both methods to exit Word and Excel. You can use the Exit command to exit a program and close an open file in one step. If you haven't saved the final version of the open file, a dialog box opens, asking whether you want to save your changes. Clicking the Save button in this dialog box saves the open file, closes the file, and then exits the program.

To exit the Word and Excel programs:

▶ **1.** On the Word title bar, click the **Close** button ✕ . Both the Word document and the Word program close. The Excel window is visible again.

   Trouble? If a dialog box opens asking if you want to save the document, you might have inadvertently made a change to the document. Click the Don't Save button.

▶ **2.** On the Ribbon, click the **File** tab to open Backstage view, and then click the **Exit** command in the navigation bar. A dialog box opens asking whether you want to save the changes you made to the workbook. If you click the Save button, the Save As dialog box opens and Excel exits after you finish saving the workbook. This time, you don't want to save the workbook.

▶ **3.** Click the **Don't Save** button. The workbook closes without saving a copy, and the Excel program closes.

Exiting programs after you are done using them keeps your Windows desktop uncluttered for the next person using the computer, frees up your system's resources, and prevents data from being lost accidentally.

REVIEW

Quick Check

1. What Office program would be best to use to write a letter?
2. How do you start an Office program?
3. What is the purpose of Live Preview?
4. What is Backstage view?
5. Explain the difference between Save and Save As.
6. True or False. In Protected View, you can see file contents, but you cannot edit, save, or print them until you enable editing.
7. What happens if you open a file, make edits, and then attempt to close the file or exit the program without saving the current version of the file?
8. What are the two ways to get Help in Office?

Practice the skills you learned in the tutorial.

PRACTICE

Review Assignments

Data Files needed for the Review Assignments: Finances.xlsx, Letter.docx

You need to prepare for an upcoming meeting at Recycled Palette. You'll open and print documents for the meeting. Complete the following:

1. Start PowerPoint, and then start Excel.
2. Switch to the PowerPoint window, and then close the presentation but leave the PowerPoint program open. (*Hint*: Use the Close command in Backstage view.)
3. Open a blank PowerPoint presentation from the New tab in Backstage view. (*Hint*: Make sure Blank presentation is selected in the Available Templates and Themes section, and then click the Create button.)
4. Close the PowerPoint presentation and program using the Close button on the PowerPoint title bar; do not save changes if asked.
5. Open the **Finances** workbook located in the Office\Review folder. If the workbook opens in Protected View, click the Enable Editing button.
6. Use the Save As command to save the workbook as **Recycled Palette Finances** in the Office\Review folder.
7. In cell A1, type your name, press the Enter key to insert your name at the top of the worksheet, and then save the workbook.
8. Preview and print one copy of the worksheet using the Print tab in Backstage view.
9. Exit Excel using the Exit command in Backstage view.
10. Start Word, and then open the **Letter** document located in the Office\Review folder. If the document opens in Protected View, click the Enable Editing button.
11. Use the Save As command to save the document with the filename **Recycled Palette Letter** in the Office\Review folder.
12. Press and hold the Ctrl key, press the End key, and then release both keys to move the insertion point to the end of the letter, and then type your name.
13. Use the Save button to save the change to the Recycled Palette Letter document.
14. Preview and print one copy of the document using the Print tab in Backstage view.
15. Close the document, and then exit the Word program.
16. Submit the finished files to your instructor.

ASSESS

SAM: Skills Assessment Manager

For current SAM information, including versions and content details, visit SAM Central (http://samcentral.course.com). If you have a SAM user profile, you may have access to hands-on instruction, practice, and assessment of the skills covered in this tutorial. Since various versions of SAM are supported throughout the life of this text, check with your instructor for the correct instructions and URL/Web site for accessing assignments.

ENDING DATA FILES

Agenda.docx

Recycled Palette Finances.xlsx
Recycled Palette Letter.docx

Teamwork

Working on a Team

Teams consist of individuals who have skills, talents, and abilities that complement each other and, when joined, produce synergy—results greater than those a single individual could achieve. It is this sense of shared mission and responsibility for results that makes a team successful in its efforts to reach its goals. Teams are everywhere. In the workplace, a team might develop a presentation to introduce products. In the classroom, a team might complete a research project.

Teams meet face to face or virtually. A virtual team rarely, if ever, meets in person. Instead, technology makes it possible for members to work as if everyone was in the same room. Some common technologies used in virtual teamwork are corporate networks, email, teleconferencing, and collaboration and integration tools, such as those found in Office 2010.

Even for teams in the same location, technology is a valuable tool. For example, teams commonly collaborate on a copy of a file posted to an online shared storage space, such as SkyDrive. In addition, team members can compile data in the program that best suits the information related to their part of the project. Later, that information can be integrated into a finished report, presentation, email message, and so on.

PROSKILLS

Collaborate with Others

At home, school, or work, you probably collaborate with others to complete many types of tasks—such as planning an event, creating a report, or developing a presentation. You can use Microsoft Office to streamline many of these tasks. Consider a project that you might need to work on with a team. Complete the following steps:

1. Start Word, and open a new document, if necessary.
2. In the document, type a list of all the tasks the team needs to accomplish. If you are working with a team, identify which team member would complete each task.
3. For each task, identify the type of Office file you would create to complete that task. For example, you would create a Word document to write a letter.
4. For each file, identify the Office program you would use to create that file, and explain why you would use that program.
5. Save the document with an appropriate filename in an appropriate folder location.
6. Use a Web browser to visit the Microsoft site at *www.microsoft.com* and research the different Office 2010 suites available. Determine which suite includes all the programs needed for the team to complete the tasks on the list.
7. In the document, type which Office suite you selected and a brief explanation of why.
8. Determine how the team can integrate the different programs in the Office suite you selected to create the files that complete the team's goal or task. Include this information at the end of the Word document. Save the document.
9. Develop an efficient way to organize the files that the team will create to complete the goal or task. Add this information at the end of the Word document.
10. If possible, sign in to SkyDrive, and then save a copy of the file in an appropriate subfolder within your Public folder. If you are working with a team, have your teammates access your file, review your notes, and add a paragraph with their comments and name.
11. Preview and print the finished document, and then submit it to your instructor.

OBJECTIVES

Session 1.1
- Plan and create a new presentation
- Create a title slide and slides with bulleted lists
- Change the theme
- Open an existing PowerPoint presentation
- Edit and format text in the Slide pane
- Use AutoCorrect
- Rearrange text in the Outline tab
- Rearrange slides in Normal and Slide Sorter view
- Delete slides
- View a slide show

Session 1.2
- Create a new presentation based on an existing one
- Animate slide titles and bulleted lists
- Apply transitions
- Insert footer text, slide numbers, and the date on slides
- Create speaker notes
- Check the spelling in a presentation
- Preview and print slides, handouts, speaker notes, and the outline

Creating a Presentation

Presenting Information About a Recreational Timeshare Company

Case | *Share-My-Toys, Inc.*

After Sandra Corwin graduated from Idaho University with a degree in business administration, she worked for a small company in Boise, Idaho, and then moved to Redding, California to work for a much larger company, Anaconda Kayaks and Canoes. After several years, she decided to return to her hometown of Montpelier, Idaho, and start her own business. Sandra grew up participating in camping, hiking, snowmobiling, boating, and other water sports. She realized that many people don't have access to the equipment to do the activities that she enjoyed as a youth.

With this in mind and her experience in the outdoor recreational equipment industry, Sandra started the company Share-My-Toys, Inc., which specializes in selling timeshares for recreational equipment, including ski boats, waverunners, snowmobiles, recreational vehicles (RVs), and all-terrain vehicles (ATVs). The company would allow everyone, even those of modest means, to have access to a wide range of recreational equipment for outdoor activities.

In this tutorial, you'll use **Microsoft PowerPoint 2010** (or simply **PowerPoint**) to begin creating a presentation that Sandra can show to potential members, and then you'll edit the presentation after Sandra finishes it. You'll then add interesting special effects to another presentation that describes Sandra's business plan for Share-My-Toys to banks and potential investors.

STARTING DATA FILES

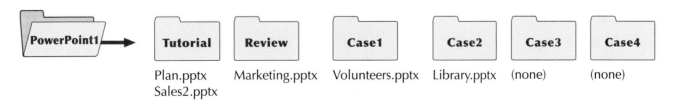

PowerPoint1 →

Tutorial	Review	Case1	Case2	Case3	Case4
Plan.pptx Sales2.pptx	Marketing.pptx	Volunteers.pptx	Library.pptx	(none)	(none)

SESSION 1.1 VISUAL OVERVIEW

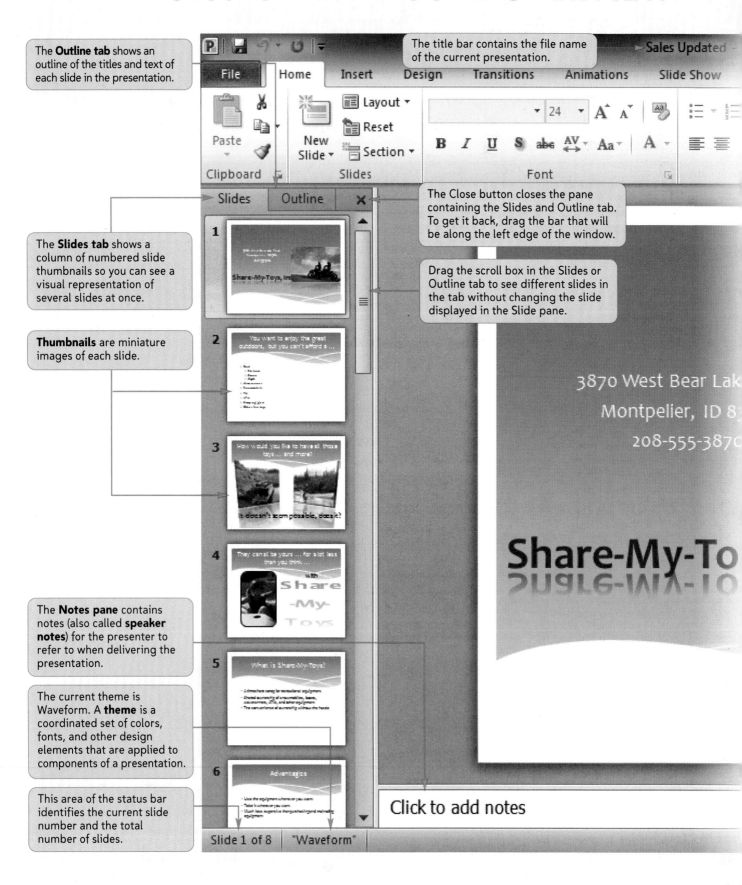

The **Outline tab** shows an outline of the titles and text of each slide in the presentation.

The title bar contains the file name of the current presentation.

The **Slides tab** shows a column of numbered slide thumbnails so you can see a visual representation of several slides at once.

The Close button closes the pane containing the Slides and Outline tab. To get it back, drag the bar that will be along the left edge of the window.

Drag the scroll box in the Slides or Outline tab to see different slides in the tab without changing the slide displayed in the Slide pane.

Thumbnails are miniature images of each slide.

The **Notes pane** contains notes (also called **speaker notes**) for the presenter to refer to when delivering the presentation.

The current theme is Waveform. A **theme** is a coordinated set of colors, fonts, and other design elements that are applied to components of a presentation.

This area of the status bar identifies the current slide number and the total number of slides.

THE POWERPOINT WINDOW

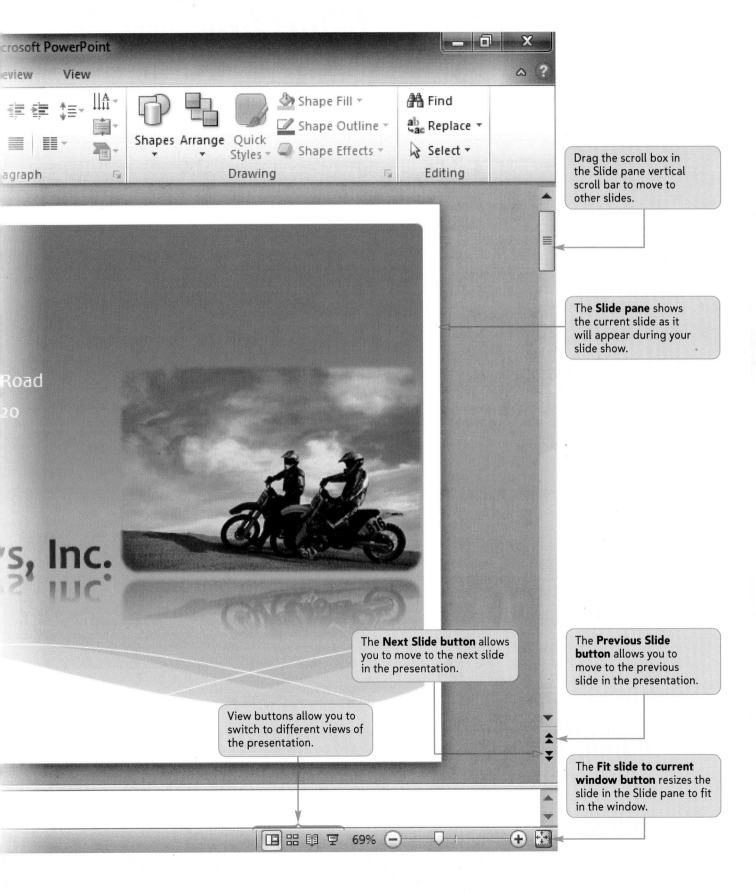

Drag the scroll box in the Slide pane vertical scroll bar to move to other slides.

The **Slide pane** shows the current slide as it will appear during your slide show.

The **Next Slide button** allows you to move to the next slide in the presentation.

The **Previous Slide button** allows you to move to the previous slide in the presentation.

View buttons allow you to switch to different views of the presentation.

The **Fit slide to current window button** resizes the slide in the Slide pane to fit in the window.

Creating a New Presentation

PowerPoint is a powerful presentation graphics program. It provides everything you need to produce an effective slide show presentation that can be shown to an audience or provided to people to view on their own.

You'll start PowerPoint now.

To start PowerPoint:

1. Click the **Start** button on the taskbar, point to **All Programs**, click **Microsoft Office**, and then click **Microsoft PowerPoint 2010**. PowerPoint starts and the PowerPoint window opens.

   Trouble? If you don't see Microsoft PowerPoint 2010 on the Microsoft Office sub-menu, look for it on a different submenu or on the All Programs menu. If you still cannot find it, ask your instructor or technical support person for help.

2. If the PowerPoint program window is not maximized, click the **Maximize** button. PowerPoint starts and displays a blank presentation. See Figure 1-1.

Figure 1-1	Blank presentation in the PowerPoint window

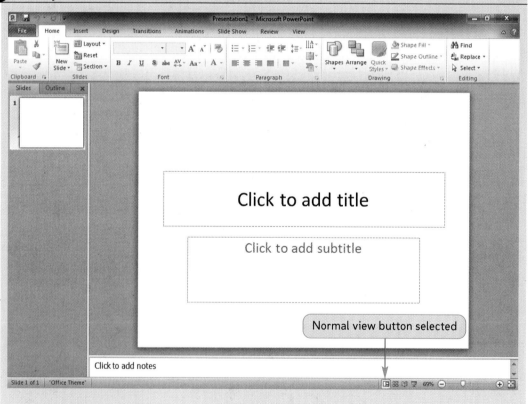

When PowerPoint starts, it displays a blank presentation in Normal view. **Normal view** displays slides one at a time in the Slide pane, allowing you to see how the text and graphics look on each individual slide, and displays thumbnails of all the slides in the Slides tab or all the text of the presentation in the Outline tab. (Refer to the Session 1.1 Visual Overview to identify elements of the PowerPoint window.)

Planning a Presentation

Sandra wants you to create a new presentation that she or other sales representatives can show to potential Share-My-Toys members. Before you create a presentation, you should spend some time planning its content.

PROSKILLS

Aa

Verbal Communication: Planning a Presentation

As you prepare your presentation, you need to consider a few key questions to help you plan what to say. Being able to answer these questions will help you create a presentation that successfully delivers its message or motivates the audience to take an action.

- **What is the purpose of your presentation?**
  In other words, what action or response do you want your audience to have? If you are making a sales pitch, you'll want the audience to buy what you're selling. If you are delivering good or bad news, you'll want the audience to hear the message clearly and take action based on the facts you provide.
- **Who is your audience?**
  Think about the needs and interests of your audience as well as any decisions they'll make as a result of what you have to say. Make sure what you choose to say to your audience is relevant to their needs, interests, and decisions, or it will be forgotten.
- **How much time do you have for the presentation?**
  Consider the amount of time available. Make sure you pace yourself as you speak. You don't want to spend too much time on the introduction and end up having to cut your closing remarks short because you run out of time. This diminishes the effectiveness of the entire presentation and weakens its impact on the audience.
- **Will your audience benefit from printed output?**
  Some presentations are effectively delivered with on-screen visuals. Others require printed support materials because there is too much information to be displayed on the screen, or the presenter wants the audience to have something to take with them to help remember what was said.

The purpose of the presentation you are going to create for Sandra is to convince people that becoming a member of Share-My-Toys will enable them to enjoy using expensive recreational equipment without the cost of purchasing and maintaining it. Normally, the presentation will be given by a presenter in a small room in slide show format. The audience will consist of potential members who have not yet decided if they will register for membership. The audience needs to know what the company offers for services and how joining as a member will benefit them. The presentation will be relatively short, no longer than 10 minutes. Sandra will have brochures on hand to give to audience members, but she will not provide a printout of the presentation itself.

With the presentation plan in place, you'll start creating it.

Creating a Title Slide

The first slide in a PowerPoint presentation is usually the title slide, which typically contains the title of the presentation and the presenter's name or a subtitle. The blank title slide contains two text placeholders. A **placeholder** is a region of a slide reserved for inserting text or graphics. A **text placeholder** is a placeholder designed to contain text. The larger text placeholder on the title slide is the **title text placeholder** and is designed to hold the presentation title. The smaller text placeholder below the title text placeholder is the **subtitle text placeholder**; it is designed to contain a subtitle for the presentation. Once you enter text into a text placeholder, it becomes a **text box**, which is simply a container that holds text.

You'll add text to the title slide.

To add text to the text placeholders in the title slide:

1. Click anywhere in the **title text placeholder**. The title text placeholder text disappears, a dashed line appears on top of the dotted line that indicates the placeholder border, and the insertion point blinks in the placeholder. See Figure 1-2.

Figure 1-2 Entering title text

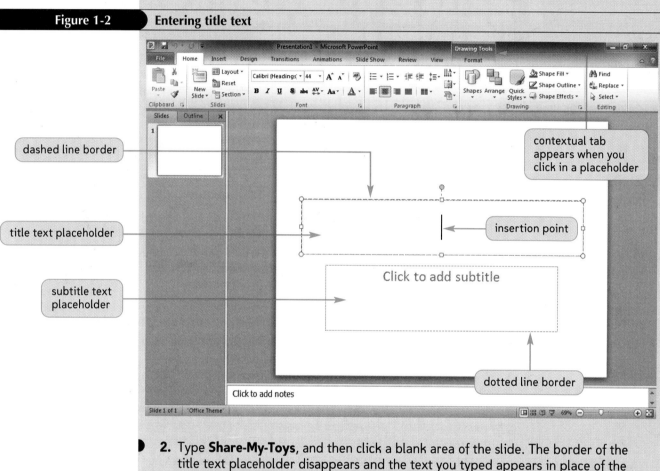

2. Type **Share-My-Toys**, and then click a blank area of the slide. The border of the title text placeholder disappears and the text you typed appears in place of the placeholder text. Notice that the thumbnail in the Slides tab also contains the text you typed. Now you can add a subtitle.

3. Click in the **subtitle text placeholder**, type your first and last name, and then click anywhere else on the slide except in the title text box. (The figures in this book show the name Sandra Corwin.) Now you need to save the presentation.

   Trouble? If PowerPoint marks your name with a wavy, red underline, this indicates that your name is not found in the PowerPoint dictionary. Ignore the wavy line for now; you'll learn how to deal with this later in the tutorial.

4. On the Quick Access Toolbar, click the **Save** button 🔲. Because this is the first time this presentation has been saved, the Save As dialog box opens.

5. Navigate to the PowerPoint1\Tutorial folder included with your Data Files, click in the File name box, type **Sales**, and then click the **Save** button. The dialog box closes, and the presentation is saved. The new filename, Sales, appears in the title bar.

Now Sandra asks you to add new slides to the presentation to describe the company.

Adding a New Slide and Choosing a Layout

When you add a new slide, the slide is formatted with a **layout**, which is a predetermined way of organizing the objects on a slide, including title text and other content (bulleted lists, photographs, charts, and so forth). All layouts, except the Blank layout, include placeholders to help you create your presentation. Slides can include several types of placeholders, but the most common are text and content placeholders. You've already seen text placeholders on the title slide. Most layouts include a title text placeholder to contain the slide title. Many layouts also contain a **content placeholder**, which contains the slide content. The slide content can be text, a table, a chart, a graph, a picture, clip art, or a movie. If you click in a content placeholder, and then add text, the content placeholder is no longer a placeholder and becomes a text box. PowerPoint provides nine built-in layouts, as described in Figure 1-3.

Figure 1-3	Built-in layouts in PowerPoint

Layout	Description
Title Slide	Contains the presentation title and a subtitle; is usually used as the first slide in a presentation
Title and Content	The most commonly used layout; can contain either a bulleted list or a graphic in addition to the slide title
Section Header	Contains a section title and text that describes the presentation section
Two Content	The same as the Title and Content layout, but with two side-by-side content placeholders, each of which can contain a bulleted list or a graphic
Comparison	The same as the Two Content layout, but includes text placeholders above the content placeholders to label the content
Title Only	Includes only a title text placeholder for the slide title
Blank	Does not contain any placeholders
Content with Caption	Contains a content placeholder, a title text placeholder to identify the slide or the content, and a text placeholder to describe the content; suitable for photographs or other graphics that need an explanation
Picture with Caption	Similar to the Content with Caption layout, but with a picture placeholder instead of a content placeholder

To insert a new slide, you use the New Slide button in the Slides group on the Home tab. If you are inserting a new slide after the title slide and you click the New Slide button, the new slide is created using the Title and Content layout. Otherwise, the new slide is created using the same layout as the current slide. If you want to choose a different layout, click the New Slide button arrow, and then select the layout you want to use from the menu that opens.

You need to create a slide that describes Share-My-Toys to potential members.

To create a new slide:

1. In the Slides group on the Home tab, click the **New Slide** button. A new Slide 2 appears in the Slide pane and in the Slides tab with the Title and Content layout applied. See Figure 1-4. Notice the content placeholder contains placeholder text that you can click to insert your own text and six icons that you can click to insert the specific items identified by the icons.

| Figure 1-4 | New slide with the Title and Content layout |

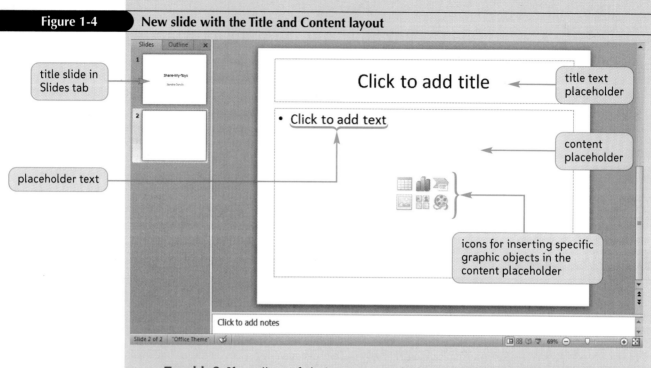

Trouble? If a gallery of choices appeared when you clicked the New Slide button, you most likely clicked the arrow on the bottom part of the New Slide button, instead of clicking the button itself. Click anywhere in the Slide pane to close the menu, and then repeat Step 1.

2. In the Slide pane, click anywhere in the **title text placeholder**, and then type **What is Share-My-Toys?**. You'll create an additional new slide.

3. In the Slides group on the Home tab, click the **New Slide button arrow**. The New Slide gallery opens displaying the nine layouts available. See Figure 1-5. You want to create a slide that will list the ways to contact the company and will have a photograph next to this list. The Two Content layout allows you to do this easily.

| Figure 1-5 | Layouts on the New Slide button menu |

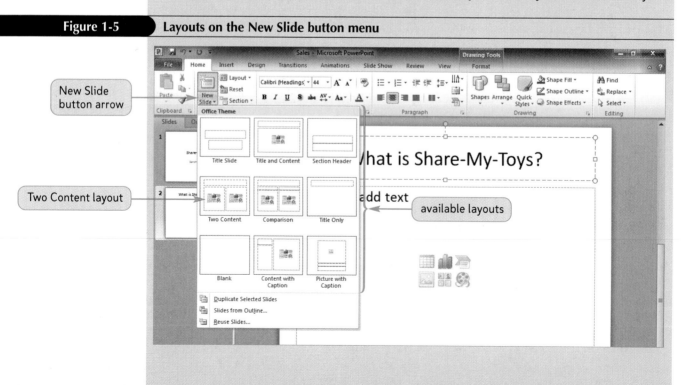

TIP

To change the layout of an existing slide, click the Layout button in the Slides group on the Home tab, and then click the desired layout.

> **4.** In the gallery, click the **Two Content** layout. A new Slide 3 is created with the Two Content layout, which consists of three placeholders: the title text placeholder and two content placeholders side by side.

> **5.** In the Slide pane, click anywhere in the title text placeholder, and then type **How do I join?**.

> **6.** In the Slide pane, at the bottom of the vertical scroll bar, click the **Previous Slide** button ⬏. Slide 2 ("What is Share-My-Toys?") appears in the Slide pane.

INSIGHT

Duplicating Slides

As you create a presentation, you might want to create a slide that is similar to another slide. In this case, it would probably be easier to start with a copy of the slide that already exists. To duplicate a slide, right-click the slide thumbnail in the Slides tab or in Slide Sorter view, and then click Duplicate Slide on the shortcut menu. You can also use the Ribbon to duplicate one or multiple slides. In the Slides group on the Home tab, click the New Slide button arrow, and then click Duplicate Selected Slides. If you select more than one slide before you use the Duplicate Selected Slides command, all of the selected slides will be duplicated.

Creating a Bulleted List

Often, text on a slide is in the form of bulleted lists to emphasize important points to the audience. A **bulleted list** is a list of "paragraphs" (words, phrases, sentences, or paragraphs) with a special symbol (dot, dash, circle, box, star, or other character) to the left of each paragraph. A **bulleted item** is one paragraph in a bulleted list.

Bullets can appear at different outline levels. A **first-level bullet** is a main paragraph in a bulleted list; a **second-level bullet**—sometimes called a **subbullet**—is a bullet below and indented from a first-level bullet. Usually, the **font size**—the size of the characters—of the text in subbullets is smaller than the font size of text in first-level bullets. A **font** is the design of a set of characters. Fonts are measured in **points**, which is a unit of measurement. One point equals 1/72 of an inch. Text in a book is typically printed in 10- or 12-point type.

To create a bulleted list describing Share-My-Toys:

> **1.** Click to the right of the bullet in the content placeholder. The placeholder text ("Click to add text") disappears, and the insertion point appears just to the right of the bullet. See Figure 1-6. In the Font group, notice that the font size in the Font Size box is 32 points.

Figure 1-6 | **Insertion point in content placeholder**

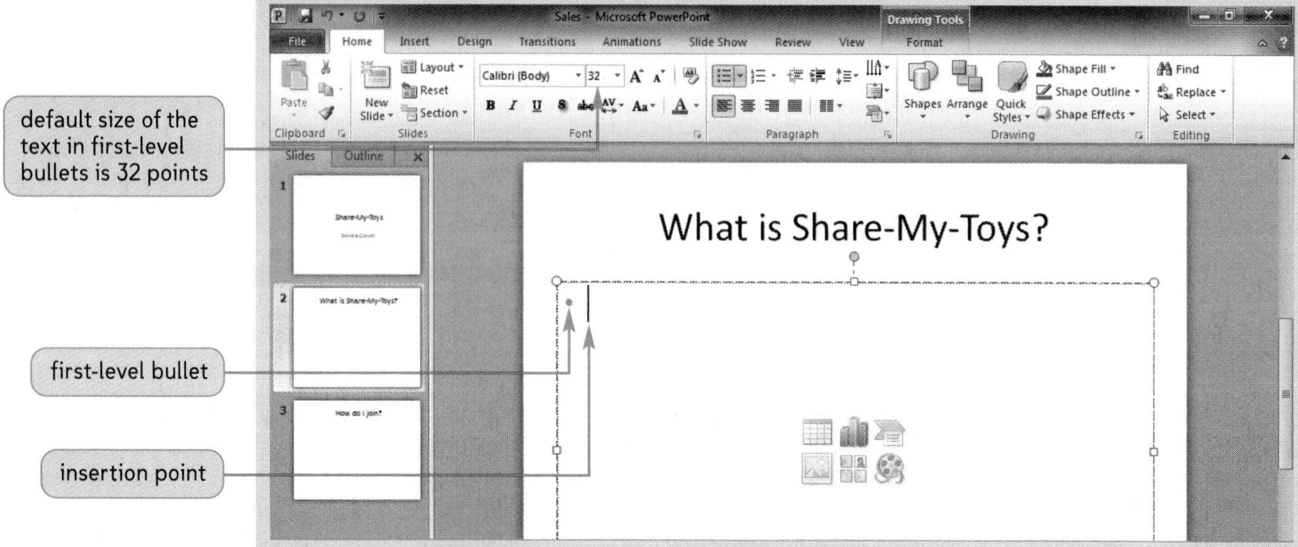

default size of the text in first-level bullets is 32 points

first-level bullet

insertion point

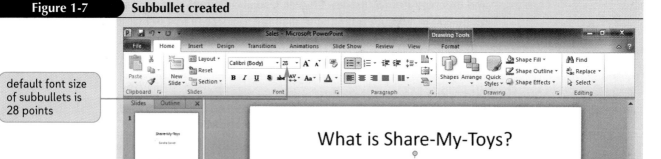

2. Type **A timeshare for recreational equipment co-op**, and then press the **Enter** key. A new bullet appears. Notice that the new bullet is lighter than the first bullet. It will darken as soon as you start typing text. If you don't type anything next to a bullet, the bullet will not appear on the slide.

3. Type **Shared ownership of:** and then press the **Enter** key. The next few lines will be subbullets below the item you just typed.

4. Press the **Tab** key. The new bullet is indented and becomes a subbullet. The subbullet is a very faint dash. See Figure 1-7. Notice that the font size of the subbullet is 28 points, which is smaller than the font size used in the first-level bullets on the slide.

Figure 1-7 | **Subbullet created**

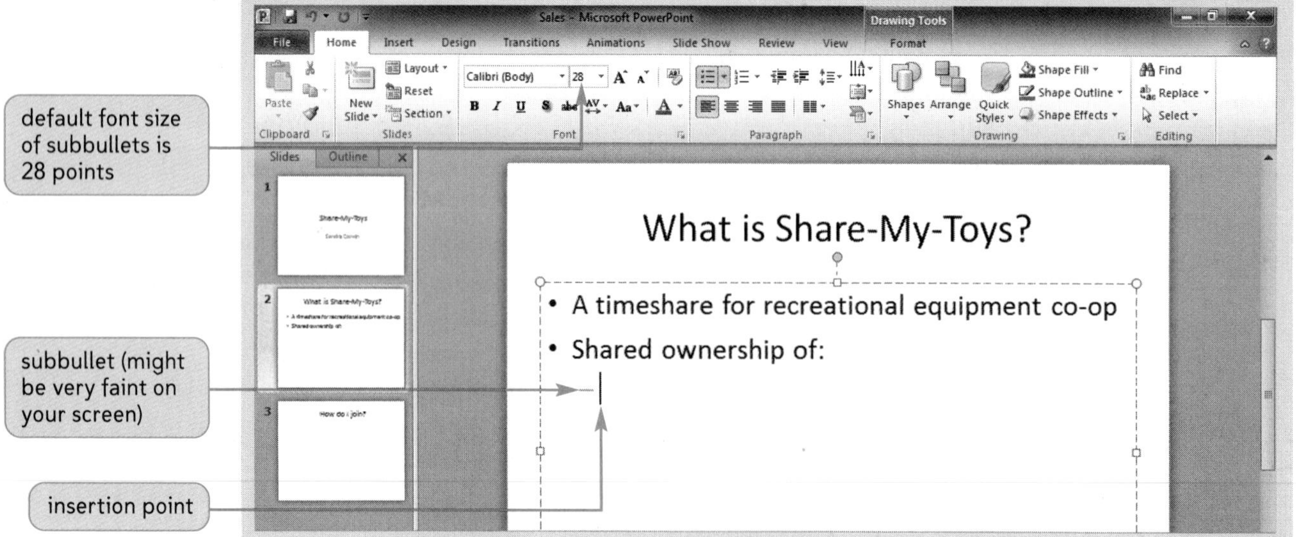

default font size of subbullets is 28 points

subbullet (might be very faint on your screen)

insertion point

What is Share-My-Toys?

- A timeshare for recreational equipment co-op
- Shared ownership of:

5. Type the following, pressing the **Enter** key after each item (do not type the commas): **Snowmobiles**, **Boats**, **Waverunners**, **ATVs**, **RVs**, and **Camping gear**. A red, wavy line appears under "Waverunners"; this means that the word is not in the built-in dictionary. You can ignore this for now.

The insertion point is blinking next to the seventh subbullet, which is positioned directly on the bottom border of the content text box. The next item you need to type is another first-level bullet.

6. Press the **Shift+Tab** keys. The subbullet changes to a first-level bullet.

As you add text to a content placeholder, the **AutoFit** feature changes the line spacing and the font size of the text if you add more text than will fit in the placeholder. The AutoFit feature is turned on by default. When you start typing the next bullet, you will see the AutoFit feature adjust the text to make it fit. If the AutoFit feature adjusts the text in a text box, the AutoFit Options button appears in the Slide pane below and to the left of the placeholder. You can click the AutoFit Options button and select an option on the menu to control the way AutoFit works.

To use the AutoFit feature:

1. Type **T**. After you type the first character in this new bullet, the line spacing in the text box tightens up slightly and the AutoFit Options button ⧧ appears next to the lower-left corner of the text box.

2. Point to the **AutoFit Options** button ⧧ so that it changes to ⧧▾, and then click the **AutoFit Options** button ⧧▾. The AutoFit Options button menu appears. See Figure 1-8. You want to AutoFit the text on this slide, so you'll close the menu without selecting anything to keep the default option of AutoFitting the text to the placeholder.

Figure 1-8	AutoFit Options button menu

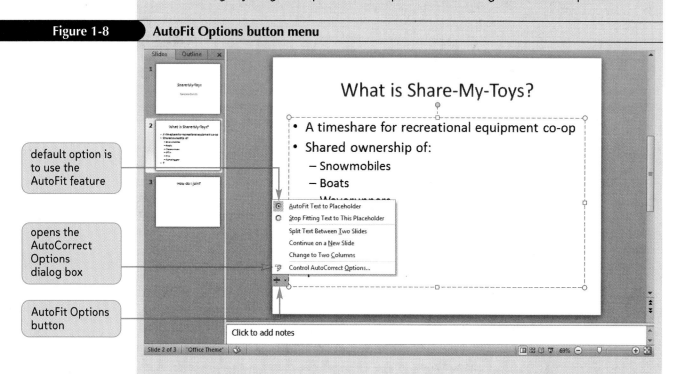

default option is to use the AutoFit feature

opens the AutoCorrect Options dialog box

AutoFit Options button

3. Click anywhere on the slide to close the AutoFit Options button menu without changing the selected default option. Now you can finish typing the bulleted item.

TIP

If you want to create a list without bullets, select the items from which you want to remove the bullets, and then in the Paragraph group on the Home tab, click the Bullets button to deselect it.

4. In the last bulleted item, click immediately after the T, type **he convenience of ownership without the hassle**. Notice that as you typed the last word, AutoFit adjusted the text again, this time by decreasing the point size of the text. The first-level bulleted items are now 30 points, and the size of the subbullets also decreased by two points.

5. Press the **Enter** key. You decide you don't need this last bullet.

6. Press the **Backspace** key twice to delete the last bullet and the blank line.

7. Click a blank area of the slide outside the content text box. The dashed line border of the text box disappears.

8. On the Quick Access Toolbar, click the **Save** button 🖫 to save your changes.

Using Themes

Plain white slides with a common font (such as black Times New Roman or Calibri) often fail to hold an audience's attention. In today's information age, audiences expect more interesting color schemes, fonts, graphics, and other effects. To make it easy to add color and style to your presentations, PowerPoint provides themes. (Refer to the Session 1.1 Visual Overview.) **Theme colors** are the colors used for the background, title text, body text, accents, background colors and objects, and graphics in a presentation. **Theme fonts** are two fonts or font styles, one for the titles (or headings) and one for text in content placeholders. In some themes, the title and body fonts are the same, just different sizes and possibly different colors. Other themes use different title and body fonts in various sizes and colors. Some themes include graphics as part of the slide background. A **graphic** is a picture, shape, design, graph, chart, or diagram.

Every presentation has a theme. Even the "blank" presentation that opens when you first start PowerPoint or when you create a new presentation without selecting another theme has the default Office theme applied.

The theme you choose for your presentation should reflect the content and the intended audience. For example, if you are presenting a new curriculum to a group of elementary school teachers, you might choose a theme that uses bright, primary colors. On the other hand, if you are presenting a new marketing plan to a mutual fund company, you might choose a theme that uses dark colors formatted in a way that conveys sophistication.

This presentation you are creating for Sandra is a sales presentation, so she asks you to choose a theme with some color in it. She also wants you to find one that reminds people of the outdoors to mirror the business objectives of Share-My-Toys.

To change the theme:

1. Click the **Design** tab on the Ribbon. The Ribbon changes to display options for setting or modifying the presentation design. In the Themes group, the first theme displayed in the group is always the currently applied theme.

2. In the Themes group, point to the first theme, which has an orange highlight around it, but do not click the mouse button. A ScreenTip appears identifying the theme, which in this case, is the Office Theme. See Figure 1-9. Note that the name of the current theme also appears at the left end of the status bar. After the currently applied theme, all the available themes are listed in alphabetical order in the Themes group, except the Office Theme, which is listed as the first available theme (so it appears twice since it is also the current theme).

Figure 1-9 | Design tab in the PowerPoint window

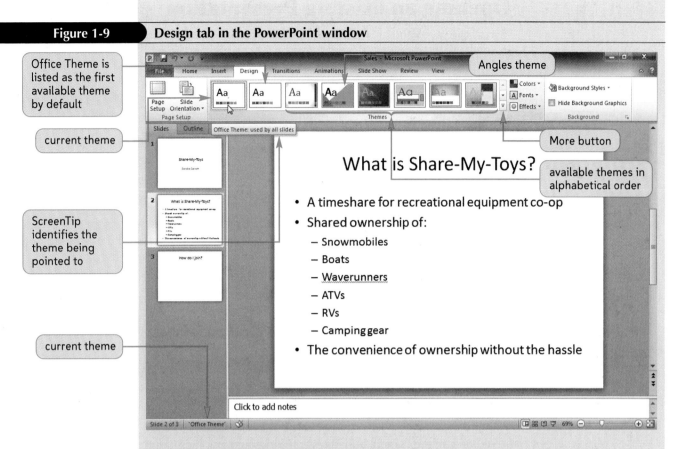

Office Theme is listed as the first available theme by default

current theme

ScreenTip identifies the theme being pointed to

Angles theme

More button

available themes in alphabetical order

current theme

3. In the Themes group, point to the fourth theme, but do not click the mouse button. The ScreenTip that appears identifies this as the Angles theme, and the Live Preview feature changes the design and colors on the slide in the Slide pane to the Angles theme.

4. In the Themes group, click the **More** button, drag the scroll bar to the bottom of the gallery list, and then point to the last theme in the last row above the Office.com section. The ScreenTip identifies this as the Waveform theme.

Trouble? If your screen is set at a different resolution than the screens shown in the figures in this book, the Waveform theme will be in a different position in the gallery. Point to each theme and use the ScreenTips to identify the Waveform theme.

5. Click the **Waveform** theme. The three slides in the presentation are changed to the design and colors of the Waveform theme, and the name of the new theme appears at the left end of the status bar. As you can see in the Slides tab, the background graphic on the title slide covers most of the slide, whereas in Slide 2 the graphic appears only at the top. Many themes arrange graphics differently on the title slide than on the content slides.

6. On the Quick Access Toolbar, click the **Save** button to save your changes. Now you will close the presentation.

7. Click the **File** tab to display Backstage view, and then click the **Close** command in the navigation bar. The presentation closes but PowerPoint remains open.

You give the presentation to Sandra so she can look it over.

Opening an Existing Presentation

If you have saved and closed a presentation, you can open it to continue working on it. Sandra worked on the sales presentation you started and saved it with a new name (Sales2). She now asks you to make a few more changes.

To open the Sales2 presentation:

▶ 1. Click the **File** tab to display Backstage view, and then click the **Open** command in the navigation bar. The Open dialog box appears.

▶ 2. Navigate to the PowerPoint1\Tutorial folder, click **Sales2**, and then click the **Open** button. You need to save the presentation with a different name so that the original presentation remains available.

   Trouble? If the yellow Protected View bar appears at the top of the presentation window, click the Enable Editing button, and then continue with Step 3.

▶ 3. Click the **File** tab to display Backstage view, and then click the **Save As** command in the navigation bar. The Save As dialog box opens.

▶ 4. Navigate to the PowerPoint1\Tutorial folder if necessary, type **Sales Updated** in the File name box, and then click the **Save** button. The presentation is saved with the new name.

   Trouble? If the slide in the Slide pane is too large or too small for the space, click the Fit slide to current window button ▦ in the lower-right corner of the window, to the right of the Zoom slider.

As you can see, Sandra added several slides and graphics to the presentation. She is happy with the graphics and doesn't need you to work on these. Rather, she wants you to edit the text on some of the slides.

Editing Text

Most presentations contain text, and you will frequently need to edit that text. You can format text, move and copy text, and create new slides by moving text. To edit text, you can work in the Slide pane or in the Outline tab.

As you have seen, when you click in a text box or a text box placeholder, the border becomes a dashed line. This indicates that the text box is **active**, which means that you can add or delete text or otherwise modify the text inside it. The small circles and squares that appear at each corner and on the sides of the active text box are **sizing handles**, which you can drag to make the text box larger or smaller. To edit text in the Slide pane, click any text to make the text box containing that text active, and then start typing or modifying the text in the text box.

Selecting and Formatting Text

If you want to emphasize specific text on a slide, you can change its font style. **Font style** refers to format attributes applied to text, such as bold and italic. To change the font style, use the formatting commands in the Font group on the Home tab, including the Bold, Italic, Underline, Shadow, and Font Color buttons. For example, on Slide 8 ("How do I join?"), Sandra wants to make it easy for the audience to identify the contact information that she added, so you will format this text in bold and with a shadow effect to make it stand out.

To format text in an active text box, you first need to select it. To select text, you can drag across it by positioning the pointer at the beginning of the text you want to select, pressing and holding the left mouse button, dragging across the text to select, and then releasing the mouse button. Another way to select text is to click at the beginning of the text you want to select, press and hold the Shift key, and then click at the end of the text to select. This procedure, sometimes called Shift-clicking, selects all the text between the two locations where you clicked. In addition, you can select nonadjacent text—that is, words or lines that are not next to each other—by first selecting text in one location, pressing and holding the Ctrl key, and then dragging the mouse over text in another location. This is sometimes called Ctrl-clicking.

Although you can edit text in the Slide pane or in the Outline tab, when you are changing the formatting of text, it is a good idea to work in the Slide pane so that you can easily see how the formatted text looks with the rest of the text on the slide.

To select and format text on Slide 8:

1. In the Slide pane, drag the **scroll box** in the vertical scroll bar down to the bottom of the scroll bar. Slide 8 ("How do I join?") appears in the Slide pane.

2. In the Slide pane, in the first line of the address in the second bulleted item, click immediately before the 3 in the street number. The text box containing the bulleted list becomes active, as indicated by the dashed line border.

3. Press and hold the **Shift** key, and then click after the 0 in the zip code. All the text between the two locations where you clicked is selected.

4. Click the **Home** tab, and then click the **Bold** button B in the Font group. The selected text is formatted with bold.

5. In the Font group, click the **Text Shadow** button S. The selected text now also has a shadow effect applied to it. See Figure 1-10. Now you need to apply bold and shadow formatting to the phone number and the Web site address.

TIP

To select adjacent text, you can also click before the first character you want to select, press and hold the Shift key, and then press the arrow keys to select adjacent text.

Figure 1-10   **Selected text formatted with bold and a shadow effect**

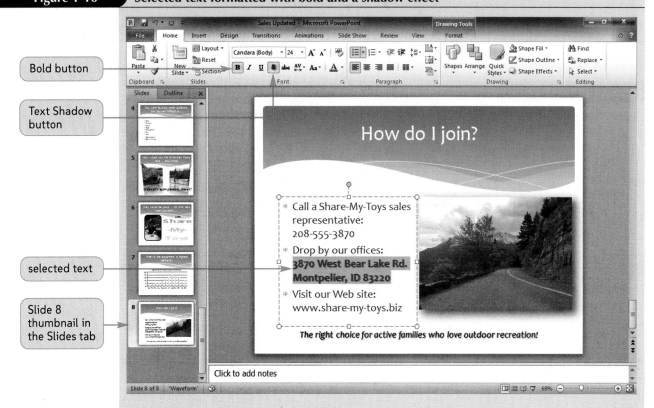

Bold button

Text Shadow button

selected text

Slide 8 thumbnail in the Slides tab

> **6.** In the Slide pane, in the first bulleted item, position the pointer to the left of the first digit in the phone number, press and hold the left mouse button, and then drag across all the numbers in the phone number. The text you dragged over is selected.

> **7.** Press and hold the **Ctrl** key, and then, in the third bulleted item, drag across **www.share-my-toys.biz** (the Web site address) the same way you dragged across the text in Step 6, and then release the **Ctrl** key. Now the URL and the phone number are selected.

> **8.** In the Font group, click the **Bold** button $\boxed{\textbf{B}}$, and then click the **Text Shadow** button $\boxed{\textbf{S}}$. The selected text is now bold and has a shadow effect applied to it.

> **9.** On the Quick Access Toolbar, click the **Save** button $\boxed{}$ to save your changes.

Editing Text in the Slide Pane

Sandra wants you to modify some of the text on Slide 3 by moving text. One technique for moving and copying text is drag-and-drop, in which you select text, and then drag it to a new location on a slide. You can do this in the Slide pane or in the Outline tab.

To move text on Slide 3 using drag-and-drop:

> **1.** In the Slides tab, drag the **scroll box** up until the ScreenTip identifies the slide as Slide 3 of 8. Slide 3 ("What is Share-My-Toys?") appears in the Slide pane.

> **2.** In the Slide pane, in the first bulleted item, double-click the word **co-op** to select it. The text box containing the bulleted list becomes active, as indicated by the dashed line border. The Mini toolbar appears because you used the mouse to select the text.

> **3.** Position the pointer on top of the selected text, press and hold the left mouse button, and then drag to the left until the vertical line that follows the pointer is positioned to the left of "for" in the first bulleted item. See Figure 1-11.

Figure 1-11 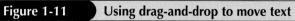 **Using drag-and-drop to move text**

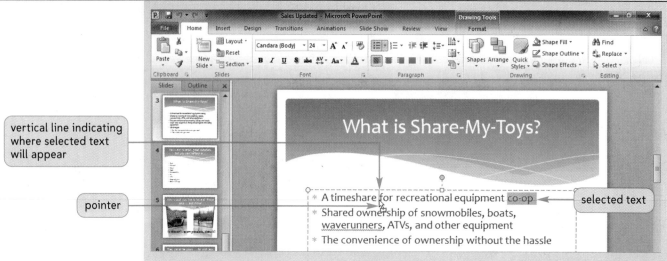

vertical line indicating where selected text will appear

pointer

selected text

TIP

To copy text using drag-and-drop, press and hold the Ctrl key while you drag.

4. With the vertical line positioned to the left of "for," release the mouse button. The selected text is moved so that it appears before the word "for."

Trouble? If a space was not inserted between "co-op" and "for," click between "co-op" and "for," and then press the spacebar.

5. In the Slide pane, position the pointer on top of the third bullet so that the pointer changes to ⊕, and then click. All of the text in the third bulleted item is selected.

6. Position the pointer on top of the third bullet so it again changes to ⊕, and then drag down without releasing the mouse button. A horizontal line follows the pointer as you drag.

7. When the horizontal line is positioned between the fourth and fifth bullet (above "Advantages"), release the mouse button. The bulleted item that starts with "The convenience of ownership" is now the fourth bulleted item.

Undoing Actions

If you make a mistake as you are working, you can undo your error by clicking the Undo button on the Quick Access Toolbar or by pressing the Ctrl+Z keys. You can undo more than one action by continuing to click the Undo button or pressing the Ctrl+Z keys, or by clicking the Undo button arrow and then selecting as many actions in the list as you want. You can also redo an action that you undid by clicking the Redo button on the Quick Access Toolbar, or by pressing the Ctrl+Y keys. Sandra wants the bulleted item "The convenience of ownership" to remain as the third bulleted item, so you will undo the action of dragging it to the fourth bulleted item position.

To undo the action of moving the bulleted item:

1. On the Quick Access Toolbar, click the **Undo button arrow** ⟲ ▾. A list of recent actions appears in a menu. See Figure 1-12.

Figure 1-12 **Undo button menu**

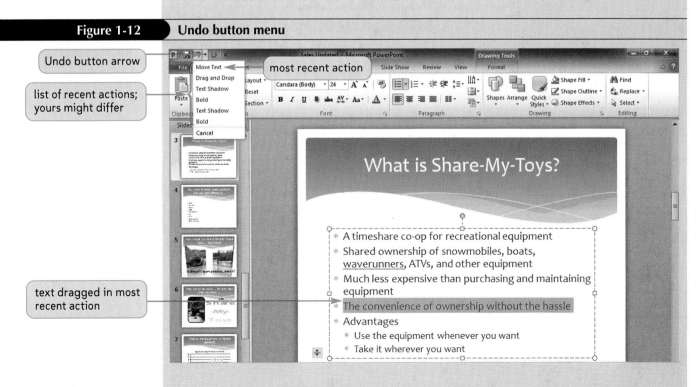

Undo button arrow

list of recent actions; yours might differ

text dragged in most recent action

> **2.** Without clicking, move the pointer down over the list. The actions you point to are highlighted. You could click any action in this list to undo it and all the actions above it. You need to undo just the most recent action, which is the Move Text action at the top of the list. You can click the top action, but you can also undo the most recent action by simply clicking the Undo button.

> **3.** Press the **Esc** key to close the menu without taking any action, and then click the **Undo** button ⟲. Your action of dragging the bulleted item "The convenience of ownership" from the third position to the fourth position is undone, and it moves back to its original position as the third bulleted item.

TIP

You can press the Ctrl+X keys to cut selected text, the Ctrl+C keys to copy selected text, and the Ctrl+V keys to paste text on the Clipboard.

Sandra wants you to copy text from Slide 3 to Slide 4. To do this, you will place the copied text on the **Clipboard**, a temporary storage area on which text or other objects are stored when you cut or copy them. To **copy** text, you select it, and then use the Copy command to place a copy of it on the Clipboard so that you can paste it somewhere else. If you want to move text from one location and paste it somewhere else, you **cut** it—that is, remove it from the original location and place it on the Clipboard using the Cut command. Note that this is different from pressing the Delete or Backspace key to delete text. Deleted text is not placed on the Clipboard.

To copy text from Slide 3 to Slide 4:

> **1.** On Slide 3 in the Slide pane, in the second bulleted item, select the text **waverunner** (do not select the "s" or the comma).

> **2.** In the Clipboard group on the Home tab, click the **Copy** button 📋. The selected text is copied to the Clipboard.

> **3.** In the Slides tab, click the **Slide 4** thumbnail, and then in the Slide pane, click in the fourth bulleted item after the word "Kayak."

> **Trouble?** If the insertion point is blinking directly next to the last letter of the word "Kayak," press the → key or the spacebar to move it so there is a space between the word and the insertion point.

> **4.** In the Clipboard group, click the **Paste** button. The text you copied is pasted at the location of the insertion point, and the Paste Options button 📋 (Ctrl) ▾ appears below and to the right of the pasted text. See Figure 1-13.

Figure 1-13   **Pasted text and the Paste Options button**

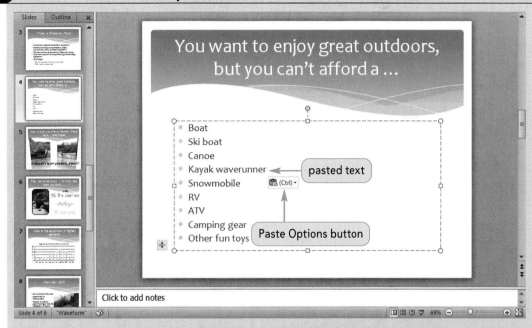

5. Click the **Paste Options** button 🅱 (Ctrl)▾. The Paste Options menu opens with four buttons on it. These buttons are described in Figure 1-14. The Paste Options menu buttons change depending on what is on the Clipboard to be pasted.

Figure 1-14   **Paste Options buttons**

Button	Button Name	Description
🖽	Use Destination Theme	Changes the formatting of the pasted text to match the theme and formatting of the paragraph in which it is pasted
🖾	Keep Source Formatting	Maintains the original formatting of the pasted text
🖼	Picture	Pastes the text as an image so it is no longer text and can be formatted with picture effects
Ⓐ	Keep Text Only	Pastes the text with no formatting so that it picks up the formatting of its new location

6. Point to (but do not click) each of the buttons in the Paste Options menu to see the ScreenTip associated with it and to see a Live Preview of the effect of clicking each button. In this case, the only button that changes the way the text is pasted is the Picture button. The default option, Use Destination Theme, is the best choice.

7. Click anywhere on the slide to close the Paste Options button menu without selecting anything. The Paste Options button remains on the screen until you click another command or start typing.

You can also click the Paste button arrow in the Clipboard group to access the Paste Options buttons before you paste the text.

Using AutoCorrect

The AutoCorrect feature automatically corrects certain words and typing errors. For example, if you accidentally type *teh* instead of *the*, as soon as you press the spacebar or the Enter key, AutoCorrect changes it to *the*. It also corrects capitalization errors, including changing the first word of sentences to an uppercase letter. In PowerPoint, AutoCorrect treats each bulleted item as a sentence and capitalizes the first word.

When AutoCorrect changes a word, the AutoCorrect symbol appears. You can point to the symbol so that it changes to the AutoCorrect Options button, and then click the button to undo the AutoCorrection or instruct AutoCorrect to stop making that particular type of correction. For example, if AutoCorrect fixed the spelling of a word, the menu choices would be to change the text back to its original spelling or to stop automatically correcting that specific word.

You need to change "waverunner" into a separate bulleted item in the list. When you do this, you will see AutoCorrect in use.

To create a new bulleted item and use AutoCorrect:

1. On Slide 4 in the Slide pane, in the fourth bulleted item, click immediately in front of the word "waverunner," and then press the **Enter** key. The text from the insertion point to the end of the line becomes a new bullet below "Kayak."

2. Click immediately after the word "waverunner" so there is no space between the final "r" and the insertion point, and then press the **spacebar**. AutoCorrect changes the first letter of "waverunner" to an uppercase W.

3. Position the pointer over the **W** in "Waverunner." The AutoCorrect symbol, a thin blue rectangle, appears below the "W." See Figure 1-15.

Figure 1-15 | AutoCorrect symbol on a slide

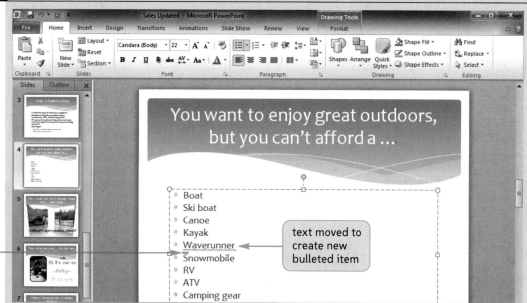

4. Position the pointer on top of the **AutoCorrect symbol** so that it changes to the AutoCorrect Options button ⚡ , and then click the **AutoCorrect Options** button ⚡ . The AutoCorrect Options menu appears. See Figure 1-16. Because the correction made was to change the capitalization, the top two choices allow you to undo the automatic capitalization or to tell AutoCorrect to stop auto-capitalizing the first letter of sentences. You want the word to be capitalized, so you'll close the menu without selecting any of the commands.

Figure 1-16   **AutoCorrect Options menu for automatic capitalization**

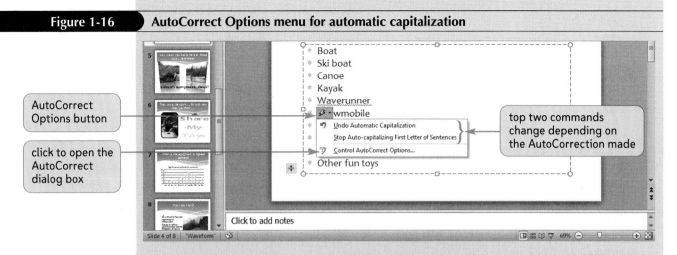

5. Click anywhere on the slide to close the menu without selecting a command. Now you will add a word to the slide title and use AutoCorrect to correct a misspelling.

6. In the title text box in the Slide pane, click immediately before the word "great," and then type **teh**.

7. Press the **spacebar**. The word you typed is changed to "the."

8. Position the pointer on top of the word "the," point to the AutoCorrect symbol that appears, and then click the **AutoCorrect Options** button ![icon]. Notice that the options on the menu are different from the options on the menu you opened when the word "waverunner" was capitalized.

9. Press the **Esc** key to close the menu without selecting a command.

Sandra examines the presentation, and asks you to make a few more edits. This time, you'll edit slide text using the Outline tab.

Editing Text in the Outline Tab

You can modify the text of a slide in the Outline tab as well as in the Slide pane. Working in the Outline tab allows you to see the outline of the entire presentation, not just the text of the single slide currently displayed in the Slide pane. When you view the outline in the Outline tab, you see only the text of the slide titles and the text in content placeholders; you do not see any graphics on the slides or any text that is not in a content placeholder. The Slide pane still displays the currently selected slide as usual.

To view slides in the Outline tab:

1. In the left pane, click the **Outline** tab. The outline of the presentation appears.

2. Drag the **scroll box** in the Outline tab down so that you can see all of the text on Slide 8 ("How do I join?") in the Outline tab. Slide 4 still appears in the Slide pane.

3. In the Outline tab, click the **Slide 8** slide icon ![icon]. All the text on Slide 8 is selected in the Outline tab, and Slide 8 appears in the Slide pane. Notice that the italicized text at the bottom of the slide in the Slide pane does not appear in the Outline tab. This text was added in a special text box that is not part of the content text box.

   Trouble? If the slide in the Slide pane is too large to fit in the window, click the Fit slide to current window button ![icon] on the right end of the status bar.

In the Outline tab, text is arranged as in an ordinary outline. Slide titles are the top levels in the outline, and the slide content—that is, the bulleted lists—are indented below the slide titles. You can use the Outline tab to see the outline of the entire presentation and easily move text around. For example, you can move a bulleted item from one slide to another, change a subbullet into a first-level bullet, or change a bulleted item into a slide title, creating a new slide.

Moving an item higher in the outline, for example, changing a second-level bullet into a first-level bullet or changing a first-level bulleted item into a slide title, is called **promoting** the item. Moving an item lower in the outline, for example, changing a slide title into a bulleted item on the previous slide or changing a first-level bullet into a second-level bullet, is called **demoting** the item.

Sandra thinks that the three specific types of boats listed on Slide 4 should be indented below the Boat bulleted item. You'll demote these items in the Outline tab.

To demote bulleted items in the Outline tab:

1. In the Outline tab, click the **Slide 4** slide icon ▦. The text on Slide 4 is selected in the Outline tab, and Slide 4 appears in the Slide pane.

2. In the Outline tab in the Slide 4 text, position the pointer over the bullet to the left of "Ski boat" so that the pointer changes to ✛, and then click. The Ski boat bulleted item is selected. See Figure 1-17.

Figure 1-17 **Bulleted item selected in the Outline tab**

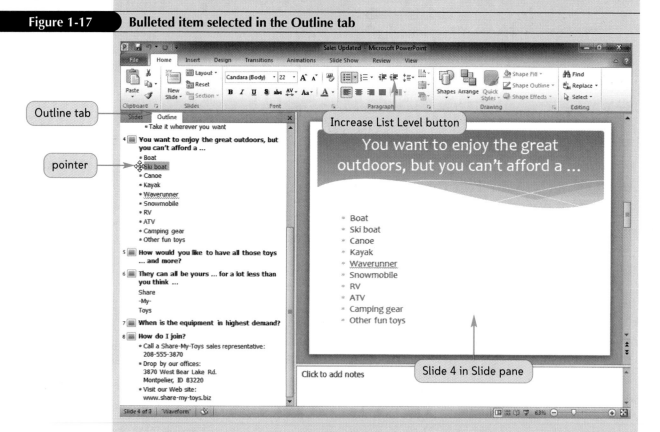

3. Press the **Tab** key. The selected first-level bulleted item is indented and becomes a second-level bulleted item. You'll demote the next two items at the same time.

4. Click the bullet next to "Canoe," press and hold the **Shift** key, and then click the bullet next to "Kayak." Both bulleted items are selected. Instead of using the keyboard, you'll use a button on the Ribbon to demote the selected items.

5. In the Paragraph group on the Home tab, click the **Increase List Level** button. The selected items are indented and become second-level bullets.

The name of the button you clicked in the Paragraph group, the Increase List Level button, is a little confusing. In an outline, the top-level items are called first-level headings, the items indented below the first-level headings are second-level headings, the items indented below those items are third-level headings, and so on. So when you change something from a second-level heading to a third-level heading by indenting it, you are *increasing* its level number from 2 to 3. That is why you click the Increase List Level button to indent an item in the Outline tab.

Sandra added text to the original "What is Share-My-Toys?" slide that you had created, but she now wants you to divide that slide's content into two slides. You'll do this by promoting a bulleted item so it becomes a slide title, thus creating a new slide.

To promote one of the bulleted items to a slide title in the Outline tab:

1. In the Outline tab, drag the **scroll box** up to the top of the scroll bar, and then click the **Slide 3** slide icon to select the text on Slide 3 in the Outline tab and display Slide 3 ("What is Share-My-Toys?") in the Slide pane.

2. In the Outline tab, in the Slide 3 text, click the bullet to the left of "Advantages." The Advantages bulleted item and the two subbullets below it are selected.

3. Press the **Shift+Tab** keys. The selected text becomes the new Slide 4. See Figure 1-18.

> **TIP**
>
> You can also click the Decrease List Level button in the Paragraph group on the Home tab to promote an item.

Figure 1-18 | **New Slide 4 created by promoting text**

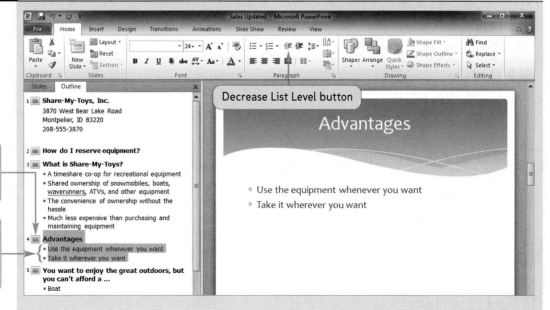

first-level bullet from Slide 3 promoted to slide title on new Slide 4

second-level bullets from Slide 3 promoted to first-level bullets on new Slide 4

The last bulleted item on Slide 3 ("What is Share-My-Toys?") should actually appear on the new Slide 4 ("Advantages"). If you need to move items from one slide to another, it is usually easier to do this in the Outline tab.

To move one of the bulleted items in the Outline tab:

▶ **1.** In the Outline tab, position the pointer over the last bullet in Slide 3 (it begins with "Much less expensive") so that the pointer changes to ✛.

▶ **2.** Press and hold the left mouse button, and then drag the bulleted item down so that the horizontal line indicating the position of the item you are dragging appears below the second bulleted item in Slide 4, as shown in Figure 1-19.

Figure 1-19   **Dragging a bulleted item in the Outline tab**

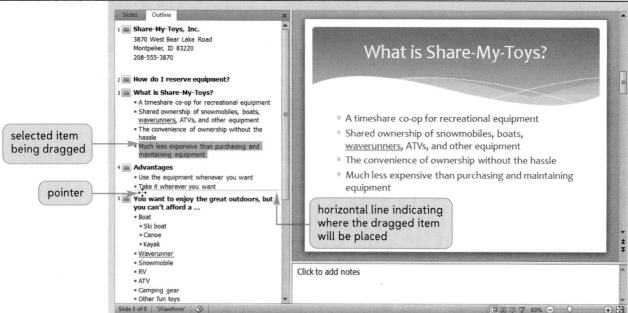

▶ **3.** With the horizontal line positioned below the second bulleted item in Slide 4, release the mouse button. The item is moved from Slide 3 to be the last item on Slide 4. Notice that the moved item also appears on Slide 4 in the Slide pane.

▶ **4.** On the Quick Access Toolbar, click the **Save** button 🔲 to save your changes.

PROSKILLS

Written Communication: Including Contact Information in a Presentation

A presentation should usually include contact information so that audience members know how to contact the presenter. In a sales presentation, the contact information might be more general, describing how to contact the company. The information should include all possible methods to contact the presenter, including the presenter's name, office phone number, cell phone number, email address, mailing address, and company Web site. If the presenter is not the only contact person at the company, or not the best contact person, include information about other people—sales representatives, marketing personnel, accountants, or other employees.

Rearranging Slides

In addition to moving bulleted items on slides or from slide to slide, you can rearrange the slides themselves. Depending on your needs, you can do this in the Slides or Outline tab in Normal view or in Slide Sorter view. **Slide Sorter view** displays all the slides in the presentation as thumbnails. This view not only provides you with a good overview of your presentation, but also allows you to easily change the order of the slides.

Because this presentation is intended to convince people to join Share-My-Toys, Sandra thinks it would be better if the first few slides after the title slide really caught the attention of the audience members and enticed them to continue watching the presentation. She wants you to move Slide 2 ("How do I reserve equipment?") so that is comes before Slide 9 ("How do I join?").You'll use the Slides tab in Normal view to move this slide.

To move Slide 2 in the Slides tab:

▶ **1.** In the left pane, click the **Slides** tab. The slide thumbnails appear.

▶ **2.** In the Slides tab, drag the **scroll box** up to the top of the vertical scroll bar.

▶ **3.** In the Slides tab, drag the **Slide 2** thumbnail down until the horizontal line following the pointer is between Slides 8 and 9, as shown in Figure 1-20.

Figure 1-20	Moving a slide in the Slides tab

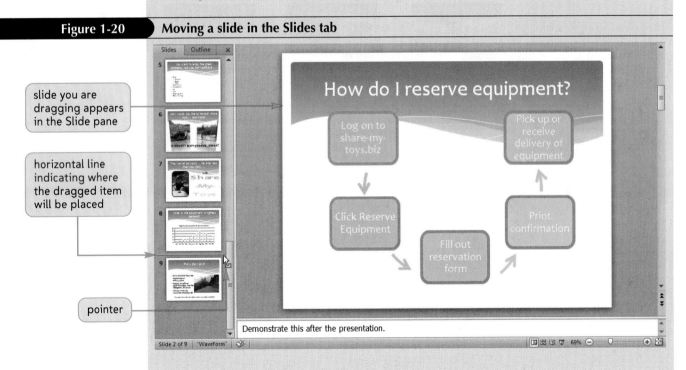

▶ **4.** With the horizontal line between Slides 8 and 9, release the mouse button. The slide titled "How do I reserve equipment?" is now Slide 8.

Now Sandra wants the new Slide 2 ("What is Share-My-Toys?") moved so it comes after Slide 6, the slide containing the picture of the woman in a boat and "Share-My-Toys" in large blue text. You'll do this in Slide Sorter view.

To move Slide 8 in Slide Sorter view:

▶ **1.** On the status bar, click the **Slide Sorter** button ⊞. The presentation appears in Slide Sorter view. A thick colored frame appears around the Slide 8 thumbnail indicating that the slide is selected.

▶ **2.** If necessary, on the Zoom slider on the right end of the status bar, click the **Zoom Out** button ⊖ to change the zoom level until you can see all nine slides arranged with four slides in the first two rows and Slide 9 in the last row.

▶ **3.** Drag the **Slide 2** thumbnail (the "What is Share-My-Toys?" slide) down so that the vertical line following the pointer is to the right of Slide 6, as shown in Figure 1-21.

Figure 1-21 ▶ **Moving a slide in Slide Sorter view**

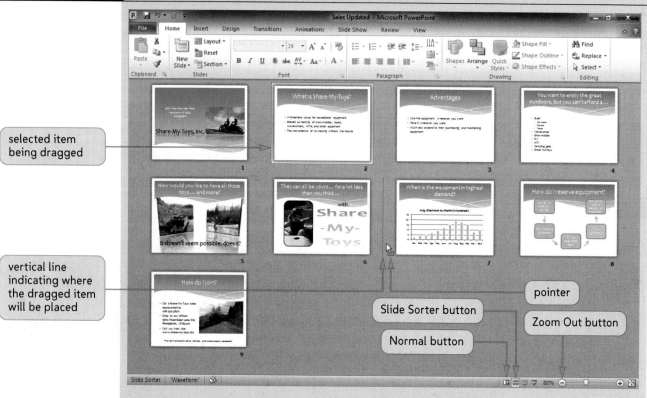

selected item being dragged

vertical line indicating where the dragged item will be placed

pointer

Slide Sorter button

Zoom Out button

Normal button

▶ **4.** Release the mouse button. The "What is Share-My-Toys?" slide is now Slide 6.

▶ **5.** On the status bar, click the **Normal** button ▦ to return to Normal view.

TIP

You could also double-click any slide thumbnail in Slide Sorter view to return to the previous view with the slide you clicked as the current slide.

You can also cut or copy and then paste slides, just as you did with text on a slide. You can do this in the Slides or Outline tab in Normal view or in Slide Sorter view.

Sandra wants you to move the current Slide 2 ("Advantages") so it follows Slide 6 ("What is Share-My-Toys"). You'll cut and paste the slide in the Slides tab in Normal view.

To cut and paste the "Advantages" slide:

▶ **1.** In the Slides tab, drag the **scroll box** up to the top of the scroll bar so that you can see Slide 2 in the Slides tab, and then click the **Slide 2** thumbnail. Slide 2 ("Advantages") appears in the Slide pane.

Be sure to click the slide thumbnail before you click the Cut button.

▶ **2.** In the Clipboard group on the Home tab, click the **Cut** button ✂. The Advantages slide is removed from the presentation and placed on the Clipboard.

Now you need to select the slide after which you want the slide you cut to appear.

3. In the Slides tab, click the **Slide 5** thumbnail. Slide 5 ("What is Share-My-Toys?") appears in the Slide pane.

4. In the Clipboard group on the Home tab, click the **Paste** button. The Advantages slide is pasted after Slide 5 as a new Slide 6.

5. On the Quick Access Toolbar, click the **Save** button 🖫 to save your changes.

Deleting Slides

When creating a presentation, you will sometimes need to delete slides. You can delete slides in the Slides and Outline tabs in Normal view and in Slide Sorter view.

REFERENCE

Deleting Slides

- In Slide Sorter view or in the Slides tab in Normal view, right-click the slide thumbnail of the slide you want to delete; or in the Outline tab in Normal view, right-click the slide title of the slide you want to delete.
- On the shortcut menu, click Delete Slide.
or
- In Slide Sorter view or in the Slides tab in Normal view, click the slide thumbnail of the slide you want to delete; or in the Outline tab in Normal view, click the slide icon of the slide you want to delete.
- Press the Delete key.

Sandra decided that she would like you to delete Slide 7 ("When is the equipment in highest demand?"). Although this is something members should know, pointing out potential difficulties in renting equipment seems out of place in a presentation designed to attract new business.

To delete Slide 7:

1. In the Slides tab, click the **Slide 7** thumbnail. Slide 7 ("When is the equipment in highest demand?") appears in the Slide pane. It's a good idea to verify that you are deleting the correct slide by first displaying it in the Slide pane.

2. In the Slides tab, right-click **Slide 7**. A shortcut menu appears. See Figure 1-22.

Figure 1-22   **Shortcut menu for a thumbnail in the Slides tab**

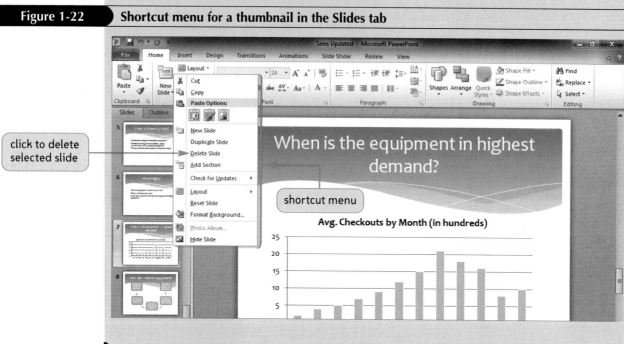

click to delete selected slide

shortcut menu

3. On the shortcut menu, click **Delete Slide**. Slide 7 is deleted and the slide titled "How do I reserve equipment?" is now Slide 7 and appears in the Slide pane.

4. Save your changes.

Running a Slide Show

Now that you have created and edited a presentation, you are ready to run the slide show. You can run the slide show in both Slide Show view and in Reading view.

Slide Show view displays each slide so that it fills the entire screen with no toolbars or other Windows elements visible on the screen, one after the other, and displays special effects applied to the slides and to the text and graphics on the slides.

As the presenter, when you switch to Slide Show view, you need to advance the slide show; that is, you need to do something to display the next slide. There are many ways to advance a slide show, including clicking the left mouse button, pressing specific keys, using commands on a shortcut menu in Slide Show view, or using the Slide Show toolbar, which appears on the screen only in Slide Show view. You will see these methods when you examine the presentation in Slide Show view.

You want to see how Sandra's presentation will appear when she shows it in Slide Show view to a potential Share-My-Toys member.

To run the slide show in Slide Show view:

1. Click the **Slide Show** tab on the Ribbon, and then in the Start Slide Show group, click the **From Beginning** button. Slide 1 appears on the screen in Slide Show view. You could also press the F5 key to start the slide show from Slide 1.

Now you need to advance the slide show. Using the keyboard, you can press the spacebar, the Enter key, the → key, or the Page Down key.

2. Press the **spacebar**. Slide 2 appears on the screen.

3. Press the **Enter** key to move to Slide 3. You can also use the mouse to move from one slide to another.

4. Click the left mouse button. The next slide, Slide 4 ("They can all be yours..."), appears on the screen. To move to the previous screen, you can press the ← key, the Page Up key, or the Backspace key.

5. Press the ← key. Slide 3 appears again. Right-clicking the mouse opens a shortcut menu. The shortcut menu allows you to jump to specific slides.

6. Right-click anywhere on the screen to display a shortcut menu. See Figure 1-23.

Figure 1-23   **Shortcut menu in Slide Show view**

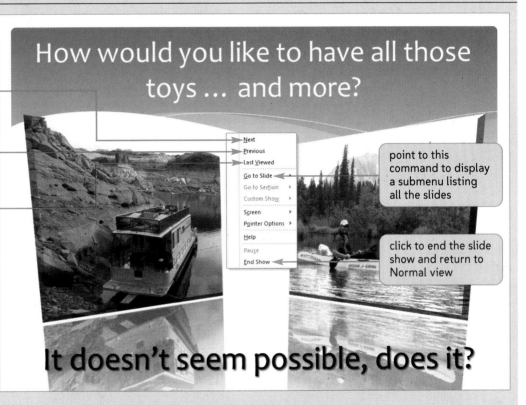

click to move to the next slide

click to move to the previous slide

click to move to the previously viewed slide

point to this command to display a submenu listing all the slides

click to end the slide show and return to Normal view

7. On the shortcut menu, point to **Go to Slide**, and then click **6 Advantages**. Slide 6 ("Advantages") appears on the screen.

8. Right-click anywhere on the screen, and then on the shortcut menu, click **Last Viewed**. The most recently viewed slide prior to Slide 6—Slide 3 ("How would you like...")—appears again.

9. Click the left mouse button twice to move to Slide 5 ("What is Share-My-Toys?"), and then move the pointer without clicking it. A very faint toolbar appears in the lower-left corner. See Figure 1-24. On this toolbar, you can click the Next ➡ or Previous ⬅ button to move to the next or previous slide, or click the Slide Show menu button 🔲 to open the same menu that appears when you right-click on the slide.

| Figure 1-24 | **Toolbar in Slide Show view** |

What is Share-My-Toys?

* A timeshare co-op for recreational equipment
* Shared ownership of snowmobiles, boats, waverunners, ATVs, and other equipment
* The convenience of ownership without the hassle

Next button

Slide Show menu button

Previous button

toolbar in Slide Show view (might be very faint on your screen)

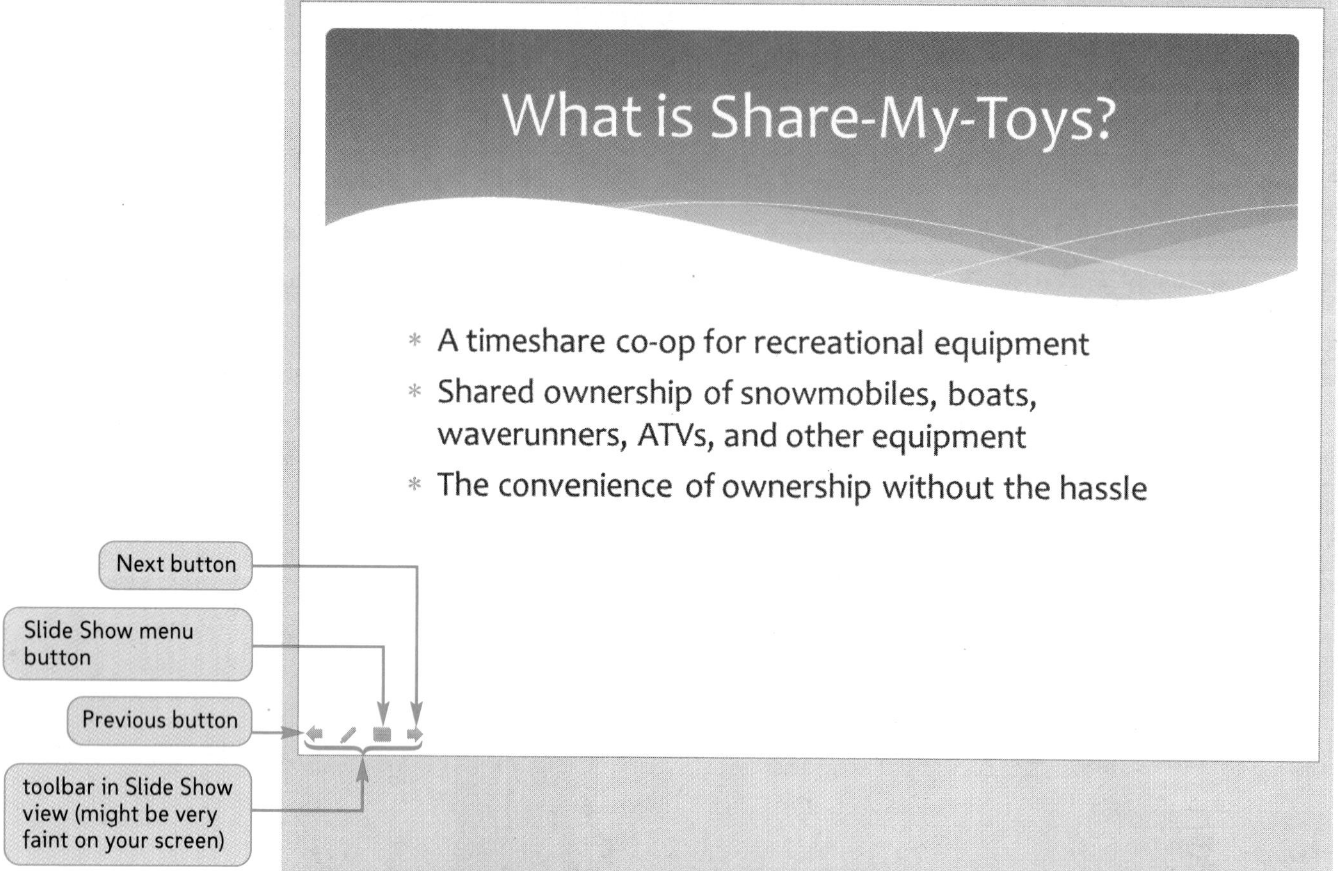

TIP

To end the slide show before you reach the last slide, press the Esc key.

▶ **10.** On the toolbar, click the **Next** button ➡. Slide 6 ("Advantages") appears.

▶ **11.** Move through the rest of the slides in the slide show using any method you want until you see a black screen after Slide 8 ("How do I join?"). As noted at the top of the screen, the black screen indicates the end of the slide show.

▶ **12.** Use any method for moving to the next slide to close Slide Show view. The presentation appears in Normal view again.

▶ **13.** Click the **File** tab to display Backstage view, and then click the **Close** command in the navigation bar to close the presentation.

Reading view is very similar to Slide Show view. **Reading view** displays each slide so that it almost fills the entire screen, but it also displays the title bar and status bar, and provides navigation buttons on the status bar for moving from slide to slide as you review the presentation. The Menu button on the status bar, similar to the Slide Show menu button on the Slide Show toolbar in Slide Show view, displays a menu that contains navigation commands as well as commands to copy and print the slide. The Menu button menu also contains the Edit Slides command; clicking this returns you to the previous view so you can edit your presentation. The view buttons also appear on the status bar in Reading view. Figure 1-25 shows Slide 1 of the Sales Updated presentation in Reading view. You use the same techniques for moving through the slide show in Reading view as you do in Slide Show view. You cannot edit the presentation in Reading view.

Figure 1-25   **Presentation in Reading view**

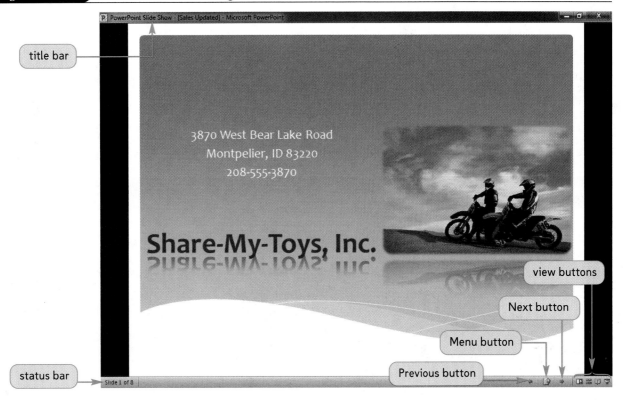

You have created a presentation, edited and formatted text in a presentation, rearranged and deleted slides, and viewed a slide show. In the next session, you'll add special effects to make the slide show more interesting, and you'll add footers and speaker notes. Then you'll check the spelling, and preview and print the presentation.

Session 1.1 Quick Check

REVIEW

1. What is the name of the view that displays the slide thumbnails or presentation outline in a tab on the left, the slides in a Slide pane, and speaker notes below the Slide pane?
2. What is a placeholder?
3. What is a layout?
4. What does AutoFit do?
5. Define theme.
6. True or False. When you demote a slide title, you are changing it to a first-level bulleted item.
7. True or False. You can rearrange slides in the Slides tab, but not in the Outline tab.
8. Describe Reading view.

SESSION 1.2 VISUAL OVERVIEW

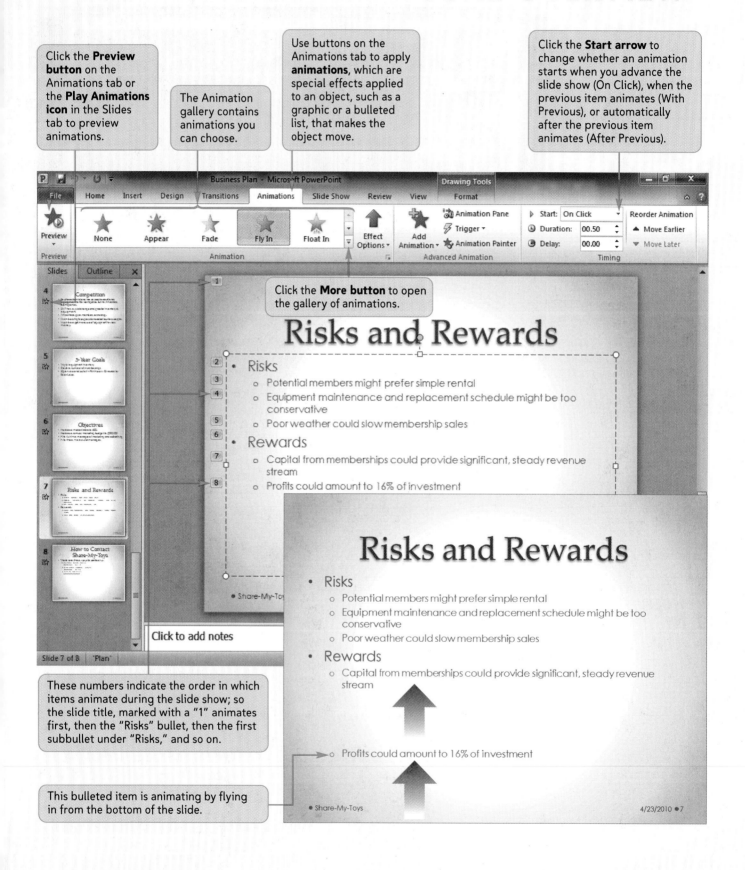

Click the **Preview button** on the Animations tab or the **Play Animations icon** in the Slides tab to preview animations.

The Animation gallery contains animations you can choose.

Use buttons on the Animations tab to apply **animations**, which are special effects applied to an object, such as a graphic or a bulleted list, that makes the object move.

Click the **Start arrow** to change whether an animation starts when you advance the slide show (On Click), when the previous item animates (With Previous), or automatically after the previous item animates (After Previous).

Click the **More button** to open the gallery of animations.

These numbers indicate the order in which items animate during the slide show; so the slide title, marked with a "1" animates first, then the "Risks" bullet, then the first subbullet under "Risks," and so on.

This bulleted item is animating by flying in from the bottom of the slide.

USING ANIMATIONS AND TRANSITIONS

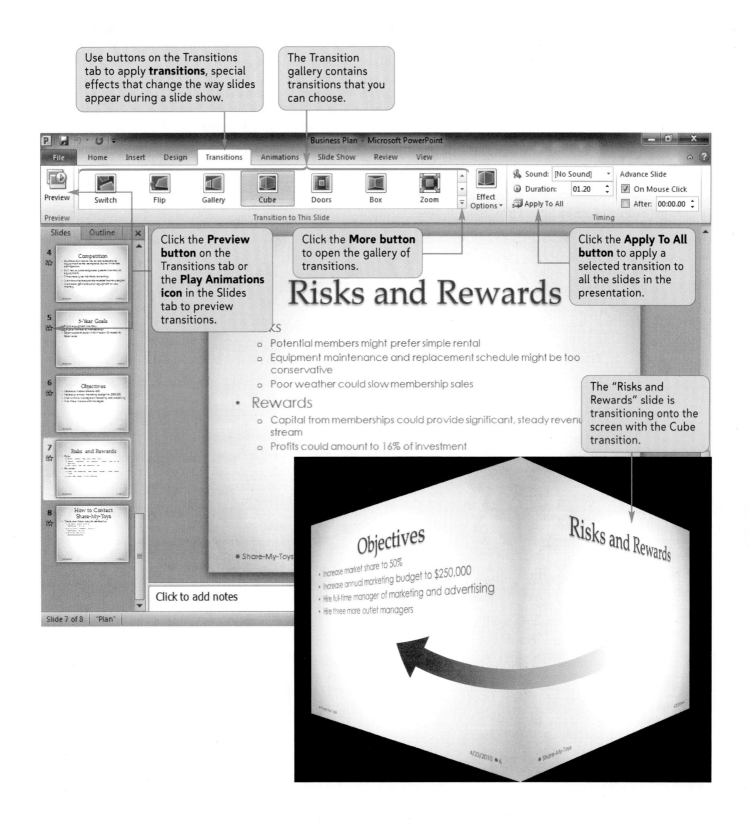

Use buttons on the Transitions tab to apply **transitions**, special effects that change the way slides appear during a slide show.

The Transition gallery contains transitions that you can choose.

Click the **Preview button** on the Transitions tab or the **Play Animations icon** in the Slides tab to preview transitions.

Click the **More button** to open the gallery of transitions.

Click the **Apply To All button** to apply a selected transition to all the slides in the presentation.

The "Risks and Rewards" slide is transitioning onto the screen with the Cube transition.

Creating a Presentation Based on an Existing Presentation

Sometimes it is easier to create a new presentation based on an existing presentation or a template. A **template** is a PowerPoint file that contains a theme, sample text, and graphics on the slides or slide background to guide you as you develop your content. When you open a template, you open a copy of the template, not the template file itself. You can treat an ordinary PowerPoint presentation as a template by opening it, and then saving it with a new name using the Save As command. But, to avoid accidentally overwriting the original file, you can use the New from existing command. When you use this command, you open a copy of the presentation, leaving the original presentation untouched.

Sandra developed a text presentation to show to potential investors to raise capital for her business. She would like you to animate the text on the slides; however, she wants you to work on a copy of the presentation so that she can refer to her original version.

To create the new presentation based on an existing presentation:

1. If you took a break after the previous session, start PowerPoint.

2. Click the **File** tab, and then click the **New** tab in the navigation bar. Backstage view changes to display the New tab. See Figure 1-26.

Figure 1-26	The New tab in Backstage view

click the Home button to return to this screen

content available on your computer or network

New tab

categories of templates and slides available on Office.com (you might see different categories on your screen)

click to open the New from Existing Presentation dialog box

▶ **3.** In the Home section, click **New from existing**. The New from Existing Presentation dialog box opens. This dialog box is similar to the Open dialog box.

   Trouble? If you clicked one of the other commands in the center pane, you can return to the list of commands for creating a new presentation by clicking the Home button at the top of the Home section of the New tab.

▶ **4.** Navigate to the PowerPoint1\Tutorial folder, and then click **Plan**. The Open button in the dialog box changes to the Create New button.

▶ **5.** Click the **Create New** button. The Plan presentation opens. Notice that the filename in the title bar is the temporary filename "Presentation2" (or another number) rather than the name of the file you opened. Now you can save it.

▶ **6.** On the Quick Access Toolbar, click the **Save** button 🔲, navigate to the PowerPoint1\Tutorial folder (if necessary), type **Business Plan** in the File name box, and then click the **Save** button. The presentation is saved with the new name.

   As you work with this presentation, you might notice a few spelling errors. You will fix these errors later in this session.

Notice that the theme name in the status bar is "Plan." When you create a new presentation based on an existing presentation or on a template, the theme in the new presentation is renamed to be the same as the name of the presentation or template on which the new presentation is based. This is to ensure that any changes you might have made to the theme in the original presentation are maintained in the new presentation.

Next, Sandra wants you to add special animation effects to the slide text.

Animating Text

Animations add interest to a slide show and draw attention to the text or object being animated. For example, you can animate a slide title to fly in from the side or spin around like a pinwheel to draw the audience's attention to that title. Refer to the Session 1.2 Visual Overview for more information about animations.

When you apply an animation to text, you are applying it to all the text in the text box. If you animate a bulleted list, the default is for the items to appear using **progressive disclosure**, an animation process in which bulleted items appear one at a time. This type of animation focuses your audience's attention on each item, without the distractions of items that you haven't discussed yet.

Animation effects are grouped into four types:

- **Entrance:** Text and objects animate as they appear on the slide; one of the most commonly used animation types.
- **Emphasis:** The appearance of text and objects already visible on the slide changes or the text or objects move.
- **Exit:** Text and objects leave the screen before the slide show advances to the next slide.
- **Motion Paths:** Text and objects follow a path on a slide.

When you choose an animation, keep the purpose of your presentation and your audience in mind. Flashy or flamboyant animations are acceptable for informal, fun-oriented presentations but would not be appropriate in a formal business, technical, or educational presentation. These types of presentations should be more conservative.

Animating Slide Titles and Bulleted Lists

The default for slide titles is to animate when the presenter advances the slide show. The default for first-level bulleted items is to appear using progressive disclosure when the presenter advances the slide show. The default for subbullets, however, is to animate at the same time as their first-level bullets.

Sandra wants you to add an animation effect to the slide titles in her presentation. Remember that this presentation is for banks and potential investors. While you want to capture their attention, you should not select an animation that appears frivolous, such as one that makes the text bounce or spin onto the screen.

To animate the slide titles:

TIP

You can also click the Add Animation button in the Advanced Animation group to open the Animations gallery.

1. Display **Slide 2** ("Mission Statement") in the Slide pane, and then click the **Animations** tab on the Ribbon. The commands on the Animations tab appear on the Ribbon; however the animations in the Animations groups are grayed out, indicating they are not available. This is because nothing is selected on the slide.

2. In the Slide pane, click anywhere on the **title text**. The animations in the Animation group darken to indicate that they are now available. All of the animations currently visible in the Animations group are entrance animations.

3. In the Animation group, point to the **Fly In** button. Live Preview shows the slide title flying in from the bottom of the slide. You'll use an Emphasis animation instead.

4. In the Animation group, click the **More** button. The Animation gallery opens. See Figure 1-27.

| Figure 1-27 | **Animations gallery open on the Animations tab** |

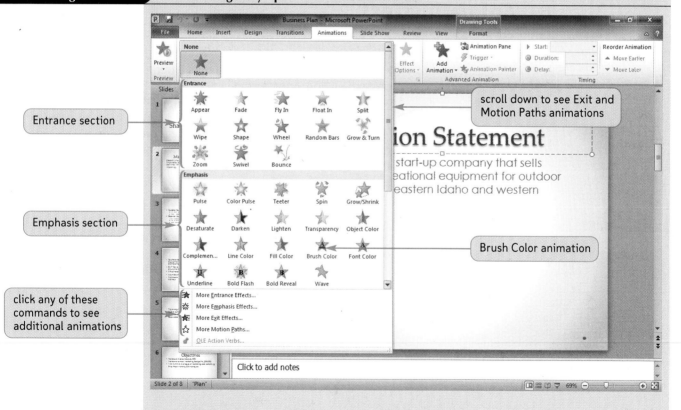

Entrance section

Emphasis section

click any of these commands to see additional animations

scroll down to see Exit and Motion Paths animations

Brush Color animation

5. In the Emphasis section, click the **Brush Color** button. The gallery closes and the animation previews in the Slide pane by changing the color of the slide title to red, brushing the new color from left to right. You can preview the animation again if you missed it.

6. In the Slides tab, under the Slide 2 slide number, click the **Play Animations** icon ⭐. The slide title animates on the slide again. After the preview is finished, notice the number 1 to the left of the slide title. This indicates that this is the first animation that will occur on the slide. In the Timing group on the Animations tab, the Start box displays the option On Click, indicating that this animation will occur when you advance the slide show. Now you need to apply the same animation to all the slide titles in the presentation.

7. Display **Slides 3** through **8** in the Slide pane one at a time, and then apply the **Brush Color** animation to the slide title on each slide.

8. Display **Slide 1** in the Slide pane, and then apply the **Brush Color** animation to the title text.

If you change your mind and decide that you don't want specific text to be animated, you can remove the animation.

To remove the animation from the title text on Slide 1:

1. In the Slide pane, on Slide 1, click the **title text**.

2. In the Animation group, click the **More** button.

3. At the top of the gallery, click the **None** button. The gallery closes and the animation is removed from the title text on Slide 1.

Next, you need to animate the bulleted lists. To do this, you follow the same process as animating the slide titles.

To animate the bulleted lists:

1. Display **Slide 8** ("How to Contact Share-My-Toys") in the Slide pane, and then click anywhere in the bulleted list to make the text box active.

   Trouble? If Slide 8 is not "How to Contact Share-My-Toys," in the Slides tab, drag the Slide 7 thumbnail down below the Slide 8 thumbnail.

2. In the Animation group, click the **Float In** button. This is an entrance animation. The animation previews in the Slide pane as the bulleted items float in from the bottom. The number 2 appears next to the bulleted items, indicating that these items will animate second on the slide (after the slide title animates).

   Sandra thinks the Float In animation is a little sluggish, so she asks you to change it to a different type.

3. In the Animation group, click the **Fly In** button. The bulleted items fly in from the bottom.

4. Apply the **Fly In** animation to the bulleted lists that appear on **Slides 3** through **7** and to the paragraph on **Slide 2**.

5. Save your changes.

Modifying the Start Timing of an Animation

When you apply an animation to a slide title or a bulleted list, the default is for the text or object to animate "On Click," which means when you advance through the slide show. However, when a bulleted list contains subbullets, as is the case with Slides 3 and 7 of Sandra's presentation, the default is for only the first-level bullets to animate when the slide show is advanced; the subbullets animate with their first-level bullet. You can change this so that the subbullets animate individually.

REFERENCE

Modifying the Start Timing of the Animation of Subbullets

- In the Slide pane, click anywhere in the text box containing the subbullets to make it active.
- Click the Animations tab on the Ribbon, and then apply an animation to the active text box.
- In the Slide pane, select all the subbullets on the slide, or select all the bulleted items on the slide, or click the dashed line box surrounding the text box so it changes to a solid line.
- On the Animations tab, in the Timing group, click the Start button arrow, and then click On Click or After Previous.

The subbullets on Slide 3 describe the CEO and CFO of Share-My-Toys. There's no need to have these subbullets appear one at a time. However, on Slide 7, the subbullets are important points that Sandra wants to emphasize, so she would like them to animate individually rather than with their first-level bullets. You'll change the start timing of the subbullets' animation now.

To modify the start timing of the animation of subbullets on Slide 7:

1. Display **Slide 7** ("Risks and Rewards") in the Slide pane, and then in the first bulleted item, double-click **Risks**. See Figure 1-28. In the Timing group, notice that On Click appears in the Start box. This indicates that this item—the first-level bullet—will animate when you advance through the slide show. Notice also that the Risks bulleted item and its subbullets all have a small number 2 next to them, indicating that all of these items will animate together as the second thing to be animated on the slide.

Figure 1-28	Start timing for the Risks bullet on Slide 7

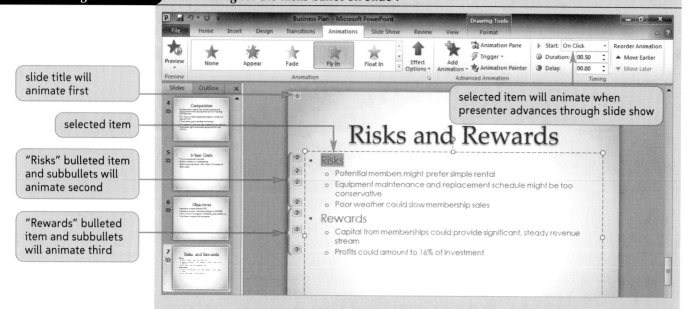

slide title will animate first

selected item

"Risks" bulleted item and subbullets will animate second

"Rewards" bulleted item and subbullets will animate third

selected item will animate when presenter advances through slide show

2. Under "Risks," click the **first subbullet**. The first subbulleted item is selected. In the Timing group, With Previous appears in the Start box. This means that the selected item will animate with—at the same time as—the previous item. You will change the animation of all of the subbullets so that they start when you advance the slide show.

Trouble? If you clicked the text of the subbulleted item, you will not see anything in the Start box. Click directly on the subbullet character.

3. Press and hold the **Ctrl** key, and then click each of the remaining four subbullets. All five subbullets on Slide 7 are now selected.

Trouble? If you accidentally clicked either of the first-level bullets, keep the Ctrl key pressed, and then click the bullet again to deselect it.

4. In the Timing group, click the **Start arrow**. The three choices for starting an animation appear. In addition to On Click and With Previous, you could choose After Previous, which animates the item after the previous animation has finished without you needing to advance the slide show.

5. Click **On Click**. Notice that each subbullet now has a different small number next to it, indicating the animation order for all the items in the bulleted list from 2 through 8. See Figure 1-29. Now the subbullets will animate individually when you advance the slide show.

Figure 1-29   Subbullets set to appear using progressive disclosure

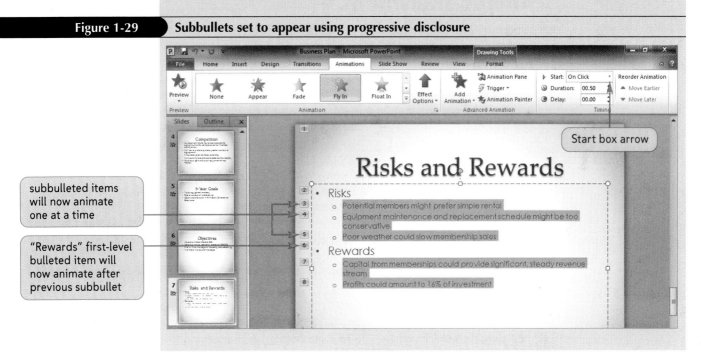

When you preview an animation, it plays automatically on the slide in the Slide pane, even if the timing setting for the animation is On Click. To make sure the timing settings are correct, you should watch the animation in Slide Show or Reading view. First, you'll preview the new animation on Slide 7, and then you'll test it in Reading view.

To preview and test the animation on Slide 7:

1. In the Preview group on the Animations tab, click the **Preview** button. The animations on Slide 7 play in the Slide pane. The Preview button is another method you can use to preview the animation. Now you will switch to Reading view.

2. On the status bar, click the **Reading View** button 📖 to start the slide show from Slide 7. Slide 7 appears in Reading view displaying only the slide title.

3. Press the **spacebar**. The slide title animates by changing color.

4. Press the **spacebar** again. The first bulleted item, "Risks," flies in from the bottom.

5. Press the **spacebar** again. The first subbullet under "Risks" flies in.

6. Press the **spacebar** five more times to display the rest of the bulleted items on Slide 7.

7. On the status bar, click the **Normal** button 🖳. The presentation appears in Normal view with Slide 7 displayed in the Slide pane.

8. Save your changes.

TIP

You can also press the Esc key or click the Menu button on the toolbar, and then click End Show to return to the previous view.

Adding Transitions

When you move from one slide to another in PowerPoint, the next slide simply appears on the screen in place of the previous slide. To make the slide show more interesting, you can add transitions between slides. You can apply transitions in Normal or Slide Sorter view.

As with animations, make sure the transitions you choose are appropriate for your audience and the presentation. In presentations with a formal tone, it's a good idea to apply one type of transition to all of the slides in the presentation. In a presentation designed to really grab the audience, such as a sales presentation, or to entertain them, such as a slide show displaying photos in a photo album, you can use a variety of transitions. The Business Plan presentation should convey an impression that Share-My-Toys will be a profitable business and is run by competent people; therefore, Sandra wants you to apply one transition to all of the slides except the last one, which contains contact information. She wants to draw attention to this information and the fact that it is the last slide in the presentation, so she asks you to apply a different, flashier transition to that slide.

REFERENCE

Adding Transitions

- In the Slides tab or the Outline tab in Normal view or in Slide Sorter view, select the slide(s) to which you want to add a transition, or, if applying to all the slides, select any slide.
- Click the Transitions tab on the Ribbon.
- In the Transition to This Slide group, click the More button to display the gallery of transition effects.
- Click the desired transition effect in the gallery.
- If desired, in the Timing group, click the Transition Sound button arrow to insert a sound effect to accompany each transition.
- If desired, in the Timing group, click the Transition Speed button arrow to modify the speed of the transition.
- To apply the transition to all the slides in the presentation, in the Timing group, click the Apply to All button.

You'll add a transition to all the slides in the presentation, and then add a different transition to the last slide.

To add transitions to the presentation:

▶ **1.** Click the **Transitions** tab on the Ribbon.

▶ **2.** In the Transition to This Slide group, click the **Push** button. You see a preview of the Push transition.

▶ **3.** In the Transition to This Slide group, click the **More** button to display the gallery of transitions, and then in the second row in the Exciting section, click the **Flip** button to see a preview of this transition.

▶ **4.** In the Transition to This Slide group, click the **Cube** button. A preview of the Cube transition appears in the Slide pane. If you miss a preview, you can see it again.

▶ **5.** In the Preview group on the Transitions tab, click the **Preview** button. Now you need to apply the transition to all of the slides.

▶ **6.** In the Timing group, click the **Apply To All** button. The selected transition is applied to all of the slides in the presentation. Now you want to apply a different transition to the last slide.

▶ **7.** In the Slides tab, click the **Slide 8** thumbnail.

▶ **8.** In the Transition to This Slide group, click the **More** button, and then in the first row in the Exciting section, click the **Blinds** button. The Blinds transition is applied to the current slide, Slide 8, and a preview of the Blinds transition appears.

Now you can test your transitions. In addition to switching to Slide Show or Reading view, you can open a small window containing the slide show on top of the program window. You'll start the slide show at Slide 6 because you don't need to run through the entire slide show, just a few of the slides.

> **TIP**
>
> Clicking the Play Animations button under the slide number in the Slides tab displays a preview of both the transition and the animations.

To test the transitions in a slide show window in Normal view:

▶ **1.** In the Slides tab, click the **Slide 6** thumbnail. Slide 6 ("Objectives") appears in the Slide pane.

▶ **2.** Press and hold the **Ctrl** key, and then in the status bar, click the **Slide Show** button ⬚. A small window opens on top of the program window, and Slide 6 transitions onto the screen in the small window. Clicking the Slide Show button in the status bar starts the slide show from the current slide. Pressing and holding the Ctrl key at the same time causes the mini Slide Show window to appear instead of the slide filling the entire screen. See Figure 1-30.

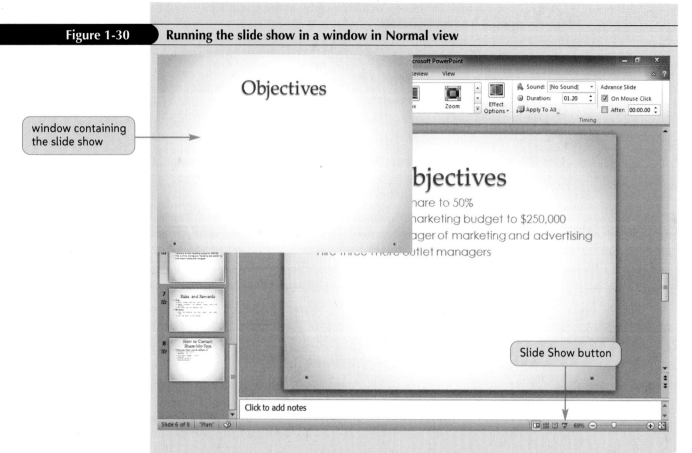

Figure 1-30 Running the slide show in a window in Normal view

window containing the slide show

Slide Show button

> **3.** Click in the small window or press the **spacebar** or **Enter** key five times to animate the title and then the bulleted list.
>
> **Trouble?** If the small slide show window disappears, you clicked in the PowerPoint program window instead of in the slide show window. Point to the PowerPoint button on the taskbar, click the PowerPoint Slide Show thumbnail, and then continue advancing the slide show.
>
> **4.** Advance the slide show. The slide show transitions to Slide 7 ("Risks and Rewards") using the Cube transition.
>
> **5.** Advance the slide show eight times to animate the title and then display the bullets and subbullets.
>
> **6.** Advance the slide show once more. The slide show transitions to Slide 8 ("How to Contact Share-My-Toys") using the Blinds transition. You don't need to test the animations on Slide 8.
>
> **7.** Right-click anywhere in the small slide show window, and then on the shortcut menu, click **End Show**. The small slide show window closes.
>
> **8.** Save your changes.

If you do not end the slide show in this window, the next time you open Slide Show view, this small window will open instead.

Inserting Footers, Slide Numbers, and the Date

In documents, a footer is text that appears at the bottom of every page. In PowerPoint, a **footer** is text that appears on every slide, but depending on the theme applied, it might not always appear at the bottom of a slide. In addition to a footer, you can display a date and the slide number. These two elements are treated separately from the footer.

Sandra would like to have the company name appear as the footer on each slide, along with the slide number and the current date. She does not want any text to appear at the bottom of the first slide, though. You'll add these elements now.

To insert the footer, slide number, and date on the slides:

1. Click the **Insert** tab on the Ribbon.

2. In the Text group, click the **Header & Footer** button. The Header and Footer dialog box opens with the Slide tab on top. See Figure 1-31. In the Preview box in the lower-right corner of the dialog box, you can see rectangles at the bottom of the preview slide. These rectangles identify where the footer, date, and slide number will appear. Their exact positions change depending on the theme applied.

Figure 1-31 | **Slide tab in the Header and Footer dialog box**

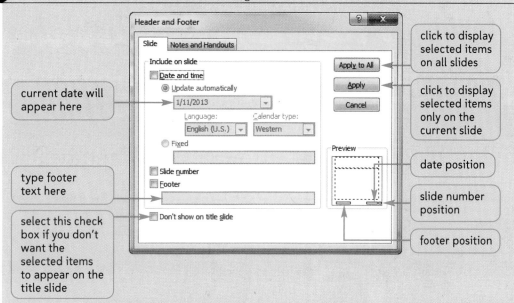

3. Click the **Footer** check box to select it. In the Preview box, the rectangle on the left turns black to indicate that the footer will appear on the slides. The insertion point is blinking in the Footer text box.

4. In the Footer text box, type **Share-My-Toys**. Now you can add the slide number.

5. Click the **Slide number** check box to select it. The right rectangle in the Preview box turns black to indicate that the slide number will appear in this location on each slide.

6. Click the **Date and time** check box. The center rectangle in the Preview box turns black, and the options under this check box darken to allow you to choose one of them. You want the current date to always appear on the slides.

7. If necessary, click the **Update automatically** option button. Now the current date will appear on the slides every time the presentation is opened. Remember that Sandra does not want this information to appear on the title slide.

8. Click the **Don't show on title slide** check box to select it.

9. Click the **Apply to All** button. The dialog box closes and all the slides except the title slide now contain the footer, slide number, and today's date.

10. Display **Slide 1** (the title slide) in the Slide pane, verify that the footer, slide number, and date do not appear on the slide, and then save your changes.

TIP

Select the Fixed option button, and then type a date in the box under this option to have that date always appear on the slides.

Using Speaker Notes

Notes (also called **speaker notes**) help the speaker remember what to say when a particular slide appears during the presentation. They appear in the Notes pane below the Slide pane in Normal view; they do not appear during the slide show. You can switch to **Notes Page view** to display each slide in the top half of the presentation window and display the speaker notes for that slide in the bottom half. You can also print notes pages with a picture of and notes about each slide.

Sandra wants you to add a note to Slide 6 ("Objectives") to remind her to pass out her marketing plan at this point in the presentation. You'll do this now.

To create the note and view slides in Notes Page view:

▶ 1. In the Slides tab, click the **Slide 6** thumbnail. Slide 6 ("Objectives") appears in the Slide pane. The placeholder text "Click to add notes" appears in the Notes pane below the Slide pane.

▶ 2. Click in the **Notes** pane, and then type **Pass out marketing plan handouts**. See Figure 1-32.

Figure 1-32   Speaker note on Slide 6

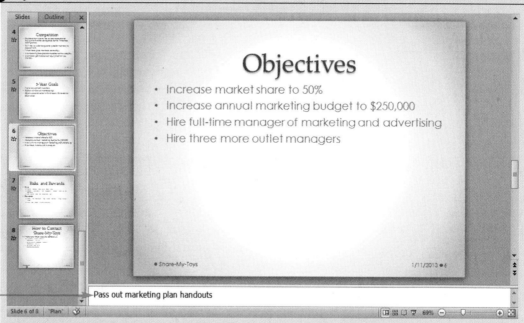

note in Notes pane

Now you want to view the slides with notes in Notes Page view.

▶ 3. Click the **View** tab on the Ribbon.

▶ 4. In the Presentation Views group, click the **Notes Page** button. Slide 6 is displayed in Notes Page view. See Figure 1-33.

| Figure 1-33 | Slide 6 in Notes Page view |

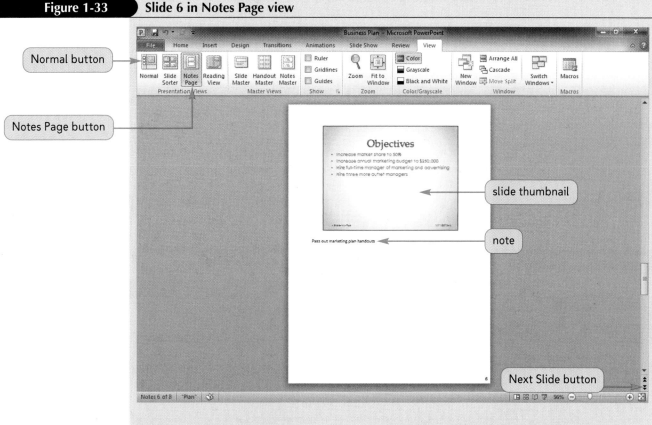

TIP

In Normal view and in Notes Page view, you can also press the Page Up key to move to the previous slide or the Page Down key to move to the next slide.

5. At the bottom of the vertical scroll bar, click the **Next Slide** button ⧩. Slide 7 ("Risks and Rewards") appears in Notes Page view. Because this slide does not contain any speaker notes, you see the notes placeholder below the slide.

6. In the Presentation Views group, click the **Normal** button. Slide 7 appears in the Slide pane in Normal view.

7. Save your changes.

Before Sandra gives her presentation, she'll print the notes pages so she'll have them available during her presentation. Next she wants to make sure there are no spelling errors in the presentation.

Checking the Spelling in a Presentation

Before you print or present a slide show, you should always perform a final check of the spelling of all the text in your presentation. This is commonly called using the spell-checker, or **spell-checking**. This helps to ensure that your presentation is accurate and professional looking.

When a word on a slide is not in the built-in PowerPoint dictionary and it doesn't AutoCorrect, the word is underlined with a wavy, red line so that you can see the word is potentially misspelled. Any word that is not in the dictionary is flagged, so proper names could be flagged as misspelled even if they are correct.

The context in which words are used can also be checked, so words that are spelled correctly but might be used incorrectly are flagged as well. For example, if you type "their" when you mean "there," the word would be flagged. This is referred to as **contextual spell-checking**. Of course, a computer program can't be 100 percent accurate in determining the correct context, especially in bulleted items that are incomplete sentences, so you still have to carefully proofread your presentation. By default, contextual spell-checking is turned off, so you need to turn this feature on.

To turn on contextual spell-checking:

1. Click the **File** tab, and then click the **Options** command in the navigation bar. The PowerPoint Options dialog box opens.

2. In the list in the left pane, click **Proofing**. The right pane of the dialog box changes to display options for proofing and correcting presentations.

3. If necessary, at the bottom of the dialog box under When correcting spelling in PowerPoint, click the **Use contextual spelling** check box to select it. A check mark appears in the check box. See Figure 1-34.

   Trouble? If the Use contextual spelling check box is already selected, do not click it or it will become deselected.

Figure 1-34	PowerPoint Options dialog box with Proofing selected

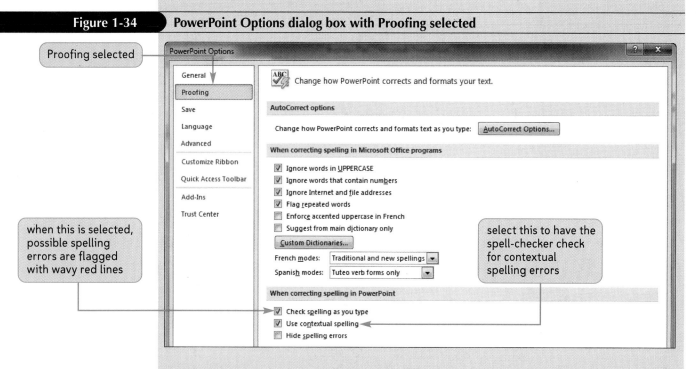

4. Click the **OK** button. The dialog box closes.

There are two ways to correct misspelled words. You can right-click a word flagged with the wavy, red line to open a shortcut menu containing suggestions for alternate spellings as well as commands for ignoring the misspelled word or opening the Spelling dialog box. Or, you can check the spelling of the entire presentation by clicking the Spelling button in the Proofing group on the Review tab.

You'll check the spelling in the Business Plan presentation. You will use the shortcut menu method first.

TIP

You can also right-click flagged words in the Outline tab.

To check the spelling of a flagged word:

1. Display **Slide 5** ("5-Year Goals") in the Slide pane. In the second bulleted item, the word "Duble" is flagged as misspelled.

2. In the Slide pane, right-click **Duble**. A shortcut menu opens. See Figure 1-35.

| Figure 1-35 | Shortcut menu for a misspelled word |

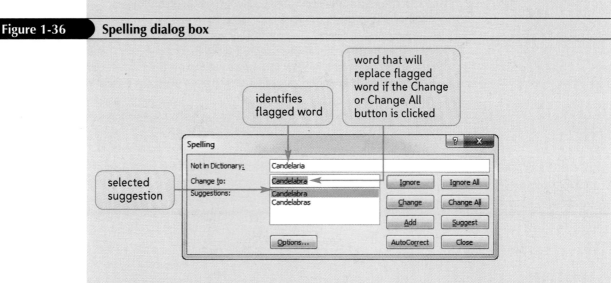

3. On the shortcut menu, click **Double**. The word changes to "Double."

Now you will check the spelling in the whole presentation.

To check the spelling in the whole presentation:

1. Click the **Review** tab on the Ribbon.

2. In the Proofing group, click the **Spelling** button. The spell-check starts from the current slide. The next slide containing a possible misspelled word, Slide 8 ("How to Contact Share-My-Toys"), appears in the Slide pane, and the Spelling dialog box opens. See Figure 1-36. Ernesto's last name is selected in the Slide pane as well. This word, however, is not misspelled; it is a surname. Ernesto's name also appears on Slide 3 ("The Team"), so you will tell the spell-checker to ignore all instances of this word.

| Figure 1-36 | Spelling dialog box |

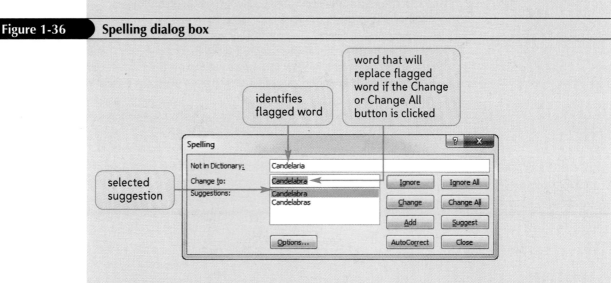

> **Trouble?** If PowerPoint doesn't flag "Candelaria," someone might have added it to the built-in dictionary. Read Step 3 but don't do it, and then continue with Step 4.

TIP

To ignore only the current instance of a flagged word, click the Ignore button instead of the Ignore All button.

3. Click the **Ignore All** button. The word is not changed on the slide, and the spell-check continues. Because Slide 8 is the last slide in the presentation and you started the spell-check on Slide 5, it cycles back to Slide 1 and continues searching. The next slide containing a possible misspelled word, Slide 2 ("Mission Statement"), appears in the Slide pane. The highlighted word "inn" is the correct spelling for a small country hotel, but it is the wrong word in this context; it should be "in." This is a contextual spelling error, so you wouldn't use the Change All command; you will change only this instance of the spelling.

   > **Trouble?** If your name on Slide 1 is flagged, click the Ignore button, and then continue with Step 4.

4. In the Spelling dialog box, make sure "in" appears in the Change to box, and then click the **Change** button. The word is corrected on the slide, the Spelling dialog box closes, and a dialog box opens telling you that the spelling check is complete.

   > **Trouble?** If another word in the presentation is flagged as misspelled, select the correct spelling in the Suggestions list, and then click the Change button.

5. In the dialog box, click the **OK** button. The dialog box closes.

6. Save your changes.

After you check the spelling, you should always reread your presentation; the spell-checker, even with the contextual spell-checking feature, doesn't catch every instance of a misused word.

Using the Research Pane

The Research pane is a feature that allows you to explore information in an encyclopedia, look up a definition, find a synonym, or translate a word. To open the Research pane, in the Proofing group on the Review tab, click the Research button. At the top of the Research pane, type the word or phrase you are looking up in the Search for box. To choose a research tool, click the arrow in the box below the Search for box at the top of the pane, and then click the tool you want to use. For example, if you want to look up a topic in the Encarta encyclopedia, select that tool from the list.

A shortcut to using the Research pane to look up a synonym is to right-click a word, and then point to Synonyms on the shortcut menu. You can also open the Research pane to the Thesaurus for currently selected word by clicking the Thesaurus button in the Proofing group on the Review tab, or by right-clicking a word, pointing to Synonyms on the shortcut menu, and then clicking Thesaurus. To open the Research pane to the Translation tool, click the Translate button in the Language group on the Review tab, and then click Translate Selected Text, or right-click a word, and then click Translate on the shortcut menu.

Now that you have proofread the presentation, Sandra asks you to run through the entire slide show to make sure that the animations and transitions appear as you expect.

To view the entire slide show:

1. Display **Slide 1** (the title slide) in the Slide pane, and then on the status bar, click the **Slide Show** button 🖵. The slide show starts with Slide 1 rolling onto the screen with the Cube transition.

2. Use any method you want to advance through the slide show until you reach Slide 8, "How to Contact Share-My-Toys," and then display the bulleted item on that slide. Each slide except Slide 8 should appear on the screen with the Cube transition. Each slide title animates by changing color, and then each first-level bulleted item flies in from the bottom one after the other. On Slide 7 ("Risks and Rewards"), the subbullets animate with progressive disclosure as well. The last slide ("How to Contact Share-My-Toys") transitions using the Blinds transition.

3. On Slide 8, point to the Web site address in the third subbullet. The pointer changes to 🖑 to indicate that this is a hyperlink. If you are connected to the Internet, you can click links during the slide show and jump to the Web sites identified by the links. (Note that the Web site address in this slide show is fictional.)

4. Press the **spacebar** to move to the black slide that indicates the end of the slide show, and then advance the slide show one more time. The presentation appears in Normal view with Slide 1 in the Slide pane. Next, you'll switch to Slide Sorter view to see the entire presentation.

5. On the status bar, click the **Slide Sorter** button 🔡, and then change the zoom to **90%** if necessary. The presentation appears in Slide Sorter view. See Figure 1-37.

Figure 1-37 | **Completed presentation in Slide Sorter view**

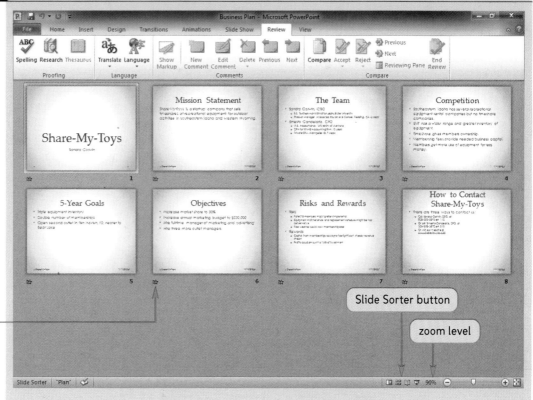

click the Play Animations button to preview transitions and animations

Slide Sorter button

zoom level

Written Communication: Creating Effective Text Presentations

Some presentations consist mainly of text, some presentations are exclusively graphics and multimedia, and others are a combination of elements. Each type of presentation has advantages for different types of audiences. A presentation consisting mostly of text allows audience members to absorb the information you are conveying by reading as well as listening. This can help audience members retain the information presented. When you create a text-based presentation, keep in mind the following:

- Make the organization of your presentation clear by using overview slides, making headings larger than subheadings, and including bulleted lists to highlight key points and numbered steps to show sequences.
- Employ the 7-7 Rule, which suggests using no more than seven bullet points per slide, with no more than seven words per bullet. Do not include so much text that your presentation consists of you reading all the bullet points aloud to the audience, leaving you with nothing else to say.
- Keep phrases parallel. For example, if one bulleted item starts with a verb (such as "Summarize"), all the other bulleted items should start with a verb (such as "Include," "List," or "Review").
- Use simple fonts in a size large enough to be read from the back of the room.
- For maximum contrast and readability, use dark-colored text on a light or white background to make it easy for the audience to quickly read the content.
- Do not layer text on top of a busy background graphic because the graphic will compete with the text.
- Always proofread your presentations. One sure way to reduce your credibility as a presenter is to have typographical errors in your presentation. It is especially important to double-check the spelling of proper names.
- Do not overly animate your slides. With too much action on the screen, the viewer might stop listening in order to watch what's happening on the slide.

Sandra now wants to preview and print her presentation. She needs several types of printouts, including handouts, notes pages, and an outline.

Previewing and Printing a Presentation

Before you deliver your presentation, you might want to print it. PowerPoint provides several printing options. For example, you can print the slides in color, grayscale, or pure black and white, and you can print one, some, or all of the slides.

You'll start by opening the Print tab in Backstage view.

To choose a printer and color options:

1. Click the **File** tab, and then click the **Print** tab in the navigation bar. Backstage view changes to display the Print tab. The Print tab contains options for printing your presentation, and a preview of the first page as it will print with currently selected options. See Figure 1-38.

Figure 1-38 **Print tab in Backstage view**

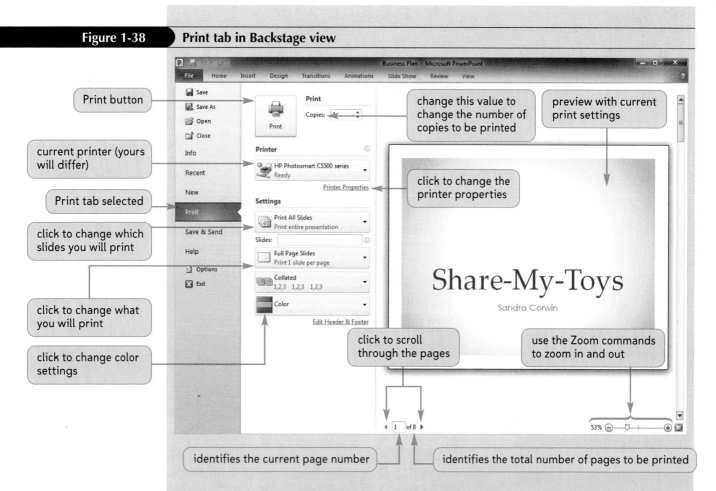

Print button

current printer (yours will differ)

Print tab selected

click to change which slides you will print

click to change what you will print

click to change color settings

change this value to change the number of copies to be printed

preview with current print settings

click to change the printer properties

click to scroll through the pages

use the Zoom commands to zoom in and out

Share-My-Toys

Sandra Corwin

identifies the current page number

identifies the total number of pages to be printed

▶ **2.** If you are connected to a network or are connected to more than one printer, make sure the printer listed in the Printer box is the one you want to use; if it is not, click the **Printer** button, and then click the desired printer from the list.

▶ **3.** Click the **Printer Properties** link to open the Properties dialog box for your printer. Usually, the default options are correct, but you can change any printer settings, such as print quality or the paper source, in this dialog box.

▶ **4.** Click the **Cancel** button to close the Properties dialog box. Now you can choose whether to print the presentation in color or black and white. Obviously, if you are connected to a black and white printer, the presentation will print in black and white or grayscale even if Color is selected in the bottom button in the Settings section. But if you plan to print in black and white or grayscale, you should change this setting so you can see what your slides will look like without color and to make sure they are legible.

▶ **5.** Click the **Color** button, and then click **Grayscale**. The preview changes to grayscale. Notice that the shading in the slide background was removed.

▶ **6.** At the bottom of the preview pane, click the **Next Page** button ▶ twice to display Slide 3 ("The Team") in the preview pane. The slides are legible in grayscale.

▶ **7.** If you will be printing in color, click the **Grayscale** button, and then click **Color**.

In the Settings section on the Print tab, you can click the Full Page Slides button to choose from among several choices for printing the presentation, as described below:

- **Full Page Slides:** Prints each slide full size on a separate piece of paper; speaker notes are not printed.
- **Notes Pages:** Prints each slide as a notes page, with the slide at the top of the page and speaker notes below the slide, similar to how a slide appears in Notes Page view.
- **Outline:** Prints the text of the presentation as an outline.
- **Handouts:** Prints the presentation with one, two, three, four, six, or nine slides on each piece of paper. When printing three slides per page, the slides appear down the left side of the page and lines for notes appear to the right of each slide. When printing four, six, or nine slides, you can choose whether to order the slides from left to right in rows (horizontally) or from top to bottom in columns (vertically).

Sandra wants you to print the title slide as a full page slide so that she can use it as a cover page for her handouts. The default is to print all the slides in the presentation as full page slides, one slide per page.

To print the title slide as a full page slide:

TIP

To print full page slides with a border around them, click the Full Page Slides button in the Settings section, and then click Frame Slides.

1. If the second button in the Settings section is not labeled "Full Page Slides," click it, and then click **Full Page Slides**.

2. In the Settings section, click the **Print All Slides** button. Note that you can print all the slides, selected slides, the current slide, or a custom range. You want to print just the title slide as a full page slide, not all eight slides.

3. Click **Custom Range**. The menu closes and the insertion point is blinking in the Slides box. The preview now is blank and at the bottom, the page number is 0 of 0.

4. In the Slides box, type **1**, and then click the **Next Page** button ▶ at the bottom of the preview pane. Slide 1 (the title slide) appears in the preview pane, and the information at the bottom indicates that you are viewing a preview of Page 1 of a total of 1 page to print. If you wanted to print a range of slides, you would type the number of the first slide you wanted to print, a hyphen, and then the number of the last slide you wanted to print. To print nonsequential slides, type a comma, and then type the next slide number.

5. At the top of the Print section, click the **Print** button. Backstage view closes and Slide 1 prints.

Next, Sandra wants you to print the slides as a handout, with all eight slides on a single sheet of paper.

To print all the slides as a handout:

1. Click the **File** tab, and then click the **Print** tab in the navigation bar.

2. In the Settings section, click the **Full Page Slides** button. A menu opens with choices for printing the presentation. See Figure 1-39. You want to print the presentation as a handout with all eight slides on one sheet of paper.

Figure 1-39   Print tab in Backstage view with print options menu open

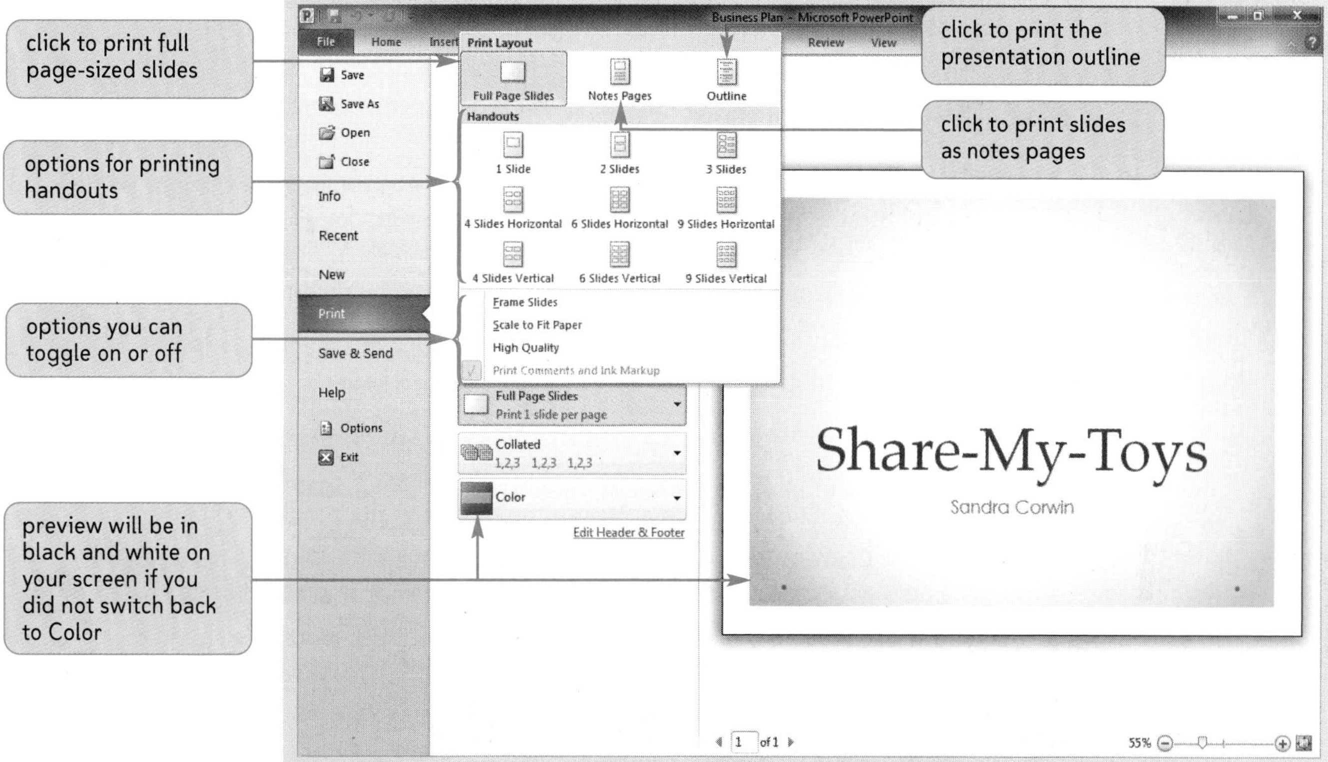

click to print full page-sized slides

options for printing handouts

options you can toggle on or off

preview will be in black and white on your screen if you did not switch back to Color

click to print the presentation outline

click to print slides as notes pages

Share-My-Toys

Sandra Corwin

3. In the Handouts section, click **9 Slides Horizontal**. The preview changes to show Slide 1 smaller and in the upper-left corner of the sheet of paper. You need to specify that all eight slides will print.

4. Below the Custom Range button, click in the **Slides** box, and then press the **Delete** or **Backspace** key. The button above the Slides box changes from Custom Range to Print All Slides, and all eight slides appear on the piece of paper in the preview pane, arranged in order in three rows from left to right.

5. At the top of the Print section, click the **Print** button. Backstage view closes and the handout prints.

Sandra would like you to print the slides that contain speaker notes as notes pages. Sandra had entered a speaker note on Slide 4 ("Competition") before she gave you the presentation to revise. There is also a speaker note on Slide 6 ("Objectives"), which you entered earlier.

To print the nonsequential slides containing speaker notes:

1. Open the Print tab in Backstage view again, and then click the **9 Slides Horizontal** button. The menu opens. "9 Slides Horizontal," one of the options for printing handouts, appeared on the button because that was the last printing option you chose. Note that the Frame Slides option at the bottom of the menu is selected—this is the default option for handouts.

2. In the Print Layout section of the menu, click **Notes Pages**. The menu closes and the preview displays Slide 1 as a Notes Page. You will verify that Slides 4 and 6 contain speaker notes.

3. At the bottom of the preview pane, click the **Next Page** button ▶ three times to display Slide 4 ("Competition") in the preview pane, and then click the **Next Page** button ▶ two more times to display Slide 6 ("Objectives"). Both slides contain speaker notes.

4. In the Settings section, click in the **Slides** box, type **4,6**, and then click a blank area of the Print tab. At the bottom of the preview pane, notice that 2 pages will print.

5. Scroll through the preview to confirm that Slides 4 and 6 will print, and then click the **Print** button. Slides 4 and 6 print as notes pages.

Finally, Sandra would like you to print the entire presentation as an outline. She will make the outline and the handout available to her audience.

To print the presentation as an outline on a single page:

1. Open the Print tab in Backstage view, click the **Notes Pages** button, and then click **Outline**. Slides 4 and 6 appear as an outline in the preview pane.

2. Click the **Custom Range** button, and then click **Print All Slides**. The entire outline appears in the preview pane. Notice that it will print on two pages.

3. At the bottom of the preview pane, click the **Next Page** button ▶ to go to page 2. Only a few lines appear on page 2. You can try to force the outline to print all on one page.

4. Click the **Outline** button, and then at the bottom of the menu, click **Scale to Fit Paper**. The menu closes and the size of the text in the outline is reduced slightly so that almost all the text now fits on one page. To avoid having a page with just a line or two of text on it, you'll deselect the scaling option.

5. In the Settings section, click the **Outline** button, and then click **Scale to Fit Paper** again.

6. At the top of the Print section, click the **Print** button. Backstage view closes and the outline prints on two sheets of paper.

You have created a new presentation based on an existing presentation, added animations and transitions to slides, created a footer for the slides, and added a speaker note. Finally, you created and printed the presentation in several formats. Your work will enable Sandra to make an effective presentation to banks and potential investors for Share-My-Toys.

REVIEW

Session 1.2 Quick Check

1. What is a transition?
2. Define progressive disclosure.
3. True or False. If you add a footer and slide number to slides, you can prevent them from appearing on the title slide.
4. How do you create speaker notes?
5. Describe contextual spell-checking and give an example.
6. What are the four ways you can print the content of a presentation?

Practice the skills you learned in the tutorial using the same case scenario.

PRACTICE

Review Assignments

Data File needed for the Review Assignments: Marketing.pptx

Calista Dymock, the new director of marketing at Share-My-Toys, asks you to prepare a PowerPoint presentation explaining the new marketing strategy. She recommends that you start with an existing presentation prepared by Sandra Corwin in her previous job. Your task is to edit the presentation according to Calista's instructions. Complete the following steps:

1. Create a new PowerPoint presentation based on the existing presentation **Marketing** located in the PowerPoint1\Review folder included with your Data Files, and then save the new presentation as **Marketing Plan** in the PowerPoint1\Review folder.

2. In Slide 1, add the title text **Share-My-Toys Membership**, and add your name as the subtitle.

3. Add a new Slide 2 using the Title and Content layout, add the slide title **Market Summary**, and then add the following first-level bulleted items: **Current memberships: 218**, **Maximum memberships: 800**, and **Current members live in:**.

4. Below "Current members live in," add the following second-level bulleted items: **Montpelier**, **ID**, **Soda Springs**, **ID**, and **Fish Haven**, **ID**.

5. Below the three second-level bullets, add the following first-level bulleted item: **Additional Target Locations**, and below that, the following second-level bulleted items: **Preston**, **ID**, **Logan**, **UT**, and **Afton**, **WY**, allowing the text to be AutoFit in the text box.

6. Add a new Slide 3 using the Comparison layout.

7. Change the theme to the Module theme.

8. On Slide 7 ("Product Definition"), format the words "Unlimited" and "Free" in bold.

9. On Slide 7, drag the text "service," (including the comma) to the left so it appears immediately before the word "maintenance," adding a space if necessary.

10. On Slide 7, drag the first subbullet down so it becomes a subbullet under the last first-level bullet.

11. Use the Undo button to put the bulleted item back as the first subbullet on the slide.

12. On Slide 7, click the first first-level bullet (begins with "Membership in Share-My-Toys") to select it and its subbullets, copy the selected items to the Clipboard, and then paste the copied text on Slide 5 ("Advantages") in front of the word "Membership"using the destination theme so that the copied bullet and subbullets appear on Slide 5 before the current bulleted item. (*Hint*: If you are working in the Outline tab, you will need to demote the pasted subbullets to their proper levels.)

13. Return to Slide 7 ("Product Definition"), cut (not copy) the second first-level bullet (begins with "Low-interest"), go to Slide 8 ("Overcoming Disadvantages"), create a new first-level bullet under the existing bulleted items, and then paste the cut text as the new first-level bulleted item using the destination theme. If a fourth bullet is created, delete it and the extra line.

14. On Slide 12 ("Advertising"), change the single bulleted item into four bulleted items that each start with an uppercase letter. Don't forget to delete the word "and" and the commas. (*Hint*: If AutoCorrect does not work the way you expected it to, make the changes manually.)

15. In the Outline tab, on Slide 2 ("Market Summary"), promote the last first-level bulleted item ("Additional target locations") and its subbullets so that it becomes a new Slide 3.

16. In the Outline tab, demote Slide 7 ("Recreational equipment rental companies") so it becomes the last first-level bullet on Slide 6 ("Advantages"), and then drag this new first-level bullet up so it is the last first-level bullet on the new Slide 5 ("Competition").

17. In the Slides tab, reposition Slide 12 ("Advertising") so it becomes the new Slide 9, and then in Slide Sorter view, reposition the new Slide 12 ("Success Metrics") so it becomes the new Slide 2.

18. Cut Slide 11 ("Contact Us"), and then paste it as the last slide in the presentation.

19. Delete Slide 5 (the slide you added using the Comparison layout), and then delete Slide 7 ("Product Definition").

20. On Slide 3 ("Market Summary") and Slide 4 ("Additional Target Locations"), animate the slide titles using the Complement animation in the Emphasis category, and then remove the animation from the presentation title on the title slide.

21. On Slide 3 ("Market Summary") and Slide 4 ("Additional Target Locations"), animate the bulleted lists and the subbulleted items so that they animate with progressive disclosure using the Wipe animation in the Entrance category.

22. Add the Gallery transition (in the Exciting category) to all the slides in the presentation, and then add the Doors transition to Slide 10 ("Contact Us").

23. Check the animations on Slide 3 ("Market Summary") and Slide 4 ("Additional Target Locations") and the transition between them in the floating slide show window on top of the PowerPoint program window, and then end the slide show to close the window.

24. Add the footer **Share-My-Toys Marketing Plan** to all the slides except the title slide, and then display the current date and the slide number on all the slides except the title slide.

25. On Slide 4 ("Additional Target Locations"), add **Point out locations on map** as a speaker note.

26. On Slide 5 ("Competition"), use the shortcut menu to correct the misspelled word "eqipment" to "equipment," and then check the spelling in the entire presentation, changing misspelled words and ignoring flagged words that are spelled correctly.

27. View the entire slide show in Slide Show or Reading view. Look carefully at each slide and check the content. If you see any errors or formatting problems, press the Esc key to end the slide show, fix the error, and then start the slide show again from the current slide.

28. Save your changes, view the slides in grayscale, and then print the following: the title slide as a full page-sized slide in color or in grayscale depending on your printer; Slides 2-10 as a handout on a single piece of paper with the slides in order horizontally; Slide 4 ("Additional Target Locations") as a notes page; and then the presentation outline on a single piece of paper. Close the presentation when you are finished.

Case Problem 1

APPLY

If you have a SAM 2010 user profile, your instructor may have assigned an autogradable version of this assignment. If so, log into the SAM 2010 Web site at www.cengage.com/sam2010 to download the instructions and start files.

Data File needed for this Case Problem: Volunteers.pptx

Department of Social Services, Yosemite Regional Hospital Mercedes Cirillo is head of Volunteer Services at Yosemite Regional Hospital in Wawona, California. One of her jobs is to recruit and train hospital volunteers. Volunteer positions include Family Surgical Liaison, Family Waiting Area Liaison, Hospitality and Escort Volunteer, Volunteer Information Ambassador, Book Cart Volunteer, Special Requests Volunteer, Flower Shop Assistant, and Pastoral Care Volunteer. Mercedes wants to give a PowerPoint presentation to individuals, couples, church groups, and service organizations on opportunities and requirements for volunteer service at the hospital. She has a rough draft of a presentation and asks you to help her revise the presentation. Complete the following steps:

1. Create a new presentation based on the existing presentation **Volunteers**, located in the PowerPoint1\Case1 folder included with your Data Files, and then save it as **Hospital Volunteers** in the PowerPoint1\Case1 folder.

2. In the title slide, add **Volunteer Service at Yosemite Regional Hospital** as the title and add your name as the subtitle.

3. AutoFit the title text to the title text box.

4. Delete Slide 3 ("Yosemite Regional Hospital").

5. Move Slide 6 ("Volunteering Procedures") so it becomes Slide 3.

6. On Slide 2 ("Our Volunteers"), add a new bulleted item to the end of the bulleted list, with the text **Volunteers work in almost all departments in the hospital**.

7. On Slide 2, add the speaker note, **Departments that don't have volunteers include Food Services, Medical Research, Security, and Custodial Services.**

8. On Slide 3 ("Volunteering Procedures"), after the second bulleted item ("Select a desired volunteer position"), insert the bulleted item **Pick up application form from Volunteer Services office**, allowing the text to AutoFit in the content text box.

9. On Slide 4 ("Volunteer Positions"), move the bulleted items "Book Cart Volunteer" and "Special Requests Volunteer" so that they appear below "Gift Shop Assistant" and above "Pastoral Care Volunteer."

10. On Slide 5 ("Requirements"), make the phrase "4 hours per week" a new first-level bullet, and then demote the bulleted items "4 hours per week" and "3-month commitment" to second-level bullets under "Minimum volunteer time."

11. On Slide 6 ("Before You Decide to Volunteer"), apply an underline to "HIPA" in the third first-level bullet.

12. Animate the slide titles for all the slides with the Grow & Turn animation in the Entrance category.

13. Remove the animation from the title on the title slide.

14. Animate all the bulleted lists using progressive disclosure for all bullet levels with the Shape animation in the Entrance category.

15. On Slide 7 ("For more information"), animate the content text box using the Font Color animation in the Emphasis category.

16. Add the Pan transition to all the slides, and then remove it from the title slide.

17. Add the footer text **Volunteering at Yosemite Regional Hospital**, and then display the footer and the slide number on all of the slides except the title slide.

18. Check the spelling throughout the presentation, and check for contextual spelling errors as well. Change misspelled words to the correct spelling, and ignore any words (such as proper names) that are spelled correctly but are not in the built-in dictionary.

19. Read each slide, proofreading for spelling errors that the spelling checker didn't detect. Notice that, on Slide 2, the word "weak" should be "week." Contextual spell-checking failed to detect this error, probably because the bulleted items are not complete sentences. Make the change and correct any other spelling errors you find.

20. View the slide show. If you see any errors, press the Esc key to end the slide show, correct the error, and then start the slide show again from the current slide. Save your changes.

21. Preview the presentation in grayscale, and then in pure black and white. If you have a color printer, switch back so the presentation will print in color.

22. Print the title slide as a full page slide, print Slides 2–7 as a handout with six slides per page arranged vertically, and then print Slide 2 as a notes page. Close the file when you are finished.

Apply your skills to create a presentation for a library volunteer program.

APPLY

Case Problem 2

Data File needed for this Case Problem: Library.pptx

Carriage Path Public Library   Davion McGechie is head of the Office of Community Outreach Services for the Carriage Path Public Library in Milford, Connecticut. Davion and his staff coordinate outreach services and develop programs in communities throughout the Long Island Sound region. These services and programs depend on a large volunteer staff. Davion wants you to help him create a PowerPoint presentation to train his staff. Complete the following steps:

1. Create a new presentation based on the existing presentation **Library**, located in the PowerPoint1\Case2 folder included with your Data Files, and then save it as **Library Outreach** in the PowerPoint1\Case2 folder.

2. In the title slide, add **Community Outreach Services** as the presentation title, and then add your name as the subtitle.

3. Change the theme to the Austin theme.

4. On the title slide, add the Shadow font effect to the presentation title.

5. On Slide 2 ("Mission Statement"), add the speaker's note **Mention that community groups include ethnic neighborhood councils, religious organizations, and civic groups.**

6. On Slide 2 ("Mission Statement"), add the following as the fourth bulleted item: **To implement outreach programs in the surrounding communities.**

7. On Slide 4 ("Community Outreach Programs"), change the first bulleted item ("Adult literacy and correctional facilities") and fourth bulleted item ("Persons with disabilities and persons without homes") into two bulleted items each. Make sure the new bulleted items start with an uppercase letter, and delete the word "and."

8. On Slide 2 ("Mission Statement"), move the second bulleted item ("To provide staff training") so that it becomes the last bulleted item.

9. On Slide 3 ("About the Library"), demote the second bulleted item ("Four central libraries with in-depth collections") and the third bulleted item ("Six neighborhood branch libraries") so that they become second-level bulleted items below the first bullet ("Consists of 10 libraries").

10. On Slide 3 ("About the Library"), promote the last first-level bulleted item ("Special Events & Programs") and its subbullets so that the first-level bulleted item becomes a new Slide 4 and its subbullets become first-level bullets on the new Slide 4.

11. Move Slide 6 ("Branch Libraries") so that it becomes Slide 5.

12. Add a new Slide 8 at the end of the presentation using the default Title and Content layout with the slide title **Volunteer Opportunities**; three first-level bulleted items: **Literacy Instructors**, **Computer Instructors**, and **Children's Hour Story Tellers**; and under the third first-level bullet, the subbullets: **After-school story hour** and **Bookmobile story hour**.

13. Animate the bulleted lists on all the slides using the Zoom animation. Do not use progressive disclosure for subbullets.

14. Add the Dissolve transition to Slide 1 ("Community Outreach Services"), add the Vortex transition to Slide 8 ("Volunteer Opportunities"), and add the Gallery transition to the rest of the slides (Slides 2–7).

15. Display the slide number on all slides, including the title slide. (*Hint*: It appears in the dark box at the top of the slides, except the title slide, where it appears at the bottom of the slide.)

16. Check the spelling in the presentation. Correct any spelling errors and ignore any words that are spelled correctly.

17. View the slide show. If you see any errors, press the Esc key to end the slide show, correct the error, and then start the slide show again from the current slide. Save your changes when you are finished.

18. Preview the presentation in grayscale, and then in pure black and white. If you have a color printer, switch back so the presentation will print in color.

19. Print the presentation as handouts with four slides per page arranged horizontally; print Slide 2 ("Mission Statement") as a notes page; and then print the presentation outline on one page if it will fit. Close the file when you are finished.

Create a new presentation about a marketing company.

CREATE

Case Problem 3

There are no Data Files needed for this Case Problem.

AfterShow, Inc.   Karla Brown is president of AfterShow, Inc., a company that markets specialized merchandise to attendees at trade shows, training seminars, and other large business events. For example, after a recent trade show of the American Automobile Manufacturers, AfterShow mailed advertisement flyers and made phone calls to the trade show participants to sell them art pieces (mostly bronze sculptures) depicting antique automobiles. In another case, after a large business seminar in which the keynote speakers were famous business leaders and athletes, AfterShow contacted participants in an effort to sell them autographed books written by the speakers. Karla asked you to create a presentation to be given to event organizers in an effort to work with those organizers in developing an after-show market and profit-sharing program. The slides in your complete presentation should look like the slides in Figure 1-40 (shown on the next page). The following instructions will help you in creating the slide show. Read all the steps before you start.

1. Create a new, blank presentation, and then save it as **AfterShow** in the PowerPoint1\Case3 folder. (*Hint:* If PowerPoint is already running, click the File tab, click New, and then click the Create button.)

2. Apply the Couture theme.

⊕ **EXPLORE**
3. Change the theme fonts to the Apothecary theme fonts. To do this, click the Design tab, and then in the Themes group, click the Fonts button.

4. On Slides 2–4 and Slide 6, increase the size of the text in the first-level bulleted items to 24 points, on Slide 2, increase the size of the text in the second-level bulleted items to 20 points, and then on the title slide, increase the size of the subtitle text to 32 points.

5. Add your name as a footer on all slides.

⊕ **EXPLORE**
6. Add your name as a header on notes pages and handouts. To do this, use the Notes and Handouts tab in the Header and Footer dialog box.

7. Apply an animation effect to the bulleted lists. This is a marketing presentation for a business, so choose one that is interesting but not silly.

8. Apply an interesting transition effect to all of the slides. Again, keep in mind that this is a marketing presentation, you can select one that is more exciting than you would select for a presentation to investors.

9. Apply a different transition to the title slide.

10. On Slide 3 ("How It Works), add as a speaker note **Pass around sample products**.

11. Check the spelling, and then run the slide show. Correct errors as needed.

12. Save your changes, and then preview the presentation in grayscale and black and white.

13. Print the presentation as handouts with three slides per page, print Slide 3 ("How It Works") as a notes page, and then print the presentation outline. Note that your name should appear as a header on the printed pages. Close the file when you are finished.

Figure 1-40 Completed presentation for AfterShow, Inc.

Use the Internet to research MP3 players and create a new presentation reviewing an MP3 player.

RESEARCH

Case Problem 4

There are no Data Files needed for this Case Problem.

Review of an MP3 Player   Your assignment is to prepare a review of an MP3 player for presentation to the class. If you own an MP3 player, you can use the Internet to search for information about it. If you do not own one, you can use the Internet to research the various brands and models, and then choose one to review. You need to organize the information into a PowerPoint presentation consisting of at least six slides. (Your instructor might also assign you to give an oral presentation based on your PowerPoint file.) Complete the following steps:

1. Go to a search engine Web site (such as Google, Bing, or Yahoo), and start your research using such terms as **MP3 player review**. Read about various brands of players to get an idea of the most popular sellers.

2. Select the brand and model of MP3 player that you want to review, and then search for additional information and reviews about that player.

⊕ **EXPLORE**

3. Create a new presentation based on the Sample presentation slides (White with blue-green design) template from the Design slides with content in the Presentations category on Office.com. To do this, open the New tab in Backstage view. In the Office.com Templates section, click Presentations, click the Design slides with content folder, click the Sample presentation slides (White with blue-green design) thumbnail, and then on the right, click the Download button. If you don't see Presentations or the Design slides with content folder, click in the Search Office.com for Templates box, type **Sample blue-green**, and then press the Enter key.

4. Save the presentation as **MP3 Player Review** in the PowerPoint1\Case4 folder included with your Data Files.

5. Delete all the slides except the title slide.

6. On the title slide, delete all the text in the title, and then type the brand and model of the MP3 player you are reviewing.

7. On the title slide, delete the subtitle text, and then type your full name.

⊕ **EXPLORE**

8. Add a new slide with the Title and Content Layout. Note that the default layout for a new slide after the title slide in this design is *not* the Title and Content layout, so you need to select this layout.

9. Title Slide 2 **Overview**, and then in the content placeholder, include basic information about your MP3 player. This information might include the brand name, model name or number, storage capacity, retail price, and street price.

10. Add a new Slide 3 using the default Title and Content layout, title the slide **Features**, and then in the content placeholder, list specific features of your MP3 player, such as number of songs the player holds, total playing time, expansion slots, battery life, and auxiliary features (for example, pictures, calendar, videos), and so forth.

11. Add a new slide after the Features slide using the default Title and Content layout, title the slide **Specifications**, and then in the content placeholder, list technical specifications (for example, size, weight, interface).

12. Add a new slide after the Specifications slide using the default Title and Content layout, title the slide **Pricing**, and then in the content placeholder, list the manufacturer's suggested retail price (MSRP) and examples of street prices, that is, prices at online vendors or prices at local stores (for example, Buy.com, Amazon.com, and Best Buy).

13. Create at least three additional slides at appropriate points in the presentation to add information or opinions about your MP3 player. Use the default Title and Content layout for these slides. Examples of slide titles are **Ease of Use** and **Reviewers' Comments**. You might also want to add a slide listing Additional Features of the MP3 player.

14. Create a final slide titled **Summary and Recommendations**. In the content place-holder, give your overall impression of the player and your recommendation for whether the player is worth buying.

15. View the presentation on the Outline tab. If necessary, change the order of the bul-leted items on the slides, or change the order of the slides.

16. If any slide contains more than about six or seven bulleted items (including subbul-lets), consider splitting the slide in two.

17. Add interesting animations.

18. Decide if you want to keep the Fade transition or use another transition (or more than one transition).

EXPLORE

19. Apply a sound to the transitions. To do this, display the Transitions tab. In the Timing group, click the Sound button arrow, and then click a sound effect. Make sure you click the Apply To All button.

20. Add a speaker note to at least one slide. Add additional speaker notes if you want.

21. Check the spelling of your presentation, and then view the slide show, correcting errors as needed. Save your changes.

22. Preview the presentation in grayscale, and then in pure black and white. If you have a color printer, switch back so the presentation will print in color.

23. Print the title slide, print any slides with speaker notes as notes pages, and then print the presentation outline on one page, if possible. Close the presentation when you are finished.

ASSESS

SAM: Skills Assessment Manager

For current SAM information, including versions and content details, visit SAM Central (http://samcentral.course.com). If you have a SAM user profile, you may have access to hands-on instruction, practice, and assessment of the skills covered in this tutorial. Since various versions of SAM are supported throughout the life of this text, check with your instructor for the correct instructions and URL/Web site for accessing assignments.

ENDING DATA FILES

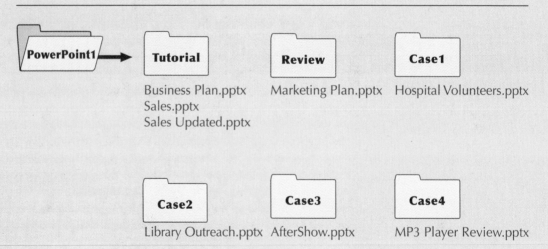

OBJECTIVES

Session 2.1
- Insert a graphic from a file
- Insert, resize, and reposition clip art
- Modify the color and shape of a bitmapped graphic
- Apply effects and styles to a graphic
- Draw and format shapes
- Add text to a shape
- Insert and format text boxes
- Flip and rotate objects

Session 2.2
- Modify the Slide Master
- Create SmartArt diagrams
- Modify a SmartArt diagram
- Apply animations to graphics
- Customize animations
- Insert headers on handouts and notes pages
- Broadcast a presentation

Adding and Modifying Text and Graphic Objects

Preparing a Presentation About a Travel Company

Case | *Alaskan Cruises and Land Tours*

Chad Morley visited Alaska for the first time in 1989, fell in love with it, and stayed to live in Anchorage. He works for Alaskan Cruises and Land Tours (ACLT), a company based in Fairbanks and with offices in Anchorage and Juneau. As a travel operator or wholesaler, ACLT arranges travel packages for travel agencies to sell to their customers. Chad's job entails educating travel agents throughout the United States and Canada about ACLT.

In this tutorial, you'll enhance a presentation by adding graphics to the slides. You will also add text boxes, format and animate the graphics you inserted, and modify the slide master. Finally, you will add headers to handouts and notes pages, and broadcast the presentation over the Internet.

STARTING DATA FILES

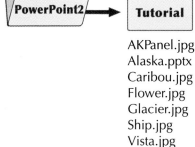

PowerPoint2 →

Tutorial	Review	Case1	Case2	Case3	Case4
AKPanel.jpg	AKRibbon.jpg	Balmoral.jpg	Campsite.jpg	ASizemore.jpg	Camera01.jpg
Alaska.pptx	LandTour.pptx	Castles.pptx	Meadow.jpg	Bodie.jpg	Camera02.jpg
Caribou.jpg	Naturalist.jpg	Edinburgh.jpg	Men.jpg	HatterasBase.jpg	Camera03.jpg
Flower.jpg	Ship2.jpg		Outfitter.pptx	HatterasStairs.jpg	Photographer.jpg
Glacier.jpg			Panel.jpg	HatterasTop.jpg	
Ship.jpg			River.jpg	LHPanel.jpg	
Vista.jpg				Lighthouses.pptx	
				Ocracoke.jpg	

SESSION 2.1 VISUAL OVERVIEW

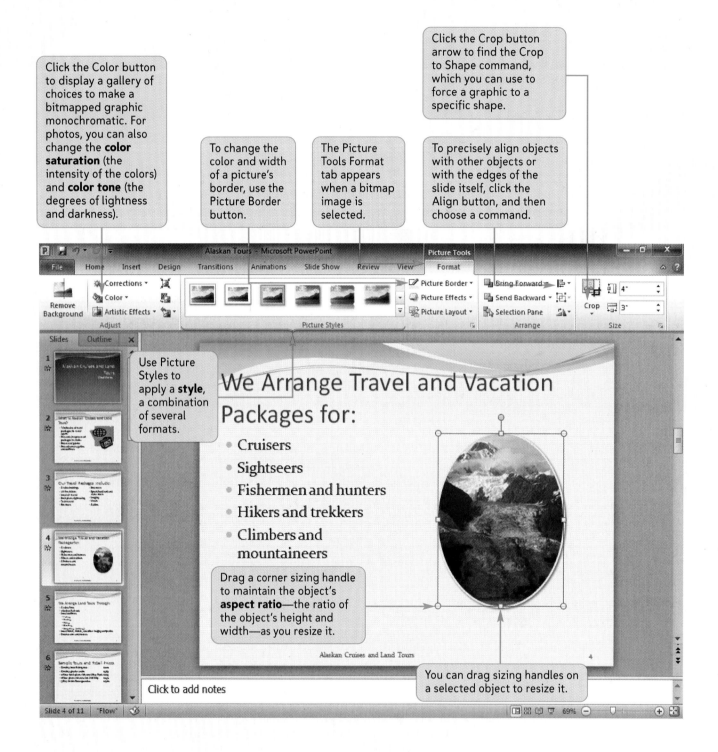

Click the Color button to display a gallery of choices to make a bitmapped graphic monochromatic. For photos, you can also change the **color saturation** (the intensity of the colors) and **color tone** (the degrees of lightness and darkness).

To change the color and width of a picture's border, use the Picture Border button.

The Picture Tools Format tab appears when a bitmap image is selected.

To precisely align objects with other objects or with the edges of the slide itself, click the Align button, and then choose a command.

Click the Crop button arrow to find the Crop to Shape command, which you can use to force a graphic to a specific shape.

Use Picture Styles to apply a **style**, a combination of several formats.

Drag a corner sizing handle to maintain the object's **aspect ratio**—the ratio of the object's height and width—as you resize it.

You can drag sizing handles on a selected object to resize it.

MODIFYING GRAPHICS

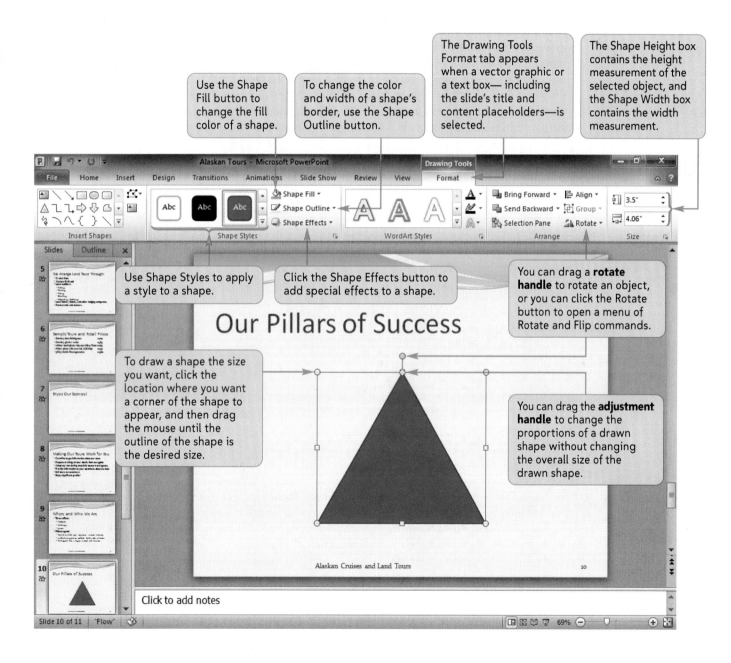

Use the Shape Fill button to change the fill color of a shape.

To change the color and width of a shape's border, use the Shape Outline button.

The Drawing Tools Format tab appears when a vector graphic or a text box— including the slide's title and content placeholders—is selected.

The Shape Height box contains the height measurement of the selected object, and the Shape Width box contains the width measurement.

Use Shape Styles to apply a style to a shape.

Click the Shape Effects button to add special effects to a shape.

You can drag a **rotate handle** to rotate an object, or you can click the Rotate button to open a menu of Rotate and Flip commands.

To draw a shape the size you want, click the location where you want a corner of the shape to appear, and then drag the mouse until the outline of the shape is the desired size.

You can drag the **adjustment handle** to change the proportions of a drawn shape without changing the overall size of the drawn shape.

Our Pillars of Success

Alaskan Cruises and Land Tours

Understanding Graphics

As you learned in Tutorial 1, a graphic is a picture, shape, design, graph, chart, or diagram. Graphics can add information, clarification, emphasis, variety, and pizzazz to a PowerPoint presentation. PowerPoint enables you to include many types of graphics in your presentation: graphics created using other programs; scanned photographs, drawings, and cartoons; and other picture files or clip art stored on your computer or network. You can also create graphics using drawing tools in PowerPoint.

Graphics are saved in a variety of file types. Photographs, generated by taking pictures with a digital camera or by scanning photos taken with conventional cameras, and pictures drawn using graphics software such as Microsoft Paint, are a type of picture file called a bitmap. A **bitmap** is a grid (or "map") of square colored dots that form a picture. The colored dots are **pixels**, which stands for picture elements. Drawings created using illustration programs such as Adobe Illustrator or CorelDRAW are vector graphics. A **vector graphic** is composed of straight and curved lines. **Metafiles** contain both bitmaps and vectors. Images are saved in several file formats, including the formats described in Figure 2-1.

Figure 2-1	Common image file formats

Format	Abbreviation	Type
Windows Bitmap	BMP	Bitmap
Tagged Image File	TIF	Bitmap
Graphics Interchange Format	GIF	Bitmap
Portable Network Graphic	PNG	Bitmap
Joint Photographic Experts Group	JPEG	Bitmap
Scalable Vector Graphic	SVG	Vector
Windows Metafile	WMF	Metafile
Enhanced Metafile	EMF	Metafile

Decision Making: Using Graphics Effectively

We live in a highly visual society. Most people are exposed to multimedia daily and expect to have information conveyed visually as well as verbally. In many cases, a graphic is more effective than words for communicating an important point. For example, if a sales force has reached its sales goals for the year, a graphic of a person summiting a mountain can convey a sense of exhilaration. You should remember the following points when deciding when and how to use graphics in a presentation:

- Use graphics to present information that words aren't able to communicate effectively, to pique interest and motivate the reader, and to increase understanding and retention of information.
- Choose graphics appropriate to your audience (their jobs, experiences, education, and culture).
- Choose graphics that support your purpose and the type of information you'll be presenting.

Chad worked with his marketing director and planned a presentation as follows:

- **Purpose of the presentation:** To encourage travel agents to sell travel packages from Alaska Cruises and Land Tours
- **Audience:** Travel agents
- **Time:** About thirty minutes
- **Handouts:** All the slides with the contact information printed as a full-page slide

After planning his presentation, Chad and his marketing director created a presentation outline. Chad wants you to add interest to the presentation by inserting some graphics.

Adding a Graphic from a File

You can insert graphics stored on your computer on a slide using the Insert Picture from File button in a content placeholder or the Picture button in the Images group on the Insert tab. Either method opens the Insert Picture dialog box. Chad gave you a photograph of a glacier that he wants you to insert on Slide 4 of his presentation.

To insert a picture on Slide 4:

1. Open the presentation **Alaska**, which is stored in the PowerPoint2\Tutorial folder included with your Data Files, and then save it to the same folder as **Alaskan Tours**. Notice in the status bar that the presentation uses the Flow theme.

   Trouble? If the status bar identifies the theme as Alaska, you used the New from existing command instead of the Open command to open the presentation. To ensure your screen matches the steps and figures, close the presentation, and then repeat Step 1.

2. Display **Slide 4** ("We Arrange Travel and Vacation Packages for:") in the Slide pane.

   Trouble? If the slide is too large for the Slide pane, click the Fit slide to current window button 🔲 on the right end of the status bar.

3. In the Slides group on the Home tab, click the **Layout** button, and then click the **Two Content** layout. The bulleted list moves to the left side of the slide in the Slide pane, and a second content placeholder appears on the right side of the slide.

4. In the content placeholder on the right side of the slide, click the **Insert Picture from File** button 🔲. The Insert Picture dialog box opens. This dialog box is similar to the Open and New from existing dialog boxes.

5. Navigate to the PowerPoint2\Tutorial folder included with your Data Files, click the picture file **Glacier**, and then click the **Insert** button. The picture appears in the Slide pane in place of the content placeholder, and the Picture Tools Format tab appears on the Ribbon and is the active tab. See Figure 2-2.

TIP

If the slide layout you are using does not contain a content placeholder, you can use the Picture button in the Images group on the Insert tab to insert a picture.

Figure 2-2   **Slide 4 after inserting picture**

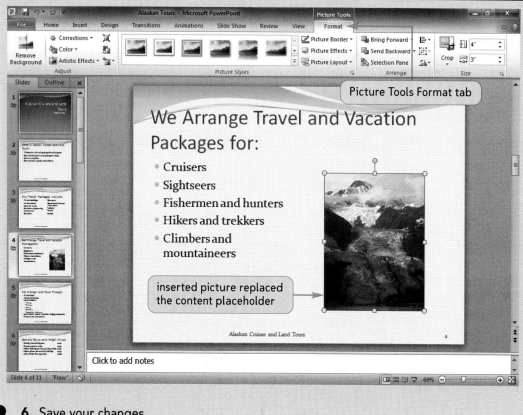

6. Save your changes.

In addition to adding pictures stored in files on your computer, you can add clip art to slides. You'll do this next.

Inserting Clip Art

Clip art includes electronic illustrations, photographs, and other graphics stored in collections so that you can easily locate and insert them into documents and presentations. Clip art is available as both bitmapped and vector graphics, and as animated GIF files. An **animated GIF file** is a series of bitmapped images that are displayed one after another so that it looks like the image is moving. In Microsoft Office programs, sounds are also included in clip art collections.

Clip art files have keywords associated with them. **Keywords** are words or phrases that describe the clip art. You use keywords to help you find clip art that suits your needs. For example, clip art of a train might have the keywords "train" and "engine" associated with it, and if the clip art is a train going over a bridge, additional keywords might be "bridge" and "trestle." If you search for clip art using any one of these keywords, that image will appear in your results, along with images of trains not on a bridge and images of bridges without any trains. The more keywords you use, the narrower (more specific) your search results will be.

REFERENCE

Inserting Clip Art on a Slide

- Switch to a layout that includes a content placeholder, and then in the content placeholder, click the Clip Art button; or click the Insert tab on the Ribbon, and then in the Images group, click the Clip Art button.
- In the Clip Art task pane, type a keyword or multiple keywords in the Search for box.
- Click the Results should be arrow, and then select the check boxes next to the types of clip art for which you want to search.
- Click the Go button.
- In the task pane, click the clip art that you want to insert into the slide.

Chad wants you to add clip art to Slide 2. First you'll change the slide layout to one with two content placeholders.

TIP

If the slide layout you are using does not contain a content placeholder, you can use the Clip Art button in the Images group on the Insert tab to insert clip art.

To change the layout of Slide 2 and add clip art:

1. Display **Slide 2** ("What Is Alaskan Cruises and Land Tours?") in the Slide pane.

2. In the Slides group on the Home tab, click the **Layout** button, and then click the **Two Content** layout.

3. In the content placeholder, click the **Clip Art** button. The Clip Art task pane appears on the right side of the PowerPoint window. See Figure 2-3.

Figure 2-3	Clip Art task pane open in the presentation window

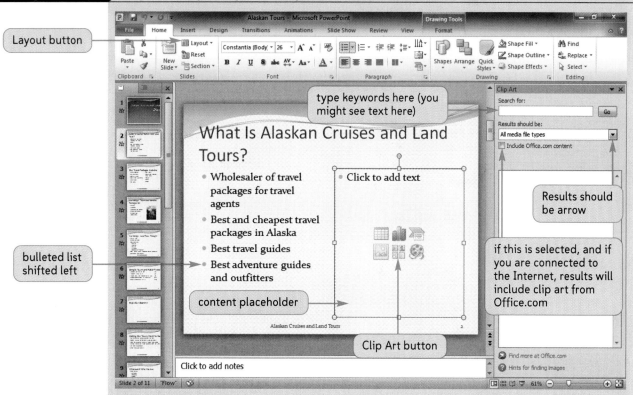

▶ **4.** At the top of the Clip Art task pane, click in the **Search for** box, delete any text in the box, if necessary, and then type **travel**.

▶ **5.** Click the **Results should be** arrow, and then if it is not selected, click the **All media types** check box.

▶ **6.** Click the **Go** button to the right of the Search for box. PowerPoint displays at least three pieces of clip art that are associated with the word "travel." (Depending on how Office was installed on your computer or if you are connected to the Internet, you might see many more clip art images.)

▶ **7.** In the Clip Art task pane, click the clip art of a globe and a suitcase. The content placeholder on the slide is replaced by the clip art you selected. Note that the image is selected, as indicated by the sizing handles in the corners and on the sides. The Picture Tools Format tab appears on the Ribbon and becomes the active tab. See Figure 2-4.

Figure 2-4 **Clip art inserted on the slide**

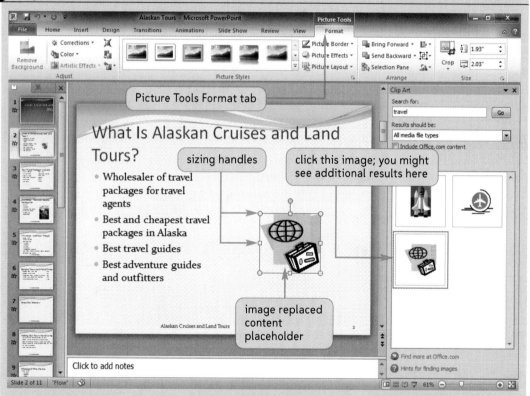

Trouble? If you don't see the image shown in Figure 2-4 in the task pane, scroll down the list. If you still can't find it, narrow the results by clicking in the Search for box, adding the keywords "baggage," "Earth," and "luggage," and then clicking the Go button again. If you still can't find it, use another image.

▶ **8.** In the upper-right corner of the Clip Art task pane, click the **Close** button ☒. The task pane closes.

▶ **9.** Save your changes.

Next, you'll modify the clip art by changing its size and repositioning it.

Resizing and Repositioning a Graphic

Chad thinks the clip art you inserted on Slide 2 is a little small in relation to the bulleted list. The easiest way to change the size of a graphic is to drag its sizing handles. You can also change a graphic's size using the Shape Height and Width boxes in the Size group on the Format tab that appears when a picture or drawing is selected.

INSIGHT

Understanding the Difference Between Bitmapped and Vector Graphics

The biggest practical difference between bitmapped and vector graphics is that you can resize a vector graphic as large as you want, and its quality will be the same as at the smaller size. When you resize a bitmapped image larger, however, the quality of the image will degrade. This is because the number of pixels used to create the image doesn't change as you make the image larger; instead, each pixel increases in size. Because pixels are square, as they get larger, you start to see the corners of each pixel, resulting in jagged edges in the image. The other important difference between the two types of files is that vector image files can be much larger than bitmapped image files. This will result in a larger presentation file size.

To resize the clip art:

▶ **1.** Position the pointer over the upper-right corner sizing handle of the clip art so that the pointer changes to ⬃, and then drag the handle up and to the right until the image is about twice its original size. Don't worry about getting the exact size. Notice that the measurements in the Shape Height and Width boxes in the Size group changed to reflect the new size of the clip art.

▶ **2.** Position the pointer anywhere on the selected clip art (except on a sizing handle) so that the pointer changes to ✛, and then drag the clip art to position it so that its upper edge is level with the top of the first bulleted item and its right edge is aligned with the right side of the word "Land" in the slide title (about one inch from the right edge of the slide).

▶ **3.** Click a blank area of the slide to deselect the image. See Figure 2-5.

| Figure 2-5 | Slide 2 with resized and repositioned clip art |

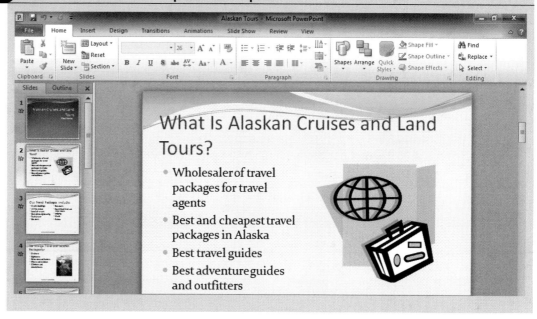

Chad asks you to align the photo you inserted on Slide 4 with the bulleted list text box on the left side of the slide. You'll use commands on the Align button menu to do this.

To align the objects on Slide 4:

1. Display **Slide 4** ("We Arrange Travel and Vacation Packages for:") in the Slide pane.

2. Click the **glacier** picture. The Picture Tools Format tab appears on the Ribbon.

3. Press and hold the **Shift** key, and then click the bulleted list text box. Both the picture and the text box are selected, and the Drawing Tools Format tab appears on the Ribbon next to the Picture Tools Format tab.

4. Click the **Picture Tools Format** tab, and then in the Arrange group, click the **Align** button 🔲 ▾ to open the Align button menu. See Figure 2-6. Notice that Align Selected Objects is selected. This means that the selected objects will align with each other rather than with the edges of the slide.

TIP

You could also click the Align button in the Arrange group on the Drawing Tools Format tab or click the Arrange button in the Drawing group on the Home tab, and then point to Align.

Figure 2-6	Commands on the Align button menu

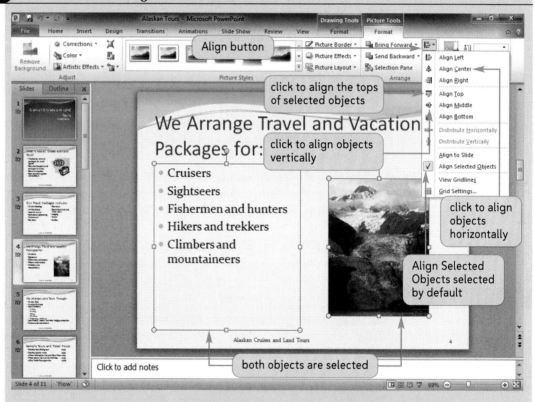

5. Click **Align Top**. The picture shifts up so that the tops of the two objects are aligned.

6. Click a blank area of the slide to deselect the objects, and then save your changes.

Next, you'll adjust the color of the photo and the clip art.

Formatting Objects

You can apply formatting to any object on a slide. Usually, you use the buttons on the contextual Format tab that appears when you select the object. Refer back to the Visual Overview for Session 2.1 to review the options on the Pictures Tools and Drawing Tools Format tabs. You can use tools on these tabs to change the format of an object; for example, you can change the colors of an object or add special effects, such as a shadow.

Adjusting the Color of a Picture

The Adjust group on the Picture Tools Format tab contains buttons you can use to apply photo editing effects, including the Color button. (This group is not on the Drawing Tools Format tab because these effects can be applied only to pictures.)

Chad thinks that the photo of the glacier looks too monochromatic (one color) and that the light blue and green colors of the clip art look washed out, so he asks you to modify the colors of these two objects.

To change the color of the photo by adjusting its saturation and tone:

1. Click the **glacier** picture, and then, if necessary, click the **Picture Tools Format** tab on the Ribbon.

2. In the Adjust group, click the **Color** button. A gallery of color options opens. See Figure 2-7. Each color option has a ScreenTip.

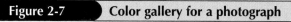

Figure 2-7   **Color gallery for a photograph**

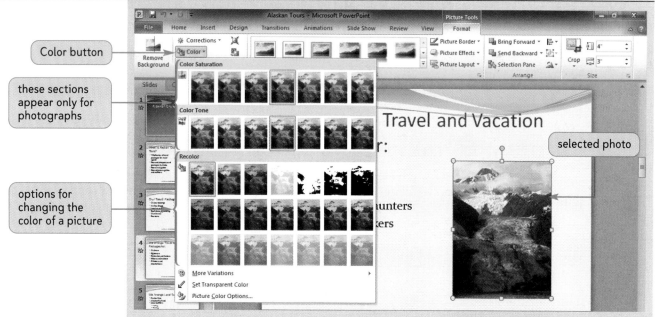

Color button

these sections appear only for photographs

options for changing the color of a picture

selected photo

3. In the Color Tone group, click the **Temperature: 7200 K** color option (the fifth option). The various elements in the picture are slightly more distinct.

4. In the Adjust group, click the **Color** button again, and then in the Color Saturation section, click the **Saturation: 66%** color option (the third option). The intensity of the colors in the photo lessens slightly. The overall effect is that the photo now appears less blue and is somewhat more striking.

Now you will modify the color of the clip art by choosing a monochromatic color option in the Color gallery.

To change the color of the clip art:

▶ 1. Display **Slide 2** ("What Is Alaskan Cruises and Land Tours?") in the Slide pane, click the **clip art** to select it, and then, if necessary, click the **Picture Tools Format** tab on the Ribbon.

▶ 2. In the Adjust group, click the **Color** button. The gallery of color options opens. Because this is not a photograph, the Color Saturation and Color Tone sections you used in the previous set of steps do not appear in the gallery.

▶ 3. Click the **Blue, Accent color 1 Dark** color option (the second color option in the second row). The colors of the clip art are changed to dark blues.

Modifying a Graphic's Border Color, Effects, and Shape

You can also change the color and width of an object's border, add special effects to an object, and change the shape of a picture. Chad asks you to add a border and shadow effect to the picture on Slide 4, and then change its shape to an oval.

To change the border color, effect, and shape of the glacier picture:

▶ 1. Display **Slide 4** ("We Arrange Travel and Vacation Packages for:") in the Slide pane again, click the **glacier** picture to select it, and then click the **Picture Tools Format** tab, if necessary.

▶ 2. In the Picture Styles group, click the **Picture Border button arrow**. A gallery of colors and a menu for borders appears.

▶ 3. Click the **Light Turquoise, Background 2** color (the third color in the first row). A very light blue border surrounds the picture.

▶ 4. In the Picture Styles group, click the **Picture Border button arrow**, point to **Weight**, and then click **3 pt**. The border is changed to a thicker border that is three points wide. You want to make the image stand out more.

▶ 5. In the Picture Styles group, click the **Picture Effects** button, point to **Shadow**, and then in the Outer section, click the **Offset Diagonal Bottom Right** shadow (the first shadow in the first row under Outer). Now you will change the picture shape.

▶ 6. In the Size group, click the **Crop button arrow**, point to **Crop to Shape**, and then under Basic Shapes, click the **Oval** shape (the first shape under Basic Shapes). See Figure 2-8.

Figure 2-8 | **Picture with modified border, shadow, and shape**

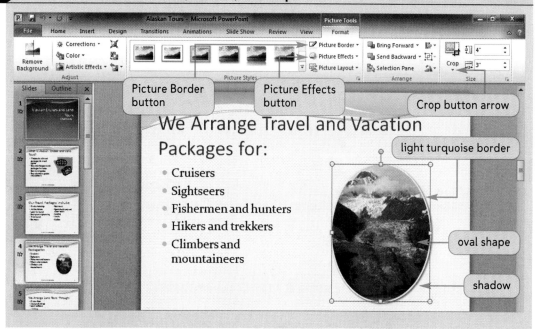

Applying a Style to a Graphic

An easy way to apply several formats at once to an object is to apply a style to it. Both of the contextual Format tabs contain a Styles gallery, in which you can click a style to apply it to the selected object. For instance, on the Picture Tools Format tab, you can click the Simple Frame, White style to apply a white border with square corners and a mitered edge seven points wide, and with a subtle shadow effect. Note that none of the Picture Styles changes the color of a picture.

Chad wants you to modify the clip art on Slide 2 by applying a style.

To apply a style to the clip art on Slide 2:

▶ **1.** Display **Slide 2** ("What Is Alaskan Cruises and Land Tours?") in the Slide pane again, click the **clip art** to select it, and then click the **Picture Tools Format** tab, if necessary.

▶ **2.** In the Picture Styles group, point to several of the styles to see the effect on the selected clip art. Notice that each style has a name that appears in a ScreenTip as you point to it.

▶ **3.** Click the **More** button, and then click the **Center Shadow Rectangle** style (the first style in the third row). A shadow effect is applied to the edges of the clip art. The Picture Styles gallery is scrolled so that the row containing the style you applied is visible. See Figure 2-9.

| Figure 2-9 | Clip art with a style and a border applied |

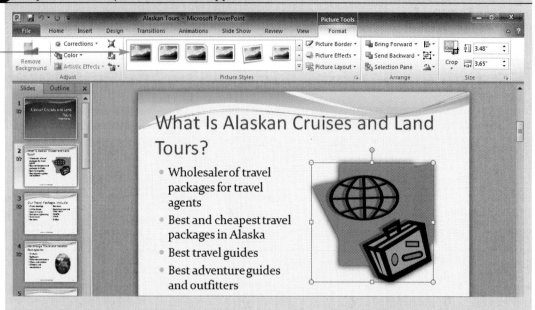

4. Click a blank area of the slide to deselect the clip art, and then save your changes.

You can combine a style with custom formatting if you like. For example, you can apply a style, and then add a custom border or modify the border that was applied with the style.

In addition to clip art and pictures stored in files on your computer, you can use the Shapes button to insert drawn shapes on slides.

Drawing and Formatting Shapes

You can add many shapes to a slide, including lines, rectangles, star shapes, and many more. To draw a shape, click the Shapes button in the Illustrations group on the Insert tab or in the Drawing group on the Home tab, and then click a shape in the gallery. To insert the shape at the default size, simply click in the slide. If you want to create a shape of a specific size, click and drag to draw the shape until it is the size you want. Shapes you draw using a selection from the Shapes gallery are vector graphics.

Chad asks you to create a graphic on Slide 10. This graphic will have text labels that will emphasize three equally important features of the company.

To insert a shape on Slide 10:

1. Display **Slide 10** ("Our Pillars of Success") in the Slide pane, and then change the layout to **Title Only**, so that the slide has no content placeholder below the title. You want to draw a triangle in a blank area of the slide.

2. In the Drawing group on the Home tab, click the **Shapes** button. The Shapes gallery opens. See Figure 2-10. The gallery is organized into nine categories of shapes, plus the Recently Used Shapes group at the top.

Figure 2-10	Shapes gallery

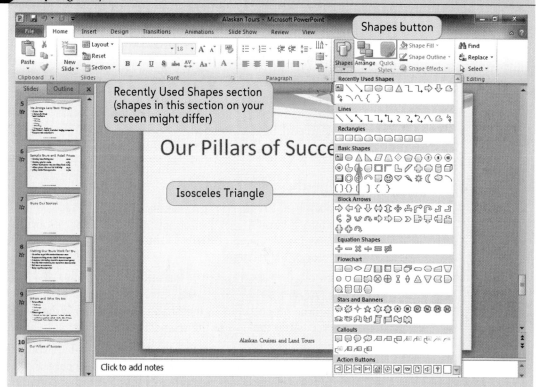

3. Click the **Isosceles Triangle** shape △, and then position the pointer one inch below the "s" in "Pillars" so that the pointer changes to +.

4. Press and hold the **Shift** key, press and hold the mouse button, and then drag the pointer down and to the right. The outline of a triangle appears as you drag. Pressing the Shift key while you drag makes the triangle equilateral.

5. Release the mouse button and the Shift key when your triangle is approximately three inches tall. Refer to Figure 2-11.

Figure 2-11	Slide 10 with an equilateral triangle

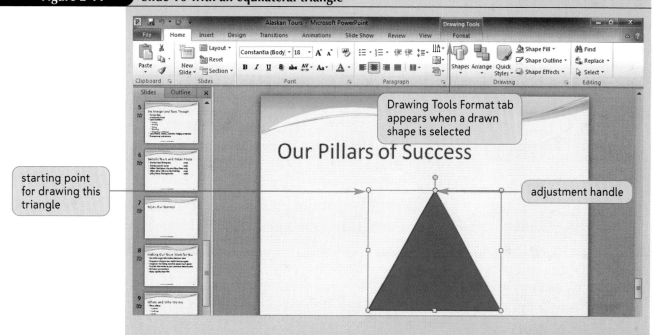

Trouble? If your triangle doesn't look like the one in Figure 2-11, resize or change its shape by dragging one or more of the sizing handles, or press the Delete key to delete it, and then repeat Steps 2 through 5 to redraw it.

▶ **6.** In the Drawing group on the Home tab, click the **Arrange** button, point to **Align**, and then click **Align Center**. The triangle is centered horizontally on the slide.

In this presentation, which has the Flow theme applied, the default color of drawn shapes is one of the blue colors from the set of theme colors. Chad wants you to change the color of the triangle to green.

To change the color and style of the triangle:

▶ **1.** Make sure the triangle is still selected, and then click the **Drawing Tools Format** tab. In the Shape Styles group, notice that an orange border appears around one of the styles. When you draw a shape, a default style is applied. First you'll change the color of the triangle.

▶ **2.** In the Shape Styles group, click the **Shape Fill button arrow**, and then click the **Lime, Accent 6** color (the last color in the top row in the palette). The triangle is now a lime green color. In the Shape Styles gallery, the default style is no longer selected. After looking at the triangle, Chad asks you to apply a shape style.

▶ **3.** In the Shape Styles group, click the **More** button to display the Shape Styles gallery, and then click the **Intense Effect – Lime, Accent 6** style (the last style in the last row). The shape is now a lime color with gradient shading (the color changes from darker to lighter inside the shape), has a beveled edge, and has a small shadow on the bottom. See Figure 2-12.

Figure 2-12   **Triangle shape with a style applied**

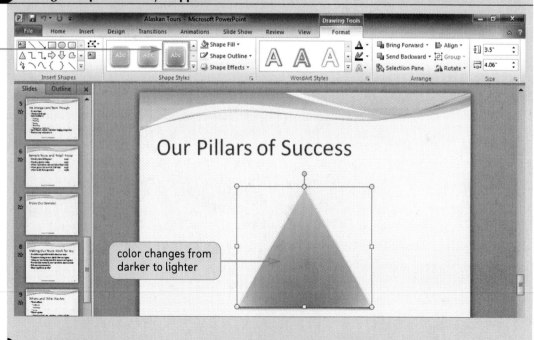

▶ **4.** Save your changes.

Next, you will add text to the shape.

Adding Text to a Shape

You can add text to a shape that you drew. Simply select the shape and start typing. Chad wants you to add the company initials to the triangle shape.

To add text to the triangle shape:

▶ **1.** Make sure the triangle is still selected.

▶ **2.** Type **ACLT**. The text you type appears in the triangle.

▶ **3.** Click a blank area of the slide to deselect the triangle.

The graphic on Slide 10 is not complete. You need to add text on each side of the triangle.

Inserting and Formatting Text Boxes

Sometimes, you need to add text to a slide in a location other than in one of the text box placeholders included in the slide layout. For example, Chad wants you to add labels to each side of the triangle you created on Slide 10 ("Our Pillars of Success"). The labels will describe three features of ACLT that Chad wants to emphasize as equally important.

To add a text box to Slide 10:

▶ **1.** Click the **Insert** tab on the Ribbon.

▶ **2.** In the Text group, click the **Text Box** button, and then position the pointer on the slide. The pointer changes to ↓.

▶ **3.** Position ↓ above the triangle, and then click. The position doesn't have to be exact. A small text box appears with the insertion point blinking in it, and the Home tab becomes active on the Ribbon.

▶ **4.** Type **Superior Tours**, and then click a blank area of the slide. You can also insert text boxes and other shapes from the Home tab.

▶ **5.** In the Drawing group, click the **Shapes** button, and then in the Recently Used Shapes section, click the **Text Box** button ▤.

▶ **6.** Click approximately two inches to the left of the triangle, type **Reasonable Prices**, and then click a blank area of the slide.

▶ **7.** Insert a third text box immediately to the right of the triangle, and then type **Excellent Guides**.

▶ **8.** Click a blank area of the slide to deselect the text box. Your slide should now look similar to the slide shown in Figure 2-13.

| Figure 2-13 | Text boxes added around the triangle |

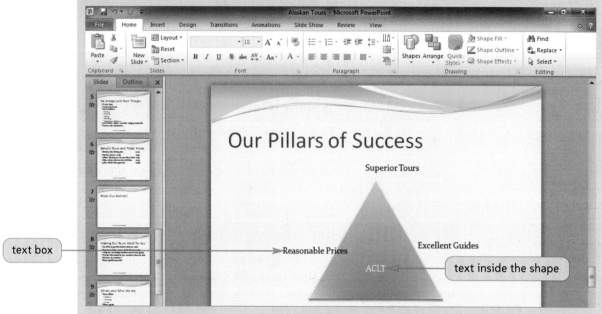

Trouble? If your text boxes are not positioned exactly as shown in Figure 2-13, don't worry. You'll reposition them later.

As you know, you can modify the formatting of text by selecting the word or words you want to format, and then clicking the appropriate button in the Font group on the Home tab. If you want to change the formatting of all the text in a text box, you can select the entire text box, and then apply the formatting. Chad asks you to change the size of the text in the three text boxes and the text inside the triangle to 24 points.

To change the size of the text in the text boxes and in the shape:

1. Click the **Superior Tours** text box, press and hold the **Shift** key, and then click the other two text boxes on the slide. All three text boxes are selected and have a solid line border around them.

2. In the Font group on the Home tab, click the **Font Size button arrow**, and then click **24**. The text in all three text boxes is now 24 points. You can also change the font size of text in a shape.

3. In the triangle, click **ACLT**, click the **dotted line border** of the triangle object, and then change the font size to **24 points**.

4. Save your changes.

Next, you'll complete the graphic by flipping the triangle and rotating the text boxes to make them parallel to the sides of the triangle.

Flipping and Rotating Objects

You can flip and rotate objects on a slide to position them so that they suit your needs. To flip an object, you can use one of the Flip commands on the Rotate menu, which you open by clicking the Rotate button in the Arrange group on the Format tab.

Chad wants you to flip the triangle so that it points down instead of up.

To flip the triangle:

▶ **1.** Make sure the **triangle** is still selected, and then click the **Drawing Tools Format** tab.

▶ **2.** In the Arrange group, click the **Rotate** button to open the menu. The top two commands rotate the object right and left, and the bottom two commands flip the triangle.

▶ **3.** Click **Flip Vertical**. The triangle flips upside down.

TIP

You can also click the Arrange button in the Drawing group on the Home tab, and then point to Rotate.

There is a problem with the triangle now; the text inside the triangle was flipped upside down as well. To avoid this problem, you can add this text to the shape using a text box.

To add a text box inside a shape:

▶ **1.** Click and drag to select the text **ACLT**, and then press the **Delete** key.

▶ **2.** In the Insert Shapes group on the Format tab, click the **Text Box** button 🔲. You cannot click to create a text box inside the shape; you must drag to create it.

▶ **3.** Position the pointer in the top half of the triangle, press and hold the mouse button, and then drag to create a text box approximately one inch wide and one-quarter inch high. The Home tab becomes the active tab on the Ribbon.

▶ **4.** Type **ACLT**. The text now appears right-side up in the triangle.

▶ **5.** Click the border of the ACLT text box to select the entire text box, change the font size to **24 points**, and then drag the right middle sizing handle to make the text box wider or narrower so that the text just fits on one line.

▶ **6.** In the Font group on the Home tab, click the **Font Color button arrow** 🅰▾, and then click the **White, Background 1** color (the first color in the first row). The text is now formatted properly.

Now you can position all of the text boxes. First you will rotate the text boxes on the left and right sides of the triangle so that the bottoms of the text boxes align with the sides of the triangle. To do this, you can use the Rotate commands on the Rotate menu, or you can drag the rotate handle on the selected object.

After the text boxes are rotated, you can drag them the same way you dragged graphics to reposition them. When you drag shapes drawn using selections from the Shapes gallery, Smart Guides appear as you drag them near other objects on the slide or vice versa. **Smart Guides** are faint blue, dashed lines that appear as you drag an object near a drawn shape to show you when edges or the center of the objects are aligned.

To rotate and move the text boxes:

▶ **1.** Click the **Excellent Guides** text box. The sizing handles and the green rotate handle appear around the text box.

▶ **2.** Position the pointer over the rotate handle. The pointer becomes 🔄.

▶ **3.** Press and hold the **Shift** key, and then drag the rotate handle counterclockwise until the top edge of the text box is parallel to the right edge of the triangle. Pressing the Shift key as you drag the rotate handle forces the object to rotate in 15-degree increments.

4. Position the pointer over a border of the **Excellent Guides** text box so that it changes to ⁺↖, and then without releasing the mouse button, drag the text box so that it is positioned against and centered on the right edge of the triangle. Smart Guides appear as you drag the text box. See Figure 2-14. Don't worry if the Smart Guides don't appear or appear in a different position. They change depending on exactly where the objects are in relation to each other.

Figure 2-14 **Positioning the rotated text box**

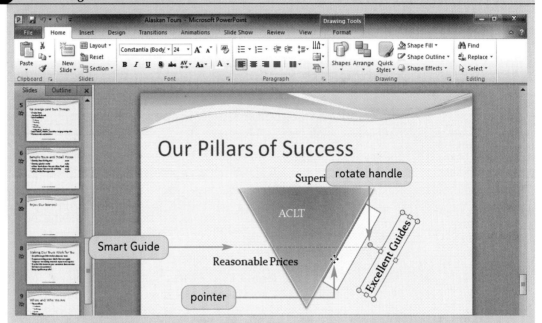

Trouble? If the edge of the text box isn't parallel to the edge of the triangle, repeat Steps 2 and 3 to fix the rotation. If necessary, try it without pressing the Shift key.

Trouble? If the text box jumps from one location to another as you drag it and you can't position it exactly where you want it, press and hold the Alt key as you drag it. The Alt key temporarily disables a feature that forces objects to snap to invisible gridlines on the slide.

5. When the text box is positioned approximately so that it is centered along the right side of the triangle and so that the top edge of the text box is resting against the side of the rectangle, release the mouse button.

6. Rotate the **Reasonable Prices** text box clockwise so that the top edge of the text box is parallel to the left edge of the triangle, and then position the text box so it's against and centered on the left edge of the triangle.

7. Drag the **Superior Tours** text box so the bottom of it is against and centered along the top edge of the triangle, using the vertical Smart Guide that appears to align the center of the text box with the point of the triangle. Now you need to adjust the alignment of the text box you drew in the center of the triangle.

8. In the triangle, click the **ACLT** text box, and then in the Paragraph group on the Home tab, click the **Center** button ≣. The text is centered in the text box you drew.

9. Click the border of the ACLT text box to select the entire text box, press and hold the **Shift** key, and then click the **triangle** to select both objects.

10. In the Drawing group, click the **Arrange** button, point to **Align**, and then click **Align Center**. The ACLT text box is centered horizontally in the triangle.

11. Click a blank area of the Slide pane to deselect the objects. Your slide should look like the slide in Figure 2-15.

Figure 2-15   **Slide 10 with completed diagram**

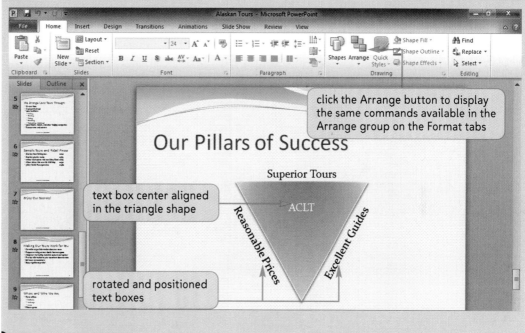

12. Save your changes.

You've added graphics and text boxes to several slides in the presentation to add visual interest and enhance the audience's understanding as Chad requested. In the next session, you'll work with the Slide Master, add a SmartArt diagram and animate it, and finish by sharing the presentation over the Internet by broadcasting it.

Session 2.1 Quick Check

REVIEW

1. What is a bitmap graphic composed of?

2. Define keywords.

3. How do you change the size of a graphic?

4. How do you format a picture, clip art, or a shape with several formats at once?

5. How do you add a shape in the default size to a slide?

6. True or False. A text box is not an object.

7. When you use the rotate handle to rotate an object, how do you force the object to rotate in 15-degree increments?

SESSION 2.2 VISUAL OVERVIEW

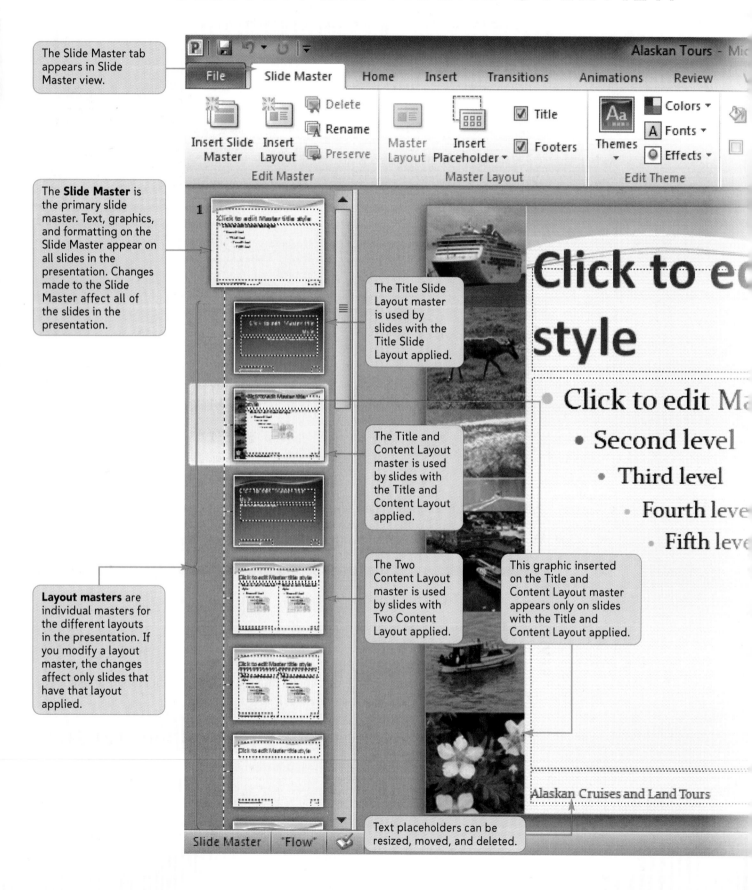

The Slide Master tab appears in Slide Master view.

The **Slide Master** is the primary slide master. Text, graphics, and formatting on the Slide Master appear on all slides in the presentation. Changes made to the Slide Master affect all of the slides in the presentation.

The Title Slide Layout master is used by slides with the Title Slide Layout applied.

The Title and Content Layout master is used by slides with the Title and Content Layout applied.

The Two Content Layout master is used by slides with Two Content Layout applied.

This graphic inserted on the Title and Content Layout master appears only on slides with the Title and Content Layout applied.

Layout masters are individual masters for the different layouts in the presentation. If you modify a layout master, the changes affect only slides that have that layout applied.

Text placeholders can be resized, moved, and deleted.

SLIDE MASTER VIEW

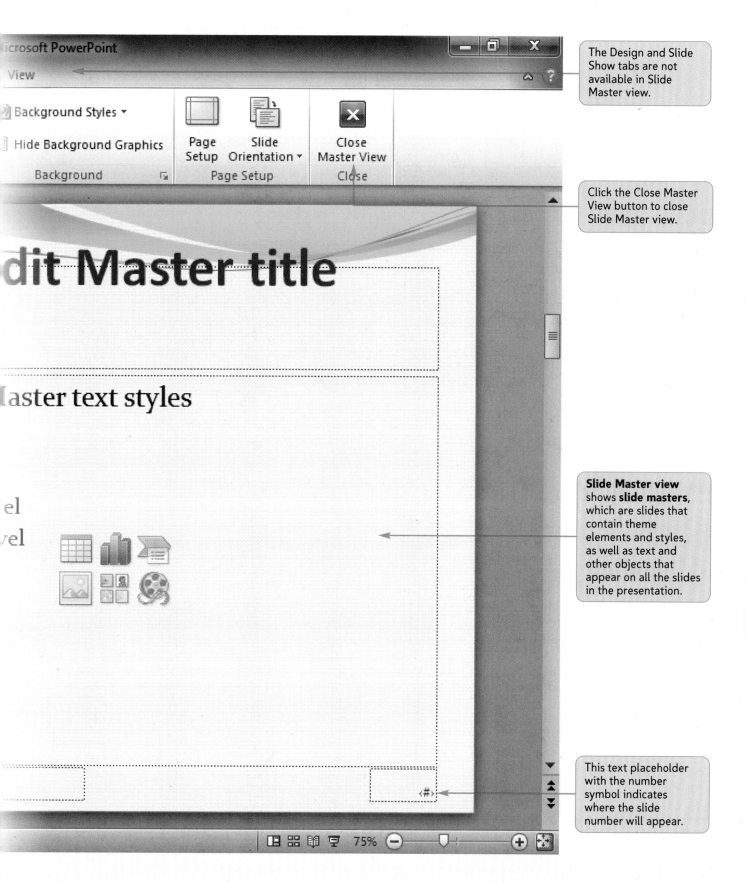

The Design and Slide Show tabs are not available in Slide Master view.

Click the Close Master View button to close Slide Master view.

Slide Master view shows **slide masters**, which are slides that contain theme elements and styles, as well as text and other objects that appear on all the slides in the presentation.

This text placeholder with the number symbol indicates where the slide number will appear.

Modifying the Slide Master

Slide masters ensure that all the slides in the presentation have a similar appearance and contain the same elements. To work with slide masters, you need to switch to Slide Master view.

To switch to Slide Master view:

1. If you took a break after the previous session, make sure PowerPoint is running, and the **Alaskan Tours** presentation you created in Session 2.1 is open in the PowerPoint window in Normal view.

2. If necessary, display **Slide 10** ("Our Pillars of Success") in the Slide pane, and then click the **View** tab on the Ribbon.

3. In the Master Views group, click the **Slide Master** button. The view changes to Slide Master view and a new tab, the Slide Master tab, appears on the Ribbon to the left of the Home tab.

4. In the pane on the left side of the window, point to the selected layout master thumbnail (at the bottom of the left pane). The ScreenTip identifies this layout master as the Title Only Layout, and indicates that it is used by Slide 10.

5. In the pane on the left, point to the top thumbnail. This is the Slide Master, as indicated by the ScreenTip. Notice that the ScreenTip includes the name of the current theme; in this case, it is the Flow Slide Master. The ScreenTip also indicates that it is used by Slides 1-11, which are all the slides in the presentation.

6. In the pane on the left, point to the third thumbnail to verify that it is the Title and Content Layout master used by Slides 5-9 and 11, and then click that layout master. (Slides 2-4 have the Two Content layout applied, and Slide 1 has the Title Slide layout applied.) The Title and Content Layout master appears in the Slide pane.

TIP

You can also press and hold the Shift key and click the Normal button on the status bar to switch to Slide Master view.

In addition to the slide masters, each presentation has a **handouts master**, which contains the elements that appear on all the printed handouts, and a **notes master**, which contains the elements that appear on the notes pages. To display these masters, click the appropriate buttons in the Master Views group on the View tab.

You can modify slide masters by changing the size and design of text in the content placeholders, adding or deleting graphics, changing the background, and making other modifications.

Chad wants you to add a bitmapped image that shows scenes of Alaska to the slide background. To create the bitmapped file of the Alaska scenes, Chad took pictures with a digital camera, and then used image-editing software to combine several pictures into one. Chad wants this graphic only on the slides that have the Title and Content layout applied, so you'll insert it on the Title and Content layout master rather than on the Slide Master. You will need to use the Picture button in the Images group on the Insert tab. You cannot use the Insert Picture from File icon in the content placeholder because you do not want to replace the content placeholder in the layout master.

To insert a graphic on the slide master:

1. Click the **Insert** tab on the Ribbon, and then click the **Picture** button in the Images group. The Insert Picture dialog box opens.

2. If necessary, navigate to the PowerPoint2\Tutorial folder included with your Data Files, click the picture file **AKPanel**, and then click the **Insert** button. The image is inserted on the slide master in the middle of the slide, and the Picture Tools Format tab appears on the Ribbon and is the active tab.

3. In the Arrange group, click the **Align** button ▤▾, and then click **Align Left**. The picture moves to the left edge of the slide. See Figure 2-16.

Figure 2-16   Title and Content Layout master with image

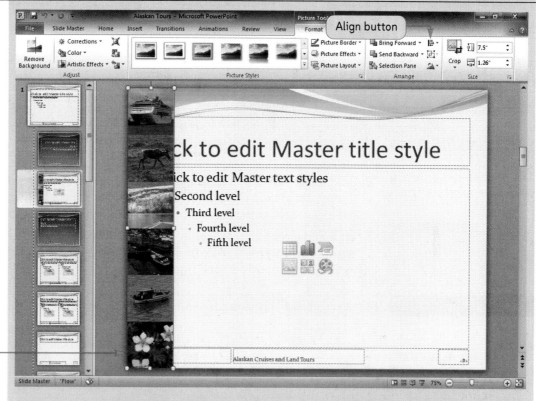

graphic aligned at left edge of the slide master

4. Save your changes.

Next, you will modify text and text placeholders in the masters.

Modifying Text Placeholders

The picture that you just inserted overlaps the title and content placeholders. Chad wants you to resize the placeholders so that their left edges are to the right of the picture. Resizing a placeholder or a text box is the same as resizing a graphic; select it, and then drag a sizing handle.

To resize the title and content placeholders:

1. In the Slide pane, click the **title text** placeholder. Sizing handles appear around the placeholder text box. You can see the left border of the title placeholder box even though that part of the box is obscured by the picture you inserted. See Figure 2-17.

Figure 2-17 Selected title text placeholder on the Title and Content Layout master

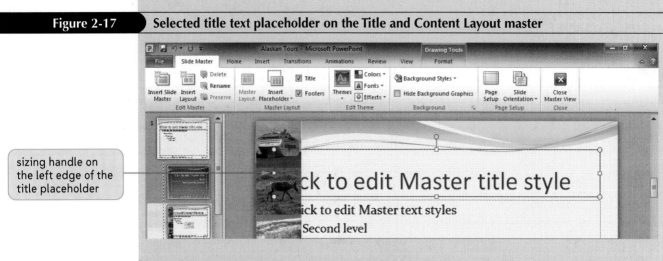

sizing handle on the left edge of the title placeholder

2. Drag the middle sizing handle on the left edge of the text box to the right until the left border of the placeholder is to the right of the bitmapped image and so there is a small amount of white space between the border and image.

3. Click in the content placeholder, and then drag its left-middle sizing handle to the right so that the left border of the content placeholder aligns with the left border of the title placeholder. See Figure 2-18.

Figure 2-18 Title and Content Layout master with resized placeholders

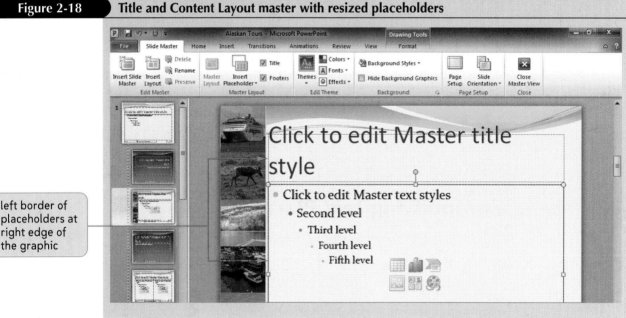

left border of placeholders at right edge of the graphic

The three placeholders at the bottom of the slide master are the Date, Footer, and Slide Number placeholders, in that order from left to right. Chad doesn't want the date to be displayed in this presentation, and he doesn't want any user to have the opportunity to add it using the Header and Footer dialog box, so he asks you to delete the Date placeholder. This will give you room to reposition the Footer and Slide Number placeholders more attractively. You want this change to affect all the slides in the presentation, so instead of working on a layout master, you will switch to the Slide Master.

To delete and reposition the text placeholders:

1. In the pane on the left side of the window, click the **Flow Slide Master** thumbnail (the top master).

2. At the bottom of the Slide pane, click the border of the Date placeholder to select it.

3. Press the **Delete** key to delete the Date placeholder. Now you need to align the Footer placeholder with the content placeholder.

   Trouble? If nothing happened when you pressed the Delete key, you didn't select the entire object. Click the edge of the placeholder so that the border changes to a solid line, and then repeat Step 3.

4. Select the **Footer** placeholder (it contains the company name), press and hold the **Shift** key, select the **content** placeholder, and then click the **Drawing Tools Format** tab.

5. In the Arrange group, click the **Align** button, and then click **Align Left**. The Footer placeholder shifts left so that its left edge is aligned with the left edge of the content placeholder above it. Whenever you make a change to the Slide Master, you should check the layout masters because sometimes the changes do not appear on the layout masters. Also, remember that you resized the placeholders on the Title and Content Layout master, so you'll need to adjust the position of the Footer placeholder on that layout master to accommodate the difference.

6. In the left pane, click the **Title and Content Layout** thumbnail. The Footer placeholder is shifted left because of the change you made on the Flow Slide Master, but the Date placeholder is still on this layout master, overlapping the Footer placeholder. See Figure 2-19. First you'll adjust the position of the Footer placeholder.

Figure 2-19	Overlapping Footer and Date placeholders

right edge of the Date placeholder

right edge of the Footer placeholder

Slide Number placeholder

...uises and Land Tours

7. Select both the **Footer** placeholder and the **content** placeholder, and then use the **Align Left** command. The content placeholder shifts left. This is not what you wanted.

8. On the Quick Access Toolbar, click the **Undo** button, and then click a blank area of the slide to deselect both placeholders. You'll move the Footer placeholder using the → key instead.

9. Select the **Footer** placeholder, and then press the → key 10 times to move the Footer placeholder to the right until its left edge is aligned with the left edge of the content placeholder. Now you need to delete the Date placeholder.

10. Click a blank area of the slide to deselect the Footer placeholder, and then click the right side of the **Date** placeholder border. See Figure 2-20.

    Trouble? If the Footer placeholder is selected instead of the Date placeholder, press the Shift+Tab keys to select the Date placeholder.

| Figure 2-20 | Selected Date placeholder |

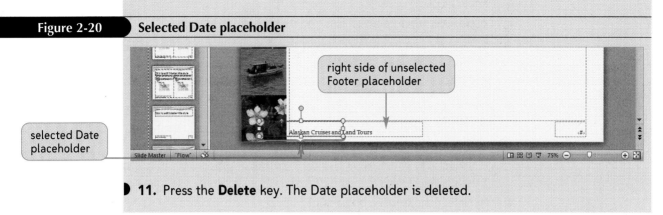

selected Date placeholder

▶ **11.** Press the **Delete** key. The Date placeholder is deleted.

Now you need to delete the Date placeholder from the Two Content Layout master and the Title Only Layout master. You don't need to delete the Date placeholder from the only other layout master used in the presentation, the Title Slide Layout master, because in the Header and Footer dialog box, the option to prevent the date, footer, and the slide number from appearing on the title slide is selected.

To delete the date from other layout masters:

▶ **1.** In the pane on the left, click the **Two Content Layout** thumbnail. As on the Title and Content Layout master, the Footer placeholder is shifted, but the Date placeholder is still there.

▶ **2.** In the Slide pane, click the **Date** placeholder, and then press the **Delete** key.

▶ **3.** In the pane on the left, click the **Title Only Layout** thumbnail, and then delete the Date placeholder from that layout master.

▶ **4.** Save your changes.

Modifying the Font Style in the Slide Master

Chad wants you to change the font style of the title text in most of the layouts from normal to bold, and the color of the title text in the Title Slide layout from light blue to yellow. It is a good idea to make this type of change in the slide masters rather than on the individual slides because you want to keep the look of the slides in the presentation consistent.

To modify the font style in the slide masters:

▶ **1.** Click the **Flow Slide Master** thumbnail at the top of the left pane, and then, in the Slide pane, select the **title text** placeholder.

▶ **2.** Click the **Home** tab on the Ribbon, if necessary, and then click the **Bold** button **B** in the Font group. The text in the title text placeholder on the Slide Master becomes bold.

   Trouble? If nothing happened when you clicked the Bold button, the title text placeholder is active, but not selected. Click directly on the border of the title text placeholder, and then repeat Step 2.

▶ **3.** In the pane on the left side of the window, click the **Title Slide Layout** thumbnail.

▶ **4.** In the Slide pane, select the **title text placeholder**.

5. In the Font group, click the **Font Color button arrow** ▲ ▾, and then, in the Standard Colors section, click the **Yellow** color. The placeholder text now matches the color of the flowers in the picture on the Title and Content Layout master. See Figure 2-21.

| **Figure 2-21** | **Modified title text placeholder on the Title Slide Layout master** |

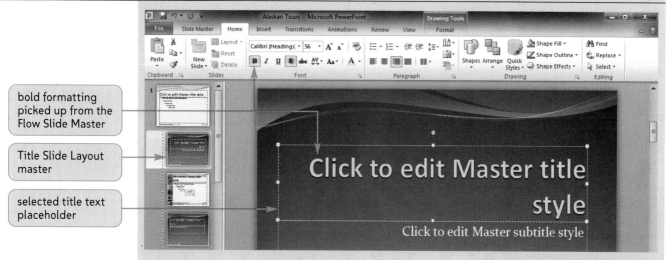

bold formatting picked up from the Flow Slide Master

Title Slide Layout master

selected title text placeholder

6. Click the **Slide Master** tab on the Ribbon, and then click the **Close Master View** button in the Close group. Slide 10 appears in the Slide pane in Normal view.

The panel of photos does not appear on Slide 10 because this slide uses the Title Only layout. However, the title text should be formatted in bold. As you saw earlier, sometimes changes you make to a Slide Master don't carry through to all the layout masters. Instead of applying the bold formatting to the Title Only Layout master, you'll change it here. Then, you'll verify that the changes you made appear on slides with the other layouts used in the presentation, the Title and Content layout and the Title Slide layout.

To fix the formatting on Slide 10 and examine other slides:

1. On Slide 10, select the **title text box**, and then apply bold formatting.

2. Display **Slide 11** ("Contact Us") in the Slide pane. This slide uses the Title and Content layout, so the title text is bold, the panel of photos appears on the left, the title and content are shifted right so that the panel of photos does not overlap them, and the footer appears in the correct position. See Figure 2-22.

Figure 2-22 **Changes from the slide masters applied to Slide 11**

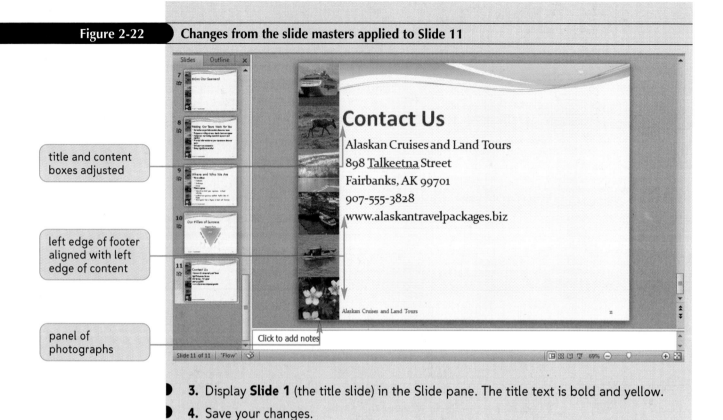

title and content boxes adjusted

left edge of footer aligned with left edge of content

panel of photographs

▶ **3.** Display **Slide 1** (the title slide) in the Slide pane. The title text is bold and yellow.

▶ **4.** Save your changes.

Creating SmartArt Diagrams

A **diagram** visually depicts information or ideas and shows how they are connected. SmartArt is a feature that allows you to create diagrams easily and quickly. In addition to shapes, SmartArt diagrams usually include text to help describe or label the shapes. You can create the following types of diagrams using SmartArt:

- **List:** Shows a list of items in a graphical representation
- **Process:** Shows a sequence of steps in a process
- **Cycle:** Shows a process that has a continuous cycle
- **Hierarchy** (including **organization charts**): Shows the relationship between individuals or units within an organization
- **Relationship** (including **Venn diagrams**, **radial diagrams**, and **target diagrams**): Shows the relationship between two or more elements
- **Matrix:** Shows information in a grid
- **Pyramid:** Shows foundation-based relationships
- **Picture:** Provides a location for a picture or pictures

There is also an Office.com category, which, if you are connected to the Internet, displays additional SmartArt diagrams available on Office.com. You also might see an Other category, which contains SmartArt diagrams previously downloaded from Office.com.

Creating a SmartArt Diagram

To create a SmartArt diagram, you can click the Insert SmartArt Graphic button in a content placeholder, or in the Illustrations group on the Insert tab, click the SmartArt button to open the Choose a SmartArt Graphic dialog box.

REFERENCE

Creating a SmartArt Diagram

- Switch to a layout that includes a content placeholder, and then in the content place-holder, click the Insert SmartArt Graphic button; or click the Insert tab on the Ribbon, and then in the Illustrations group, click the SmartArt button.
- In the Choose a SmartArt Graphic dialog box, select the desired SmartArt category in the list on the left.
- In the center pane, click the SmartArt diagram you want to use.
- Click the OK button.

Chad asks you to use SmartArt in the Picture category to add photos to Slide 7.

TIP

If the slide layout you are using does not contain a content placeholder, you can use the SmartArt button in the Illustrations group on the Insert tab to insert a SmartArt diagram.

To create a picture diagram using SmartArt:

1. Display **Slide 7** ("Enjoy Our Scenery!") in the Slide pane, and then in the content placeholder, click the **Insert SmartArt Graphic** button. The Choose a SmartArt Graphic dialog box opens. See Figure 2-23. The first diagram in the first row is selected. The pane on the right identifies this as the Basic Block List and provides a description of this diagram.

Figure 2-23	Choose a SmartArt Graphic dialog box

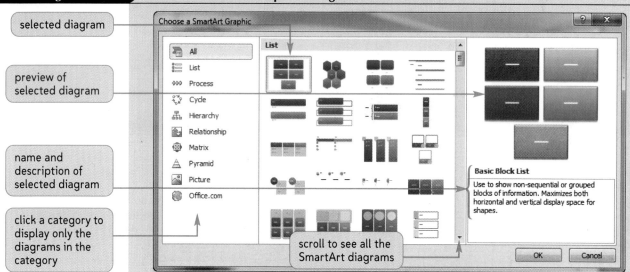

selected diagram

preview of selected diagram

name and description of selected diagram

click a category to display only the diagrams in the category

scroll to see all the SmartArt diagrams

2. In the list of diagram categories on the left, click **Picture**. The gallery in the middle of the dialog box changes to display various types of Picture diagrams.

3. In the gallery, point to the first diagram in the first row. The ScreenTip identifies it as Accented Picture.

4. Click the **Accented Picture** diagram. The pane on the right changes to show a preview and description of the selected diagram.

5. Click the **OK** button. The dialog box closes and the SmartArt diagram you selected appears on the slide. You might see a Text pane labeled "Type your text here" to the left of the diagram.

▶ **6.** If the Text pane is visible, click the **Close** button ⊠ in its upper-right corner. See Figure 2-24. The diagram consists of a large picture placeholder, three smaller picture placeholders, and four text placeholders, one associated with each picture placeholder. The border around the diagram defines the borders of the entire SmartArt diagram object. Finally, note the two SmartArt Tools contextual tabs that appear on the Ribbon.

Figure 2-24	Accented Picture SmartArt diagram on the slide

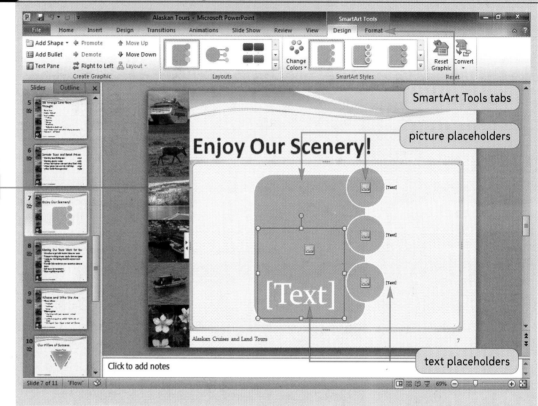

Now that you've added the diagram to the slide, you need to add content to it. In this case, you will first add pictures, and then you will add text in the text placeholders to describe those pictures.

To add pictures to the Picture diagram:

▶ **1.** In the largest picture placeholder on the left side of the diagram, click the **Insert Picture from File** button. The Insert Picture dialog box opens.

▶ **2.** In the PowerPoint2\Tutorial folder included with your Data Files, click **Ship**, and then click the **Insert** button. The dialog box closes and a picture of a ship replaces the large picture placeholder in the diagram.

▶ **3.** In each of the three small picture placeholders, insert the following picture files, from top to bottom: **Vista**, **Caribou**, and **Flower**.

Chad feels this slide would be more effective if the panel of photos on the left did not appear.

Be sure to click the picture icon in the top small picture placeholder and not the border of the large picture you just inserted.

4. Click the **Home** tab, click the **Layout** button in the Slides group, and then click the **Title Only** layout. The layout changes and the panel of photos that appears on slides with the Title and Content layout disappears. Remember that the bold formatting you applied to the title text on the Slide Master did not carry through to the Title Only layout master.

5. Modify the title so that it is bold. See Figure 2-25.

Figure 2-25   **SmartArt picture diagram with the Title Only layout applied**

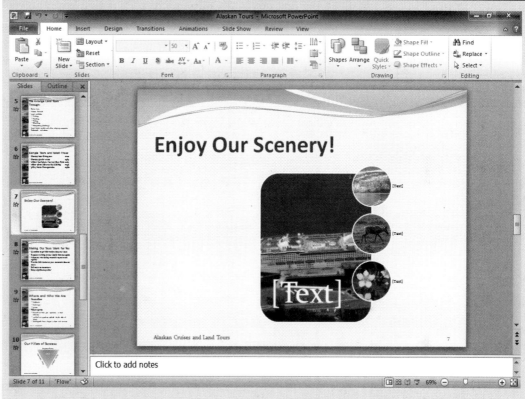

Next, you will add labels to the SmartArt picture diagram.

To add labels to the SmartArt Picture diagram:

1. In the picture of the ship, click the **text** placeholder. The placeholder text disappears and the insertion point is blinking, waiting for you to start typing.

2. Type **One of our cruise ships**. The text appears on top of the picture.

3. Next to the top small photo, click the **text** placeholder, and then type **Approaching a glacier**. As you type, the pictures are shifted to the left within the SmartArt object to make room for the text you are typing, and the font size of the text you are creating shrinks to fit the placeholder.

4. Replace the middle text placeholder with **Caribou**, and then replace the bottom text placeholder with **Wildflower**. The size of the text in the labels for the three small photos overwhelms the photos, so Chad asks you to decrease the font size of these labels.

▶ 5. Select **Approaching a glacier**.

▶ 6. In the Font group, click the **Font Size button arrow**, and then click **28**.

▶ 7. Reduce the font size of **Caribou** and **Wildflower** to **28** points. With the text size of all three labels reduced, the photos shift right again so that they are more centered. Now you want to decrease the size of the white text on the large picture and reposition it so it is on top of the water in the picture.

▶ 8. Reduce the font size of **One of our cruise ships** to **32** points.

▶ 9. Drag the text box in the large picture up until the top border of the text box touches the top border of the SmartArt.

▶ 10. Drag the bottom, middle sizing handle of the text box up until the text box outline fits within the water above the boat in the picture. See Figure 2-26.

| Figure 2-26 | **Final SmartArt diagram with labels** |

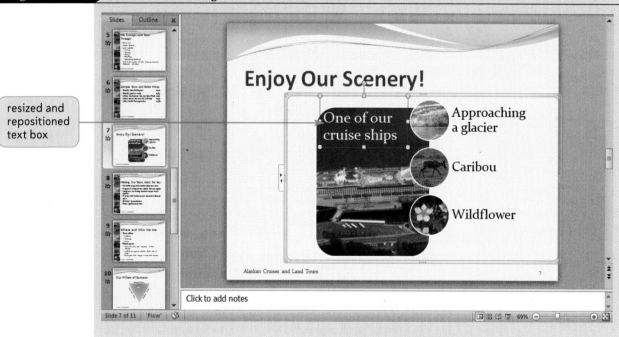

Converting a Bulleted List into a SmartArt Diagram

You can convert an existing bulleted list into a SmartArt diagram by using the Convert to SmartArt button in the Paragraph group on the Home tab.

Converting a Bulleted List into a SmartArt Diagram

- Click anywhere in the bulleted list.
- In Paragraph group on the Home tab, click the Convert to SmartArt Graphic button, and then click More SmartArt Graphics.
- In the Choose a SmartArt Graphic dialog box, select the desired SmartArt category in the list on the left.
- In the center pane, click the SmartArt diagram you want to use.
- Click the OK button.

Chad wants you to convert the bulleted items in Slide 8 ("Making Our Tours Work for You") into a process diagram to show the steps for using ACLT services.

To convert the bulleted list on Slide 8 into a SmartArt diagram:

1. Display **Slide 8** ("Making Our Tours Work for You") in the Slide pane, and then click anywhere on the bulleted list. The dashed line text box border appears.

2. In the Paragraph group on the Home tab, click the **Convert to SmartArt Graphic** button. A gallery opens displaying twenty SmartArt diagrams.

3. Point to several of the diagrams and watch Live Preview change the bulleted list into the various SmartArt diagrams.

4. In the third row, the third column, click the **Continuous Block Process** diagram. The text on Slide 8 converts to a SmartArt diagram, and the SmartArt Tools tabs appear on the Ribbon, with the Design tab active. See Figure 2-27.

TIP

You can open the Choose a SmartArt Graphic dialog box by clicking More SmartArt Graphics.

Figure 2-27   Slide 8 with a process diagram

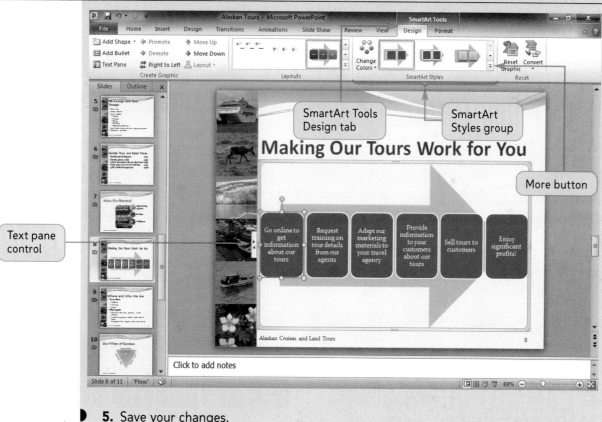

5. Save your changes.

Modifying a SmartArt Diagram

A SmartArt diagram is a larger object composed of smaller objects. You can modify the diagram by adding or deleting shapes, modifying the text by changing the font attributes, and changing the way the shapes look. You can also modify the diagram as a whole.

Adding a Shape to a SmartArt Diagram

- Click the shape next to the position where you want to insert the shape.
- Click the SmartArt Tools Design tab on the Ribbon.
- In the Create Graphic group, click the Add Shape button arrow, and then click the appropriate command on the menu.
- Type the text in the new shape.

or

- Click the Text pane control to open the Text pane.
- Click at the end of the bulleted item corresponding to the shape after which you want to add the shape; or click at the beginning of the bulleted item before which you want to add the shape.
- Press the Enter key.
- Click next to the new bullet if necessary, and then type the text of the new shape.

Chad decides he doesn't need the last box in the diagram, but he wants you to add a shape before the "Sell tours…" shape.

To delete a shape from and add a shape to the SmartArt diagram:

1. Make sure the SmartArt diagram is selected.

2. On the left border of the diagram, click the **Text pane control**. The Text pane contains the text in the diagram as a bulleted list. See Figure 2-28. You can edit the text in the shapes in the diagram, or you can edit the bulleted list in the Text pane.

Figure 2-28 **Text pane open on SmartArt diagram**

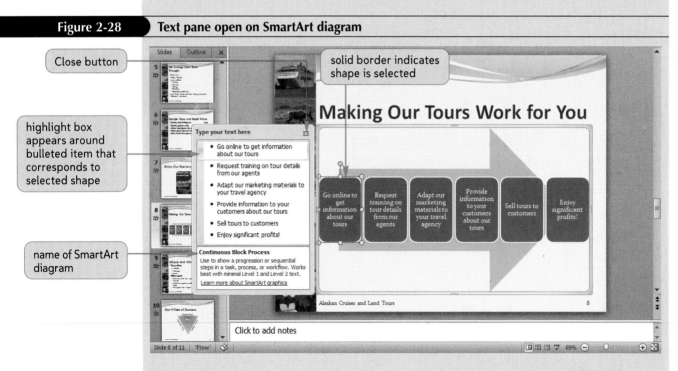

3. In the diagram, position the pointer on the border of the last shape ("Enjoy significant profits!") so that it changes to ↖, click to select the shape, and then press the **Delete** key. The shape is removed, and the corresponding bulleted item is removed from the Text pane. The "Sell tours…" shape is now selected.

TIP

To add a new shape, you can also work in the Text pane. It works just like bulleted lists in a content placeholder.

4. In the Create Graphic group on the Design tab, click the **Add Shape button arrow**. The top command on the menu is the default command that would be executed if you clicked the icon on the Add Shape button. The commands in gray on the menu are available when different SmartArt diagrams are on the slide.

5. Click **Add Shape Before**. The menu closes and a new shape is added to the diagram before the selected shape, and the new shape is selected. A corresponding bullet appears in the Text pane.

6. Type **Check our Web site for updates on sales and promotions**. The text appears in the new shape and next to the corresponding bullet in the Text pane.

7. Click a blank area of the SmartArt diagram. The "Check our Web site" shape is deselected, but because you clicked inside the border of the SmartArt diagram, the diagram is still selected.

8. In the upper-right corner of the Text pane, click the **Close** button ☒. The Text pane closes.

Now that you have all the correct shapes and text in your diagram, you can add formatting to the shapes in the diagram using the options on the SmartArt Tools Format tab. You can also use options on the SmartArt Tools Design tab to apply special effects to the diagram. Chad asks you to apply a style to the diagram.

To apply a style to the SmartArt diagram:

1. In the SmartArt Styles group on the SmartArt Tools Design tab, click the **More** button to open the gallery of styles available for the graphic.

2. In the gallery, click the **Metallic Scene** style (the first style in the last row in the 3-D section). The style of the graphic changes to the one you chose. See Figure 2-29.

Figure 2-29   **SmartArt diagram with a style applied**

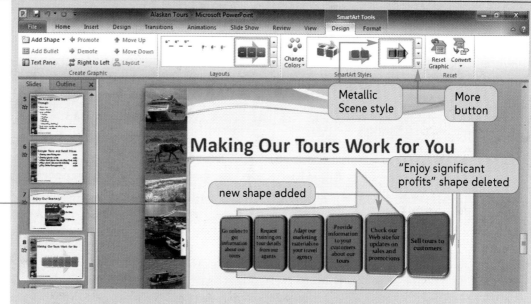

3. Save your changes.

Next, you will animate the clip art on Slide 2, the photo on Slide 4, and the SmartArt process diagram.

Animating Objects

You can add interest to a slide show by animating objects on the slides. When you animated text in Tutorial 1, you actually animated the text boxes, which are objects. You can animate any object on a slide, including photos and clip art. Even SmartArt diagrams can be enhanced by applying animations.

Animating Graphics

To animate a graphic, you simply select the graphic, and then select an animation in the Animation group on the Animations tab. Chad wants you to animate the clip art on Slide 2 and the picture on Slide 4 with entrance animations.

To animate the graphics on Slides 2 and 4:

1. Display **Slide 2** ("What Is Alaskan Cruises and Land Tours?") in the Slide pane, and then click the **clip art** to select it.

2. Click the **Animations** tab.

3. In the Animation group, click the **More** button, and then in the top row in the Entrance section, click the **Split** animation. The animation previews on the slide.

4. Display **Slide 4** ("We Arrange Travel and Vacation Packages for:") in the Slide pane, and then apply the **Split** animation to the photograph.

Changing the Sequence of an Animation

If you apply animation to a SmartArt diagram, you can choose to have the entire diagram animate at once as a single object, as individual objects but all at the same time, or as individual objects one at a time. Chad wants you to animate the process diagram on Slide 8 so that each object in the diagram appears one after the other.

To animate the SmartArt diagram and change the sequence:

1. Display **Slide 8** ("Making Our Tours Work for You") in the Slide pane, and then click anywhere on the **SmartArt diagram**. You want the diagram to fly in.

2. In the Animation group, click the **Fly In** animation. The animation previews and the entire diagram flies up from the bottom.

3. In the Animation group, click the **Effect Options** button. See Figure 2-30. The options on this menu change depending on the selected animation and on the object being animated. The options in the Sequence section reflect that you are animating an object composed of multiple objects.

Figure 2-30   **Effect Options menu for the Fly In animation applied to a SmartArt diagram**

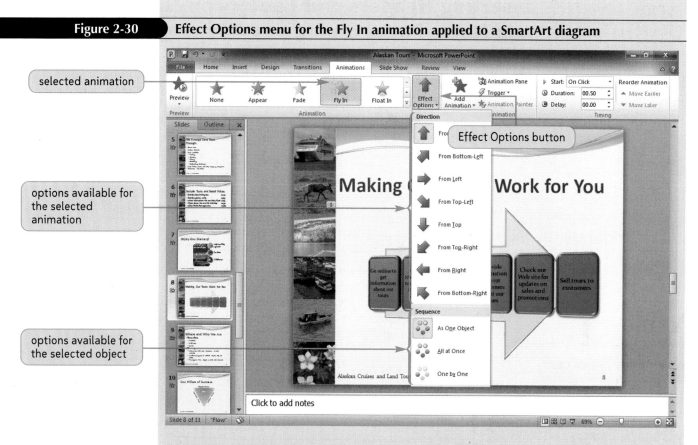

> **4.** In the Sequence section at the bottom of the menu, click **One by One**. The animation previews again and each shape flies in individually.

As you saw when you animated a bulleted list, the default for the list is to animate each first-level bulleted item one at a time. If you opened the Effect Options menu for an animated bulleted list, you would see that the Sequence options are similar to those for SmartArt, but that last option is By Paragraph instead of One by One.

Customizing the Direction of an Animation

Now that you have customized the sequence of the SmartArt animation, you can change the direction of the animation. Chad thinks it would be more effective if the objects in the SmartArt diagram could fly onto the slide from the direction indicated by the arrow, from the left. You can adjust this using the Effect Options menu.

To customize the animation direction:

> **1.** In the Animation group on the Animations tab, click the **Effect Options** button. The Effect Options menu appears.

> **2.** In the Direction section, click **From Left**. The animation previews and each object in the top row in the diagram flies in from the left.

> **3.** Save your changes.

Inserting Headers and Footers on Handouts and Notes Pages

In Tutorial 1, you learned how to add footers to slides in a slide show. Recall that a footer is text that appears at the bottom of each slide. You can also insert footers on handouts and notes pages. Similar to footers, a **header** is text that appears at the top of every page in a document. In PowerPoint, you cannot insert a header on slides in the presentation, but you can insert a header in handouts and notes pages. Because handouts and notes pages are printed documents, the options for inserting headers differ from the footer options for slides that you used in Tutorial 1.

To add a header and footer to the handouts and notes pages:

▶ 1. Click the **Insert** tab, and then click the **Header & Footer** button in the Text group. The Header and Footer dialog box opens with the Slide tab on top.

▶ 2. Click the **Notes and Handouts** tab. See Figure 2-31. Notice the options on this tab are different than the options available for inserting footers on slides. Unlike the Slide tab, this tab contains a Header check box and a box in which you can type a header. Also note that instead of the Slide number check box, this tab includes a Page number check box that is selected by default.

| Figure 2-31 | Notes and Handouts tab in the Header and Footer dialog box |

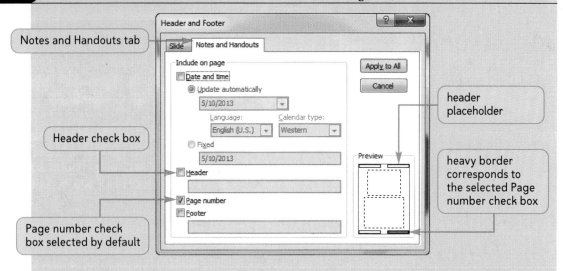

▶ 3. Click the **Header** check box to select it. A thick border appears around the place-holder in the upper-left corner of the Preview. That is where the header will appear.

▶ 4. In the Header box, type **Information for Travel Agents**.

▶ 5. Click the **Footer** check box, and then in the Footer box, type **Alaskan Tours 2013**.

▶ 6. Click the **Apply to All** button to close the dialog box.

The header will appear on handouts and any notes pages you print. (Slide 5 contains a speaker note that Chad added to his original presentation.)

Decision Making: Are Handouts Necessary?

Before taking the time to create handouts for your presentation, there are a few factors to consider, such as when to provide the handouts to the audience and whether the audience will find value in having the handout. Many speakers provide printed copies of their presentation slides to the audience at the beginning of their presentation. Often, this reduces the need for the audience to take notes on each slide as it's presented. However, sometimes the audience starts to read through the handouts as soon as they are distributed, getting ahead of the speaker. This might also cause the audience to stop listening because they are focused more intently on the printed text. And as they turn the pages, the rustle of paper can cause a distraction. To avoid this problem, first decide if handouts are truly necessary. If you decide they are, instead of handing out materials before the presentation, consider providing handouts at the end of your presentation session. If you need to provide a handout specifically designed to support a specific part of your presentation, wait and distribute this handout when you get to that point. Thinking about these factors beforehand will help you decide how and when it is of value to provide handouts.

Your presentation is complete. You should always check the spelling in your presentation, proofread it, and view it in Slide Show or Reading view to make sure everything works as expected.

To check and view the presentation:

1. Click the **Review** tab on the Ribbon, and then click the **Spelling** button in the Proofing group to start checking the spelling of your presentation. Decide how to handle each word that is flagged because it was not found in the PowerPoint dictionary.

2. Display **Slide 1** (the title slide) in the Slide pane, and then click the **Slide Show** button 🖳 on the status bar. The slide show starts in Slide Show view. The transition that Chad chose for Slide 1 is the Ripple transition. He thought that was appropriate for a presentation from a company that provides travel packages that include a cruise.

3. Press the **spacebar** or click the mouse button to advance through the slide show. Notice that Chad used the Wipe transition on the rest of the slides. He thought the Ripple transition was too distracting to use for all of the slides.

4. If you see any problems while you are watching the slide show, press the **Esc** key to exit the slide show and return to Normal view, make the necessary corrections, and then return to Slide Show view.

5. Switch to Slide Sorter view, increase the zoom so that the slide thumbnails are as large as possible but still all appear within the Slide Sorter window (about 80% zoom), and then save your changes to the presentation. Compare your presentation to Figure 2-32.

Figure 2-32 Completed presentation in Slide Sorter view

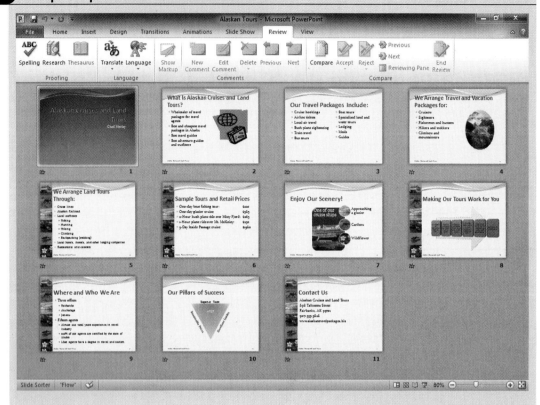

6. Submit the finished presentation to your instructor, either in printed or electronic form, as requested.

Chad is pleased with the additions and modifications you made to the presentation. He is eager to give the presentation to travel agents. He will do so using the Broadcast feature.

Broadcasting a Presentation

You can broadcast a presentation over the Internet and anyone with the URL (the address for a Web page on the Internet) for the presentation and a browser can watch it. When you **broadcast** a presentation, you send the presentation to a special Microsoft server that is made available for this purpose. (If you have access to a SharePoint server, you can send the presentation to that server instead.) A unique Web address is created, and you can send this Web address to anyone you choose. Then, while you run your presentation on your computer in Slide Show view, your remote audience members can view it on their computers in a Web browser at the same time. In order to use the broadcast feature, you need a Windows Live ID (or access to a SharePoint server) and you need to be connected to the Internet.

Chad would like to present his slide show to travel agents all over the country and in Canada. He asks you to try out the Broadcast feature. First you need to obtain a Windows Live ID.

Note: If you are not connected to the Internet, read, but do not perform the steps in this section. If you already have a Windows Live ID, you can skip this next set of steps.

To obtain a Windows Live ID:

▶ **1.** Start your browser, and then go to **www.windowslive.com**.

   Trouble? If the URL doesn't bring you to the page where you can sign in to Windows Live, use a search engine to search for "Windows Live."

▶ **2.** Click the **Sign up** button. The Create your Windows Live ID page appears.

▶ **3.** Follow the instructions on the screen to create an ID with a new, live.com email address or create an ID using an existing email address.

▶ **4.** After completing the process, if you signed up with an existing email address, open your email program or go to your Web-based email home page, and open the email message automatically sent to you from the Windows Live site. Click the link to open the Sign In page again, sign in with your user name and password, and then click the **OK** button in the page that appears telling you that your email address is verified.

▶ **5.** Exit your browser and return to the PowerPoint window.

Once you have a Windows Live ID, you can connect to the broadcast service from within your PowerPoint presentation to create the unique Web address and start the broadcast.

REFERENCE

Broadcasting a Presentation

- Click the Slide Show tab on the Ribbon, and then in the Start Slide Show group, click the Broadcast Slide Show button; or click the File tab on the Ribbon, and then in the navigation bar click the Save & Send tab; in the Save & Send section, click Broadcast Slide Show; and then in the pane on the right, click the Broadcast Slide Show button.
- In the Broadcast Slide Show dialog box, click the Start Broadcast button.
- In the dialog box that asks for your Windows Live credentials, type your Windows Live ID user name and password, and then click the OK button.
- In the dialog box that displays the unique link for your presentation, click Copy Link to copy the link to the Clipboard, paste the copied link in an email message or other form of electronic communication and send it to the people you are inviting to your broadcast; or click Send in Email to start your email program and place the link in a new message.
- Ask audience members to click the link to open the Web page or to paste the link in the Address bar of their browser, and then press the Enter key to go to the Web page.
- In the Broadcast Slide Show dialog box, click the Start Slide Show button.
- Advance through the slide show, and then end the slide show.
- In the yellow Broadcast View bar, click the End Broadcast button; or in the Broadcast group on the Broadcast tab, click the End Broadcast button.
- In the confirming dialog box, click the End Broadcast button.

TIP

You can also click the File tab, in the navigation bar, click the Share tab, and then click Broadcast Slide Show.

To broadcast the slide show:

1. Click the **Slide Show** tab, and then click the **Broadcast Slide Show** button in the Start Slide Show group. The Broadcast Slide Show dialog box opens. See Figure 2-33.

Figure 2-33 Broadcast Slide Show dialog box

2. Click the **Start Broadcast** button. The dialog box changes to show that you are connecting to the PowerPoint Broadcast Service, and then another dialog box opens asking for your Windows Live ID credentials. See Figure 2-34.

Figure 2-34 Dialog box asking for your Windows Live ID credentials

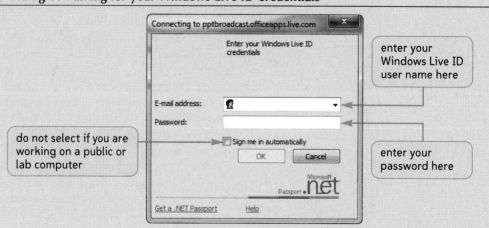

3. In the E-mail address box, type your Windows Live ID user name, click in the Password box, type your Windows Live ID password, and then click the **OK** button. The dialog box closes, and the Broadcast Slide Show dialog box displays the progress of the connection. After a few moments, the Broadcast Slide Show dialog box changes to display the link to your presentation on the PowerPoint Broadcast server. See Figure 2-35. Notice that in the presentation window behind the dialog box, the tabs on the Ribbon are gone, replaced by the Broadcast tab, and a yellow Broadcast View bar appears below the Ribbon indicating that you are broadcasting the presentation and you cannot make changes.

Figure 2-35   **Broadcast Slide Show dialog box and presentation after broadcast has started**

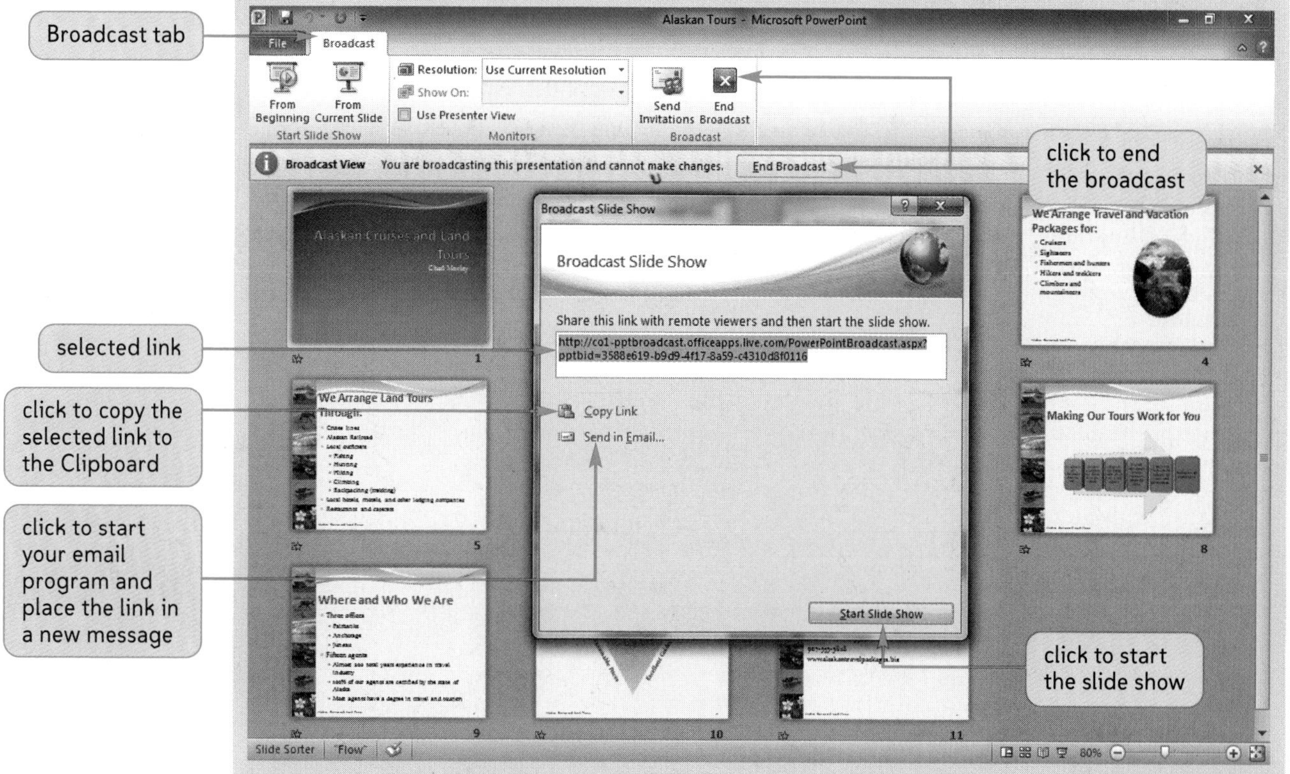

Broadcast tab

click to end the broadcast

selected link

click to copy the selected link to the Clipboard

click to start your email program and place the link in a new message

click to start the slide show

Next, you need to invite people to watch your broadcast.

To invite people to your broadcast:

1. In the dialog box, make sure the link is still selected in the white box, and then click **Copy Link**. The link is copied to the Clipboard.

2. Send the link to a friend if possible, or send it to yourself by pasting it into the body of an email message, a Facebook post, or any other method of communicating over the Internet.

Now you can start the broadcast. You can start the broadcast even if no one is watching it. It will look like ordinary Slide Show view to you. Anyone watching it will see a view similar to Slide Show view in their browser window. If people go to the Web site before you start the slide show, they will see a message in the middle of the window telling them that the site is waiting for the broadcast to begin.

To broadcast the presentation:

1. In the dialog box, click the **Start Slide Show** button. The Slide Show starts in Slide Show view. Anyone watching the broadcast in their browser sees the screen shown in Figure 2-36.

Figure 2-36 Title slide of your presentation in the Internet Explorer browser during a broadcast

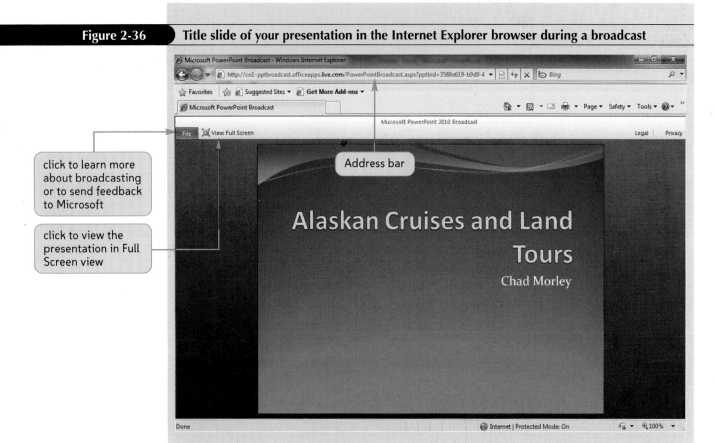

▶ **2.** Advance to Slide 2. You see the Wipe transition, but people watching the broadcast see the Fade transition. People watching the broadcast will see only the Fade transition, no matter what transitions you have applied. Animations are also limited.

▶ **3.** Continue advancing through the slide show until you see the black slide that indicates the end of the show, and then press the **spacebar** once more to exit Slide Show view on your computer. Anyone watching the slide show continues to see the black slide that indicates the end of the slide show. Now you can end the broadcast.

TIP

You can also click the End Broadcast button in the Broadcast group on the Broadcast tab on the Ribbon.

▶ **4.** In the yellow Broadcast View bar below the Ribbon, click the **End Broadcast** button. A dialog box opens warning you that remote viewers will be disconnected.

▶ **5.** In the dialog box, click the **End Broadcast** button to confirm that you do want to end the broadcast. The dialog box closes, the yellow Broadcast View bar below the Ribbon disappears, and the ordinary tabs on the Ribbon reappear, replacing the Broadcast tab. The last slide displayed during your broadcast disappears from the browser window of anyone watching your broadcast, and a message telling them that the broadcast is over appears in its place.

▶ **6.** Close the presentation.

INSIGHT

Viewing the Broadcast on the Same Computer as the Slide Show

If you want to test your broadcast so that you see exactly the same thing your remote viewers will see, you can preview the broadcast. Make sure the PowerPoint window containing the presentation you want to broadcast is the only window maximized on your computer. Copy the broadcast link from the Broadcast Slide Show dialog box, and then start your browser. Right-click the address in the Address bar, click Paste on the shortcut menu, and then press the Enter key to go to the broadcast Web site. Now you need to display the two windows side by side with the PowerPoint window on the left. To do this, first click the PowerPoint button on the taskbar to make the PowerPoint window the active window. Right-click the Windows taskbar, and then on the shortcut menu, click Show windows side by side. Finally, in the PowerPoint window, display Slide 1 in the Slide pane, press and hold the Ctrl key, and then click the Slide Show button on the status bar to start the slide show in the small slide show window. (You can't run the slide show normally because it will fill the entire screen and you won't be able to see the browser window.) You'll see the broadcast start in the browser window a few seconds later. Advance through the slide show, and make sure you end the slide show in the small slide show window.

Chad is pleased with how easy it is to use the broadcast feature. He plans to set up conference calls with groups of travel agents and broadcast the presentation while speaking to them on the phone.

REVIEW

Session 2.2 Quick Check

1. What is the difference between the Slide Master and a layout master?
2. What is a diagram?
3. True or False. If you want to use the text in a bulleted list in a diagram, you can convert it to a SmartArt diagram.
4. True or False. The process for animating a photo or clip art is completely different from the process of animating any other object.
5. When you animate a SmartArt diagram, how do you change the animation so that the individual elements animate one at a time rather than having the entire diagram animate all at once?
6. True or False. You can add headers to handouts and notes pages.
7. What happens when you broadcast a presentation?

Practice the skills you learned in the tutorial using the same case scenario.

PRACTICE

Review Assignments

Data Files needed for the Review Assignments: AKRibbon.jpg, LandTour.pptx, Naturalist.jpg, Ship2.jpg

In addition to the presentation on general information about Alaskan Cruises and Land Tours, Chad wants presentations on information about the specific cruises and land tours that his company operates. He wants you to modify a presentation he created about one of the Alaskan land tours. Complete the following steps:

1. Open the **LandTour presentation**, located in the PowerPoint2\Review folder included with your Data Files, and then save the file as **Denali Tours** in the same folder. Replace "Chad Morley" in the subtitle in Slide 1 with your name.

2. In Slide 3 ("Expert Guide"), change the layout so you can place a picture on the right, and insert the picture file **Naturalist** located in the PowerPoint2\Review folder. Increase the size of the Naturalist picture without changing the aspect ratio until the picture height is about the same height as the entire bulleted list (about four-and-a-half-inches high), and then align the middles of the photo and the bulleted list.

3. Change the color saturation of the picture to 66%, and then change the color tone of the picture to Temperature: 7200 K.

4. Apply the picture style Reflected Rounded Rectangle to the photo.

5. In Slide 2 ("Whittier to Denali"), change the layout so you can place clip art to the right of the bulleted list, and then insert a clip art image of a yellow bus (by searching for **bus** in the Clip Art task pane).

6. Drag the clip art so its top is aligned with the top of the first bulleted item, and then increase the size of the clip art while maintaining the aspect ratio so that it is approximately the same height as the bulleted list. Reposition it, if necessary, so it is centered in the space to the right of the bulleted list.

7. Change the color of the clip art to Gold, Accent color 1 Light.

8. Change the layout of Slide 7 ("Five-Point Advantage") so that the only placeholder on it is the title text placeholder, and then draw a Regular Pentagon (the eighth shape in the first row under Basic Shapes) about four inches high with five sides of equal length. (*Hint:* Press and hold down the Shift key while dragging to draw the shape.) Use the Align Center command to position the pentagon in the middle of the slide.

9. Change the outline of the pentagon shape to a line 2¼ points wide, colored with the Red, Accent 6 color (last color in the top row under Theme Colors). Apply the Soft Round bevel effect.

10. Add the text **Cruise with ACLT!** to the pentagon shape.

11. Flip the pentagon so a flat edge is on top and a corner is pointing down.

12. Delete the text inside the pentagon, and then create a text box inside the pentagon, remembering to drag to create the text box. Type **Cruise with ACLT!** in the text box. Resize the text box, if necessary, to fit the text, center the text in the text box, and then format the text in the text box so it is bold, white, and 28 points.

13. Insert a text box on each side of the pentagon, starting with the top of the pentagon and going clockwise around it, with the phrases **Exciting tours**, **Low prices**, **Expert guides**, **Full amenities**, and **Flexible schedules**.

14. Rotate and reposition these text boxes so they are flush with their respective sides of the pentagon. (The bottom two text boxes should be positioned so that the tops of the text boxes are aligned with the sides.) Press the Alt key if you need to override the snap-to-grid feature.

15. Switch to Slide Master view, and then, in the Title Slide Layout master, insert the picture from the file **AKRibbon**, located in the PowerPoint2\Review folder. Use an Align command to position the picture along the bottom of the slide. It will cover up the footer and page number placeholders, which is not a problem because you don't want to display those items on the title slide.

16. In the Module Slide Master, delete the Date placeholder, and then align the left edges of the Footer and content placeholders. Check the Title and Content, Two Content, and Title Only Layout masters, and repeat this process if necessary.

17. In the Module Slide Master, increase the font size of the title text to 48 points, and then change the color of the text in the content placeholder to Gold, Accent 1, Lighter 60% (third color, fifth column under Theme Colors in the Font Color gallery).

18. Return to Normal view, and then on Slide 4 ("The Best Cruise Lines"), create a SmartArt diagram using the Snapshot Picture List diagram (the last diagram in the first row in the Picture category). Use the picture icon to insert the picture **Ship2**, located in the PowerPoint2\Review folder included with your Data Files. In the text placeholder below the photo, type **We arrange cruise packages through:**, and then in the text placeholder to the right of the photo, type the following, pressing the Enter key after each name: **Carnival**, **Celebrity**, **Holland America**, **Princess**, **Royal Caribbean**.

19. On Slide 5 ("Sample Land-Tour Sequence…"), convert the bulleted list to the Continuous Block Process SmartArt diagram (the first diagram in the third row in the Process category).

20. Delete the first shape in the diagram, add a new shape after the last shape ("Fly-fish for salmon"), type **Hike through Denali National Park** in the new shape, and then apply the Brick Scene SmartArt style to the diagram.

21. Animate the SmartArt diagram so it Wipes from the left one-by-one.

22. On Slide 2 ("Whittier to Denali"), animate the clip art to Fly In from the left.

23. Add your name as the header on the handouts and notes pages, and then add **Alaskan Cruises and Land Tours** as a footer on the handouts and notes pages and on all the slides except the title slide. Display the slide numbers on all slides except the title slide.

24. Check the spelling in the presentation, view the slide show, fix any problems you see, and then save your changes.

25. Broadcast your presentation, and then submit the completed presentation to your instructor, either in printed or electronic form, as requested. Close the file.

Case Problem 1

APPLY

Data Files needed for this Case Problem: Balmoral.jpg, Castles.pptx, Edinburgh.jpg

Castles of Scotland   Moyra Torphins is a sales representative for Johnson Hodges Incorporated (JHI), a sales promotions company in Scarsdale, New York. JHI provides incentives packages and giveaways for large companies that hold internal sales competitions. Moyra, originally from Scotland, has been assigned to do research on castles in Scotland and to present her research to the other sales representatives. You will help her prepare a PowerPoint presentation on castles of Scotland. Complete the following steps:

1. Open the file **Castles**, located in the PowerPoint2\Case1 folder included with your Data Files, replace the name in the subtitle on Slide 1 with your name, and then save the file to the same folder using the filename **Scottish Castles**.

2. On the Foundry Slide Master, change the color of the title text so it's the light-blue theme color Sky Blue, Accent 3.

3. Add the footer **Scottish Castles** and slide numbering to all the slides, including the title slide, and then add your name as a header on the notes pages and handouts.

4. On Slide 2 ("Successful Promotional Packages"), convert the bulleted list to the Basic Venn SmartArt diagram.

5. Change the font size of all the text in the Venn diagram text boxes to 24 points. Insert a hyphen between the two "*m*"s in "Accommodations" so that the word is split at this location.

6. Near the upper-left side of the Venn diagram, insert a text box with the phrase **The Intersection of Success**. Change the text to 20-point, light-green text using the Light Green, Accent 2 color.

7. Resize the text box by decreasing its width and increasing its height so that "The Intersection" is on one line and "of Success" is on another line, and then reposition it, if necessary, so the text box is about an inch to the left of the top circle in the diagram and about an inch above the bottom-left circle.

8. Use the Arrow shape in the Lines category to draw an arrow from the text box to the center of the Venn diagram, and then change its color to black by using the Shape Outline button in the Shape Styles group on the Drawing Tools Format tab.

9. Animate the Venn diagram using the entrance animation Grow & Turn.

10. Apply the option to animate the objects in the diagram one by one.

11. Animate the text box and the arrow to appear on the screen together when you advance the slide show using the Wipe animation, modified to wipe from the left.

12. On Slide 3 ("Successful Promotional Package"), change the layout to Two Content, insert clip art that reflects travel (for example, a picture of luggage or an airplane), and then resize and reposition the clip art to fit nicely on the right side of the slide. If the clip art you chose is a bitmapped graphic, change its color to Sky Blue, Accent color 3 Light.

13. On Slide 4 ("Scottish Castles"), insert a SmartArt diagram using the Vertical Chevron List process diagram. In the green, chevron points, enter the following from top to bottom: 1093, 1230, 1626. In the top white rectangle, enter **Edinburgh Castle** in the top text placeholder and **Located in Edinburgh** in the bottom text placeholder; in the second white rectangle, enter **Urquhart Castle** and **Located in Inverness**; and in the bottom white rectangle, enter **Craigievar Castle** and **Located in Aberdeen**.

14. Add two new shapes to the diagram. The first contains **1636** in the green chevron, and **Fraser Castle** and **Located in Aberdeen** in the white rectangle, and the second contains **1854** in the green chevron, and **Balmoral Castle** and **Located in Aberdeen** in the white rectangle.

15. Apply the Inset SmartArt style to the diagram.

16. On Slides 5 and 6, change the layouts as needed, and insert the appropriate picture of the castle from the files in the PowerPoint2\Case1 folder. Format the photos with the Simple Frame, White picture style.

17. Animate the photos you added to Slides 5 and 6 using the Shape animation. Keep the default timing of On Click.

18. Check the spelling, view the slide show, fix any problems you see, and then save the presentation using the default filename.

19. Broadcast the presentation. Submit the complete presentation to your instructor, either in printed or electronic form, as requested, and then close the file.

Apply your skills to modify a presentation for a backpacking company.

APPLY

Case Problem 2

Data Files needed for this Case Problem: Campsite.jpg, Meadow.jpg, Men.jpg, Outfitter.pptx, Panel.jpg, River.jpg

The Backpacker's Outfitter Several years ago, Blake Stott started a new company, The Backpacker's Outfitter, which provides products for hiking, mountain climbing, rock climbing, and camping and services including guided backpacking and climbing expeditions and courses. Blake gives presentations to businesses, youth groups, clubs, and other organizations. He asks you to help him prepare a PowerPoint presentation explaining his products and services. Complete the following steps:

1. Open the presentation **Outfitter**, located in the PowerPoint2\Case2 folder included with your Data Files, change the subtitle to your name, and then save the file to the same folder using the filename **Backpacker's Outfitter**.

2. In the Solstice Slide Master, select and delete the three circular objects located in the upper-left corner.

3. Insert the picture file **Panel** in the Solstice Slide Master, and then position the picture near the top of the tan panel so it is approximately centered between the left and right edges of the tan pane. Align the tops of picture and the title text placeholder.

4. Still in the Solstice Slide Master, delete the Date placeholder (located at the bottom of the slide), and then align the left edges of the footer and content placeholders. Repeat this if necessary on the Title Slide Layout master, the Title and Content Layout master, Two Content Layout master, and the Title Only Layout master.

5. In the Solstice Slide Master, change the font size of the footer and slide number placeholder boxes to 20 points, and then increase the width of the slide number placeholder box so that the symbol "<#>" fits on one line.

⊕ EXPLORE

6. In the Two Content Layout master, change the space before each paragraph and before each line of text to 0 points. To do this, first select both content placeholders. Next, in the Paragraph group on the Home tab, click the Line Spacing button, and then click Line Spacing Options. In the Paragraph dialog box, in the Spacing section, set the value in the Before text box to 0.

7. In Normal view, insert the footer **Backpacker's Outfitter**, turn on slide numbering for all the slides except the first one, and then add your name as a header to the notes pages and handouts.

8. On Slide 2 ("Overview"), change the slide layout to Two Content, and then add the bitmapped image **River** to the content placeholder.

9. Apply the picture style Rotated, White to the photo, and then drag the photo to position it so no part of the formatted picture is hanging off the slide.

10. On Slide 5 ("Courses"), repeat Steps 8 and 9, except insert the image **Men**, located in the PowerPoint2\Case2 folder. Decrease the width of the bulleted list text box so "Level" appears on the second line in the bulleted list in which it appears.

11. On Slide 4 ("Guided Trips (continued)"), change the layout to Two Content. Modify the size and shape of the content placeholders so that they are horizontal rectangles, and so that the one currently on the left is positioned above the one currently on the right.

12. Add the **Campsite photo**, located in the PowerPoint2\Case2 folder, to the lower content placeholder. Resize the image proportionately, until the width of the image is five inches, and then drag the photo so that it's centered between the left and right edges of the white background of the slide and between the bottom of the bulleted list and the footer. Make sure the picture and text don't overlap.

13. Apply a 10-point soft edge effect to the photo.

14. On Slide 9 ("For More Information"), change the layout to Two Content, and then repeat Step 12, except insert the image **Meadow**, located in the PowerPoint2\Case2 folder, and don't change its size. The text in the top content text box should be 20 points. Apply a 10-point soft edge effect to the photo.

15. On Slide 6 ("Backpacking Equipment"), use the Picture command on the Insert tab, and then insert the picture in the file **River**, located in the PowerPoint2\Case2 folder. Resize the photo so that it is almost as large as the white area of the slide without covering the footer and slide. (*Hint*: Start by dragging the corners of the photo to resize it proportionately, and then drag the side sizing handles.)

16. Change the color of the photo using the Washout color effect.

⊕ EXPLORE

17. Send the photo behind the text on the slide. To do this, click the Send Backward button in the Arrange group on the Picture Tools Format tab as many times as needed.

18. On Slide 7 ("Phases of a Successful Backpacking Trip"), draw a large, equilateral, Regular Pentagon in the middle of the blank area of the slide below the title, and then invert the pentagon so it's pointed down. Add the text **Have Fun!** to the shape.

19. Apply the Moderate Effect – Gold, Accent 2 shape style to the pentagon.

20. Add five text boxes just outside the pentagon, one on each side, using the phrases (starting at the top of the pentagon and going clockwise): **Planning**, **Conditioning**, **Training**, **Equipment**, and **Trip Site**.

21. Change the font of the text boxes to Verdana, and then rotate the text boxes so they are parallel to their respective sides of the pentagon.

22. Animate the pentagon with any emphasis animation you wish, and then animate each text box with the Fly In or Wipe animation. Change the timing so that they appear automatically, one after the other starting with the one on top and working clockwise. Change the direction of the animation for each text box so that they animate to their positions without crossing over the pentagon.

23. Check the spelling, view the slide show, fix any problems you see, and then save your changes.

24. Submit the completed presentation in printed or electronic form, as requested by your instructor, and then close any open files.

Create a new presentation about lighthouses by using and expanding on the skills you learned in this tutorial.

CHALLENGE

Case Problem 3

Data Files needed for this Case Problem: ASizemore.jpg, Bodie.jpg, HatterasBase.jpg, HatterasStairs.jpg, HatterasTop.jpg, LHPanel.jpg, Lighthouses.pptx, Ocracoke.jpg

Historic Preservation of Lighthouses   Ardith Sizemore is a field representative for the Division of Historic Preservation for the Massachusetts State Historical Society. She visits lighthouses of historical significance. She has asked you to prepare a PowerPoint presentation on lighthouses of the Outer Banks of North Carolina. The nine slides in your completed presentation should look like the slides shown in Figure 2-37. Use the following information to create the slide show.

1. Base your presentation on the presentation file named **Lighthouses**, located in the PowerPoint2\Case3 folder included with your Data Files, and save it as **NC Lighthouses** in the same folder.

⊕ EXPLORE

2. Change the background to a medium blue that varies in intensity. To do this, click the Design tab, and then in the Background group, click the Background Styles button. Click Style 7 in the gallery.

3. Make the following changes to the Slide Master:

   a. The picture on the left edge of Slides 1, 2, and 9 is in the file **LHPanel**, located in the PowerPoint2\Case3 folder. It is resized so to stretch the height of the slide. It is added to the Title Slide Layout and the Title and Content Layout masters. (*Hint*: Insert the image on one of the masters, modify it as described in Steps b, c, and d, and then copy it to the other master.)

   b. The LHPanel image is colored with the Blue, Accent color 1 Dark color.

⊕ EXPLORE

   c. The contrast and brightness of the LHPanel image is adjusted so that the image is 40% brighter. To do this, click the Corrections button in the Adjust group on the Picture Tools Format tab, and then apply the setting under Brightness and Contrast named Brightness: +40% Contrast: 0% (Normal).

   d. The soft edge effect is applied to the LHPanel picture with a 25-point edge.

   e. On the Title and Content Layout and the Two Content Layout masters, the font size of the footer and slide number placeholder is 24 points, the width of the footer placeholder is increased and its position is adjusted, and the title text placeholder is aligned with the top of the slide.

Figure 2-37   **Completed NC Lighthouses presentation**

f. The placeholders on the masters with the LHPanel photo are adjusted so that they don't overlap the LHPanel picture. (Do not do anything to the Date placeholder.)

g. The title text placeholders on the Title and Content Layout and on the Two Content Layout masters are adjusted so they align with the top of the slide, and the height of the content placeholders on those masters is increased to fill in the space.

EXPLORE

h. The title text placeholder on the Office Theme Slide Master animates with the Expand entrance effect automatically after the slides transition. To find the Expand effect, open the Animations gallery, and then click More Entrance Effects.

4. Change the layouts to add pictures to Slides 4–8. You'll find all these images in the PowerPoint2\Case3 folder. Each picture has the Drop Shadow Rectangle picture style applied.

5. Change the layout on Slide 3 to the Pictures Custom Layout, a layout that was created for this presentation. Then, add the same photos you inserted on Slides 4–8 in the placeholders. Format all five photos with the Soft Edge Rectangle picture style.

6. On Slide 3, delete the footer and slide number text boxes.

EXPLORE

7. On Slide 3 only, remove the blue background. To do this, right-click the Style 1 background on the Background Styles button menu in the Background group on the Design tab, and then click Apply to Selected Slides.

8. Animate the photos on Slide 3 using the entrance animation Spiral In so that after you click once to make the first photo spiral in, the rest of the photos automatically spiral in one after the other, in any order you want.

9. On Slide 9, resize the content text box so it is approximately half its current width, and then use the Picture command in the Images group on the Insert tab to insert the photo **ASizemore**, located in the PowerPoint2\Case3 folder. Modify it to fill the space on the right, and then add the Beveled Matte, White picture style.

10. Use any entrance animation you want to animate the photo on Slides 4–8 so that the photo appears automatically after the slide title animates. On the slides with captions under the photos, animate the caption with the same animation as the photo and set it to animate with the photo.

11. On Slide 4, animate the bulleted list with any entrance animation you want, using progressive disclosure. Keep the timing for the bulleted list animation as On Click.

⊕ **EXPLORE** 12. On Slide 4, add the Fade exit animation to the bulleted list. To do this, click the Add Animation button in the Advanced Animation group. Change the effect options so it fades out as one object. Keep the timing set to On Click.

⊕ **EXPLORE** 13. Use the Animation Painter to copy the animations applied to the bulleted list on Slide 4 to the bulleted lists on Slides 5–8. To do this, select the bulleted list text box on Slide 4, click the Animation Painter button in the Advanced Animation group, click the next slide, and then click anywhere in the bulleted list on that slide.

⊕ **EXPLORE** 14. On Slides 4–8, add a motion path animation to the photo so that it slides to the left after the bulleted list fades out so that it is centered on the slide. Use the Add Animation button, choose the Lines motion path animation, and then change the effect options to change the direction of the animation. Change the timing so the motion path animation happens automatically after the text box exits. Also add this animation to the captions under the photos on Slides 6 and 7. (Note that you cannot use the Animation Painter to copy this animation because the animation order does not copy correctly.)

15. Apply any transitions you think are appropriate.

16. Change the subtitle on the title slide to your name, check the spelling, view the slide show, fix any problems you see, and then save your changes.

17. Broadcast the slide show.

18. Submit the completed presentation in printed or electronic form, as requested by your instructor, and then close any open files.

Create a presentation about digital cameras using information from the Internet.

RESEARCH

Case Problem 4

Data Files needed for this Case Problem: Camera01.jpg, Camera02.jpg, Camera03.jpg, Photographer.jpg

Digital Cameras   Prepare a description of a digital camera for a presentation. Organize your information into a PowerPoint presentation with at least eight slides. Use the photos supplied in the PowerPoint2\Case4 folder included with your Data Files as needed to add interest to your presentation. Complete the following steps:

1. Gather information on a digital camera of your own choice. You can start with the Web site *www.dpreview.com*, but you will probably want to find others.

2. Create a new PowerPoint presentation. Type the brand and model of the camera on the title slide, and then type your name as the subtitle.

3. Create one or two slides with general information about digital cameras.

4. Create at least three slides with information about the camera you have chosen. Your slides might include information about the body and design, lens, operation, picture resolution options, picture format options, storage card, battery, viewfinder, LCD (liquid crystal display), boot-up time, retake time, automatic and manual features, upload method, or software. The information might also include lists of advantages and disadvantages.

5. Modify the Slide Master by adding a text box or graphics object, changing the font attributes, or making some other desired change that will appear on all the slides.

6. Include the slide number and an appropriate footer on each slide, except the first title slide. In the Slide Master, change the font style, size, color, or position of the footer and slide number text.

7. Include sample photographs, if possible.

8. If possible, include a photo of the camera itself.

9. Include in your presentation at least one clip-art image, and change its color.

 EXPLORE

10. Include a table in your presentation. You might include a table of features, with the feature name (Price, Body Material, Sensor, Image Sizes, File Format, Lens, and so forth) in the left column, and the corresponding feature data in the right column. To add a table, use the Table button in the Tables group on the Insert tab. Apply a style from the Table Styles group on the Table Tools Design tab.

11. Include at least one SmartArt diagram. For example, you might create a process diagram for setting up the camera, or you might create a Venn diagram showing how the elements of taking a good photograph come together.

12. Add appropriate animations and transitions.

13. Check the spelling in your presentation, view the slide show, and then save the presentation to the PowerPoint2\Case4 folder using the filename **Digital Camera**.

14. Submit the completed presentation in printed or electronic form, as requested by your instructor, and then close the file.

SAM: Skills Assessment Manager

For current SAM information, including versions and content details, visit SAM Central (http://samcentral.course.com). If you have a SAM user profile, you may have access to hands-on instruction, practice, and assessment of the skills covered in this tutorial. Since various versions of SAM are supported throughout the life of this text, check with your instructor for the correct instructions and URL/Web site for accessing assignments.

ENDING DATA FILES

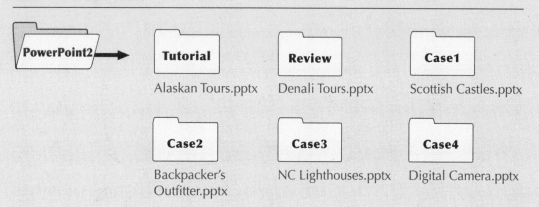

PowerPoint2 →

Tutorial — Alaskan Tours.pptx

Review — Denali Tours.pptx

Case1 — Scottish Castles.pptx

Case2 — Backpacker's Outfitter.pptx

Case3 — NC Lighthouses.pptx

Case4 — Digital Camera.pptx

Verbal Communication

Rehearsing Your Presentation

The best presentations are planned well in advance of their delivery. Once the content has been created, enhanced, and perfected, it is time to prepare you, the presenter. Presenters who try to stand up and "wing it" in front of a crowd usually reveal this amateur approach the moment they start speaking—by looking down at their notes, rambling off topic, or turning their back on the audience frequently to read from the slides displayed on-screen.

To avoid being seen as an amateur, you need to rehearse your presentation. Even the most knowledgeable speakers rehearse to ensure they know how the topic flows, what the main points are, how much time to spend on each slide, and where to place emphasis. Experienced presenters understand that while practice may not make them perfect, it will certainly make them better.

Where you practice isn't that important. You can talk to a mirror, your family, or a group of friends. If you have a video camera, you can record yourself, and then review the video. Watching video evidence of your performance often reveals the weaknesses you don't want your audience to see and that your friends or family may be unwilling or unable to identify. Whatever you choose to do, the bottom line is this: If you practice, you will improve.

As you rehearse, you should remember to focus on the following steps:

- Practice speaking fluently.
- Work on your tone of voice.
- Decide how to involve your audience.
- Become aware of your body language.
- Check your appearance.

Speaking Fluently

Be sure to speak in an easy, smooth manner, and avoid using nonwords and fillers. Nonwords consist of ums, ahs, hms, and other such breaks in speech. Fillers are phrases that don't add any value yet add length to sentences. Both can dilute a speaker's message because they are not essential to the meaning of what's being spoken. At best, they can make you sound unprofessional. At worst, they can distract your audience and make your message incomprehensible.

Considering Your Tone of Voice

When delivering your presentation, you usually want to speak passionately, with authority, and with a smile. If you aren't excited about your presentation, how will your audience feel? By projecting your voice with energy, passion, and confidence, your audience will automatically pay more attention to you. Smile and look directly at your audience members and make eye contact. If your message is getting across, they will instinctively affirm what you're saying by returning your gaze, nodding their heads, or smiling. There's something compelling about a confident speaker whose presence commands attention. However, be careful not to overdo it. Speaking too loudly or using an overly confident or arrogant tone will quickly turn off an audience and make them stop listening altogether.

Involving Your Audience

If you involve your audience in your presentation, they will pay closer attention to what you have to say. When an audience member asks a question, be sure to affirm them before answering. For example, you could respond with "That's a great question. What do the rest of you think?" or "Thanks for asking. Here's what my research revealed." An easy way to get the audience to participate is to start with a question and invite responses, or to stop partway through to discuss a particularly important point.

Being Aware of Your Body Language

Although the content of your presentation plays a role in your message delivery, it's your voice and body language during the presentation that make or break it. Maintain eye contact to send the message that you want to connect and that you can be trusted. Stand up straight to signal confidence. Conversely, avoid slouching, which can convey laziness, lack of energy, or disinterest, and fidgeting or touching your hair, which can signal nervousness. Resist the temptation to glance at your watch; you don't want to send a signal that you'd rather be someplace else. Finally, be aware of your hand movements. The best position for your hands is to place them comfortably by your side, in a relaxed position. As you talk, its fine to use hand gestures to help make a point, but be careful not to overdo it.

Evaluating Your Appearance

Just as a professional appearance makes a good impression during a job interview, an audience's first impression of a speaker is also based on appearance. Before a single word is spoken, the audience sizes up the way the presenter looks. You want to make sure you look professional and competent. Make sure your appearance is neat, clean, and well-coordinated, and dress in appropriate clothing.

As you spend time practicing your presentation, you will naturally develop appropriate body language, tone of voice, and a fluent delivery, ensuring a clear connection with your audience and a professional delivery of your presentation's message.

PROSKILLS

Create and Deliver a Training Presentation

If you hold a job for any length of time, as part of your employment, you might have to train new employees in their work tasks. For example, if you work in a library, you might have to explain how to process returned books, or if you work in a chemistry stockroom at a college, you might have to describe how to make up solutions for the school's chemistry laboratories. A PowerPoint presentation can be an effective way to start the training process. With a presentation, you can give an overview of the job without needing to repeat yourself to explain basic aspects of the job. Then you can customize the rest of the training to fit the needs of the specific employee.

In this exercise, you'll create a presentation containing information of your choice, using the PowerPoint skills and features presented in Tutorials 1 and 2, and then you will practice techniques for delivering the presentation.

ProSkills

Note: Please be sure *not* to include any personal information of a sensitive nature in the documents you create to be submitted to your instructor for this exercise. Later on, you can update the documents with such information for your own personal use.

1. Create a new PowerPoint presentation and apply an appropriate theme. Make sure you choose a theme that is relevant to the job you are describing and to your audience.

2. On Slide 1, make the presentation title the same as the title of your job or the job for which you are giving the training. Add your name as a subtitle.

3. On the Slide Master, add the logo of the business for which you are creating your presentation. You can usually get a digital image of the logo from the business's Web site.

4. Look at each of the layout masters. Is the logo appropriately placed on each one? If not, move it.

5. Create a new slide for each major category of tasks. For example, task categories for a library job might be "Punching In," "Checking in with Your Supervisor," "Gathering Books from Drop-Off Stations," "Scanning Returned Books into the Computer," "Checking Books for Damage or Marks," "Processing Abused Books," "Processing Late Books," "Sorting Books," "Shelving Books," and "Punching Out."

6. On each slide, create a bulleted list to explain the particular task category or to provide the steps required to perform the task, or consider if a graphic would better illustrate your point.

7. Where applicable, include clip art or a photograph. For example, you might include a photograph of the punch clock (time clock) used by hourly workers in the library, or a photograph of a book with serious damage relative to one with normal wear.

8. If certain jobs require a set process, convert a bulleted list into a process diagram using SmartArt graphics.

9. On one or more slides, insert a shape, such as a rectangle, triangle, circle, arrow, or star. For example, you might want to place a small colored star next to a particularly important step in carrying out a task.

10. Examine your outline. Are you using too many words? Can any of your bulleted lists be replaced with a graphic?

11. Re-evaluate the theme you chose. Do you think it is still appropriate? Does it fit the content of your presentation? If not, apply a different theme.

12. Add appropriate transitions and animations. Remember that the goal is to keep your audience engaged without distracting them.

13. Check the spelling, including contextual spelling, of your presentation, and then proofread your presentation.

14. Rehearse the presentation. Consider your appearance, and decide on the appropriate clothing to wear. Practice in front of a mirror and friends or family, and if you can, create a video of yourself. Notice and fine tune your body language, tone of voice, and fluency to fully engage your audience.

15. Save the presentation, and submit the completed presentation to your instructor in printed or electronic form, as requested.

Adding and Customizing Media and Charts

Preparing a Sales Presentation

OBJECTIVES

Session 3.1
- Insert slides from another presentation
- Insert and format a video on a slide
- Trim a video clip
- Set a poster frame
- Insert a sound clip
- Create and format a table
- Create and format a chart
- Apply a second animation to an object
- Change the speed of an animation

Session 3.2
- Change theme fonts
- Change theme colors
- Reset slides
- Apply a gradient background
- Add a picture to the background
- Add a textured background
- Customize bullets
- Create and apply a custom theme
- Apply a second theme to a presentation

Case | *Classic Flowers, Inc.*

Sophie De Graff is a horticulturalist who works as the sales manager at Classic Flowers, Inc., in Bainbridge, Georgia. Classic Flowers grows and distributes flowers to retail stores throughout the state. One of Sophie's responsibilities is to obtain and manage new accounts. This involves giving sales presentations to large retail stores (Sam's Club, Costco, Wal-Mart, Piggly Wiggly, Kroger, and so forth) that have floral departments. Sophie asks you to help her prepare the PowerPoint presentation. She emphasizes the importance of preparing a high-quality presentation that includes a custom theme, video, graphics, sound effects, animations, charts, and other elements to maximize the visual effects.

In this tutorial, you'll insert slides from one presentation into another presentation, add video and sound, examine and modify the animation settings for video and sound, create a table and a chart, animate a chart, and apply a second animation to an object. You will also change theme fonts and create custom theme colors, modify the background and bullets, create a custom theme, and apply a second theme to a presentation.

STARTING DATA FILES

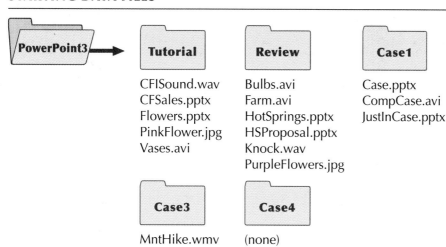

PowerPoint3 →

Tutorial
CFISound.wav
CFSales.pptx
Flowers.pptx
PinkFlower.jpg
Vases.avi

Review
Bulbs.avi
Farm.avi
HotSprings.pptx
HSProposal.pptx
Knock.wav
PurpleFlowers.jpg

Case1
Case.pptx
CompCase.avi
JustInCase.pptx

Case2
Wedding01.jpg
…
Wedding10.jpg
(10 photos)

Case3
MntHike.wmv
MntMap.jpg
MntPlateau1.jpg
MntPlateau2.jpg

Case4
(none)

SESSION 3.1 VISUAL OVERVIEW

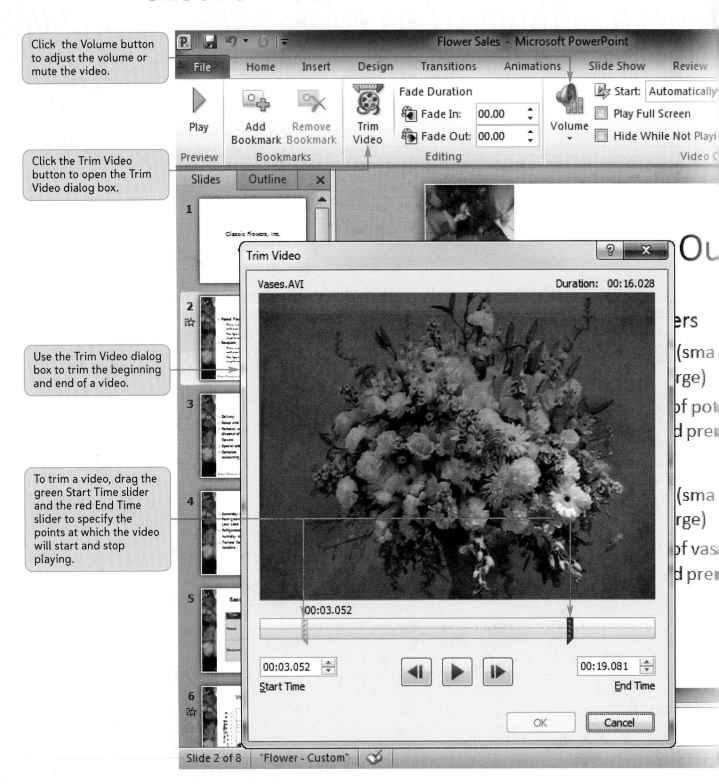

Click the Volume button to adjust the volume or mute the video.

Click the Trim Video button to open the Trim Video dialog box.

Use the Trim Video dialog box to trim the beginning and end of a video.

To trim a video, drag the green Start Time slider and the red End Time slider to specify the points at which the video will start and stop playing.

WORKING WITH VIDEO

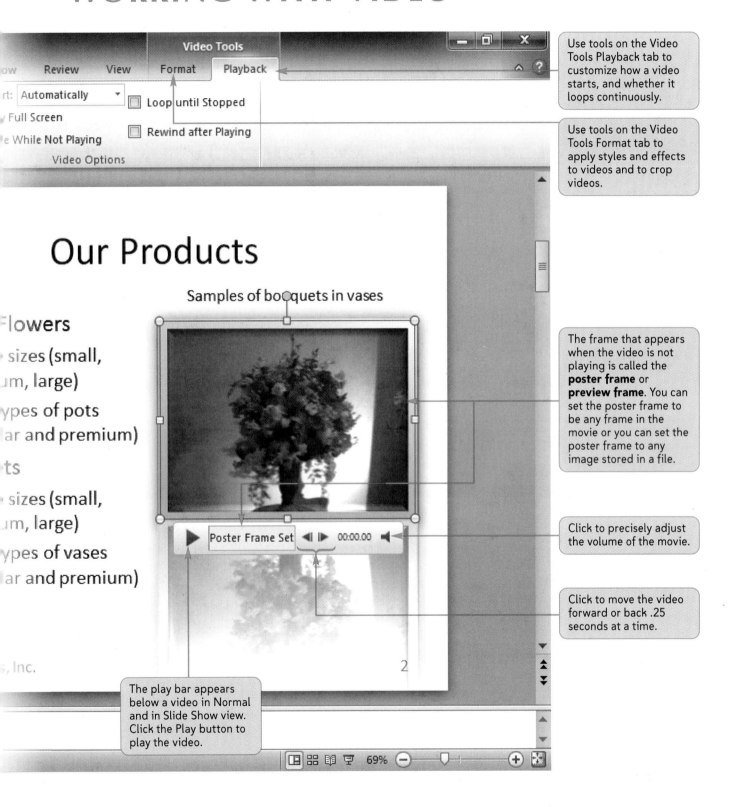

Use tools on the Video Tools Playback tab to customize how a video starts, and whether it loops continuously.

Use tools on the Video Tools Format tab to apply styles and effects to videos and to crop videos.

The frame that appears when the video is not playing is called the **poster frame** or **preview frame**. You can set the poster frame to be any frame in the movie or you can set the poster frame to any image stored in a file.

Click to precisely adjust the volume of the movie.

Click to move the video forward or back .25 seconds at a time.

The play bar appears below a video in Normal and in Slide Show view. Click the Play button to play the video.

Inserting Slides from Another Presentation

You can combine slides from two presentations to create one presentation. Sophie gives you two presentation files: Flowers, which contains text and pictures to describe the products and services, and CFSales, a presentation that includes additional information about Classic Flowers' sales. First, you'll open the Flowers presentation, and then, you'll add slides to it from the CFSales presentation.

To open the Flowers presentation and save it with a new name:

1. Open the presentation **Flowers** located in the PowerPoint3\Tutorial folder included with your Data Files, and then save the presentation file as **Flower Sales** in the same folder. See Figure 3-1.

Figure 3-1 | **Slide 1 of Flower Sales**

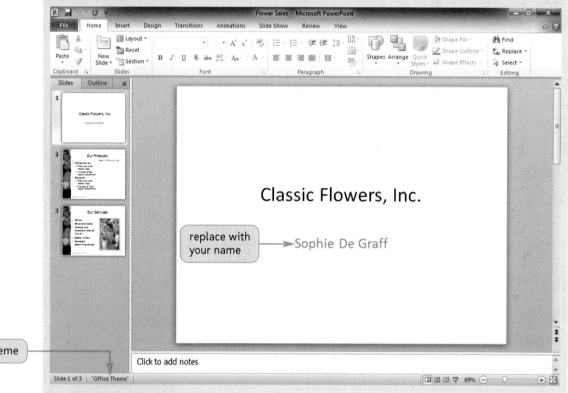

2. Change the subtitle ("Sophie De Graff") to your name, and then look through the three slides of the presentation so you have an idea of its content. Notice that the Office theme is applied and there is a long, slender photograph ("panel") of pink flowers on the slides with bulleted lists.

You use the Reuse Slides command on the New Slide menu to insert specific slides from any other presentation. If the inserted slides have a different design than the current presentation, the design of the current presentation will override the design of the inserted slides by default.

REFERENCE

Inserting Slides from Another Presentation

- Display the slide after which you want to insert slides from another presentation.
- In the Slides group on the Home tab, click the New Slide button arrow, and then click Reuse Slides to display the Reuse Slides task pane.
- In the task pane, click the Browse button, and then click Browse File to open the Browse dialog box.
- Navigate to the location of the presentation that contains the slides you want to insert, click the file, and then click the Open button.
- In the task pane, make sure the Keep source formatting check box is *not* selected, to force the inserted slides to use the theme in the current presentation or click the Keep source formatting check box to retain the theme of the slides you want to import.
- In the task pane, click each slide that you want to insert into the current presentation.

Sophie asks you to insert all six slides from the CFSales presentation into the Flower Sales presentation.

To insert slides from the CFSales presentation:

▶ **1.** Display **Slide 3** ("Our Services") in the Slide pane.

▶ **2.** In the Slides group on the Home tab, click the **New Slide button arrow**. The gallery of available layouts opens with a menu below the gallery.

▶ **3.** On the menu, click **Reuse Slides**. The Reuse Slides task pane opens on the right side of the window.

▶ **4.** Click the **Browse** button in the task pane, and then click **Browse File**. The Browse dialog box opens.

▶ **5.** Navigate to the PowerPoint3\Tutorial folder, and then double-click **CFSales**. Thumbnails of the five slides from the CFSales presentation appear in the Reuse Slides task pane. The Apex theme is applied to these slides. See Figure 3-2. At the bottom of the task pane, the Keep source formatting check box is unchecked. You don't want to keep the formatting of the inserted slides, but rather you want the new slides to take on the theme and modifications of the slide master of the current Flower Sales presentation, so you will keep this unchecked.

Figure 3-2 CFSales presentation slides in the Reuse Slides task pane

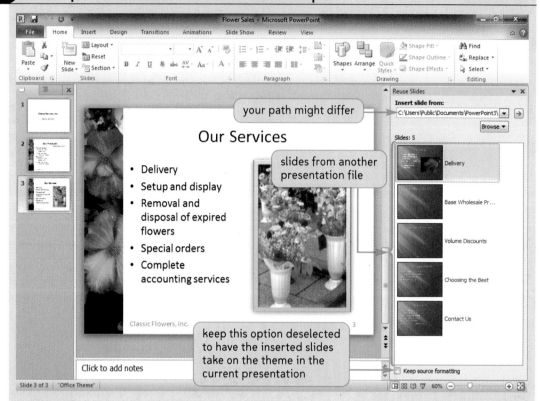

6. In the task pane, point to the first slide, "Delivery." The slide increases in size so that you can read its content.

7. Click the **Delivery** slide. It is inserted into the Flower Sales presentation after the current slide (Slide 3), and the Office Theme is applied instead of the Apex theme used in CFSales.

8. Insert the other four slides, one at a time. When you are finished, the presentation will have eight slides, and the last slide inserted, "Contact Us," will be displayed in the Slide pane.

9. In the Reuse Slides task pane title bar, click the **Close** button ⊠.

10. Save your changes.

The five slides from CFSales are now Slides 4 through 8 of the Flower Sales presentation. One of the new slides contains text and a photo; the rest contain only text.

Adding Video

You can insert digital video in slides or in slide masters. PowerPoint supports various file formats, but the most commonly used are the Audio Visual Interleave format (listed in Explorer windows as the Video Clip file type), which uses the filename extension ".avi," and the Windows Media Video format, which uses the filename extension ".wmv." After you insert a video, you can modify it by changing the length of time the video plays, changing playback options, and applying formats and styles to the video.

Inserting a Video in a Slide

You can insert a video clip in two different ways. You can change the layout to one of the content layouts, and then click the Insert Media Clip button, or you can use the Video button in the Media group on the Insert tab. If you want to add a video to a slide master, you must use the Video button on the Insert tab; otherwise you will replace the content placeholder on all slides using that master. You'll add the video now using the Insert Media Clip button in a content layout.

REFERENCE

Inserting a Video into a Presentation

- In Normal view, display the slide in which you want to insert the video in the Slide pane; or in Slide Master view, display the layout master in which you want to insert the video.
- In Normal view, in a content placeholder, click the Insert Media Clip button; or in Normal or Slide Master view, click the Insert tab on the Ribbon, and then in the Media group, click the Video button.
- In the Insert Video dialog box, navigate to the folder containing the video, click the video file, and then click the Insert button.

Sophie wants you to insert a short video showing some of the vase arrangements that Classic Flowers sells as part of Slide 2, "Our Products."

To add a video to Slide 2:

1. Display **Slide 2** ("Our Products") in the Slide pane. The Two Content layout is applied to this slide. Notice that there is a text box above the content placeholder.

2. In the content placeholder on the right, click the **Insert Media Clip** button 🎬. The Insert Video dialog box opens.

3. Navigate to the PowerPoint3\Tutorial folder included with your Data Files, click **Vases**, and then click the **Insert** button. The movie is inserted in place of the content placeholder. See Figure 3-3.

Figure 3-3   **Slide 2 with video**

Figure 3-3   Slide 2 with video

4. On the play bar below the movie, click the **Play** button ▶, and then watch the video.

Inserting a Video Behind Objects on a Slide

You can insert videos behind other objects on a slide. Video added to a slide background can add visual interest to your presentation for audiences that are accustomed to multimedia. To do this, insert the video as usual. On the Video Tools Format tab, in the Arrange group, click the Send Backward button arrow, and then click Send to Back. The video object will move behind the rest of the objects on the slide; for example, if the slide contains a bulleted list, the bulleted list will appear on top of the video. If you choose to add a video to the background, it should not include too much action, or your audience will have difficulty making out the text or images in the foreground. Sometimes, applying a washout or gray color effect to background video produces the effect you need.

Changing Video Playback Options

You can change several options for how a video plays. These options are listed in Figure 3-4.

Figure 3-4   Video Playback options

Video Option	Function
Volume	Change the volume of the video from high to medium or low or mute it.
Start	Change how the video starts, either when the presenter advances the slide show (On Click) or automatically when the slide appears during the slide show.
Play Full Screen	The video fills the screen during the slide show.
Hide While Not Playing	The video does not appear on the slide when it is not playing; make sure the video is set to play automatically if this option is selected.
Loop until Stopped	The video plays continuously until the next slide appears during the slide show.
Rewind after Playing	The video rewinds after it plays so that the first frame or the poster frame appears again.

When you insert a video, the default is for it to play On Click. You can change this by changing the Start setting on the Video Tools Playback tab to Automatically. When you set a video to play automatically, you can override this, or after the video has played once, you can play it again by clicking the video or clicking the Play button under the video to start playback.

Sophie wants the video you inserted on Slide 2 to play automatically when the slide appears during the slide show. You'll change the start setting now.

To change video options to play the video automatically:

1. With the movie selected, click the **Video Tools Playback** tab. The options for changing how the video plays are in the Video Options group. See Figure 3-5.

Figure 3-5   Video Tools Playback tab

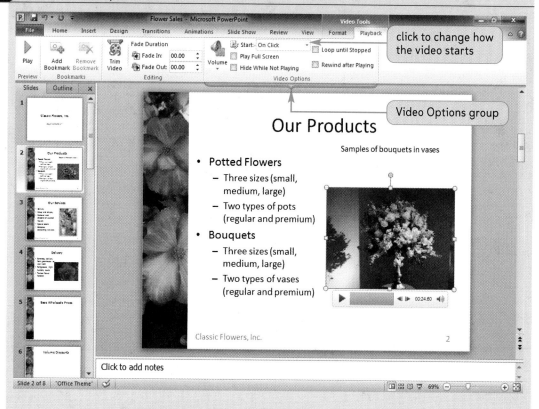

> **2.** In the Video Options group, click the **Start** arrow, and then click **Automatically**. Now the video will play automatically when the slide appears during the slide show.

You can also set volume options for video. The video was filmed in a noisy atmosphere. Sophie thinks the background noise in the video will be distracting during her presentation, so she asks you to set the volume to mute while the video is playing.

To adjust the volume of the video:

> **1.** In the Video Options group, click the **Volume** button. A menu opens with four options for adjusting the volume.

> **2.** Click **Mute**. The menu closes. You can check the options you set in Slide Show view.

> **3.** On the status bar, click the **Slide Show** button 🖵. The video plays automatically and the background noise is muted.

> **4.** After the video is finished playing, press the **Esc** key to end the slide show.

Trimming a Video

If a video is too long, or if there are parts you don't want to show during the slide show, you can trim it. To do this, you click the Trim Video button in the Editing group on the Video Tools Playback tab, and then, in the Trim Video dialog box, drag the sliders to indicate where you want the video to start and stop. Refer to the Session 3.1 Visual Overview for more information about using the Trim Video dialog box.

After reviewing the video, Sophie decides that the last bouquet in the video clip looks too similar to the first one. She asks you to trim the video so it ends at the point where the camera zooms in on the pink bouquet. She also wants you to trim a few seconds off the beginning of the video so that the movement starts a little sooner.

To trim the video:

> **1.** In the Editing group on the Video Tools Playback tab, click the **Trim Video** button. The Trim Video dialog box opens.

> **2.** On the bar below the video, drag the red **End Time slider** to the left to approximately the 19-second mark. The time in the End Time box changes to match the time point that you dragged the slider to. The video will stop playing at this point.

> **3.** Drag the green **Start Time slider** to the right to approximately the 3-second mark. The time in the Start Time box changes to match the time point that you dragged the slider to. The video will now start playing at this point.

> **4.** Click the **OK** button. You can watch the trimmed video in Normal view.

> **5.** On the play bar, click the **Play** button ▶. The trimmed video plays.

Setting a Poster Frame

The default poster frame for a video is the first frame of the video. You can change this so that any frame from the video or any image stored in a file is the poster frame. Sophie wants the poster frame to show one of the pink bouquets.

To set a poster frame for the video:

1. In the Slide pane, position the pointer on top of the play bar so that you see a ScreenTip identifying the time at the point where the pointer is positioned.

2. Move the pointer until it is at approximately the 14-second mark, and then click. The gray indicator in the play bar moves back to the 14-second mark, and the bouquet with pink flowers appears.

3. Click the **Video Tools Format** tab.

4. In the Adjust group, click the **Poster Frame** button. A menu opens.

5. Click **Current Frame**. The menu closes and a note appears in the Play bar indicating that this will be the poster frame. See Figure 3-6. This frame will now be the poster frame for this video clip.

Figure 3-6   Video after the poster frame is set

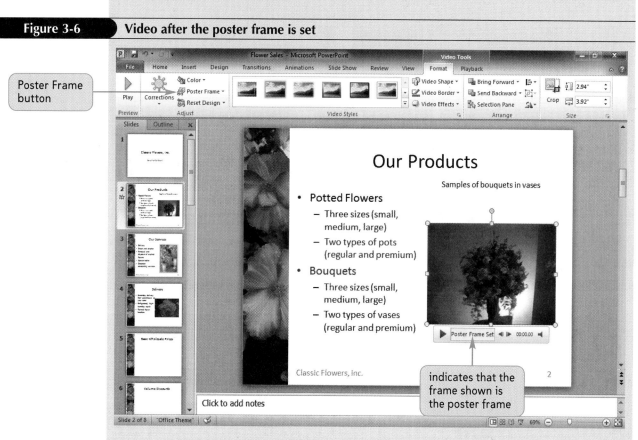

Formatting a Video

You can format videos just like you format pictures. For example, you can crop the sides of a video, or you can resize it by dragging the sizing handles. You should be careful doing this. Normally, you don't want to change the proportions of a video because it will distort the image. You can also apply styles and special effects to videos.

The photograph on Slide 3 has the Metal Frame style applied to it, so Sophie asks you to apply the same style to the video on Slide 2. She also wants you to add a reflection effect to the video clip. When you apply a style or add an effect to a video, you see the style and effect when the video plays.

To apply a style and a reflection effect to the video:

▶ **1.** In the Video Styles group on the Video Tools Format tab, click the **More** button. The gallery opens.

▶ **2.** Click the **Metal Frame** style (the last style in the gallery). See Figure 3-7. Now the frame around the movie photo matches the frame around the picture on Slide 3. Next, you can apply the reflection effect.

| Figure 3-7 | Metal Frame style applied to the video |

▶ **3.** In the Video Styles group, click the **Video Effects** button. A menu appears listing special effects that you can apply to a video.

▶ **4.** Point to **Reflection**, and then click the **Full Reflection, touching** style (the last reflection style in the first row under Reflection Variations). A reflection of the poster frame appears under the video. Now you will reposition the video a little higher on the slide.

▶ **5.** Position the pointer on the selected video so that it changes to ⬆️, and then drag the video up so that the top of the video is approximately aligned with the "Potted Flowers" bullet, and then click a blank area of the slide. See Figure 3-8. Next, you'll check the effects you applied in Slide Show view.

Figure 3-8   **Reflection effect applied to the video**

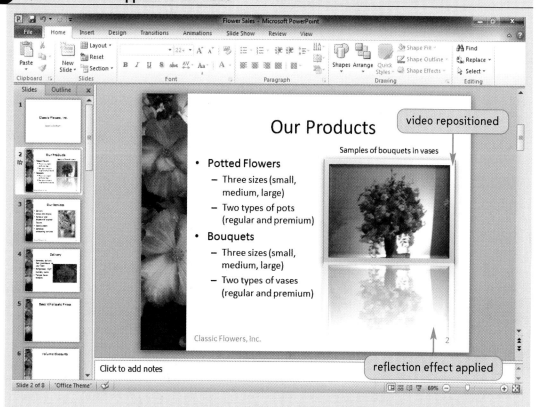

6. On the status bar, click the **Slide Show** button. Slide 2 appears in Slide Show view, and the video clip plays. Notice that the video played in the reflection as well.

7. Press the **[Esc]** key to end the slide show, and then save your changes.

PROSKILLS

Decision Making: Choosing Video to Enhance Your Message

Inserting and manipulating video in PowerPoint slides is easy to do. A video can convey information in a way that bulleted items can't match. Video in the background can add a powerful visual punch to a presentation. However, the content of video in a presentation should clearly convey, illustrate, or support your message. Always carefully consider the purpose of a video, and evaluate the video to make sure it enhances rather than distracts from your presentation.

In addition to inserting a video, you can insert a sound clip on a slide. You'll do this next.

Inserting a Sound Clip

Sophie wants you to add two sound clips to the presentation—a recording of a welcome message on Slide 1 and a sound clip of music that will play across all the slides in the presentation except the first one. The recorded message is a Wave file, which is the most common file format for short sound clips. (Wave files use the filename extension ".wav.") The music you will insert is an MP3 file, another sound file format that PowerPoint supports.

To add a sound clip to a slide, use the Audio button in the Media group on the Insert tab.

Inserting a Sound into a Presentation

- In Normal view, display the slide in which you want to insert the sound in the Slide pane.
- Click the Insert tab on the Ribbon, and then click the Audio button in the Media group; or, click the Insert tab on the Ribbon, click the Audio button arrow in the Media group, and then click Audio from File.
- In the Insert Audio dialog box, navigate to the folder containing the sound clip, click the audio file, and then click the Insert button.

First, you will add a welcome message to Slide 1.

To add a sound clip to Slide 1:

1. Display **Slide 1** in the Slide pane, and then click the **Insert** tab on the Ribbon.

2. In the Media group, click the **Audio** button. The Insert Audio dialog box opens.

3. Navigate to the PowerPoint3\Tutorial folder, click **CFISound**, and then click the **Insert** button. A sound icon appears in the middle of the slide with a play bar below it. See Figure 3-9.

| Figure 3-9 | Slide 1 with sound icon |

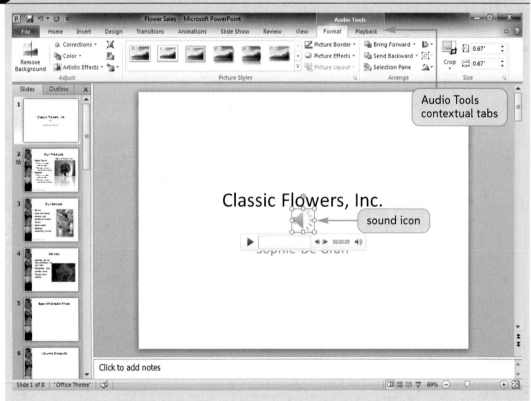

4. On the play bar, click the **Play** button ▶. You hear the sound clip, which is a welcome message. As with videos, the default start setting is On Click. You can verify this.

5. Click the **Audio Tools Playback** tab.

▶ **6.** In the Audio Options group, confirm that the Start box displays On Click as the current setting.

▶ **7.** Position the pointer on top of the border of the sound icon so that it changes to ⬍, and then drag the sound icon to the lower-right corner of the slide.

Sophie wants you to keep the sound icon visible on Slide 1 because she will need to click it to play the message during the slide show. If you don't need to click the icon to play the sound—that is, if you set it to play automatically—you can hide the icon on the slide.

Sophie wants you to insert another clip to play soft music in the background throughout the rest of the slides in the slide show.

To add a sound clip to Slide 2:

▶ **1.** Display **Slide 2** ("Our Products") in the Slide pane. You'll insert one of the sample songs provided with Windows.

▶ **2.** Click the **Insert** tab.

▶ **3.** In the Media group, click the **Audio** button.

▶ **4.** In the navigation pane on the left, click **Music**, and then double-click the **Sample Music** folder.

Trouble? If you are using Windows Vista or XP, navigate to the Music or the Public Music folder, and then double-click the Sample Music folder.

▶ **5.** Click **Sleep Away**, and then click the **Insert** button. The sound icon and play bar appear in the middle of the slide.

Trouble? If you are using Windows Vista or XP, select any music in the Sample Music folder. Try to choose one that has no vocals.

To have this sound play throughout the rest of the slide show, you need to change the Start setting. You also will set the sound icon to be hidden during the slide show. Similar to videos, the options for changing how the sound plays during the slide show appear on the Audio Tools Playback tab. They are the same options that appear on the Video Tools Playback tab, except there is no option to play full screen.

To change playback options for the sound clip on Slide 2:

▶ **1.** Click the **Audio Tools Playback** tab on the Ribbon.

▶ **2.** In the Audio Options group, click the **Start arrow**. You can choose to play the sound On Click, automatically, or across slides.

▶ **3.** Click **Play across slides**. Because you want the sound clip to start over if it ends before the slide show is finished, you will set the sound clip to play continuously.

▶ **4.** In the Audio Options group, click the **Loop until Stopped** check box. Now you will set the option to hide the icon during the slide show.

▶ **5.** In the Audio Options group, click the **Hide During Show** check box to select it. See Figure 3-10. Because this is supposed to be quiet background music, you will adjust the volume to low.

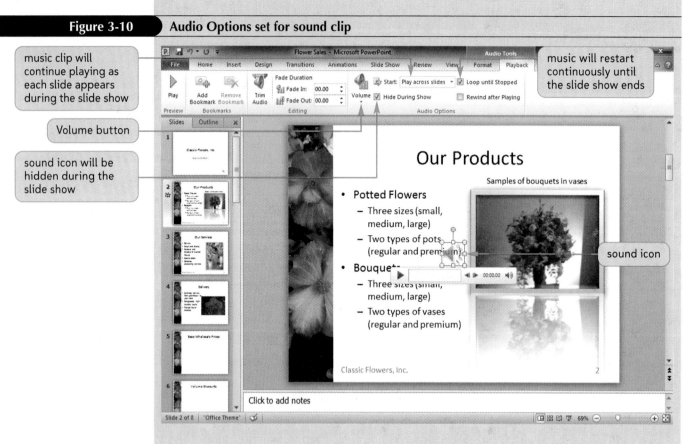

Figure 3-10 Audio Options set for sound clip

6. In the Audio Options group, click the **Volume** button, and then click **Low**. Now you can test your settings.

7. On the status bar, click the **Slide Show** button. Slide 2 appears in Slide Show view, and the flower video plays. When the video of the flowers finishes, the sound starts playing.

8. Advance the slide show. Slide 3 appears on the screen and the music keeps playing.

9. Advance through the rest of the slides until you reach Slide 8 ("Contact Us"). The music continues playing as each slide appears.

10. Wait until the music clip ends. The Sleep Away clip is three minutes and 20 seconds long. When the song is finished, there is silence for a moment, and then it starts again because you set it to Loop until Stopped.

11. End the slide show.

Understanding Video and Audio Animation Effects

Why did the music audio not start until the flower video was over? When you insert video and audio clips, Media animation effects are applied to the clip automatically, and the start setting of these animation effects is tied to the Start setting of the media clip. When you insert a media clip, the default Start setting is On Click. A Play animation is also automatically applied to the clip and it too is set to start On Click. To fix the music clip settings so that it starts playing when the slide appears, as Sophie wants, you'll first examine the animation settings applied to the media clips you inserted.

To examine the Media animation effects for the sound and video clips:

▶ 1. Display **Slide 1** in the Slide pane, and then click the **sound icon** in the lower-right corner.

▶ 2. Click the **Animations** tab on the Ribbon. As shown in Figure 3-11, the Play animation is selected in the Animation gallery, and the Pause and Stop animations appear in the gallery as well. In the Timing group, the start of the selected animation is set to On Click.

| Figure 3-11 | Animations tab when a sound clip is selected |

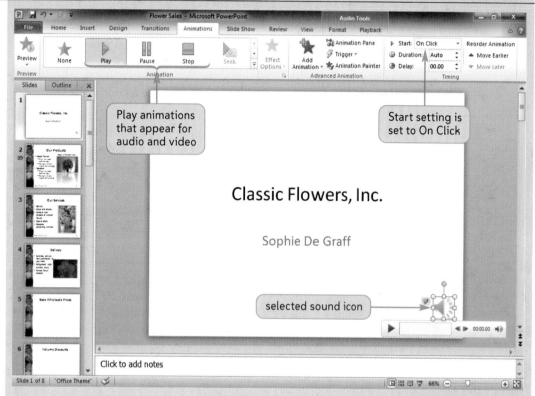

▶ 3. In the Animation group, click the **More** button. Notice that a new Media category is listed in the gallery. The Media category appears in the Animation gallery only when an audio or media clip is inserted.

▶ 4. Press the **Esc** key to close the gallery, display **Slide 2** ("Our Products") in the Slide pane, and then click the **sound icon** in the middle of the slide. The Play animation is selected in the Animation gallery again, and After Previous appears in the Start box. When you set a sound to play across slides, the Play animation setting changes from On Click to After Previous.

▶ 5. In the Slide pane, click the **flower video**. Multiple is selected in the Animation gallery.

▶ 6. Click the **0 animation sequence icon** to the left of the flower video. Play is selected in the Animation gallery, and After Previous appears in the Start box. The Start setting changes from On Click to After Previous when you change the Playback setting from On Click to Automatically.

Remember that if you want an animation to play at the same time as the previous animation or when the slide transitions, you can change the play animation start setting to With Previous. You'll do this now, so the music starts playing when the Vases video starts playing.

To change the start setting for the Play animation applied to the sound clip on Slide 2:

▶ **1.** In the Slide pane, click the **sound icon** in the middle of Slide 2.

▶ **2.** In the Timing group on the Animations tab, click the **Start** arrow, and then click **With Previous**. Next you will check the setting in Slide Show view.

▶ **3.** On the status bar, click the **Slide Show** button 🖵. Slide 2 appears in Slide Show view, the video starts, and the music starts playing.

▶ **4.** After the video finishes, advance the slide show to Slide 3. The music continues playing.

▶ **5.** End the slide show.

Creating a Table on a Slide

Sophie wants you to add a table of the base wholesale prices of Classic Flowers' products to Slide 5. A **table** is information arranged in horizontal rows and vertical columns. The area where a row and column intersect is called a **cell**. Each cell contains one piece of information. A table's structure is indicated by borders, which are lines that outline the rows and columns.

REFERENCE

Inserting a Table

- Switch to a layout that includes a content placeholder, and then click the Insert Table button in the content placeholder; or, click the Insert tab on the Ribbon, click the Table button in the Tables group, and then click Insert Table.
- Specify the desired table size—the numbers of columns and rows—and then click the OK button.

or

- Click the Insert tab on the Ribbon, and then in the Tables group, click the Table button.
- Click a box in the grid that opens to create a table of that size.

The table of wholesale prices that you'll create will have three columns—one for the type of arrangement, one for the size of the arrangement, and one for the price. The table needs to have seven rows—one row for column labels and six rows for data.

To create a table on Slide 5:

▶ **1.** Display **Slide 5** ("Base Wholesale Prices") in the Slide pane.

▶ **2.** In the content placeholder, click the **Insert Table** button ▦. The Insert Table dialog box opens.

▶ **3.** In the Number of columns box, type **3**.

▶ **4.** Press the **Tab** key to move to the Number of rows box, and then type **7**.

▶ **5.** Click the **OK** button. The dialog box closes, a table with three columns and seven rows appears on the slide, and the Table Tools contextual tabs appear on the Ribbon. The insertion point is blinking in the first cell. See Figure 3-12.

Figure 3-12 | Slide 5 with table

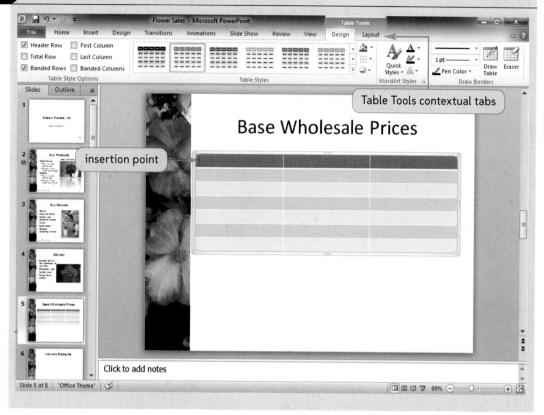

Now you're ready to fill the blank cells with the information about the available arrangements. To enter data in a table, you click in the cell in which you want to enter data. Use the Tab and arrow keys to move from one cell to another.

To add information to the table:

1. With the insertion point blinking in the upper-left cell, type **Type**, and then press the **Tab** key. The insertion point moves to the second cell in the first row.

2. Type **Size**, press the **Tab** key to move to the third cell in the first row, and then type **Price**. These are the column labels.

3. Press the **Tab** key again. The insertion point moves to the first cell in the second row.

4. Type **Potted**, press the **Tab** key, type **Small**, press the **Tab** key, and then type **$3.85**. This completes the first row of data.

5. In the third row, click in the **second cell** (the cell under "Small") to place the insertion point in that cell.

6. Type **Medium**, press the **Tab** key, and then type **$5.25**.

7. Press the **Tab** key twice, type **Large**, press the **Tab** key, and then type **$6.75**.

8. In the next row, starting with the first cell, type **Bouquets**, **Small**, **$6.95**.

9. In the next row, skip the first cell in the row, and then type **Medium**, **$8.50**.

10. In the last row, skip the first cell in the row, and then type **Large**, **$10.25**. The table should look like Figure 3-13.

> **TIP**
>
> To add new rows and columns to the table, use the buttons in the Rows & Columns group on the Table Tools Layout tab.

Figure 3-13   Completed table

Trouble? If you have a blank row at the bottom of your table, you probably pressed the Tab key after entering the data in the last cell, which inserted a new, blank row at the bottom of the table. On the Quick Access Toolbar, click the Undo button to undo the creation of the extra row.

Changing the Table Style

PowerPoint comes with built-in table styles for each theme. Table styles include the borders around the table and cells and color schemes. You can use Live Preview to see how your table will look with different table styles. Sophie wants you to add color and borders to the table, so you will apply a style with a header row (for the column labels), horizontal borders, and some color to add visual interest.

To change the table style:

▶ **1.** If necessary, click the **Table Tools Design** tab on the Ribbon.

   Trouble? If the Table Tools contextual tabs are not on the Ribbon, click anywhere in the table.

   Trouble? If you see presentation themes on the Ribbon instead of table styles, you clicked the Design tab next to the Insert tab. Click the Design tab farther to the right under the Table Tools label.

▶ **2.** In the Table Style Options group, make sure the **Header Row** check box is selected, click the **Banded Rows** check box to deselect it, and then make sure the rest of the check boxes in the Table Style Options group are not selected.

3. In the Table Styles group, click the **More** button. Notice that the default style is the second style in the second row under Medium.

4. In the Medium section, click the **Medium Style 2 – Accent 4** style (the fifth style in the second row under Medium). The style you selected is applied, and the first row is formatted in bold because the Header Row check box was selected. See Figure 3-14.

Figure 3-14 Table with a table style applied

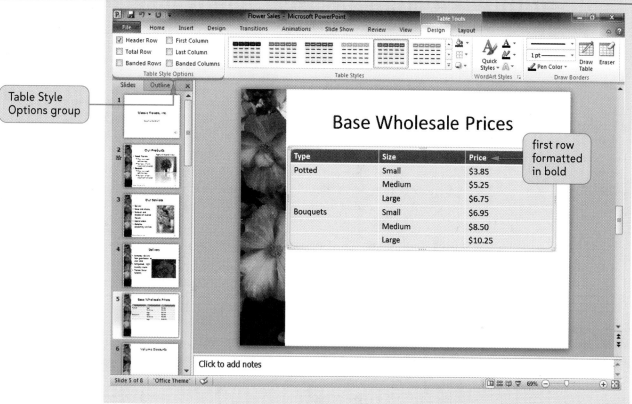

Changing the Table Layout

After you insert data into a table, you usually need to adjust the layout so it fits nicely on the slide and is readable. Commands on the Table Tools Layout tab on the Ribbon let you remove rows, add and remove columns, combine cells, split cells, position text in cells, and perform other modifications to the table. As you can see, all three columns of the table are of equal width. All of the columns could be narrower, and the column labels might be clearer if the numbers were centered in the cells. Before making these changes, you will merge the cells containing the "Potted" and "Bouquet" labels with the empty cells beneath them, and then vertically center the labels in the merged cells.

To change the table layout:

1. Click the **Table Tools Layout** tab on the Ribbon.

2. Click in the first cell in the second row (the cell containing "Potted"), press and hold the mouse button, and then drag down to the fourth row to select the first cells in rows 2, 3, and 4. These are the cells you want to merge.

3. In the Merge group on the Layout tab, click the **Merge Cells** button. The cells are merged into one cell.

4. Merge the cell containing "Bouquets" and the two cells under it. Next, you will resize the columns to better fit the data.

5. Position the pointer on the divider between the first two columns so that the pointer changes to ◀║▶, and then double-click. The first column shrinks so that it is just wide enough to fit the widest entry in the column.

6. Position the pointer on the divider between the last two columns so that the pointer changes to ◀║▶, and then drag the border to the left until the second column is approximately two inches wide.

7. Position the pointer just to the left of the border on the right side of the table so that the pointer changes to ◀║▶, and then drag to the left until the third column is approximately two inches wide. Next, you will horizontally center the text in the first row in the table and vertically center the text in the first column of the table.

Trouble? If the entire table moved, you dragged the table border instead of the column border. On the Quick Access Toolbar, click the Undo button 🔄, and then repeat Step 7, taking care to position the pointer just to the left of the table border so that it changes to ◀║▶.

8. Drag across all the text in the first row of the table to select it, and then click the **Center** button ≣ in the Alignment group on the Table Tools Layout tab. The contents of the cells in the first column are center-aligned in the cells.

9. Drag to select all the text in the second and third columns below the header row, and then center the selected text.

10. Drag to select the text in the two merged cells containing "Potted" and "Bouquets," and then click the **Center Vertically** button ≣ in the Alignment group. See Figure 3-15.

Figure 3-15 | **Table after changing the layout**

The font size of the text in the table is a little small, so Sophie asks you to increase it. You will also make the entire table larger, and then center it on the slide.

To resize and reposition the table:

1. Position the pointer on one of the table borders so that it changes to ⬚, and then click the **border** to select the entire table.

2. Click the **Home** tab on the Ribbon.

3. In the Font group, click the **Increase Font Size** button 𝖠̇ twice to change the font size to 24 points.

4. Position the pointer on the lower-right corner of the table border so that the pointer changes to ⬉, and then drag the lower-right corner of the table down and to the right until the table is approximately 6½ inches wide and 4½ inches tall and the right side of the table is aligned with the right side of the title.

5. Drag the table to position it approximately in the center of the white space on the slide. Compare your finished table to Figure 3-16.

| Figure 3-16 | Finished table |

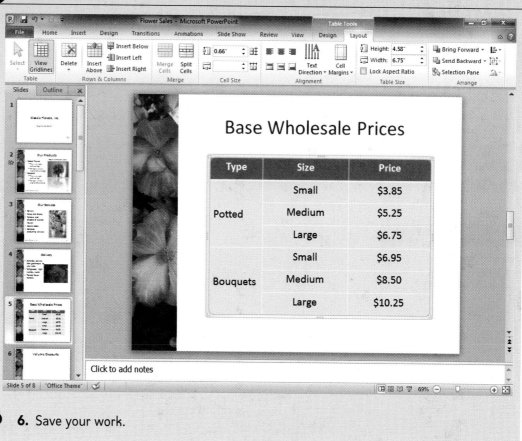

6. Save your work.

Sophie likes the way the table looks on the slide. Next, she wants you to create a chart on Slide 6.

Creating a Chart

A **chart** is a visual depiction of data in a spreadsheet. A **spreadsheet**, called a worksheet in Microsoft Excel, is a grid of cells that contain numbers and text. When you create a chart in a slide, a Microsoft Excel program window opens with a worksheet containing sample data that you can change to the data to be depicted in your chart. As in a table, the intersection of a row and a column is a **cell**, and you add data and labels in cells. The columns are labeled A, B, C, and so on, and the rows are numbered 1, 2, 3, and so forth. You can use a chart to show an audience data trends and patterns or to visually compare data.

REFERENCE

Creating a Chart

- Change the slide layout to one of the content layouts, and then click the Insert Chart button in the content placeholder to open the Insert Chart dialog box; or click the Insert tab, and then, in the Illustrations group, click the Chart button to open the Insert Chart dialog box.
- Click one of the chart icons in the Insert Chart gallery, and then click the OK button.
- In the Excel worksheet that opens, edit the information in the worksheet for the data that you want to plot.
- In the Excel window, click the Close button.

Sophie wants you to create a chart in Slide 6 to show the volume discount prices from the base wholesale prices given in Slide 5.

To insert a chart on Slide 6:

1. Display **Slide 6** ("Volume Discounts") in the Slide pane.
2. In the content placeholder, click the **Insert Chart** button ![]. The Insert Chart dialog box opens, displaying a gallery of charts. See Figure 3-17.

Figure 3-17 | Insert Chart dialog box

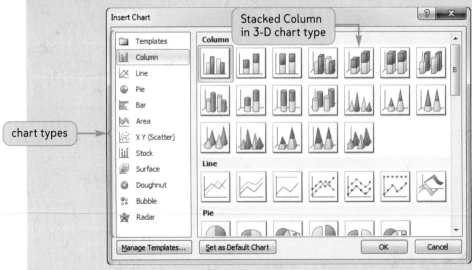

3. Click the **Stacked Column in 3-D** chart type, which is the fifth chart in the first row in the gallery, and then click the **OK** button. A sample chart is inserted in Slide 6, the PowerPoint program window is resized to fit half of the screen, and a Microsoft Excel worksheet opens on the right side of the screen with sample data. See Figure 3-18. Notice that some of the groups on the Home tab on the Ribbon in both windows are collapsed into buttons.

Figure 3-18	Excel spreadsheet with data for chart

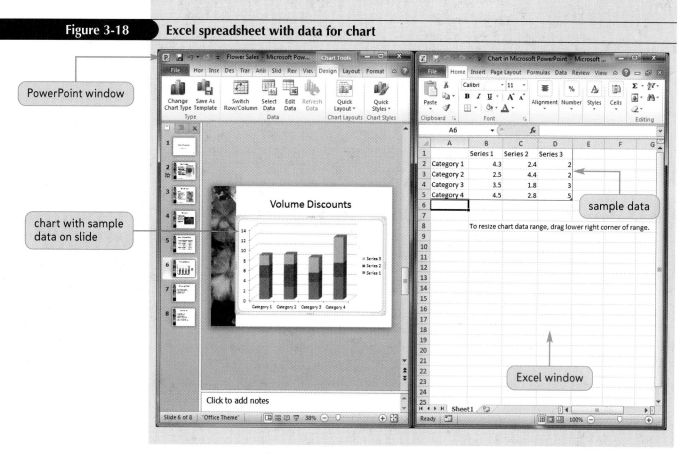

To create the chart for Sophie's presentation, you simply edit the information in the sample worksheet in the Excel window. When you work with a worksheet, the cell in which you are entering data is the **active cell**. The active cell has a thick black border around it. In this chart, Sophie wants only two columns, one with the number of units ordered (per month) and one with the percent discount. You'll begin by deleting the third and fourth columns of data in the worksheet.

To enter the data for the chart:

1. In the Excel worksheet, click anywhere in column D. Notice the blue border around the sample data.

2. On the Home tab in the Excel worksheet, click the **Cells** button, click the **Delete button arrow**, and then click **Delete Table Columns**. Column D is deleted from the worksheet, the blue border adjusts to exclude column D, and the chart in the slide is redrawn to match the worksheet.

Trouble? If you see the Cells group instead of the Cells button on the Home tab, click the Delete button arrow located in that group.

▶ **3.** Delete column C. The blue border adjusts again.

▶ **4.** Click cell **B1**, which currently contains the column label "Series 1."

▶ **5.** Type **Discount %**, and then press the **Enter** key. The text you typed replaces the text in cell B1. Notice that the legend and the title in the chart in the PowerPoint window change as well.

TIP

If you want to widen the columns in the Excel window, double-click the column divider to resize the column to fit the widest entry or drag the column divider to resize the column to a specific width.

▶ **6.** Click cell **A2** ("Category 1"), type **11-50 Units/Mo**, and then press the **Enter** key. The text is entered into cell A2, and cell A3 becomes the active cell. You can't see all of the text in cell A2 because the column is too narrow to fit it. This doesn't matter because the worksheet will not appear on the slide.

▶ **7.** Type **51-100 Units/Mo** in cell A3, press the **Enter** key, type **101-300 Units/Mo** in cell A4, press the **Enter** key, type **>300 Units/Mo** in cell A5, and then press the **Enter** key.

▶ **8.** Enter **3** in cell B2, **8** in cell B3, **15** in cell B4, and **20** in cell B5. The new values appear in cells B2 through B5 in Excel and are reflected in the chart in PowerPoint. See Figure 3-19.

Figure 3-19 **Completed Excel worksheet with data for chart**

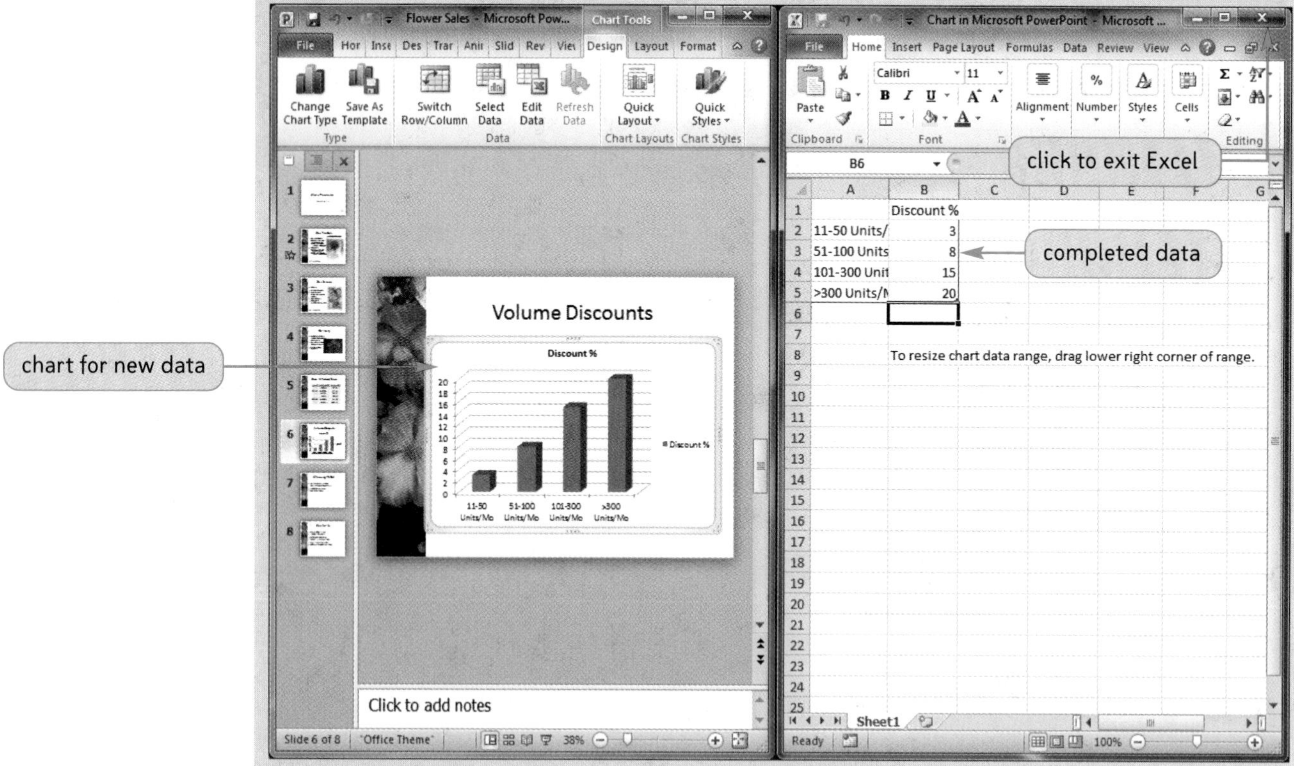

▶ **9.** In the Excel window, click the **Close** button ![X] on the Excel title bar. The Excel window closes, the Excel data is saved in the PowerPoint presentation, and the PowerPoint window expands to fill the full screen. The new chart is selected in Slide 6, as shown in Figure 3-20, and three Chart Tools contextual tabs appear on the Ribbon.

| Figure 3-20 | Slide 6 with chart |

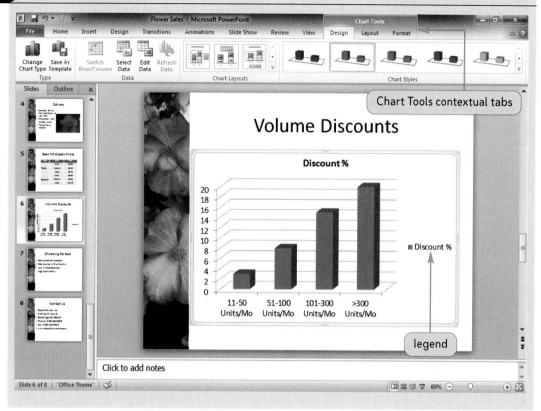

Modifying a Chart

Once the chart is on the slide, you can modify it by changing or formatting the various elements of the chart. For example, the legend on the right side of the chart is unnecessary because all the columns in the chart refer to the discount percentage, so you can choose to delete it. You can apply a chart style to your chart to change its look. You can also add gridlines and labels or edit or remove a chart's title.

Sophie wants you to modify the chart by deleting the legend, applying a style, and adding gridlines and labels. You'll do this now.

To edit and format the chart:

1. Click the **legend** to select it, and then press the **Delete** key. The legend is removed from the chart, and the chart expands to fill the space that was occupied by the text box you deleted. You can also change the chart style.

2. If necessary, click the **Chart Tools Design** tab on the Ribbon.

3. In the Chart Styles group, click the **More** button, and then click **Style 14**, the purple style in the second row in the gallery. The column colors change from blue to purple. See Figure 3-21.

TIP

You can also delete the legend by clicking the Chart Tools Layout tab on the Ribbon, clicking the Legend button in the Labels group, and then clicking None.

Figure 3-21   **Chart after deleting legend and applying a style**

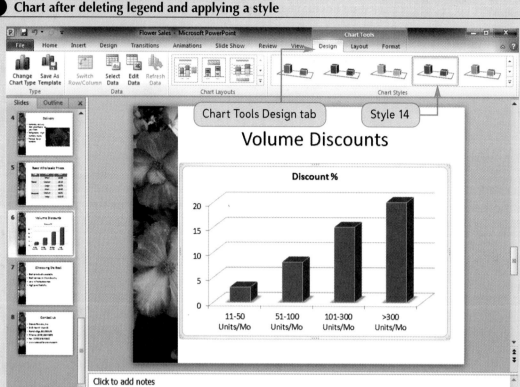

▶ **4.** Click the **Chart Tools Layout** tab on the Ribbon.

▶ **5.** In the Labels group, click the **Data Labels** button, and then click **Show**. Now the actual values of the discount percent appear on the columns in the chart. Next, you'll add vertical gridlines to the chart.

▶ **6.** In the Axes group, click the **Gridlines** button, point to **Primary Vertical Gridlines**, and then click **Major Gridlines**. Now you can see not only horizontal but also vertical gridlines. See Figure 3-22. Next, Sophie wants you to add a label to the vertical axis on the left. You'll add rotated text along that axis.

Figure 3-22   **Chart after displaying column values and gridlines**

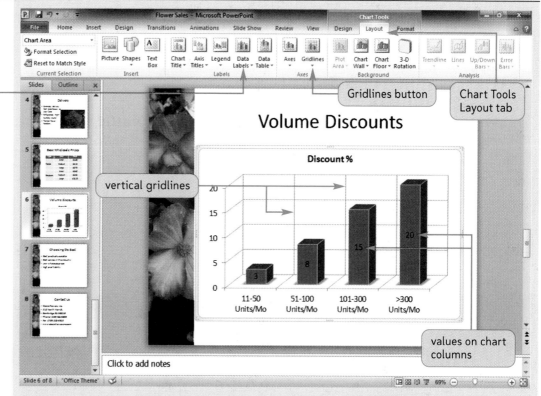

7. In the Labels group, click the **Axis Titles** button, point to **Primary Vertical Axis Title**, and then click **Rotated Title**. A text box, rotated so it reads bottom to top parallel to the vertical axis, appears on the chart with the text "Axis Title." The new text box is selected, so you can just start typing to replace the temporary axis title.

8. Type **Percent Discount**. The text "Axis Title" is changed to "Percent Discount." The slide title describes the chart, so you will delete the chart title.

9. In the Labels group, click the **Chart Title** button, and then click **None**. Compare your chart to the one shown in Figure 3-23.

Figure 3-23 Completed chart

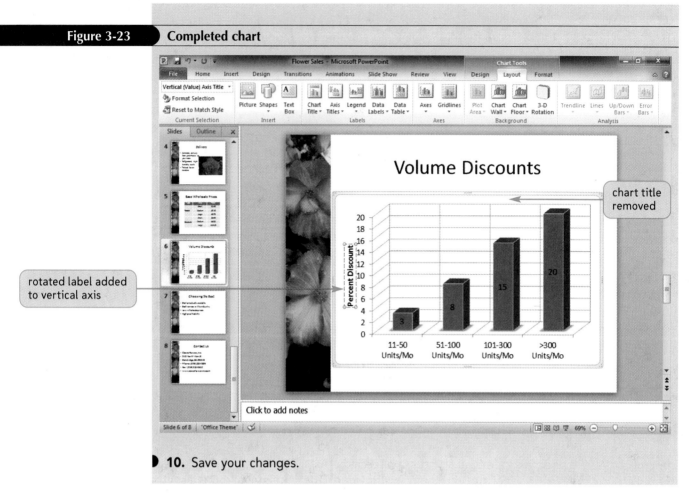

10. Save your changes.

Animating a Chart

Sophie now wants you to apply an entrance animation effect to the chart in Slide 6. To apply an animation to a chart, you use the same technique as animating any other object on a slide.

To animate the chart:

1. Click the **Animations** tab on the Ribbon. The chart should still be selected.

2. In the Animations gallery, click the **More** button, and then in the second row under Entrance, click **Random Bars**. The animation previews. One animation sequence icon appears next to the chart. The default is for the chart to animate as one object (the same as SmartArt), but you want each bar to appear one after the other.

3. In the Animation group, click the **Effect Options** button. Notice that there are five options under Sequence.

4. Click **By Element in Series**. The animation previews with the chart appearing with the Random Bars effect followed by each bar, one after the other. Five animation sequence icons now appear next to the chart; the first icon, number 1, is for the chart grid, and numbers 2 through 5 are associated with each bar.

Adding a Second Animation to an Object

After Sophie spends some time discussing the information on this slide during her presentation, she wants to draw her audience's attention back to the chart. To do this, she asks you to apply an emphasis animation to occur after the entrance animation.

To add a second animation to the chart and change its speed:

1. Make sure the chart is still selected.

2. In the Advanced Animation group, click the **Add Animation** button. The same gallery that opens when you click the More button in the Animation group appears.

3. In the first row under Emphasis, click **Pulse**. This effect causes the object to pulse—that is, to zoom in slightly and then shrink back. Notice the additional five animation sequence icons next to the chart. See Figure 3-24. Although the default for charts is to animate as one object, because you changed the Entrance animation so that each bar in the chart animates one series at a time, the default for this second animation that you applied to the chart is By Element in Series as well. It's too distracting to have the chart pulse one bar at a time, so Sophie suggests that since both animations must have the same sequence effect, it would be better to have them animate as one object.

Figure 3-24	Chart with two animations set to animate by element in series

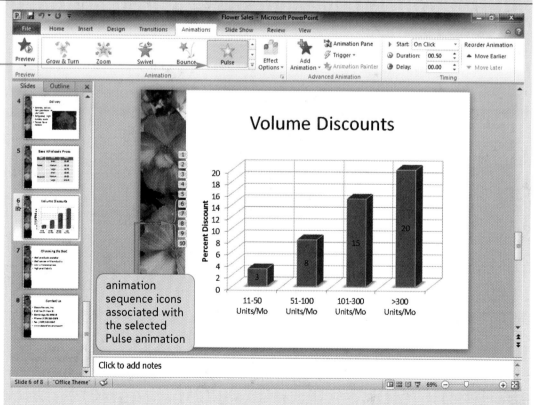

4. In the Animation group, click the **Effect Options** button, and then click **As One Object**. Now just two animation sequence icons appear next to the chart.

Changing the Speed of Animations

You can adjust the speed of animations. For the chart, Sophie wants the entrance animation to progress more slowly than the default setting of one-half second, and she wants the Pulse animation to occur more quickly. To change the speed of an animation, you change the time in the Duration box in the Timing group on the Animations tab.

To change the speed of the chart animations:

1. Click the animation sequence icon with the number 1 in it. Random Bars is selected in the Animation group on the Animations tab.

2. In the Timing group, click the **Duration up arrow** twice. See Figure 3-25. The Random Bars animation will now take one second instead of one-half second.

| Figure 3-25 | Speed of the Random Bars animation modified |

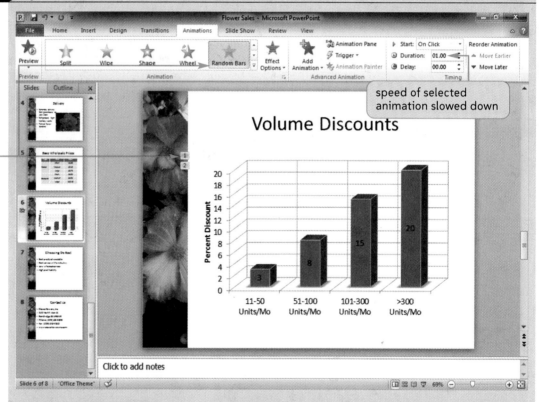

3. Click the animation sequence icon with the number 2 in it. Pulse is selected in the Animation group.

4. In the Timing group, click the **Duration down arrow** to change the Duration to .25 seconds.

5. In the Preview group, click the **Preview** button to preview the chart animations.

6. Save your changes.

You have created content for Sophie's sales presentation by inserting slides from another presentation and adding video, sound, a table, and a chart. You have also added a second animation to an object and changed the speed of animations. In the next session, you will customize the theme by changing the theme fonts and colors and modifying the slide background and bullet styles, and then save the modified theme as a custom theme. You will also apply a different theme to one slide in the presentation.

REVIEW

Session 3.1 Quick Check

1. Describe how you insert slides from one presentation into another.
2. What happens when you add a reflection effect to a video?
3. How do you shorten a video's playback?
4. True or False. You cannot set a sound clip to play across multiple slides.
5. When you apply a table style, how do you quickly identify columns or rows that should be formatted differently?
6. What program opens when you insert a chart on a slide?
7. True or False. To add a second animation to an object, you click the second animation in the Animation gallery.
8. How do you change the speed of an animation?

SESSION 3.2 VISUAL OVERVIEW

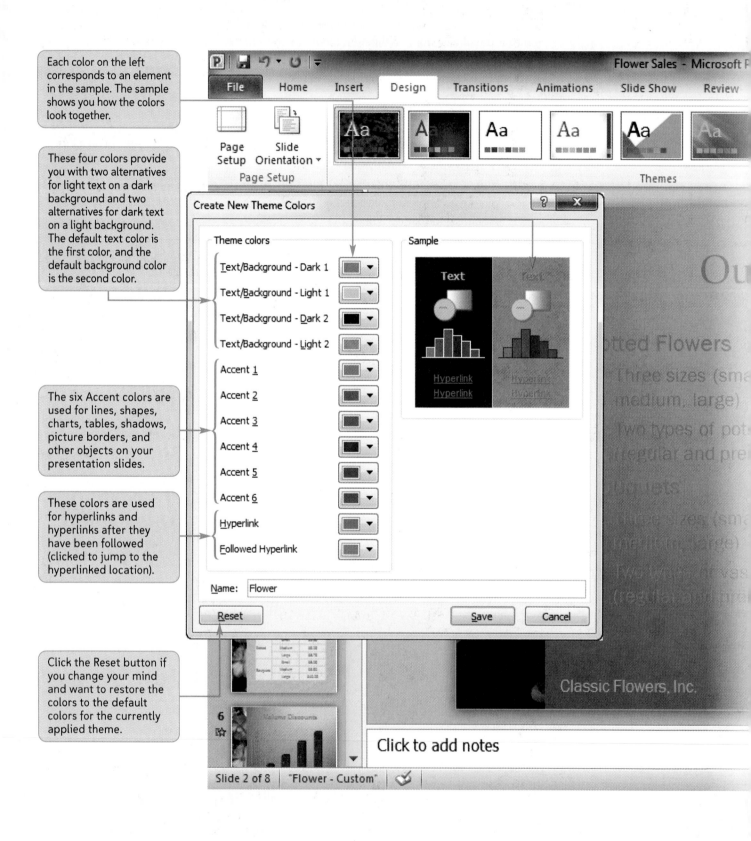

Each color on the left corresponds to an element in the sample. The sample shows you how the colors look together.

These four colors provide you with two alternatives for light text on a dark background and two alternatives for dark text on a light background. The default text color is the first color, and the default background color is the second color.

The six Accent colors are used for lines, shapes, charts, tables, shadows, picture borders, and other objects on your presentation slides.

These colors are used for hyperlinks and hyperlinks after they have been followed (clicked to jump to the hyperlinked location).

Click the Reset button if you change your mind and want to restore the colors to the default colors for the currently applied theme.

THEME COLORS AND BACKGROUNDS

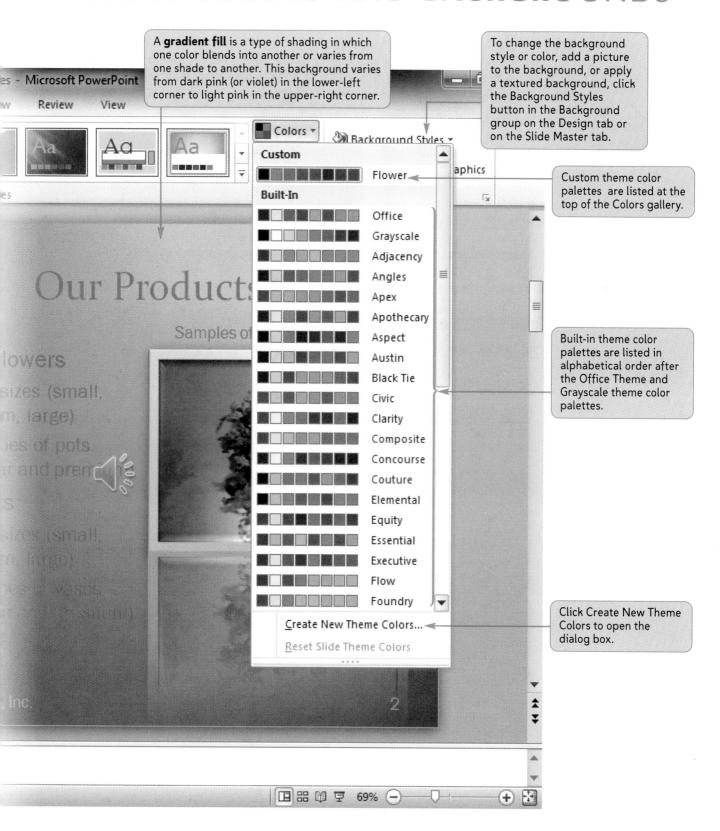

A **gradient fill** is a type of shading in which one color blends into another or varies from one shade to another. This background varies from dark pink (or violet) in the lower-left corner to light pink in the upper-right corner.

To change the background style or color, add a picture to the background, or apply a textured background, click the Background Styles button in the Background group on the Design tab or on the Slide Master tab.

Custom theme color palettes are listed at the top of the Colors gallery.

Built-in theme color palettes are listed in alphabetical order after the Office Theme and Grayscale theme color palettes.

Click Create New Theme Colors to open the dialog box.

Changing Theme Fonts and Colors

The 20 built-in themes provide many choices for personalizing the design of a presentation. However, if you don't like the specific colors or fonts that come with a theme, you can change them easily. You could change the fonts used for the slide titles and content and the colors used for elements shown in the slide masters, but this would not change the default font used for text boxes you draw, the text used in shapes and tables, the text used for labels in charts, and so on. Instead, you can change the set of theme fonts and theme colors.

Changing Theme Fonts

Recall from Tutorial 1 that theme fonts are two coordinating fonts or font styles, one for the titles (or headings) and one for text in content placeholders and other text elements on a slide. To change the theme fonts, you click the Fonts button in the Themes group on the Design tab, and then select the coordinating set of fonts from another theme.

The Flower Sales presentation is based on the Office theme, and the font used for all the text in the presentation is Calibri. Sophie would like to use a different set of theme fonts in the Flower Sales presentation. You'll change the theme fonts now.

To change the theme fonts:

▶ 1. If you took a break after the last session, make sure the **Flower Sales** presentation you created in Session 3.1 is open in the PowerPoint window in Normal view.

▶ 2. Display **Slide 1** in the Slide pane, and then click the **Design** tab on the Ribbon.

▶ 3. In the Themes group, click the **Fonts** button. The gallery of theme fonts opens.

▶ 4. Scroll down the alphabetical list, and then point to **Pushpin**. Live Preview shows the fonts change from Calibri, used in the Office theme, to Constantia for the slide titles and Franklin Gothic Book for text in the content text boxes, the fonts used in the Pushpin theme. See Figure 3-26.

| Figure 3-26 | Fonts gallery |

5. Click **Pushpin**. The menu closes and the fonts in the presentation are changed to the fonts used with the Pushpin theme.

6. Save your changes.

You can also customize a theme by choosing a different set of theme colors.

Changing Theme Colors

Each of the built-in PowerPoint themes, including the default Office theme, has a set of 12 theme colors associated with it. Recall that theme colors are the coordinating colors used for the background, title fonts, body fonts, and other elements of the presentation. Refer to the Session 3.2 Visual Overview for more information about theme colors.

The current presentation uses the color theme called "Office," which is the default set of colors used when the Office theme is applied. The default background color is white and the default text color is black (except for the gray subtitle on the title slide). Sophie feels that this simple theme doesn't fit well with the sales presentation on potted flowers and bouquets. She would like you to choose a theme that uses a brighter set of theme colors.

You choose a different set of theme colors using the Colors button in the Themes group on the Design tab.

To change the theme colors in the presentation:

▶ **1.** In the Themes group on the Design tab, click the **Colors** button to display the Colors gallery. See Figure 3-27. Office and Grayscale appear at the top of the list, followed by an alphabetical list of theme color sets. Grayscale is not a theme, but is available as a set of theme colors if you want to create a presentation using only shades of gray.

| Figure 3-27 | Colors gallery |

▶ **2.** Scroll down the list, and then click **Perspective**. This set of theme colors uses brighter colors than those used in the Office theme. Because the text and background colors for the Perspective theme are also black and white, the only change that happens in the presentation is that the table and chart on Slides 5 and 6 changed color slightly.

Customizing Theme Colors

The color change was not as dramatic as Sophie had hoped. She decides she would like you to customize the theme colors by changing the color of text to green and the color of the background to pink. To do this, you need to create a new, custom set of theme colors. Refer back to the Session 3.2 Visual Overview for more information about how each color is assigned to an element and how to change these colors.

To create custom theme colors:

▶ **1.** In the Themes group, click the **Colors** button, and then at the bottom of the gallery, click **Create New Theme Colors**. The Create New Theme Colors dialog box opens. You want to change the color of text from black to green.

▶ **2.** Click the **Text/Background – Dark 1** button to display the complete Theme Colors and Standard Colors palettes. Because no dark-green tile appears in the palette, you'll look at more colors.

▶ **3.** At the bottom of the palette, click **More Colors** to display the Colors dialog box, and then, if necessary, click the **Standard** tab. See Figure 3-28.

Figure 3-28 — Standard tab in the Colors dialog box

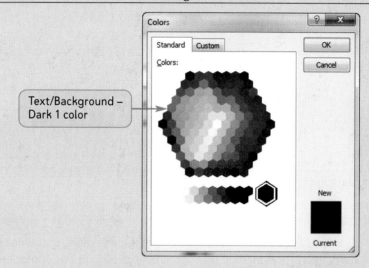

Text/Background – Dark 1 color

▶ **4.** Refer to Figure 3-28, click the dark green tile labeled **Text/Background – Dark 1** in the figure, and then click the **OK** button. The Colors dialog box closes. The Text/Background – Dark 1 color changes from black to dark green, and the text in the panel on the right in the Sample area of the Create New Theme Colors dialog box changes to dark green also. Next, you'll change the color of the light color background.

▶ **5.** Click the **Text/Background – Light 1** button to display the Colors gallery.

▶ **6.** Under Theme Colors, click the **Dark Purple, Accent 4, Lighter 80%** color (the pink color in the eighth column, second row). The text in the panel on the left in the Sample area changes to light pink. Even though the text in the left panel changed, the Text/Background – Light 1 color will be applied to the slide background. Since you created a new set of theme colors, you need to save them in order to apply them to the presentation.

▶ **7.** In the **Name** box, delete the text "**Custom 1**," and then type **Flower**.

▶ **8.** Click the **Save** button. The dialog box closes and the custom theme colors are applied to the presentation. As you can see in Slide 1, the title text is now dark green and the background is light pink. The subtitle text changed to a complementary color to the title text. See Figure 3-29.

TIP

Never select dark text on dark background or light text on light background.

Figure 3-29	New theme colors applied to the presentation

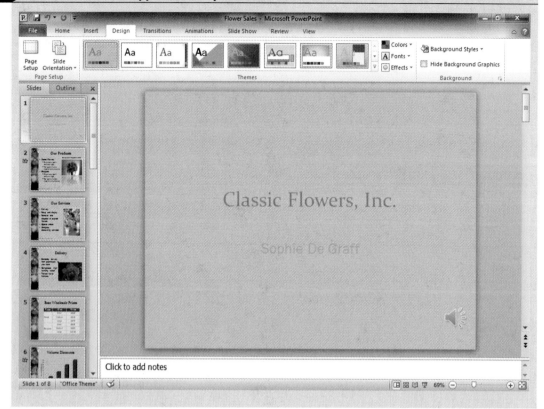

Now that you have saved the custom theme colors, that color palette is available to apply to any presentation that you create or edit on this computer.

Deleting Custom Theme Colors

You can delete a custom theme or theme colors. If you've applied the theme or the theme colors to a presentation, and then saved that presentation, the theme and colors will still be applied to that presentation even if you delete the theme or theme colors from the hard drive. You'll delete the custom theme color palette you created from the computer you are using.

To delete the custom theme colors:

▶ **1.** In the Themes group, click the **Colors** button. The Flower custom color theme you created appears at the top of the Colors gallery under "Custom."

▶ **2.** Right-click the **Flower** theme color palette, and then click **Delete** on the shortcut menu. A dialog box opens asking if you want to delete these theme colors.

▶ **3.** Click the **Yes** button. The dialog box closes and the custom theme colors are deleted.

▶ **4.** In the Themes group, click the **Colors** button, and confirm that the Flower theme color palette is deleted.

▶ **5.** Click a blank area of the window to close the menu without making a selection.

▶ **6.** Save your changes.

Resetting Slides

When you create custom theme colors or change the theme fonts, you should examine the slides to make sure they look as you expect. When you change theme or slide master elements in a presentation, you sometimes need to reset the slides so that they pick up the new formatting. In this case, the new text color did not get picked up by the existing slides in the presentation. You can fix this by resetting the slides. When you reset slides, you reset every object on the slides, so you might need to reposition objects or reapply styles. Slide 1 is fine and does not need to be reset.

To reset the slides:

▶ **1.** Display **Slide 8** ("Contact Us") in the Slide pane. The text on this slide did not change to the new green color.

▶ **2.** Click the **Home** tab on the Ribbon.

▶ **3.** In the Slides group, click the **Reset** button. The text changes to the green color you selected.

▶ **4.** Reset **Slide 7** ("Choosing the Best"), **Slide 6** ("Volume Discounts"), and **Slide 5** ("Best Wholesale Prices"). When you reset Slide 5, the table moved back to its original position on the slide.

▶ **5.** Drag the **table** to position it approximately in the center of the pink area of the slide below the slide title.

▶ **6.** Reset **Slide 4** ("Delivery"). The text changed to green, and the flower picture on the slide moved down. You'll leave this as it is for now.

▶ **7.** Reset **Slide 3** ("Our Services"). In addition to the text changing to green, the Metal Frame style is removed from the picture. You'll reapply that style.

▶ **8.** Select the picture, click the **Picture Tools Format** tab, and then in the Picture Styles group, click the **Metal Frame** style (the third style in the gallery).

▶ **9.** Reset **Slide 2** ("Our Products"). The text changed to green, but the reflection effect and the Metal Frame style are removed from the video and the video moved back down to its original position on the slide. This is a case where resetting the slide made the problem worse, not better. You can undo your change.

▶ **10.** On the Quick Access Toolbar, click the **Undo** button ⟲. The changes made to the image are undone, but the text in the title and content text boxes is still green. This is because the color of the text is directly connected to the theme, and therefore the slide master and the Reset command simply fixed something that should have been changed when the theme changes were made.

▶ **11.** In the text box above the image, drag across the text to select it.

▶ **12.** In the Font group on the Home tab, click the **Font Color button arrow**, and then click the **Green, Text 1** color in the first row under Theme Colors—even if it is already selected.

▶ **13.** Click a blank area of the slide, and then save your changes.

Now that you've created a new set of theme colors for the presentation, you'll change the background style of the slides.

Modifying the Slide Background

The background of a slide can be as important as the foreground when you are creating a presentation with a strong visual impact. You can modify the background style and colors, add a picture or even video as the slide background, or add a textured background. You can change the background from the Design tab or from the Slide Master tab.

Adding a Gradient

You can change the background for one or all slides using the Background Styles gallery, which lists the four colors used for the Text/Background colors in the Create New Theme Colors dialog box. Gradient shading added to the background of slides can add interest and a professional touch to the presentation. You can make this change in Normal or Slide Master view.

You changed the background color to a light pink. Sophie thinks that a gradient background will look a little more interesting, so you'll add a gradient fill.

To change the background style to a gradient fill:

▶ **1.** Click the **Design** tab on the Ribbon.

▶ **2.** In the Background group, click the **Background Styles** button. The Background Styles gallery opens. See Figure 3-30. The Background Styles gallery includes 12 styles—four solid colors along the top row corresponding to the four Text/Background theme colors and two gradient styles for each of those colors.

TIP

To change the background style on only one slide, right-click the style you want to apply, and then on the shortcut menu, click Apply to Selected Slides.

Figure 3-30   **Background Styles gallery**

3. Click **Style 5**, which is the first background style in the second row. The background of the slides now vary from dark pink (or violet) in the lower-left corner to light pink in the upper-right corner.

As you can see from the Slide pane and the slide thumbnails in the pane on the left, all of the slides now have a background with a gradient fill. You'll now add a picture to the background of Slide 1.

Adding a Background Picture

Sophie wants you to add a photo of a bed of flowers to the background of Slide 1. Although you can change the background style in Normal or Slide Master view, if you want a background picture to become part of the theme, you need to add it to the slide background in Slide Master view. You want to be able to apply the formatting changes you made in this presentation to future presentations, so you'll add the picture to the Title Slide Layout master. Recall that the slide master contains the objects that appear on the slide layouts, and the Title Slide layout master contains the objects that appear only on the title slide.

Adding a Picture to a Background

- Click the Design tab on the Ribbon; or, switch to Slide Master view, and then click the Slide Master tab on the Ribbon, if necessary.
- In the Background group, click the Background Styles button, and then click Format Background to open the Format Background dialog box.
- Click the Picture or texture fill option button.
- Click the File button to open the Insert Picture dialog box.
- Click the image you want to use, and then click the Insert button.
- Click the Close button if you want to apply the textured background just to the current slide, or click the Apply to All button if you want to apply the textured background to all the slides in the presentation.

You'll add a photo of flowers to the background of the Title Slide Layout master now.

To add a background picture to the Title Slide Layout master:

1. Click the **View** tab on the Ribbon.

2. In the Master Views group, click the **Slide Master** button. Slide Master view opens.

3. If necessary, click the **Title Slide Layout** thumbnail (the second thumbnail from the top in the pane on the left).

4. In the Background group on the Slide Master tab, click the **Background Styles** button. The Background Styles gallery opens.

5. Below the gallery in the menu, click **Format Background**. The Format Background dialog box opens with Fill selected in the left pane.

6. Click the **Picture or texture fill** option button. The dialog box changes to display commands for customizing a background with a texture or a picture. See Figure 3-31. The default background for this option—the Papyrus textured background—appears on the slide behind the dialog box.

TIP

If you decide you do not want a picture or a textured background, click the Reset Background button in the Format Background dialog box.

| Figure 3-31 | Format Background dialog box with Fill options |

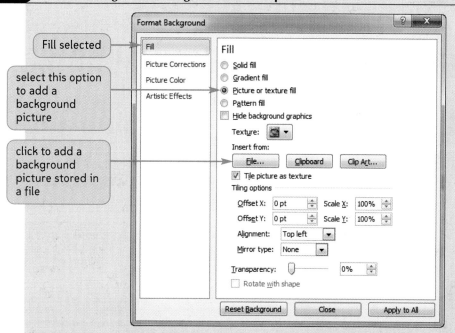

Fill selected

select this option to add a background picture

click to add a background picture stored in a file

7. In the Insert from section in the center of the dialog box, click the **File** button. The Insert Picture dialog box opens.

8. Navigate to the PowerPoint3\Tutorial folder, click the picture file **PinkFlower**, and then click the **Insert** button. The Insert Picture dialog box closes and the picture is inserted into the background of the Title Slide Layout, which is visible behind the Format Background dialog box.

The new background makes it difficult to read the text on the slide, so Sophie asks you to adjust the brightness and contrast. Because the image is part of the background, you must adjust the brightness and contrast in the Format Background dialog box; you cannot adjust it on the Picture Tools Format tab.

To change the brightness and contrast of the background image:

TIP

You can also open the Format Background dialog box by right-clicking a blank area of the slide, and then clicking Format Background.

1. In the left pane of the Format Background dialog box, click **Picture Corrections**. The dialog box changes to include commands for modifying the picture on the background. See Figure 3-32.

Figure 3-32   **Format Background dialog box with Picture Corrections options**

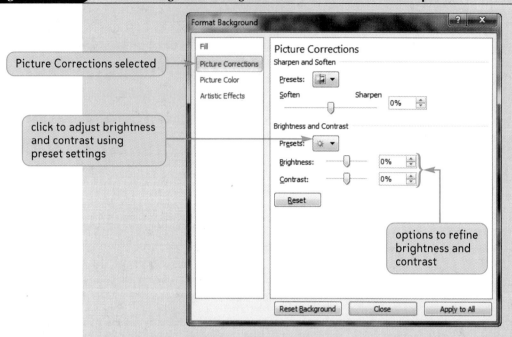

Picture Corrections selected

click to adjust brightness and contrast using preset settings

options to refine brightness and contrast

▶ **2.** In the Brightness and Contrast section, click the **Presets** button. The Brightness and Contrast gallery opens.

Trouble? If you see only one row of styles, you clicked the Presets button in the Sharpen and Soften section. Click the Presets button to close the gallery without selecting anything, and then repeat Step 2.

▶ **3.** In the first row, click the **second style** (its ScreenTip is Brightness -20% Contrast -40%). The brightness and contrast of the image changes behind the Format Background dialog box. You want the image to be a little darker.

▶ **4.** Drag the **Brightness** slider to the left until the box indicates **-30%**. The picture behind the dialog box darkens slightly.

Trouble? If you can't position the slider exactly, click the up or down arrow in the box containing the percentage as needed, or drag to select the percentage and then type -30.

▶ **5.** Click the **Close** button in the dialog box.

The backgrounds appear as Sophie wants them, but she now wants you to make the title text on the slides stand out more. You'll modify the color of the text.

To change the color of the presentation title and subtitle:

▶ **1.** With the Title Slide Layout master still selected, click the border of the title text placeholder, which currently contains dark-green text.

▶ **2.** Click the **Home** tab on the Ribbon.

▶ **3.** In the Font group, click the **Font Color button arrow** A ▾ to display the theme colors palette.

4. Under Standard Colors, click the **Yellow** color (the fourth color in the row).

   Trouble? If the title text color did not change, you probably clicked inside the title text placeholder instead of directly on the border. Click directly on the border to select the entire placeholder, and then repeat Steps 3 and 4.

5. Change the color of the subtitle text to the Standard Color **Orange** (the third color in the row under Standard Colors).

6. Deselect the text box. See Figure 3-33.

Figure 3-33   **Title Slide Layout master with modified title text**

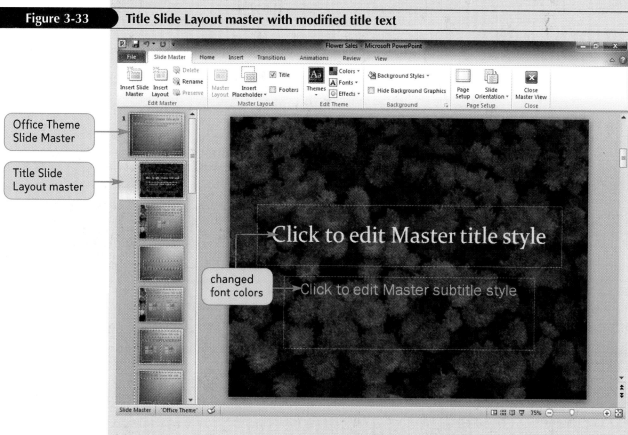

7. Close Slide Master view, and then display **Slide 1** (the title slide) in the Slide pane so that you can examine the changes you made.

8. Save your changes.

Adding a Textured Background

In addition to changing the background style and adding a picture to the background, you can apply a textured background to a slide. Sophie asks you to change the background of Slide 5, which contains a table of the base wholesale prices of Classic Flowers' products, to highlight that slide. Because this change will highlight Slide 5 only—not all the slides with the Title and Content Layout master applied—you'll make this change in Normal view.

REFERENCE

Applying a Textured Background

- Click the Design tab on the Ribbon.
- In the Background group, click the Background Styles button, and then click Format Background to open the Format Background dialog box.
- Click the Picture or texture fill option button.
- Click the Texture button to display a gallery of textured backgrounds.
- Click the desired texture and then click the Close button if you want to apply the textured background just to the current slide, or click the Apply to All button if you want to apply the textured background to all the slides in the presentation.

You'll now apply a "pink tissue paper" texture to the background of Slide 5.

To add a textured background to Slide 5:

1. Display **Slide 5** ("Base Wholesale Prices"), and then click the **Design** tab.

2. In the Background group, click the **Background Styles** button, and then click **Format Background**. The Format Background dialog box opens with Fill selected on the left.

3. Click the **Picture or texture fill** option button. The dialog box changes to include commands for inserting a picture or a fill.

4. Click the **Texture** button. A gallery of textured backgrounds appears.

5. Click the **Pink tissue paper** texture, located in row 4, column 3. The background of the slide changes to pink tissue paper behind the dialog box.

6. Click the **Close** button. The pink tissue paper texture is applied to the current slide. See Figure 3-34.

| Figure 3-34 | Slide 5 with textured background |

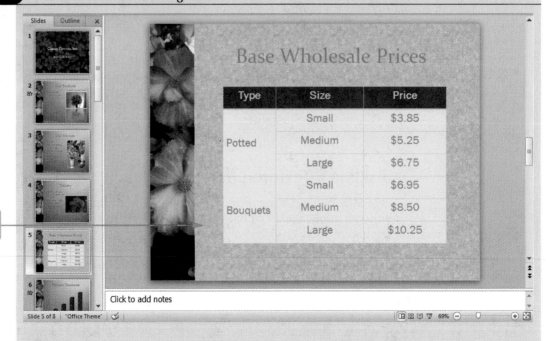

pink tissue paper texture background

7. Save your changes.

Sophie looks over the presentation, and asks you to change the bullets to a more distinctive style. You'll do this next.

Modifying Bullet Styles

You can change the style, size, and color of bullets. Like font changes, this change should be made in the slide master so that all the bullets in the presentation look the same.

First, you'll change the first-level bullets to a picture bullet that looks a little like the yellow center of a flower. You want the new bullet style to be applied to all the content text boxes in the presentation, so you'll make this change in Slide Master view.

To change the first-level bullets to a picture bullet:

1. Switch to Slide Master view.

2. In the pane on the left, scroll up, and then click the **Office Theme Slide Master** thumbnail to display the Slide Master in the slide pane.

3. Click anywhere in the first bulleted item, which says "Click to edit Master text styles."

4. Click the **Home** tab on the Ribbon.

5. In the Paragraph group, click the **Bullets button arrow** ≔ ▾ to display the Bullets gallery.

6. Click **Bullets and Numbering** at the bottom of the Bullets gallery to display the Bullets and Numbering dialog box with the Bulleted tab on top.

7. Click the **Picture** button. The Picture Bullet dialog box opens.

8. Scroll down until the scroll box is about one-third the way down the scroll bar, so that you see the picture bullet shown in Figure 3-35.

Figure 3-35 Picture Bullet dialog box

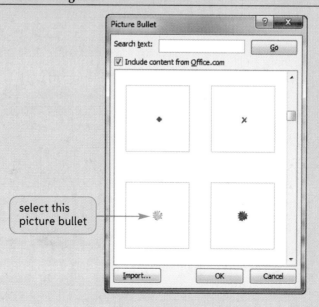

select this picture bullet

9. Click the bullet indicated in Figure 3-35, and then click the **OK** button. Both dialog boxes close, and the picture bullet you selected becomes the first-level bullet in the content placeholder.

Now you'll change the second-level bullet. For this bullet, Sophie asks you to use one of the standard bullet styles.

To change the second-level bullets to a standard bullet symbol:

▶ **1.** Click anywhere in the "Second level" bulleted item.

▶ **2.** Click the **Bullets button arrow** :≡ ▾. The Bullets gallery opens. See Figure 3-36.

Figure 3-36   Bullets gallery

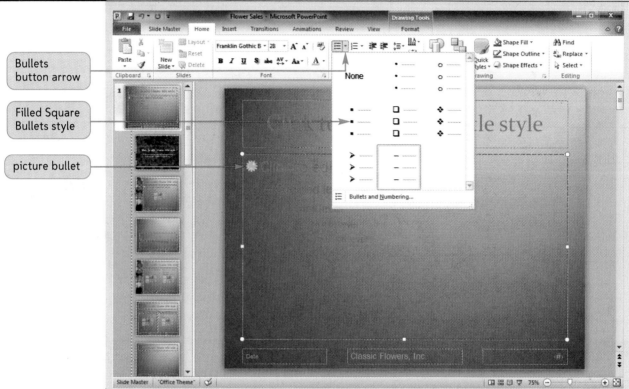

▶ **3.** In the second row, click the **Filled Square Bullets** style. The Bullets gallery closes, and the second-level item bullet changes to the Filled Square Bullet style.

To make the second-level bullet stand out a little more, Sophie asks you to change the color of these bullets to yellow and increase their size.

To change the color and size of the second-level bullets:

▶ **1.** With the insertion point still in the "Second level" bulleted item, click the **Bullets button arrow** :≡ ▾, and then click **Bullets and Numbering**.

▶ **2.** Click the **Color** button in the lower-left corner of the dialog box, and then click the **Yellow** color in the first row under Standard Colors. You want the bullet to be a little larger.

▶ **3.** In the Size box, drag to select **100**, and then type **120**. The bullet will be 120% of the size of the text. See Figure 3-37.

Figure 3-37   Bullet tab in the Bullets and Numbering dialog box

set the size of the bullet as a percentage of the size of the text

click to change the color of bullets

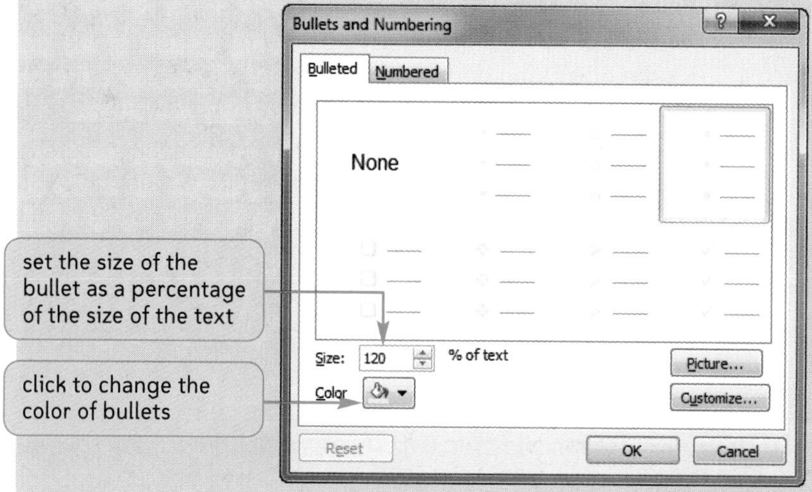

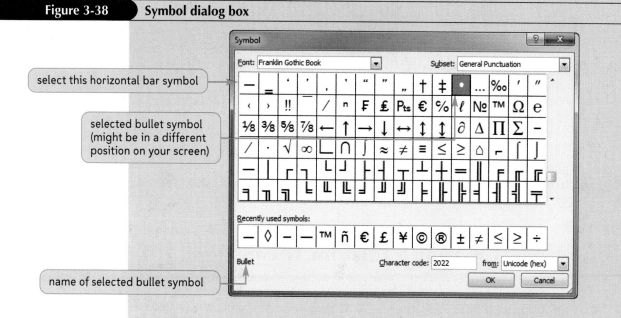

4. Click the **OK** button to close the dialog box.

Now you will change the third-level bullets. For this bullet, you use a bullet symbol in the Symbol dialog box.

To change the third-level bullets to a nonstandard bullet symbol:

1. Click anywhere in the "Third level" bulleted item, and then open the Bulleted tab in the Bullets and Numbering dialog box. You want to use a bullet symbol, but you want to use a dash, which does not appear in the gallery of standard bullet symbols.

2. Click the **Customize** button. The Symbol dialog box opens. The bullet symbol is selected and is identified at the bottom-left of the dialog box. See Figure 3-38.

Figure 3-38   Symbol dialog box

select this horizontal bar symbol

selected bullet symbol (might be in a different position on your screen)

name of selected bullet symbol

TIP

You can scroll through the entire list of symbols, or you can click the Subset arrow to move to a subset of symbols. You can also change the symbols shown by using the Font arrow to change the current font.

▶ **3.** Scroll up or down a few rows to locate and then click the **Horizontal Bar** symbol. At the bottom of the dialog box, the name of the symbol, Horizontal Bar, appears.

Trouble? If the name of the symbol at the bottom of the dialog box is Em Dash, click the other long horizontal bar symbol. If you can't find the Horizontal Bar symbol, use the Em Dash or any other symbol you choose.

▶ **4.** Click the **OK** button. The horizontal bar symbol you selected now appears as the last symbol in the Bullets gallery on the Bulleted tab in the Bullets and Numbering box, and it is highlighted to indicate that it is the current bullet symbol.

▶ **5.** Click the **OK** button. The dialog box closes and the new symbol appears next to the "Third level" item. See Figure 3-39. You don't have any fourth- or fifth-level bulleted items, so you do not need to make any changes to these bullet styles.

Figure 3-39 **Slide Master with modified bullets**

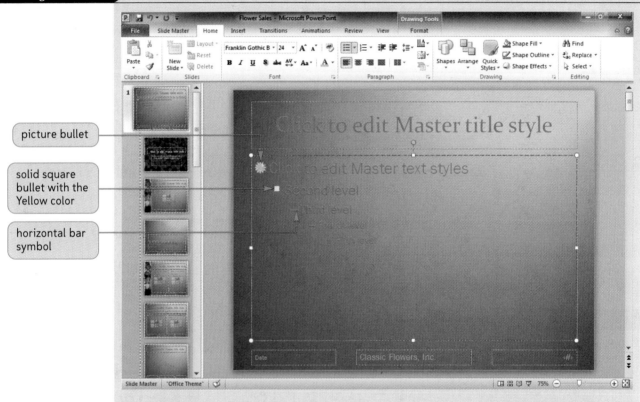

picture bullet

solid square bullet with the Yellow color

horizontal bar symbol

▶ **6.** Close Slide Master view, and then display **Slide 2** ("Our Products") in the Slide pane. You see the new first- and second-level bullets on Slide 2.

▶ **7.** Save your changes.

Sophie likes the way the new bullets look. She wants to save the presentation as a custom theme.

Creating a Custom Theme

In earlier tutorials, you applied built-in themes by clicking the Design tab on the Ribbon to display the Themes group, and then selecting the desired theme. For this presentation, you started with a presentation using the Office theme, and then made changes to customize the theme colors, theme fonts, slide background, and bullet styles—essentially creating a custom theme to suit your needs. You can save this custom theme so that you can apply it to other presentations.

Sophie wants you to save the formatting changes you made to the Flower Sales presentation as a custom theme. When you do so, the custom theme becomes an **Office theme file**, with the filename extension ".thmx". You can use an Office theme file to apply a custom theme to an existing PowerPoint presentation, or you can create a new presentation based on the custom theme.

INSIGHT

Understanding the Difference Between a Theme and a Template

When you save a PowerPoint presentation as a theme, only the design elements (including background graphics) are saved, not the content, that is, not the text or objects applied to the slides. If you want to save a theme with the contents for use in other presentations, you would instead save the presentation as a PowerPoint template.

The default location for saving a custom theme is the Document Themes folder located in the Templates folder, but you can save a theme in any folder. If you save a custom theme in the Document Themes folder, it will appear in the Themes gallery. If you save a theme to a different folder, you can apply it to a presentation by clicking the More button in the Themes group on the Design tab, and then clicking Browse for Themes. You can also use this command to apply a theme from any existing presentation, not just a theme file.

REFERENCE

Saving a Custom Theme

- Click the Design tab on the Ribbon.
- In the Themes group, click the More button, and then click Save Current Theme to open the Save Current Theme dialog box with Office Theme already selected in the Save as type box; or click the File tab, in the navigation bar click Save As to open the Save As dialog box, click the Save as type arrow, and then click Office Theme.
- Navigate to the desired location, type a filename, and then click the Save button.

You've saved your work as a normal PowerPoint presentation. Now you'll save it as a custom theme as Sophie requested, and then test it by creating a new presentation based on this theme.

To save the presentation as a theme:

1. Click the **Design** tab on the Ribbon.

2. In the Themes group, click the **More** button, and then below the gallery, click **Save Current Theme**. The Save Current Theme dialog box opens with Office Theme selected as the Save as type, and the current folder in the Address bar changes to Document Themes. See Figure 3-40.

Figure 3-40 Save Current Theme dialog box

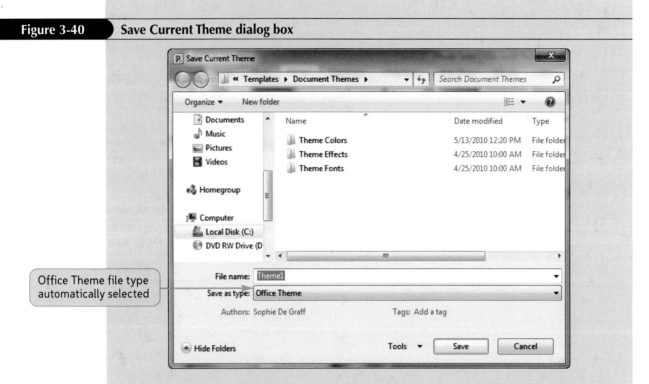

Office Theme file type automatically selected

3. Click the **Save as type** arrow. The Save as type list opens. The list shows only one file type because by clicking the Save Current Theme command, you restricted the file type to the Office Theme file type.

4. Edit the text in the File name box to **Flower – Custom**, and then click the **Save** button. Because you didn't change the default folder, the theme will be listed as a Custom theme in the Themes gallery. Now you will save the theme file in the same location where you saved the Flower Sales presentation (in the PowerPoint3\ Tutorial folder included with your Data Files). This time, you will use the Save As command to save the theme.

5. Click the **File** tab, and then click **Save As** in the navigation bar. The Save As dialog box opens.

6. Click the **Save as type** arrow. A list of file types opens. See Figure 3-41.

Figure 3-41	Save as type list in the Save As dialog box

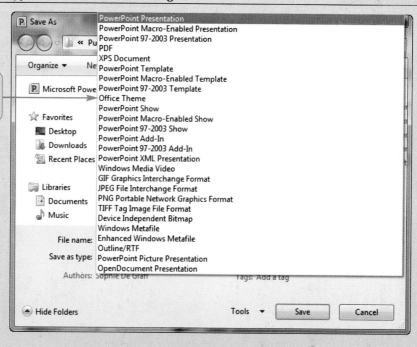

click Office Theme to save presentation theme as a custom theme

7. In the list, click **Office Theme**. The current folder changes to the Document Themes folder.

8. Navigate to the PowerPoint3\Tutorial folder included with your Data Files, edit the text in the File name box to **Flower**, and then click the **Save** button. PowerPoint saves the file as a theme in the folder you specified.

You have now created a custom theme that Sophie and others can use with any new presentation. You decide to apply the saved theme to the Flower Sales presentation so that the custom theme name appears in the status bar.

To apply the custom theme in the Themes gallery to the presentation:

1. Click the **Design** tab on the Ribbon.

2. In the Themes group, click the **More** button. The Themes gallery opens. A new section labeled Custom appears above the Built-In section, and the custom theme you created and saved in the Document Themes folder appears in this section.

3. In the Custom section, point to the theme. The ScreenTip identifies this theme as Flower – Custom. See Figure 3-42.

Figure 3-42 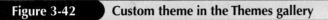 **Custom theme in the Themes gallery**

custom theme saved in the Themes folder

ScreenTip

click to browse for themes not stored in the Themes folder

▶ **4.** Click the **Flower – Custom** theme. The Flower theme is applied to the presentation. The slides don't change much, because you had already applied the changes to the slides, but the theme name in the status bar now is Flower – Custom. See Figure 3-43.

Figure 3-43 **Custom theme applied to the presentation**

custom theme name

▶ **5.** Save your changes.

PROSKILLS

Problem Solving: How Should You Create Your Own Theme?

PowerPoint comes with professional designed themes, theme colors, and theme fonts. The various combinations give you hundreds of professional designs from which to choose. If you decide you need to create a custom theme, you can start "from scratch" and assign every theme color and create your own combination of fonts. But unless you are a graphics designer, consider creating a custom theme as was done in this tutorial—by starting with a theme or theme colors that most closely match the colors you want to use, and then selectively customize some of the colors, fonts, or styles. By creating a theme this way, you can take advantage of the professional designs available in PowerPoint to create your own custom look.

You decide to test your new custom theme on a new presentation. This time, you'll apply the theme you saved to the PowerPoint3\Tutorial folder.

To create a new presentation using the custom theme:

1. Click the **File** tab to open Backstage view.

2. Click **New** in the navigation bar, and then with the Blank presentation button selected in the Available Templates and Themes section, click the **Create** button. PowerPoint creates a new presentation with the default Office Theme applied.

3. Click the **Design** tab on the Ribbon.

4. In the Themes group, click the **More** button. You could click the custom theme in the Custom section of the gallery, but instead, you'll apply the theme that you saved to the PowerPoint3\Tutorial folder.

5. Below the Themes gallery, click **Browse for Themes**. The Choose Theme or Themed Document dialog box opens listing presentations, templates, and theme files stored in this folder. You can choose any of the PowerPoint file types to apply the theme used in that presentation.

6. Navigate to the PowerPoint3\Tutorial folder included with your Data Files, and then double-click the Office Theme file **Flower**. The custom theme Flower is applied to the new presentation.

7. Close the presentation without saving it. Keep Flower Sales open in PowerPoint.

When you save a theme to the Document Themes folder, it is available to anyone who works on that computer. You can easily delete a custom theme.

To delete the custom theme from the Themes gallery:

1. In the Themes group, click the **More** button. The Themes gallery opens again.

2. Right-click the **Flower – Custom** theme, and then click **Delete** on the shortcut menu. A warning dialog box opens asking if you want to delete this theme.

3. Click the **Yes** button. The dialog box closes.

4. In the Themes group, click the **More** button. The custom theme you saved to the Document Themes folder is no longer listed.

5. Click a blank area of the window to close the gallery without making a selection.

Applying a Different Theme to Individual Slides

Normally, all your slides in one presentation will have the same theme. On occasion, however, you might want to apply a different theme to only one, or a few, of the slides in your presentation. Sophie wants you to change the theme for Slide 8, "Contact Us," so that this slide stands out from the others because it lists the contact information.

To apply a different theme to Slide 8:

▶ 1. Display **Slide 8** ("Contact Us") in the Slide pane.

▶ 2. In the Themes group on the Design tab, click the **More** button.

▶ 3. Right-click the **Opulent** theme (the third theme in the fourth row under "Built-In"), and then click **Apply to Selected Slides**. Because Slide 8 is the only selected slide, the Opulent design theme is applied only to that slide. The title text overlaps the panel of flowers on the slide master. You can change the layout to one that doesn't have the flower panel on its master. Remember, the photo panel appears only on the Title and Content and Two Content slides.

▶ 4. Click the **Home** tab on the Ribbon.

▶ 5. In the Slides group, click the **Layout** button. The Layout gallery appears. Notice that it now contains two sections, one for each theme used in the presentation. See Figure 3-44.

Figure 3-44 **Layout menu when two themes are applied to a presentation**

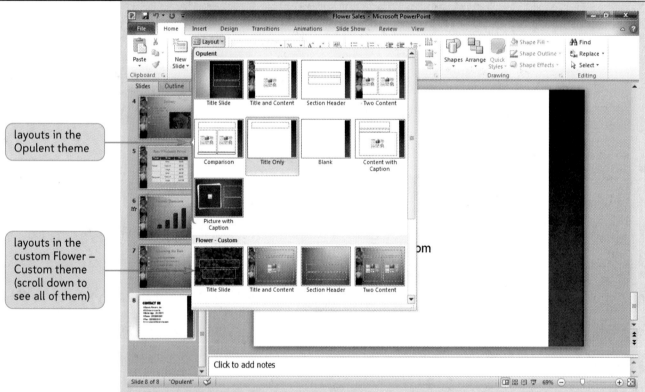

layouts in the Opulent theme

layouts in the custom Flower – Custom theme (scroll down to see all of them)

▶ 6. In the Opulent section, click the **Title Only** layout. The Opulent Title Only layout is applied to the current slide, and the flower panel photo is removed.

▶ 7. Click anywhere on the bulleted list, and then drag the left middle sizing handle to the right approximately one-half inch so that the left edge of the content text box is aligned with the left edge of the slide title.

▶ 8. Save your changes.

If you apply a second theme to a presentation, slide masters for that theme are applied to the presentation. You can see the second set of masters if you switch to Slide Master view.

To examine the slide masters for the second theme:

1. Switch to Slide Master view. In the pane on the left, the Title Only Layout master is selected, and "Opulent" appears in the status bar.

2. In the pane on the left, drag the scroll box about halfway up in the scroll bar, and then click the **Opulent Slide Master** thumbnail. See Figure 3-45. The number 2 next to the Opulent Slide Master indicates that the masters following this slide are associated with the second theme used in the presentation.

Figure 3-45   Slide Master view when two themes are applied to a presentation

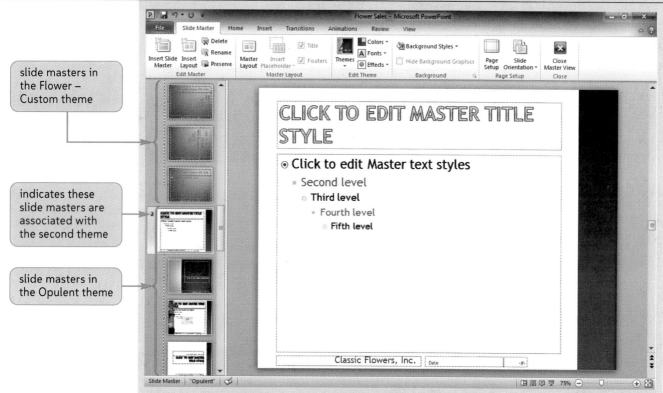

slide masters in the Flower – Custom theme

indicates these slide masters are associated with the second theme

slide masters in the Opulent theme

3. Scroll to the top of the left pane, and then click the **Flower – Custom Slide Master** thumbnail. Notice that the number 1 appears next to this Slide Master. When a presentation uses multiple themes, the themes are listed in Slide Master view in alphabetical order.

4. Scroll back down until the **Opulent Slide Master** is the top thumbnail in the left pane, and then click and examine, in turn, the **Title Slide Layout** master, the **Title and Content Layout** master, and the **Two Content Layout** master. Notice that the flower panel was picked up from the Flowers – Custom theme, but the text boxes were not resized. Since none of the slides in the presentation use these layouts, you don't need to fix these masters.

5. Close Slide Master view.

6. Display the presentation in Slide Sorter view at 90% zoom. Compare your screen to Figure 3-46.

Figure 3-46   **Final presentation in Slide Sorter view**

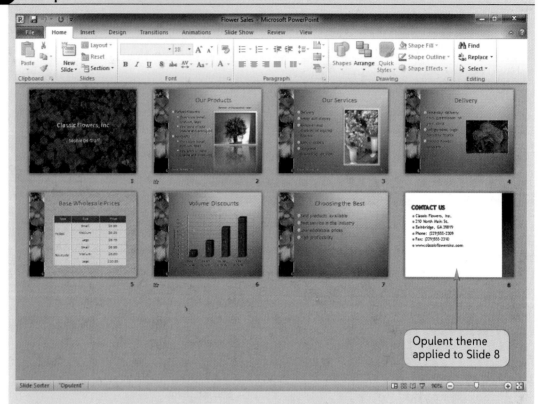

Opulent theme applied to Slide 8

▶ **7.** Save your changes, and then submit the finished presentation to your instructor, either in printed or electronic form, as requested.

▶ **8.** Close the presentation.

Sophie looked over your presentation, and she is happy with it. She thinks that the customized theme elements enhance her presentation and will help identify her company for her audience.

Session 3.2 Quick Check

REVIEW

1. How do you change theme fonts?
2. Once you have created a set of theme colors in the Create New Theme Colors dialog box, what should you do so that they are available for applying to other presentations?
3. True or False. You can delete a custom theme color set.
4. How do you apply a textured background to a slide?
5. True or False. You can change a bullet to a picture bullet.
6. Describe how you save a custom theme as an Office Theme file.
7. True or False. You can apply only one theme at a time to a presentation.

Review Assignments

Data Files needed for the Review Assignments: Bulbs.avi, Farm.avi, HotSprings.pptx, HSProposal.pptx, Knock.wav, PurpleFlowers.jpg

The chief horticulturalist for Classic Flowers, Inc., Kathleen Bahlmann, recently became aware that a particular farm in southern Georgia is for sale. The farm is special because it has a natural hot spring on its premises. The farm owner has set up a system to use water from the spring to heat his barns during the winter. Now that the farm is for sale, Kathleen sees this as an opportunity to improve the profitability of Classic Flowers by purchasing the farm, converting the barns to greenhouses, and using the water from the hot spring to heat the greenhouses. This has the potential of saving millions of dollars on heating expenses over the next several years. Kathleen wants to present her idea to the board of directors of Classic Flowers, and she has asked you to help her create the PowerPoint presentation. She has already created a couple of PowerPoint presentation files; one contains a title slide with some elements that she wants to use for a design theme, and the other contains some of the text that she wants in the final presentation. Complete the following steps:

1. Open the file **HSProposal**, located in the PowerPoint3\Review folder included with your Data Files, change the subtitle from "Kathleen Bahlmann" to your name, and then save the file as **Hot Springs Proposal** in the same PowerPoint3\Review folder.

2. Insert Slides 2 through 8 (that is, all but the first slide) from the file **HotSprings**, located in the PowerPoint3\Review folder.

3. In Slide 8 ("Farm for Sale"), add the movie **Farm** located in the PowerPoint3\Review folder. Set it to start Automatically, and loop until stopped, and set the poster frame to the frame at the three-second mark.

4. Apply the Rounded Diagonal Corner, White style to the video, and then apply the Half Reflection, touching reflection effect.

5. In Slide 7 ("Sample Bulbs"), add the movie **Bulbs**, located in the PowerPoint3\Review folder. Trim the video so that it starts at the 3-second mark and ends at the 24-second mark. Mute the volume.

6. In Slide 2 ("Opportunity Knocks"), insert the sound clip **Knock**, located in the PowerPoint3\Review folder. Set it to start automatically, and hide the icon during the slide show.

7. In Slide 3 ("Problem with a Solution"), insert the music file **Maid with the Flaxen Hair** from the Sample Music folder included with Windows 7. (*Hint:* If you are using Windows Vista or XP, insert any music file from the Sample Music folder. Try to find one without vocals.) Set the music to play across slides, set it to loop until it is stopped, change the volume to low, and hide the icon during the slide show.

8. In Slide 8 ("Farm For Sale"), change the Play animation so that it starts with the previous action. (*Hint:* Click the zero animation sequence icon.)

9. In Slide 6 ("Proposed Flats For Sale") insert a table with three columns and seven rows. Insert the following labels and data in the table:

Type	Size	Price
Flowers	Small flat	$5.29
	Large flat	$8.49
Vegetables	Small flat	$6.59
	Large flat	$9.69
Herbs	Small flat	$5.99
	Large flat	$8.99

10. Apply the Dark Style 1 – Accent 1 table style with a header row and banded rows, and then change the color of the text in all the rows except the header row to Dark Green, Text 1.

11. Modify the table layout by changing the width of each column in the table to approximately two inches wide and merging the cells containing "Flowers," "Vegetables," and "Herbs" with the empty cells below each of them.

12. Resize the table so it is approximately eight inches wide and four-and-a-half inches high, change the font size of the text in the table to 28 points, and then drag the table to center it on the slide.

13. Center the text in the cells in the first row, and then vertically center the text in the cells in the first column in all the rows except the first one.

14. In Slide 5 ("Heating Costs and Profits over Five Years"), insert a chart using the 3-D Clustered Column style.

15. In the Excel spreadsheet for the PowerPoint chart, do the following:
    a. Delete column D.
    b. Change cell B1 to **Heating Costs (in millions)**.
    c. Change cell C1 to **Profits (in millions)**.
    d. Change the labels in cells A2 through A5 to the years **2009** through **2012**, and then add **2013** in cell A6. Click the OK button in the warning dialog box that appears.
    e. In cells B2 through B6 (below Heating Costs), replace the current cell contents with **1.8**, **2.2**, **2.7**, **3.3**, **4.1**.
    f. In cells C2 through C6 (below Profits), replace the current cell contents with **3.2**, **3.1**, **2.9**, **2.7**, **2.5**.
    g. Drag to select cells B2 through C6. On the Home tab in the Excel window, click the Number button, and then click the Accounting Number Format button to format these numbers as currency.

16. Close the Excel window, and then in the chart, show the data labels, and add vertical major gridlines.

17. Animate the chart with the entrance animation Split, and then add the Teeter emphasis animation to the chart.

18. Increase the speed of the Split animation so it takes .25 seconds, and then increase the speed of the Teeter animation so it takes .5 seconds.

19. Change the theme fonts to the Solstice fonts and the Theme colors to the Perspective colors.

20. Modify the theme colors by changing the Text/Background – Light 1 color to the Dark Purple, Accent 4, Darker 25% theme color, and changing the Text/Background – Light 2 color to the White, Text 1 color. Save the new color set using the name **HotSprings**.

21. Change the background style so it has a gradient by applying the background style Style 9.

22. Apply the Stationery textured background to Slide 5 ("Heating Costs and Profits over Five Years").

23. Add the PurpleFlowers picture located in the PowerPoint3\Review folder to the background of the Title Slide Layout master. Adjust the brightness to -40% and the contrast to +40%, and change the color of the subtitle to Yellow.

24. In the Office Theme Slide Master, do the following:
    a. Change the first-level bullet to a picture of a yellow-gold square.
    b. Change the second-level bullet to the Arrow Bullets symbol, and then change the color of the bullet to Brown, Accent 2.
    c. Change the third-level bullet to the Lozenge symbol—a diamond outline located in the last visible row in the Symbol dialog box—and change the size of the bullet to 90% of the size of the text.

25. Save your changes to the presentation, and then save the theme to the PowerPoint3\
    Review folder using the filename **Flower2**.
26. Apply the custom theme Flower2 to the presentation.
27. Change the theme of Slide 4 ("The Culprit") to the Executive theme.
28. View the slide show in Slide Show view. Remember to click the Bulbs video on Slide
    7 to play it. If you see any errors in the presentation, press the Esc key to end the
    slide show, fix the error, and then start the slide show again from the current slide.
29. Delete the custom color set HotSprings.
30. Submit the presentation in printed or electronic format, as directed by your instructor.

*Apply the skills
you learned
to create a
presentation for
an eBay store.*

APPLY

Case Problem 1

Data Files needed for this Case Problem: Case.pptx, CompCase.avi, JustInCase.pptx

Just in Case   Jergen Oleson is a small-electronics aficionado. He had the latest in electronic gadgets—MP3 player, cell phone, palm computer, laptop, GPS receiver, digital
camera, and so forth. But he was always frustrated in trying to find proper cases for these
items. He was surprised, in fact, by the dearth of companies that sold cases for electronic
gadgets. So he decided to start his own company, which he called Just in Case, and to
sell his products through his own eBay store. He now asks you to help him create a
theme for his PowerPoint presentations and to start creating a presentation that he will
give to potential manufacturers of his cases. Complete the following steps:

1. Open the presentation file **JustInCase**, located in the PowerPoint3\Case1 folder
   included with your Data Files. This is a file with the Just in Case logo placed on three
   of the slide masters and with modifications to the size, location, and text justification
   of some of the placeholders. You'll continue creating the Office Theme file from here.
2. Change the theme fonts to the Apex fonts, and change the theme colors to the
   Elemental theme colors.
3. Create a new set of theme colors by changing the Text/Background – Dark 1 color to
   White, Text 1, and then changing the Text/Background – Light 1 color to a Dark Blue
   color by using the More Colors command, and selecting the last cell in the top row
   of the color diagram in the Colors dialog box. Save the theme colors using the name
   JustInCase.
4. Change the background style to Style 5.
5. In the Office Theme Slide Master, do the following:
   a. Change the first-level bullet to a yellow filled-square bullet.
   b. Change the second-level bullet to a filled round bullet colored Teal, Accent 5 and
      sized 110% of the size of the normal bullet.
   c. Change the third-level bullet to a white, hollow, round bullet.
   d. Change the second-level text color to Yellow.
6. Save the presentation as an Office Theme file to the PowerPoint3\Case1 folder using
   the filename **Just in Case**. Close the file without saving it.
7. Open a new, blank presentation and apply the Just in Case theme. Delete the
   JustInCase theme color set.
8. On the title page, insert the title **Case Manufacturing and Order Fulfillment
   Services**. Insert your name as the subtitle.
9. Save the presentation in the PowerPoint3\Case1 folder using the filename **Case
   Manufacturing**.
10. Insert into this presentation file all six slides from the file **Case**, located in the
    PowerPoint3\Case1 folder.

11. In Slide 3, insert the movie **CompCase**, so that it plays when clicked during a slide show, and then apply the video style Reflected Rounded Rectangle. Set the poster frame to the frame at the .5-second mark, and rewind the video when it is finished playing.

12. In Slide 6, insert a chart as follows:

   a. Insert the Line with Markers chart, in the Line section in the Insert Chart dialog box.

   b. Change "Category 1" through "Category 4" to **2010**, **2011**, **2012**, and **2013** to represent the years.

   c. Change "Series 1" to **Sales (in $Thousands)** and "Series 2" to **Profits (in $Thousands)**.

   d. In the Sales column (cells B2 through B5), insert the values **850**, **1000**, **1100**, **1250**.

   e. In the Profits column (cells C2 through C5), insert the values **80**, **180**, **280**, **400**.

   f. Delete column D.

13. Change the Chart Style to Style 28.

14. In Slide 7, add the Denim textured background.

15. In Slide 2, animate the picture to enter the screen using the Fly In entrance effect, then add the Teeter emphasis effect.

16. Change the speed of the Fly In animation to .75 seconds.

17. To all the slides, apply the Push slide transition.

18. Run the slide show, and make any needed corrections. Save your changes.

19. Submit the presentation in printed or electronic format, as directed by your instructor.

Go beyond the skills you've learned to create a self-running presentation for a photographer.

CHALLENGE

Case Problem 2

Data Files needed for this Case Problem: Wedding01.jpg through Wedding10.jpg

Ultimate Slideshows   Sharah-Renae Wabbinton has a home business shooting or scanning photos for special occasions—primarily graduations, weddings, family reunions, and religious events—and preparing self-running, animated slide shows using the Photo Album feature in PowerPoint. She gives you 10 photographs from a recent wedding, and has asked you to prepare not only a PowerPoint presentation using those photos but also a custom Office theme for her business.

Complete the following steps:

1. Start a new, blank presentation (using the Office theme).

⊕**EXPLORE**   2. Change the background style to a gradient fill, with the preset colors design called Peacock. Apply this background to all slides. (*Hint*: Use the Preset colors button in the Format Background dialog box.)

3. Change the theme fonts to the Waveform theme font set.

⊕**EXPLORE**   4. In the Office Theme Slide Master, change all the text placeholders to white text, and then draw a rectangle that is the same shape and almost the same size as the entire slide, so that a white border appears between the rectangle and the outer edges of the slide approximately one-quarter of an inch from the edge of the slides. (*Hint*: Use the rectangle Shape tool to draw the rectangle so that it completely covers the slide of the Slide Master, and then, while holding down the Alt key, drag the resize handles to slightly reduce the size of the rectangle on all four sides.)

⊕**EXPLORE**   5. Set the Shape Fill of the rectangle to No Fill, and set the Shape Outline to a white, 3-point line.

⊕**EXPLORE**   6. With the Slide Master still in the slide pane, set the slide transition to any transition in the Exciting section.

⊕**EXPLORE**   7. Set up the slide show to advance automatically from one slide to the next, with about 5 seconds for each slide. (*Hint*: With the Slide Master still in the slide pane, on the Transitions tab in the Timing group, deselect the On Mouse Click check box, and then select the After check box. Change the After time from 00:00.00 to 00:05.00)

8. In Normal view, save the presentation as an Office theme named **Wedding** in the PowerPoint3\Case2 folder included with the Data Files. Save the presentation again as an Office theme named **Wedding** in the default Document Themes folder.

9. Close the current presentation without saving it, and then create a new, blank presentation.

EXPLORE 10. In the Images group on the Insert tab, use the Photo Album button to insert all 10 photographs, **Wedding01** through **Wedding10**, located in the PowerPoint3\Case2 folder. Do not close the Photo Album dialog box. (*Hint*: In the Photo Album dialog box, click the File/Disk button, navigate to the folder containing the pictures, select all the pictures, and then click the Insert button.)

EXPLORE 11. With the Photo Album dialog box still open, in the Album Layout section, set the Picture layout to 1 picture (meaning, 1 picture per slide). Set the Frame shape to Simple Frame, White. Apply the Wedding theme you created and saved in the PowerPoint3\Case2 folder. Click the Create button at the bottom of the Photo Album dialog box to create the photo album. (*Hint*: If you already closed the Photo Album dialog box, click the Photo Album button arrow, and then click Edit Photo Album.)

12. In Slide 1, change the title to **Curtis and Cassandra**. The name in the subtitle is the name of the registered user on your computer. If your name does not appear as the subtitle, change the name in the subtitle to your own.

13. In Slides 2 through 11, apply a different Entrance animation effect to each photograph. Change the Start setting for each animation to With Previous, and change the duration to two seconds.

EXPLORE 14. Set up the presentation to loop automatically so that it starts over when it reaches the end. (*Hint*: On the Slide Show tab, in the Set Up group, click the Set Up Slide Show button, and then click the Loop continuously until 'Esc' check box.)

15. Start the slide show and make sure that it runs on its own and continues to run until you press the Esc key.

16. Save the presentation as **Wedding Slideshow** in the PowerPoint3\Case2 folder.

17. Delete the Wedding custom theme from the Themes gallery.

18. Submit the presentation in printed or electronic format, as directed by your instructor.

Case Problem 3

Use the skills you learned to create a custom theme and presentation for a cartography company.

CREATE

Data Files needed for this Case Problem: MntHike.avi, MntMap.jpg, MntPlateau1.jpg, MntPlateau2.jpg

Cartography Research Systems Barrett Worthington is founder and president of Cartography Research Systems (CRS), a company that maps geological formations and nearby areas. Sample geological areas include glaciers, caves, canyons, river beds, and wilderness sites. CRS clients mostly are energy and mineral exploration companies, but they also include the National Parks Service and land developers. Barrett has asked you to create and save a design theme that his company can use for their presentations to clients. He then asks you to help him prepare a portion of a presentation to one of his clients, Eckstein Energy.

Complete the following steps:

1. Create a new presentation, change the theme colors to Flow, and then modify them as shown in Figure 3-47. Your colors don't have to be exactly the same as those shown in the figure. Just try to select each theme color as close as you can. Save the theme colors as **CRScolors**.

Figure 3-47   **Selections for custom theme colors**

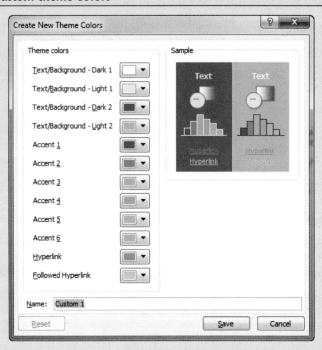

2. Use the slide masters to apply the background style, font attributes, and bullets shown in Figure 3-48. If you're not sure of a particular color, just pick any theme color that is close.

Figure 3-48   **Selections for background style, font attributes, and bullets**

Dark blue font color and bold

picture bullet

Filled Square

Style 6 Background Style

Click to edit Master title style

Click to edit Master text styles
- Second level
  - Third level
    - Fourth level
      - Fifth level

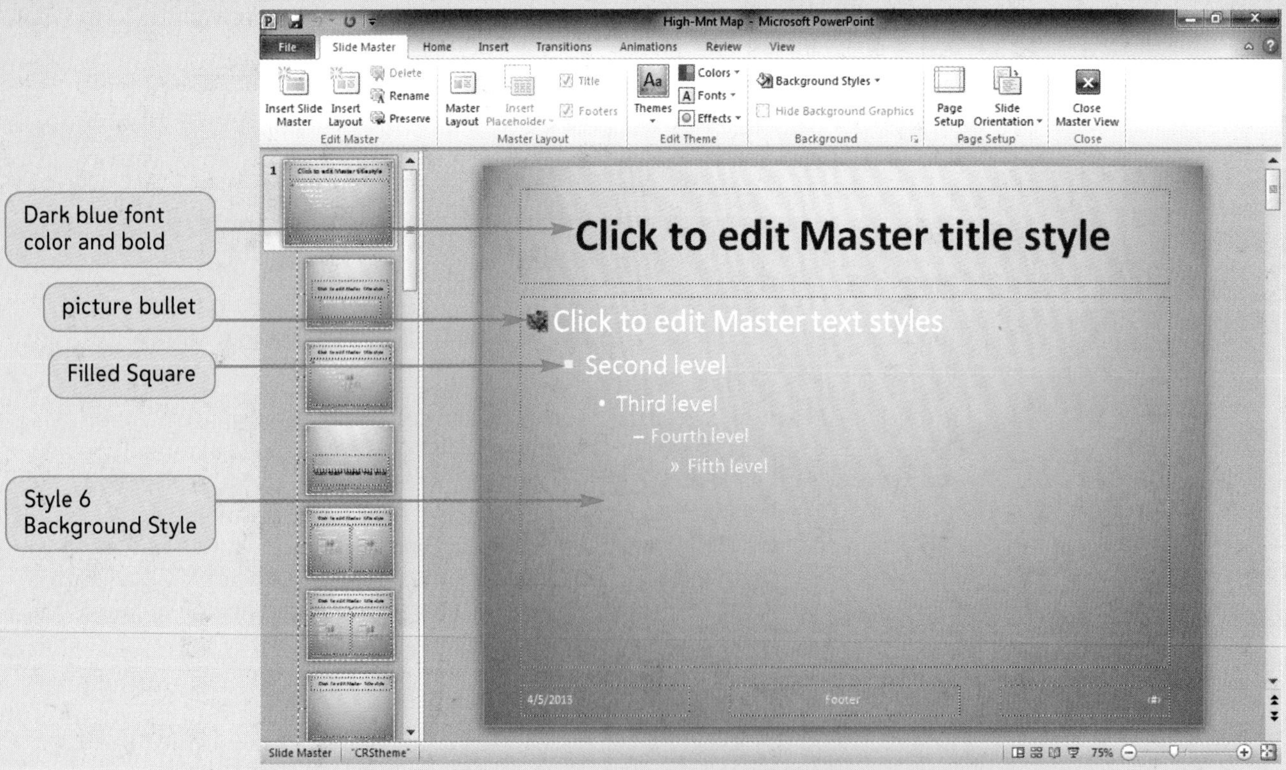

3. Save the file as an Office Theme file in the PowerPoint3\Case3 folder using the file-name **CRStheme**, and then close the presentation without saving changes.

4. Start a new PowerPoint presentation, and then apply the CRStheme you created. Save the presentation in the PowerPoint3\Case3 folder using the filename **High-Mnt Map**. Delete the CRScolors theme color set.

5. Add content to the new presentation, as shown in Figure 3-49. Refer to the following as you add the content:

a. In Slide 1, add the title shown, but use your own name for the subtitle.

b. In Slide 2, insert the photos **MntPlateau1** and **MntPlateau2**, and then apply the picture style called Snip Diagonal Corner, White.

c. In Slide 3, add the video **MntHike**. Set the poster frame to the frame at the 13-second mark. Trim the video so that it ends just before it fades to black, at approximately the 18-second mark. Set the video to play automatically, and to play full screen.

EXPLORE

d. Crop off the black borders on the video. To do this, select the video, and then in the Size group on the Video Tools Format tab, click the Crop button. Drag the middle crop handles on the top, bottom, and sides of the video to remove the black borders.

e. In Slide 4, insert the picture **MntMap**, and then apply the picture style called Metal Frame.

f. In Slide 4, insert, rotate, and then color the text boxes that label the reservoir, springs, creeks, and trails, as shown.

g. In Slide 5, create an elevation chart using the Line type chart format called Line with Markers. In the Excel window, first, delete columns C and D, then drag the lower right corner of the blue border down so the blue border surrounds cells A1 through B16. Enter the following data in this table:

	Altitude feet		Altitude feet
0	6800	8	8200
1	7400	9	8800
2	8200	10	8400
3	9500	11	9400
4	8800	12	7600
5	8000	13	7200
6	7400	14	6800
7	7700		

h. Remove the legend, and then add axis titles to the horizontal and vertical axes, as shown on Slide 5 in Figure 3-49. Along the primary horizontal (x) axis, the text is **Miles from Trailhead**, and along the primary vertical (y) axis, the text is **Elevation above Sea Level (feet)**.

i. In Slide 6, after you enter the information, apply the textured background called Medium Wood.

Figure 3-49 CRS presentation content

High-Mountain Map for Eckstein Energy, Jackson, WY

Barrett Worthington

1

High Mountain Terrain

2

3

Geological Map

4

Altitude Profile of Jeep Trail

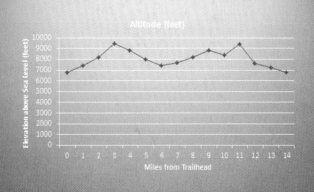

5

Contact Information

Barrett Worthington
- President, Cartography Research Systems
- 5412 Eagle Road
- Great Falls, MT 59403
- 406-555-8220

6

6. Animate all the text boxes on Slide 4 using the Appear entrance effect.

7. On Slide 2 ("High Mountain Terrain"), apply an entrance animation to each photograph.

8. On Slide 2 ("High Mountain Terrain"), add audio clip art of a camera shutter sound. (*Hint:* In the Media group on the Insert tab, click the Audio button arrow, and then click Clip Art Audio. To find a camera sound, you need to be connected to the Internet, and the Include Office.com content check box must be selected. If you are not connected to the Internet, use another sound.)

EXPLORE

9. Change the Start setting for the Play animation of the camera sound to With Previous, and then change the order of the selected animation so it has the same animation sequence number as the first photograph. (*Hint:* With the animation selected, click the Move Earlier button in the Timing group on the Animations tab as many times as needed.)

10. Select the sound icon, and then add a second Play animation. Change its start to With Previous.

11. Run the slide show, and correct any errors.

12. Save your changes, and then submit the presentation in electronic or printed form, as requested.

Use the skills you learned to create a presentation about a collection for a volunteer group.

CREATE

Case Problem 4

There are no Data Files needed for this Case Problem.

Cabot Collectibles Cabot Collectibles is a group of volunteer collectors who create PowerPoint presentations about personal collections. They make these presentations available to anyone who wants to present information on collectibles to schools, churches, civic organizations, clubs, and so forth. They rely on collectors to prepare the PowerPoint presentations. Complete the following steps

1. Select a type of collectible—stamps, coins, foreign currency, baseball cards, jewelry, comic books, artwork, rocks, dolls, figurines, chess sets, or almost anything else.

2. Plan your presentation so the audience learns basic information about your chosen collectible and sees pictures, with descriptions, of sample items from the collection.

3. Acquire pictures or a video of sample items. You can take the pictures yourself with a digital camera, take the pictures with a film camera and scan the photographs, scan flat items directly (stamps, bills, cards, book covers, and so forth), or get pictures from the Web.

4. Gather information about the items depicted in your graphics. You might want to include some of the following—name of item, age of item, origin (purchase location or place of manufacture), date of purchase, dimensions, and special characteristics (handmade, natural dyes, first edition, and so forth).

5. Create a custom theme appropriate for your presentation. In selecting theme fonts and theme colors, take into account the nature of the collection and the common colors found in the graphics that you're going to include. Your theme should include the following:

    a. Custom theme colors

    b. At least one graphic—logo, picture, ready-made shape (rectangle, circle, triangle, and so forth), or textured background

    c. A custom set of bullets, including a picture bullet for the first-level bulleted items

    d. Progressive disclosure, with dimming, of the bulleted lists

6. Create a new presentation based on your custom theme.

7. Include a title slide, at least two slides with bulleted lists, and at least six slides with pictures of collectibles.

8. Apply slide transitions to your slide presentation.

9. Animate at least one graphic with two animations.

 EXPLORE

10. If you have access to a microphone on your computer, create at least one sound clip and insert it in your presentation. Keep the recording shorter than three seconds. For example, record your voice saying a hard-to-pronounce noun or a foreign word associated with a collectible item, or record a sound effect, like a knock on the door, a bell, or a whistle. (*Hint*: Use the Sound Recorder installed with Windows. Click the Start button, point to All Programs, click Accessories, and then click Sound Recorder. With your microphone ready, click the Start Recording button. When you're finished recording, click the Stop Recording button.)

11. Save the presentation in the PowerPoint3\Case4 folder using the filename **Collection**.

12. Save the theme in the PowerPoint3\Case4 folder using the filename **Collectible**.

13. Run the slide show and correct any errors. Save your changes.

14. Submit your presentation in electronic or printed form, as requested by your instructor.

SAM: Skills Assessment Manager

For current SAM information, including versions and content details, visit SAM Central (http://samcentral.course.com). If you have a SAM user profile, you may have access to hands-on instruction, practice, and assessment of the skills covered in this tutorial. Since various versions of SAM are supported throughout the life of this text, check with your instructor for the correct instructions and URL/Web site for accessing assignments.

ENDING DATA FILES

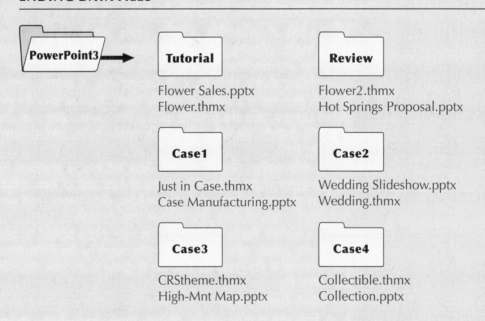

PowerPoint3 →

Tutorial
Flower Sales.pptx
Flower.thmx

Review
Flower2.thmx
Hot Springs Proposal.pptx

Case1
Just in Case.thmx
Case Manufacturing.pptx

Case2
Wedding Slideshow.pptx
Wedding.thmx

Case3
CRStheme.thmx
High-Mnt Map.pptx

Case4
Collectible.thmx
Collection.pptx

POWERPOINT

Integrating PowerPoint and Collaborating with Others

Presenting Clinical Trial Results

OBJECTIVES

Session 4.1
- Import, modify, and export a Word outline
- Import graphics
- Copy an object from another presentation
- Remove the background from photographs
- Embed and modify a table from Word
- Link and modify an Excel chart
- Create and edit hyperlinks
- Add action buttons

Session 4.2
- Apply a dynamic content transition
- Customize handout masters
- Mark slides during a slide show
- Work with comments and compare presentations
- Inspect documents for private or hidden data
- Identify features not supported by previous versions of PowerPoint
- Mark a presentation as final
- Save a presentation in other formats

Case | *Landon Pharmaceuticals Testing*

Alyssa Byington is director of customer service at Landon Pharmaceuticals Testing (LPT), a company that performs clinical trial testing of medicinal drugs developed by other pharmaceutical companies. Alyssa asks you to help create a PowerPoint presentation on the results of a clinical trial for a client, Pamerleau Biotechnologies. Pamerleau has developed a drug, with the code name Asperitol and code number PB0182, for the treatment of autoimmune diseases such as rheumatoid arthritis and lupus.

In this tutorial, you'll add data from Word and Excel files and hyperlinks to a presentation. You'll also apply dynamic content transitions, customize handout masters, and mark slides during a slide show. Finally, you'll learn how to add and review comments, compare presentations, and save a presentation in other formats.

STARTING DATA FILES

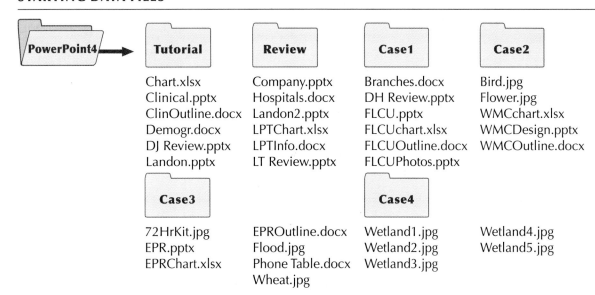

PowerPoint4 →

Tutorial
Chart.xlsx
Clinical.pptx
ClinOutline.docx
Demogr.docx
DJ Review.pptx
Landon.pptx

Review
Company.pptx
Hospitals.docx
Landon2.pptx
LPTChart.xlsx
LPTInfo.docx
LT Review.pptx

Case1
Branches.docx
DH Review.pptx
FLCU.pptx
FLCUchart.xlsx
FLCUOutline.docx
FLCUPhotos.pptx

Case2
Bird.jpg
Flower.jpg
WMCchart.xlsx
WMCDesign.pptx
WMCOutline.docx

Case3
72HrKit.jpg
EPR.pptx
EPRChart.xlsx

EPROutline.docx
Flood.jpg
Phone Table.docx
Wheat.jpg

Case4
Wetland1.jpg
Wetland2.jpg
Wetland3.jpg

Wetland4.jpg
Wetland5.jpg

SESSION 4.1 VISUAL OVERVIEW

source file (Word outline)

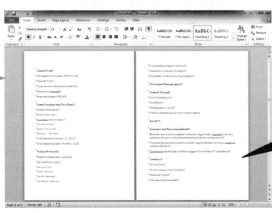

The program used to create the object is called the **source program**; the file that initially contains the object is called the **source file**.

When you **import** an object, a copy of an object created in the source program becomes part of the destination file; you can edit the object with the tools available in the destination program.

source file (Word table)

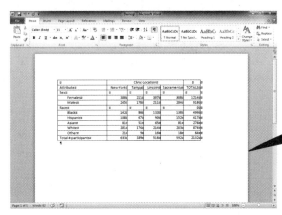

When you **embed** an object, a copy of the object along with a one-way connection to the source program become part of the destination file, and you can edit the object using the source program's commands. Changes made do not appear on the source file.

source program

You must have access to the source program to edit an embedded object; however, you do not need access to the source file.

source file (Excel chart)

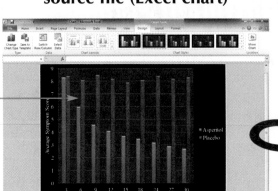

When linking an object, you must have access to the source file if you want to make changes to the source object.

SHARING DATA

**destination file
(Powerpoint presentation)**

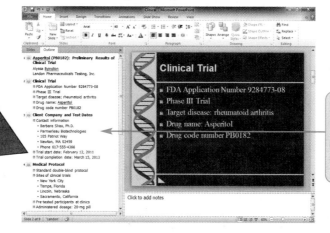

The program used to create the file where you want to insert the object is called the **destination program**; the file where you want to insert the object is called the **destination file**.

**destination file
(Powerpoint presentation)**

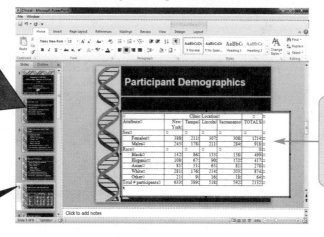

There is no connection between an embedded object and its source file; therefore, changes made to the object in the source file do not appear in the destination file.

When you **link** an object, a direct connection is created between the source and destination programs, so that the object exists in only one place—the source file—but the link displays the object in the destination file as well.

**destination file
(Powerpoint presentation)**

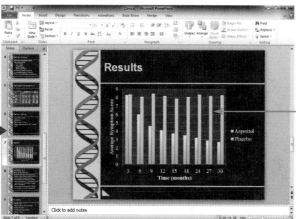

If you edit a linked object in the source file, the link ensures that the changes appear in the destination file.

Importing and Exporting a Word Outline

If your presentation contains quite a bit of text, it might be easier to create the outline of your presentation in Word, so that you can take advantage of the extensive text-editing features available in that program. Fortunately, if you create an outline in a Word document, you don't need to retype it in PowerPoint. You can import it directly into your presentation.

You can also use Word to create handouts. Although you can create handouts in PowerPoint, sometimes you might want to take advantage of Word's formatting commands to make the text easier to read. You might also want to use the presentation outline as the basis for a more detailed document. To do this, you can export the outline to a Word document.

Importing a Word Outline

As you know, when you work in the Outline tab in PowerPoint, each level-one heading (also called Heading 1 or A head) automatically becomes a slide title; each level-two heading (a Heading 2 or B head) automatically becomes a level-one bulleted paragraph; each level-three heading (a Heading 3 or C head) automatically becomes a level-two bulleted paragraph, and so forth. Similarly, Word lets you assign heading levels to text. To create text at the first level, you apply the built-in Heading 1 style; to create text at the second level, you apply the built-in Heading 2 style, and so forth.

Alyssa created a Word document in which she applied heading styles to create an outline with text at various levels. She asks you to import her outline into a PowerPoint presentation that she created with a custom theme named Landon.

To import the Word outline:

1. Open the file **Clinical** from the PowerPoint4\Tutorial folder included with your Data Files, and then save the file with the new filename **Clinical Report** to the same folder. The title slide appears on the screen with the name of the presenter, Alyssa Byington, in the subtitle text box. See Figure 4-1. Alyssa's custom theme includes the color scheme with a solid brown background, yellow title text, white body text, and a background graphic of a DNA double helix. Notice that the presentation includes only this one slide, and a footer identifying the company name and the slide number appears at the bottom of the slide.

Figure 4-1	Title slide of Clinical Report presentation

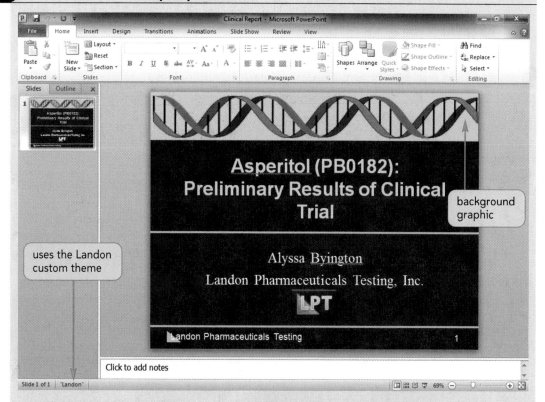

2. In the Slides group on the Home tab, click the **New Slide button arrow**, and then click **Slides from Outline**. The Insert Outline dialog box opens.

3. Navigate to the PowerPoint4\Tutorial folder included with your Data Files, click **ClinOutline**, and then click the **Insert** button. The Word outline is inserted as new slides after the current slide in the PowerPoint presentation, with all the level-one text becoming new slide titles. Slide 2 appears in the Slide pane and is currently selected in the Slides tab. Notice that PowerPoint applies the fonts and text colors of the outline document rather than of the presentation theme. A new layout, Title and Text, was created and applied to all of the slides that were inserted. You need to apply the Title and Content layout and then reset the slides.

4. Press and hold the **Shift** key, scroll down the Slides tab, and then click **Slide 9** (the last slide) to select Slides 2 through 9.

5. In the Slides group, click the **Layout** button, and then click **Title and Content**. The Title and Content layout is applied to the selected slides. Now you need to reset the slides to the default settings from the Slide Master.

6. In the Slides group, click the **Reset** button. The font style and color are reset to the presentation theme. The slide number and footer that appeared on Slide 1, however, do not appear on all the slides.

7. Click the **Insert** tab on the Ribbon.

8. In the Text group, click the **Header & Footer** button to display the Header and Footer dialog box. The footer that appears on Slide 1 is in the Footer box, but the Slide number and Footer check boxes are not selected.

9. Click the **Slide number** check box, click the **Footer** check box, and then click the **Apply to All** button. Now the footer and page number appear on all the slides. See Figure 4-2. The imported Word outline is now in the PowerPoint slides with the Landon theme applied.

Figure 4-2 | **Presentation with imported Word outline**

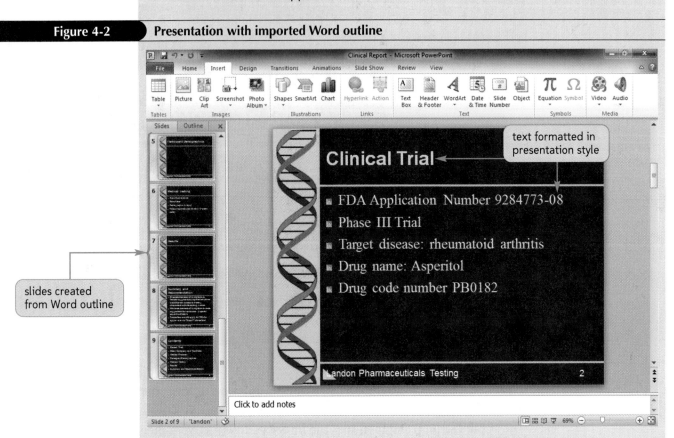

Because you imported the outline, the text is now part of PowerPoint and has no relationship with the Word file ClinOutline. Any changes you make to the PowerPoint presentation will have no effect on the ClinOutline file.

Exporting an Outline to Word

After looking over the presentation, Alyssa decides that she wants Slide 9 ("Contents") to become Slide 2, so that her audience gets an overview of the presentation contents near the beginning. She then wants you to export the revised text as a Word document so that she can create a written report based on the revised outline. You'll do this now.

To modify the presentation outline in Slide Sorter view:

1. Switch to Slide Sorter view.

2. Drag the **Slide 9** thumbnail to the right of the Slide 1 thumbnail (and to the left of the Slide 2 thumbnail). The Contents slide becomes the new Slide 2.

3. Double-click **Slide 1** to return to Normal view, and then click the **Outline** tab in the pane on the left so you can see the text of the outline. See Figure 4-3.

| Figure 4-3 | Presentation outline after "Contents" slide is moved |

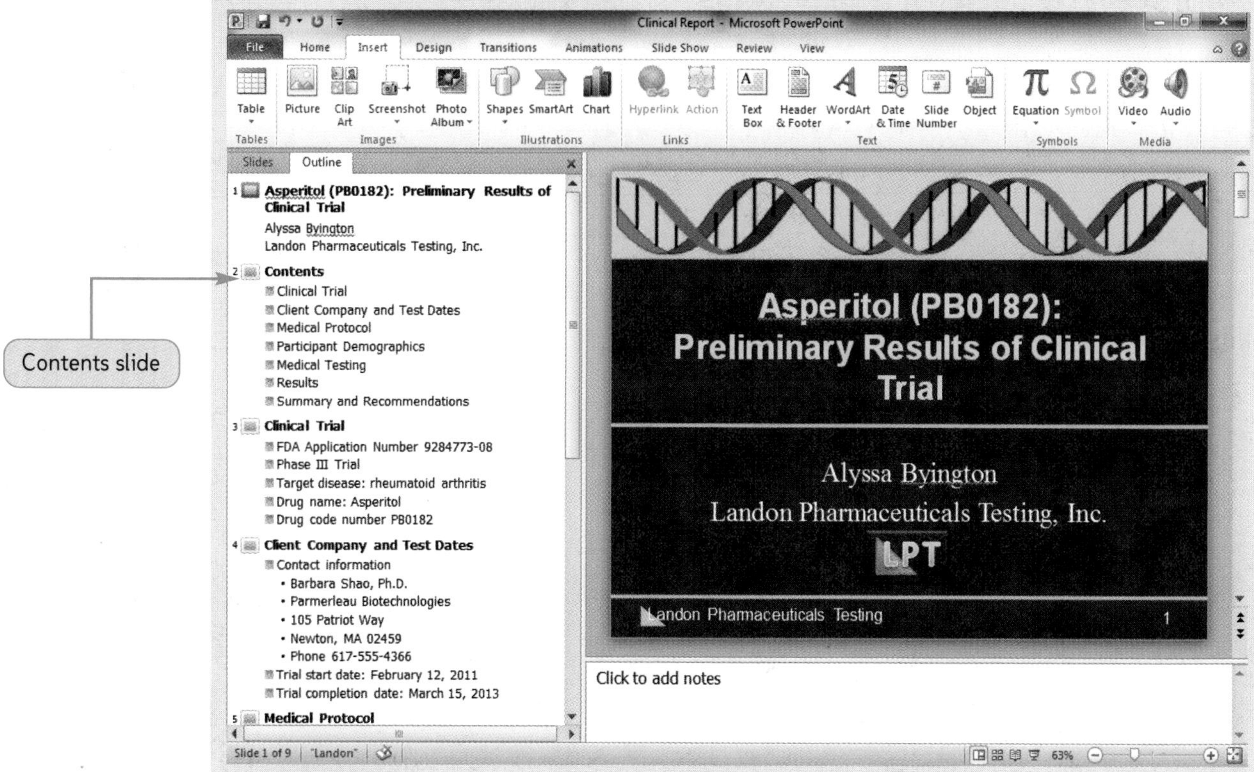

Contents slide

Now you'll export the revised outline to a Word file.

To export the outline to Word:

1. Click the **File** tab, and then click the **Save As** command in the navigation bar. The Save As dialog box opens.

2. Click the **Save as type** arrow, and then click **Outline/RTF**. "RTF" stands for Rich Text Format, which is a text format that preserves most formatting and can be read by most word processors.

3. Navigate to the PowerPoint4\Tutorial folder, if necessary, change the filename to **Report Outline**, and then click the **Save** button. PowerPoint saves the text of the PowerPoint file as an RTF file.

4. Start Microsoft Word 2010, and then open the document **Report Outline**, located in the PowerPoint4\Tutorial folder. The text is barely visible because PowerPoint created the RTF file using the same font sizes and colors as in the presentation, so in this case, it is yellow or white text on a white background. You'll make the text more visible.

5. Press the **Ctrl+A** keys to select all the text in the document.

6. Change the font to **Calibri**, change the font size to **12**, and then change the font color to **Automatic** (black).

   Trouble? If you are unfamiliar with Microsoft Word 2010, skip Steps 6 and 7.

7. Click anywhere to deselect the text. Now you can read the text. See Figure 4-4.

TIP

You can also click the File tab, click Save & Send in the navigation bar, click Create Handouts, and then click the Create Handouts button. In the Send To Microsoft Word dialog box, click the Outline Only option button.

Figure 4-4	Exported outline in Microsoft Word

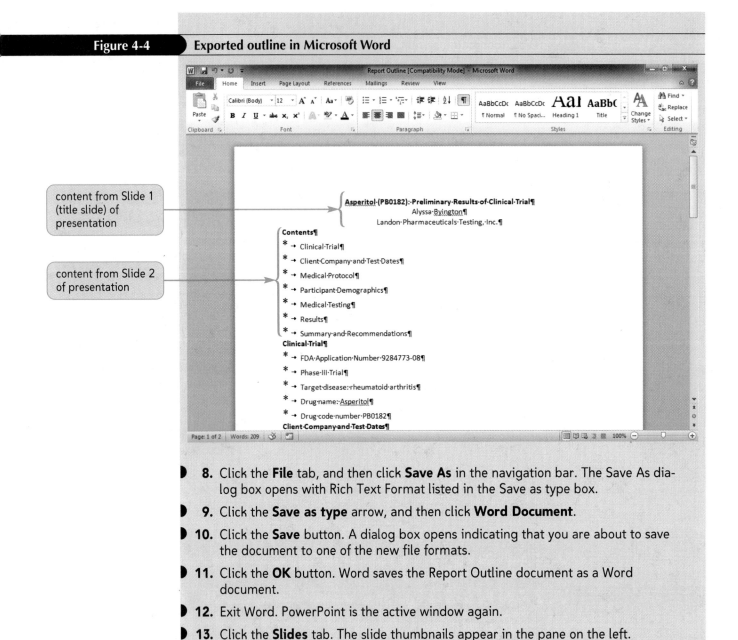

8. Click the **File** tab, and then click **Save As** in the navigation bar. The Save As dialog box opens with Rich Text Format listed in the Save as type box.

9. Click the **Save as type** arrow, and then click **Word Document**.

10. Click the **Save** button. A dialog box opens indicating that you are about to save the document to one of the new file formats.

11. Click the **OK** button. Word saves the Report Outline document as a Word document.

12. Exit Word. PowerPoint is the active window again.

13. Click the **Slides** tab. The slide thumbnails appear in the pane on the left.

Next Alyssa wants you to insert a photograph into the presentation by copying it from another presentation.

Copying an Object from a Different Presentation

You can copy an object from one presentation and paste it into another using the Copy and Paste commands and the Clipboard. A photograph of Asperitol pills is included in a short presentation that Alyssa's assistant created. Alyssa asks you to copy that photograph to Slide 3 in the Clinical Report presentation.

To copy an object from the Landon presentation:

1. With the Clinical Report presentation open in the PowerPoint window, open the presentation **Landon**, which is located in the PowerPoint4\Tutorial folder.

2. Display **Slide 3** ("Latest Phase III Trial: Asperitol") in the Slide pane, and then click the photo of the pills to select it.

3. In the Clipboard group, click the **Copy** button 📋. The photo is copied to the Clipboard.

4. In the title bar, click the **Close** button ❌ to close the Landon presentation and return to the Clinical Report presentation.

5. Display **Slide 3** ("Clinical Trial") in the Slide pane, and then change the layout to the **Two Content** layout. The bulleted list appears in the content text box on the left and a content placeholder appears on the right.

6. In the Clipboard group, click the **Paste** button. The photograph of the pills appears in the center of the slide. It did not replace the content placeholder.

7. Click the border of the content placeholder on the right, and then press the **Delete** key. The content placeholder on the right is deleted.

8. Drag the photograph to approximately center it in the area to the right of the bulleted list, and then click a blank area of the slide to deselect the pasted object. See Figure 4-5.

Figure 4-5   Slide 3 with pasted photograph

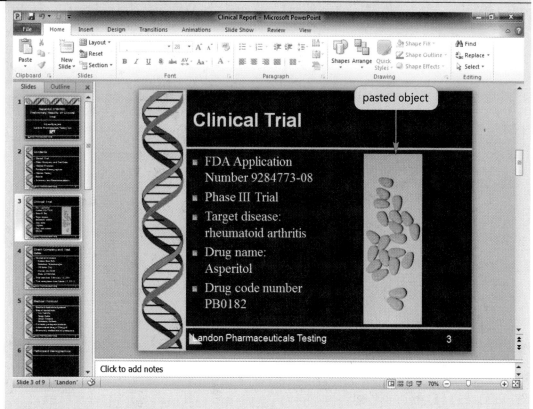

9. Save your changes.

Next, you'll modify the photograph you pasted by removing its background.

Removing the Background from Photographs

Alyssa thinks that the photograph of the pills on Slide 3 would look better without the gray background. You can remove the background in photographs with the Remove Background tool. When you click the Remove Background button, the photograph is analyzed; part of it is marked to be removed and part of it is marked to be retained.

REFERENCE

Removing the Background of a Photograph

- Click the photograph, and then click the Picture Tools Format tab on the Ribbon.
- In the Adjust group, click the Remove Background button.
- Drag the sizing handles on the remove background border to make broad adjustments to the area marked for removal.
- In the Refine group on the Background Removal tab, click the Mark Areas to Keep or the Mark Areas to Remove button, and then click or drag through an area of the photo that you want marked to keep or remove.
- Click a blank area of the slide or click the Keep Changes button in the Close group to accept the changes.

You'll remove the background on the photograph now.

To remove the background of the photograph:

1. In the Slide pane, click the photograph to select it, if necessary, and then click the **Picture Tools Format** tab on the Ribbon.

2. In the Adjust group, click the **Remove Background** button. The areas of the photograph marked for removal are colored purple. A sizing box appears around the general area of the photograph that will be retained, and a new tab, the Background Removal tab, appears on the Ribbon and is the active tab. See Figure 4-6. Notice several of the pills are marked to be removed as well. You can adjust the area of the photograph that is retained by dragging the sizing handles.

Figure 4-6   **Photograph after clicking the Remove Background button**

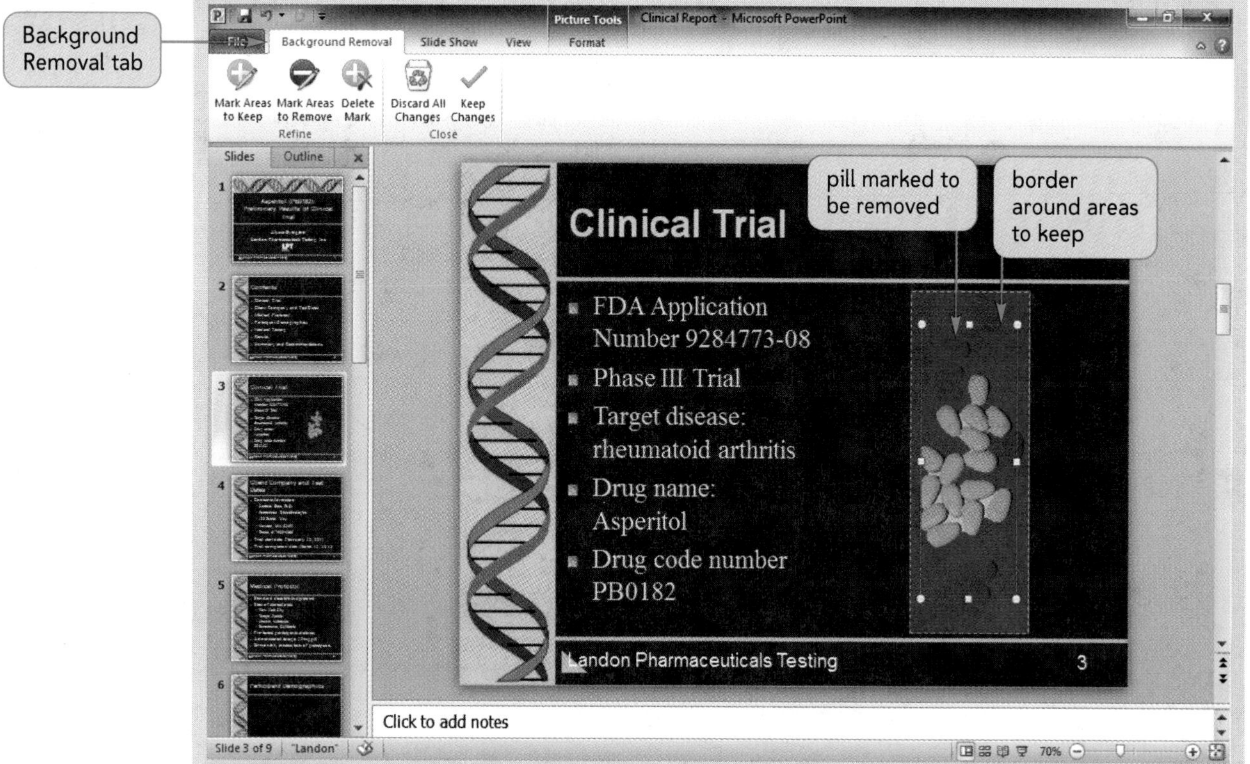

Background Removal tab

pill marked to be removed

border around areas to keep

3. Drag the **right middle sizing handle** to the right edge of the photograph. The pill on the right that had been marked for removal is colored normally again.

4. Drag the **left middle sizing handle** to the left edge of the photograph. The pills on the left that had been cut off are colored normally. There are still three pills at the top and two pills at the bottom that are marked for removal.

5. Drag the **bottom middle sizing handle** down to about halfway between the bottom pill in the photograph and the bottom border of the photograph. Now all the pills are inside the border, but one at the top and two at the bottom are still marked for removal. Also, some of the gray background is visible again. See Figure 4-7. You can fine tune the removal if adjusting the sizing handles doesn't work.

Trouble? If your photograph doesn't look exactly like the one in Figure 4-7, don't be concerned. You will adjust it in the next few steps.

Figure 4-7 **Border resized around area to keep**

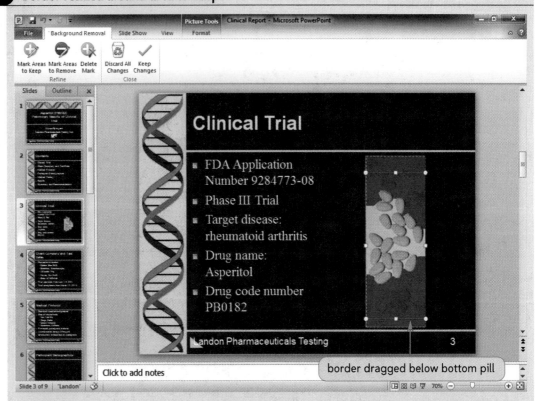

6. In the Refine group on the Background Removal tab, click the **Mark Areas to Remove** button, and then position the pointer on top of the photo. The pointer changes to ⌀.

7. On the right side of the photograph, click in the gray area below the rightmost pill. A circle with a minus sign appears, and a portion of the gray area near where you clicked might be marked for removal. If you drag through an area that you want to remove or keep, you provide more information about the exact portions to keep or remove. To see the difference, first, you'll undo the change you just made.

8. On the Quick Access Toolbar, click the **Undo** button ↺.

9. In the Refine Group, click the **Mark Areas to Remove** button again, and then on the right side of the photograph, drag down from between the cluster of pills on the right to the bottom part of the gray area, taking care not to touch any of the pills. The gray area you dragged through is marked for removal, and a dotted line indicating the path you dragged through appears on either side of the circle with the minus sign. See Figure 4-8.

Figure 4-8 | **Photograph after marking a specific area to remove**

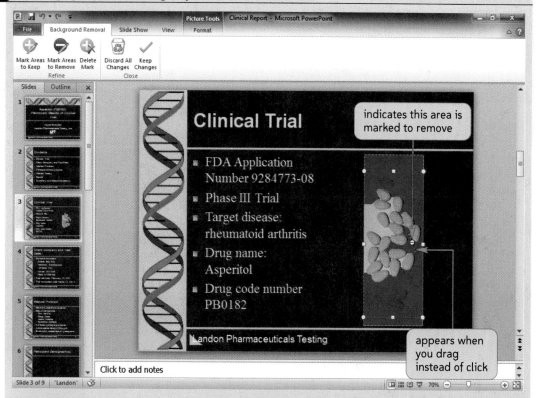

10. On the left side of the photograph, click in the gray area to the left of the pills, and then click the other gray areas in the photograph. The gray areas are now all marked for removal.

   Trouble? If a pill is marked for removal, don't be concerned. In the next step, you will mark areas to keep.

11. In the Refine group, click the **Mark Areas to Keep** button, and then click the top pill. The top three pills are now marked to appear in the final photo.

   Trouble? If there are still pills at the top of the photograph that are marked for removal, make sure the Mark Areas to Keep button is still selected, and then click them.

12. At the bottom of the photograph, click one of the two pills marked for removal, and then click any other pills that are marked for removal. All the pills are now colored normally and most of the gray background is marked for removal.

   Trouble? If any pills are still marked for removal, click them with the Mark Areas to Keep pointer.

13. In the Close group, click the **Keep Changes** button. The changes you made are applied to the photograph, and the Background Removal tab disappears from the Ribbon. See Figure 4-9.

Figure 4-9   **Photograph of pills with the background removed**

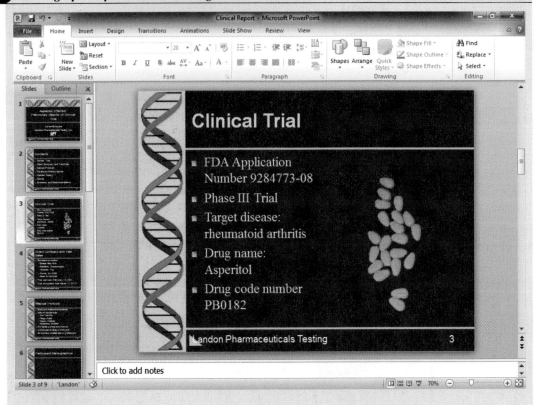

14. Save your changes.

If you change your mind and decide that you want the background after all, you can click the Reset Picture button in the Adjust group on the Picture Tools Format tab. Alyssa likes the way the photograph looks without the gray background.

Embedding and Modifying a Word Table

You know how to use PowerPoint commands to create a table in a slide, but what if you've already created a table using Word? You don't have to re-create it in PowerPoint; instead, you can copy the table and paste it in a slide. If you embed the table, you can then edit it using Word table commands. You can use copy and paste commands to embed a Word table, but if the Word file contains only the Word table, you can use the Object command instead. The Object command inserts the entire file in a slide.

REFERENCE

Embedding a Word Table in a Slide Using the Object Command

- Click the Insert tab, and then click the Object button in the Text group to open the Insert Object dialog box.
- Click the Create from file option button.
- Click the Browse button to open the Browse dialog box, navigate to the drive and folder containing the file with the table, and then click the OK button.
- Make sure the Link check box is deselected in the Insert Object dialog box.
- Click the OK button.

Alyssa created a table in a Word document that lists the demographics of the participants in the trials, and she asks you to embed the table in Slide 6 in her presentation. Alyssa created the table with a black font on a white background, so it is legible in a Word document. But as you'll see, it's not legible against the dark background in the PowerPoint presentation.

To embed a Word file in the presentation:

1. Display **Slide 6** ("Participant Demographics") in the Slide pane, and then click the **Insert** tab on the Ribbon.

2. In the Text group, click the **Object** button. The Insert Object dialog box opens. You can create a new embedded file or use an existing one. You'll use the existing file that Alyssa created.

3. Click the **Create from file** option button, and then click the **Browse** button to open the Browse dialog box.

4. Navigate to the PowerPoint4\Tutorial folder included with your Data Files, click **Demogr**, and then click the **OK** button. The Browse dialog box closes, and the path and filename of the file you selected appear in the File box in the Insert Object dialog box. See Figure 4-10.

Figure 4-10	Insert Object dialog box

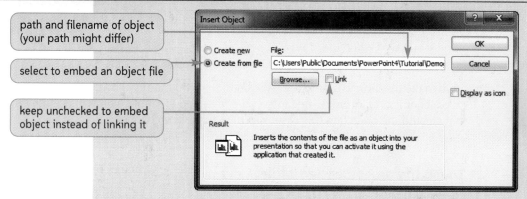

5. Make sure the **Link** check box is not selected, as shown in Figure 4-10, and then click the **OK** button. The embedded table appears in Slide 6.

6. Resize the table by dragging the corner sizing handles so that the table is as large as possible and still fits on the middle of the slide without overlapping background objects. You will have to drag the object border beyond the edges of the slide to make the table as big as possible. See Figure 4-11.

Figure 4-11   Slide 6 with embedded Word table

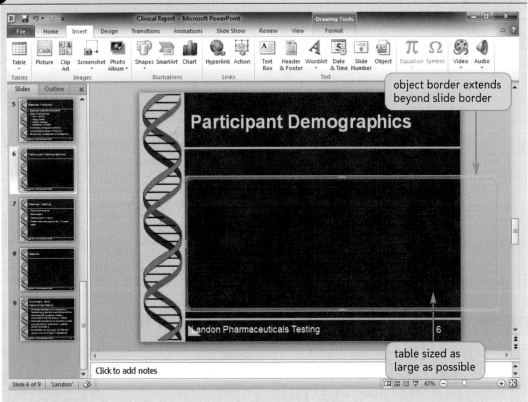

To make the table easier to see, Alyssa asks you to modify it by changing the table color scheme and font size. Because you embedded the table, you will use the program that created the object (in this case, Word) to make the changes.

To modify an embedded table:

1. Double-click anywhere in the table in Slide 6. The embedded table object becomes active in Word, and the Word Ribbon replaces the PowerPoint Ribbon. See Figure 4-12.

Figure 4-12	Slide 6 with embedded Word table made active

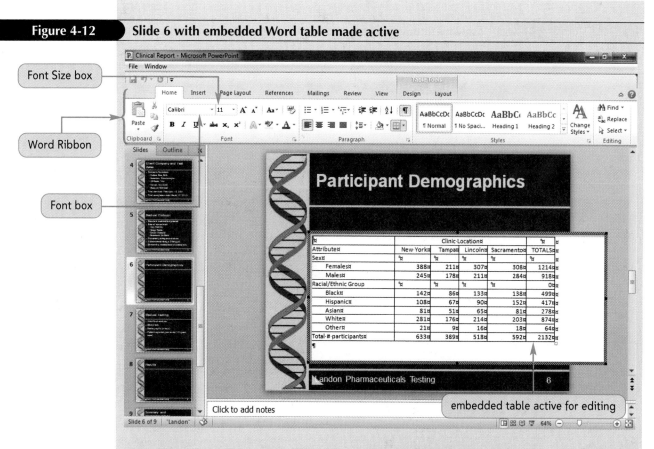

2. Drag the mouse pointer from the upper-left cell to the bottom-right cell to select the entire table.

3. In the Font group on the Home tab, click the **Font box arrow**, and then scroll to locate and select **Times New Roman**.

4. Click in the **Font Size** box, type **13**, and then press the **Enter** key. The text of the table is now 13-point Times New Roman.

5. Click the **Font Color button arrow** ▲▾, and click the **White, Background 1** color. The font in the Word window seems to disappear, because it is white on a white background. On Slide 6, which has a dark brown background, the text will show up nicely.

6. In the Paragraph group, click the **Borders button arrow** ⊞▾, and then click **Borders and Shading** at the bottom of the gallery. The Borders and Shading dialog box opens.

7. Click the **Color** arrow, and then click the **Yellow** color under Standard Colors to change the table grid lines to yellow.

8. Click the **OK** button, click a blank area of the slide to exit Word and return to PowerPoint, and then click a blank area again to deselect the table. See Figure 4-13.

TIP

Use the Shading button in the Table Styles group on the Table Tools Design tab to fill a cell with gradient color, a texture, or a picture.

Figure 4-13   **Slide 6 with modified table**

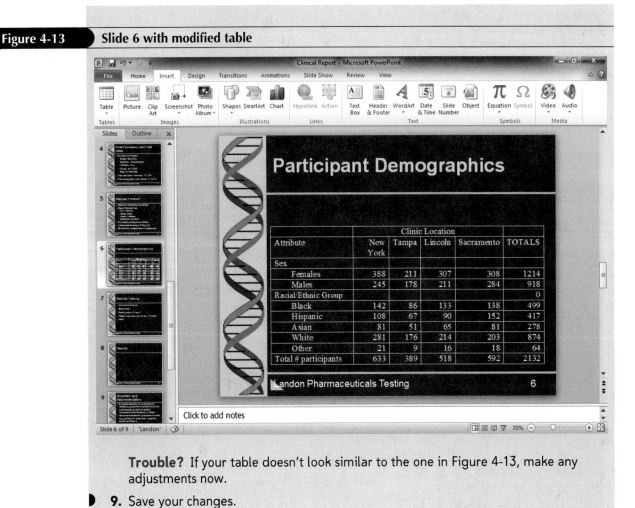

Trouble? If your table doesn't look similar to the one in Figure 4-13, make any adjustments now.

9. Save your changes.

Keep in mind that the changes you made to the embedded object did not change the original table in the Word document because embedding maintains a connection only with the program that was used to create the object, not with the original object itself.

Next, you'll link an Excel chart to the presentation.

Linking and Modifying an Excel Chart

Now you know how to insert objects into a PowerPoint slide by importing them and by embedding them. What if you needed to include in your presentation data that might change? For example, you might need data from an Excel worksheet, but you know that the final numbers won't be available for a while or that the numbers will change over time. In this case, you can link the data. Then, when the source file is updated, you can automatically update the linked object in the destination file so that it reflects the changes made to the source file.

Linking an Excel Chart to a Slide Using Copy and Paste

- Start Excel (the source program), open the file containing the chart to be linked, select the chart you want to link to the destination program, and then in the Clipboard group on the Home tab, click the Copy button.
- In the PowerPoint file that will contain the linked chart (the destination file), in the Clipboard group on the Home tab, click the Paste button, click the Paste Options button, and then click the Use Destination Theme & Link Data button or click the Keep Source Formatting & Link Data button; or click the Paste button arrow, and then click the Use Destination Theme & Link Data or Keep Source Formatting & Link Data button.

Alyssa wants to include a bar chart of the results of the drug clinical trial in the presentation. She wants to use a bar chart because it emphasizes the effects of the drug on trial participants. The bar chart was created using Excel, based on data in an Excel workbook, but Alyssa anticipates that she will have to modify the chart after she creates the PowerPoint presentation because some of the trial results were incomplete. Alyssa wants any changes made to the chart to be reflected in the PowerPoint file, so she asks you to link the Excel chart to the PowerPoint presentation.

To insert a chart linked to an Excel worksheet:

1. Display **Slide 8** ("Results") in the Slide pane, and then change the slide layout to **Title Only**.

2. Start Microsoft Office Excel 2010, open the file **Chart** located in the PowerPoint4\ Tutorial folder, and then save it as **Clinical Chart** in the same folder. Now you can make changes to the chart without modifying the original document.

3. Click the edge of the chart to select it, click the **Home** tab, and then click the **Copy** button 🗎 in the Clipboard group to copy the chart to the Clipboard.

In order for link commands to appear as paste options, do not exit Excel.

4. On the taskbar, click the **PowerPoint** button 🅟. The Clinical Report presentation appears with Slide 8 in the Slide pane.

5. In the Clipboard group, click the **Paste** button to paste the chart into Slide 8. The chart is pasted in the slide.

6. Below the lower-right corner of the chart, click the **Paste Options** button 🖺 (Ctrl) ▾. Notice that the default selected button is the Use Destination Theme & Link Data button 🖺. This is what you want, so you don't need to select a different option on the menu.

7. Click the **Paste Options** button 🖺 (Ctrl) ▾ to close the menu without making a selection.

8. Resize the chart so it fits within the large blank region of the slide, and then drag the entire chart to approximately center it in the blank area of the slide. Compare your screen to Figure 4-14.

TIP

When you copy and paste an object from another program into a PowerPoint presentation, the object is normally imported, not embedded or linked, except when you copy and paste a chart from Excel into PowerPoint; in this case, the chart is linked.

Figure 4-14 **Slide 8 with linked Excel chart**

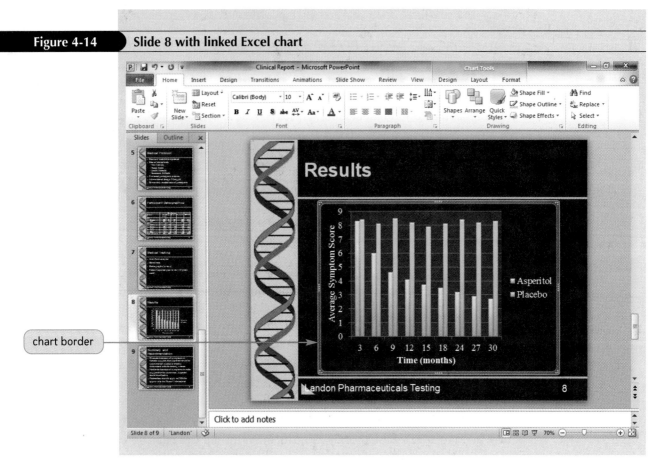

chart border

After you linked the chart, Alyssa received updated information about one of the results in the clinical trial report. The scientists at Landon had estimated that the average symptom score after 30 months would be 2.7, but after all the data was collected, the value was actually 3.1. Alyssa asks you to make changes to the Excel worksheet data, which will then be reflected in the chart, both in the Excel and PowerPoint files.

To modify the linked chart:

1. Click the **Chart Tools Design** tab on the Ribbon.

2. In the Data group, click the **Edit Data** button. The PowerPoint program window is resized to fit in the left half of the screen, and the Excel window containing the linked chart appears on the right. See Figure 4-15.

Figure 4-15   Adding a chart in Slide 8

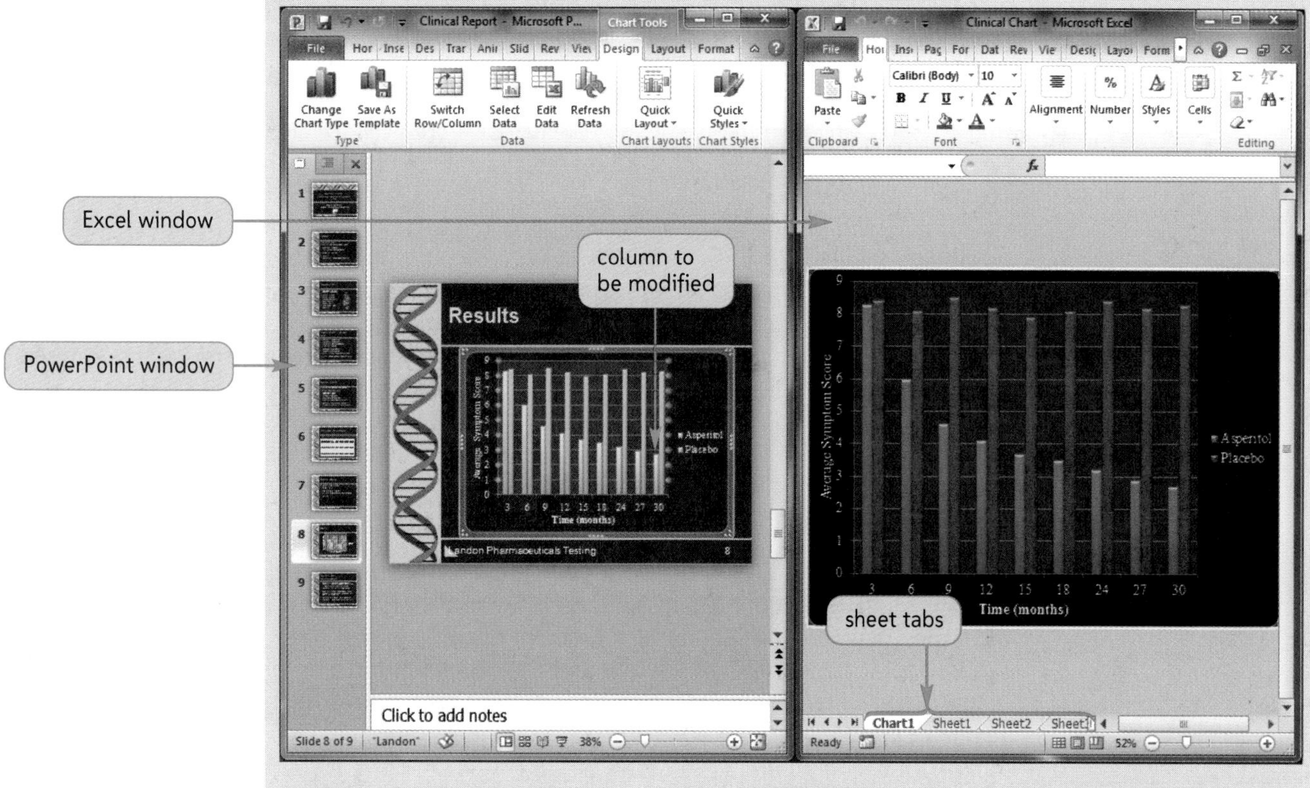

3. In the Excel window, click the **Sheet1** tab at the bottom of the window, and then click cell **B10** (the intersection of column B and row 10).

4. Type **3.1**, but don't press the Enter key yet. Look at the chart in the PowerPoint window on the left. Focus on the rightmost yellow bar, which indicates the average symptom score at 30 months.

5. Press the **Enter** key. The rightmost yellow bar in the chart in the PowerPoint window changed.

6. In the Excel window, click the **Close** button [X], and then click the **Save** button when asked if you want to save the changes to the Excel file. PowerPoint now fills the screen again.

7. Save your changes to the presentation.

You have now linked and edited an Excel chart in a PowerPoint presentation. If you decide later to make further changes to the chart, you can do so either by directly starting Excel and opening the Clinical Chart workbook, or accessing the workbook by clicking the Edit Data button in PowerPoint. Either way, any changes made to the workbook will be reflected in the linked object in the PowerPoint slide.

Decision Making: Comparing Import, Embed, and Linking Options

Both linking and embedding involve inserting an object into a destination file; the difference lies in where their respective objects are stored. Each type of integration has advantages and disadvantages. The advantage of embedding an object instead of linking it is that the source file and the destination file can be stored separately. You can use the source program commands to make changes to the object in the destination file, and the source file will be unaffected. The disadvantage is that the destination file size is somewhat larger than it would be if the object were simply imported as a picture or text or linked. The advantage of linking an object instead of embedding it is that the object remains identical in the source and destination files, and the destination file size does not increase as much as if the object were embedded. The disadvantage is that the source and destination files must be stored together. When you need to copy information from one program to another, consider which option is the best choice for your needs.

Creating and Editing Hyperlinks

A **hyperlink** (or **link**) is a word, phrase, or graphic image that you click to "jump to" (or display) another location, called the **target**. The target of a link can be a location within the same document (presentation), a different document, or a page on the World Wide Web. Graphic hyperlinks are visually indistinguishable from graphics that are not hyperlinks, except when you move the mouse pointer over the link, the pointer changes to 👆. Text links are usually underlined and are a different color than the rest of the text. After clicking a text link during a slide show, the link changes to another color to reflect the fact that it has been clicked, or **followed**.

Formatting Text as a Hyperlink

Alyssa is expecting that some in her audience will be eager to see the results of the clinical trial, before the details of the trial are presented. Therefore, she wants to be able to easily move from Slide 2, which lists the presentation contents, to Slide 8 showing the chart summarizing the trial results. Therefore, she asks you to create a hyperlink between the Results bullet in Slide 2 and the corresponding Slide 8 in the presentation, and then to create a hyperlink from Slide 8 back to Slide 2.

Creating a Hyperlink to Another Slide in a Presentation

- Select the text or object from which you want to create the hyperlink.
- Click the Insert tab, and then click the Hyperlink button in the Links group.
- In the Insert Hyperlink dialog box, under Link to, click Place in This Document.
- In the Select a place in this document list, click the slide to which you want to link.
- Click the OK button.

You will create this hyperlink next.

To create a hyperlink from text on Slide 2 to Slide 8:

1. Display **Slide 2** ("Contents") in the Slide pane.
2. In the bulleted list, select the text **Results**.
3. Click the **Insert** tab, and then click the **Hyperlink** button in the Links group. The Insert Hyperlink dialog box opens. See Figure 4-16. You need to identify the file or location to which you want to link. In this case, you're going to link to a place in the existing document, so you'll want to select that option in the Link to panel on the left side of the dialog box.

| Figure 4-16 | Insert Hyperlink dialog box |

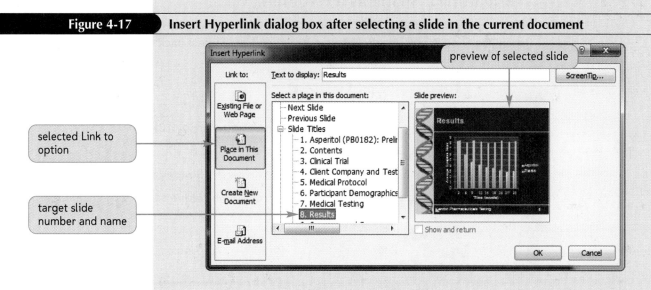

4. In the Link to panel on the left side of the dialog box, click **Place in This Document**. The dialog box changes to list all of the slides in the presentation.
5. In the Select a place in this document list, click **8. Results**. The Slide preview area on the right side of the dialog box displays Slide 8. This is the slide to which the text will be linked. See Figure 4-17.

| Figure 4-17 | Insert Hyperlink dialog box after selecting a slide in the current document |

6. Click the **OK** button, and then click a blank area of the slide to deselect the text. The text "Results" is now a hyperlink, and it is now formatted as green and underlined. (Recall that you can specify the hyperlink color when you customize the theme colors.) See Figure 4-18.

| Figure 4-18 | Slide 2 with a hyperlink to Slide 8 |

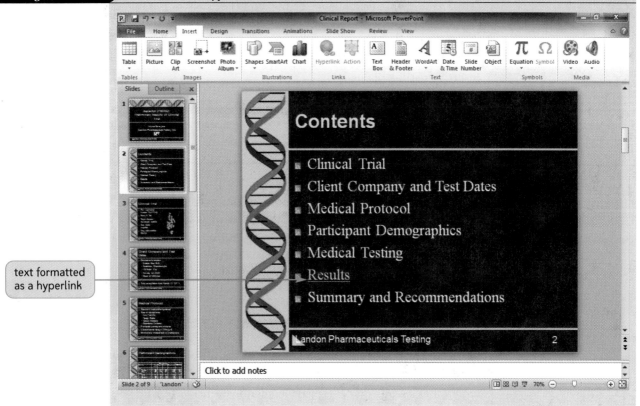

text formatted as a hyperlink

Formatting a Shape as a Hyperlink

Now that you have formatted the Results bullet in Slide 2 as a hyperlink to the corresponding Slide 8, you need to create a hyperlink from Slide 8 back to Slide 2. To do this, you will create a shape to format as a hyperlink.

You'll first create the shape.

To insert the shape that you will format as a hyperlink:

1. Display **Slide 8** ("Results") in the Slide pane.

2. In the Illustrations group on the Insert tab, click the **Shapes** button.

3. In the Basic Shapes section of the gallery, click the **Plaque** shape, as indicated in Figure 4-19.

Figure 4-19 | **Slide 8 with the Shapes gallery open**

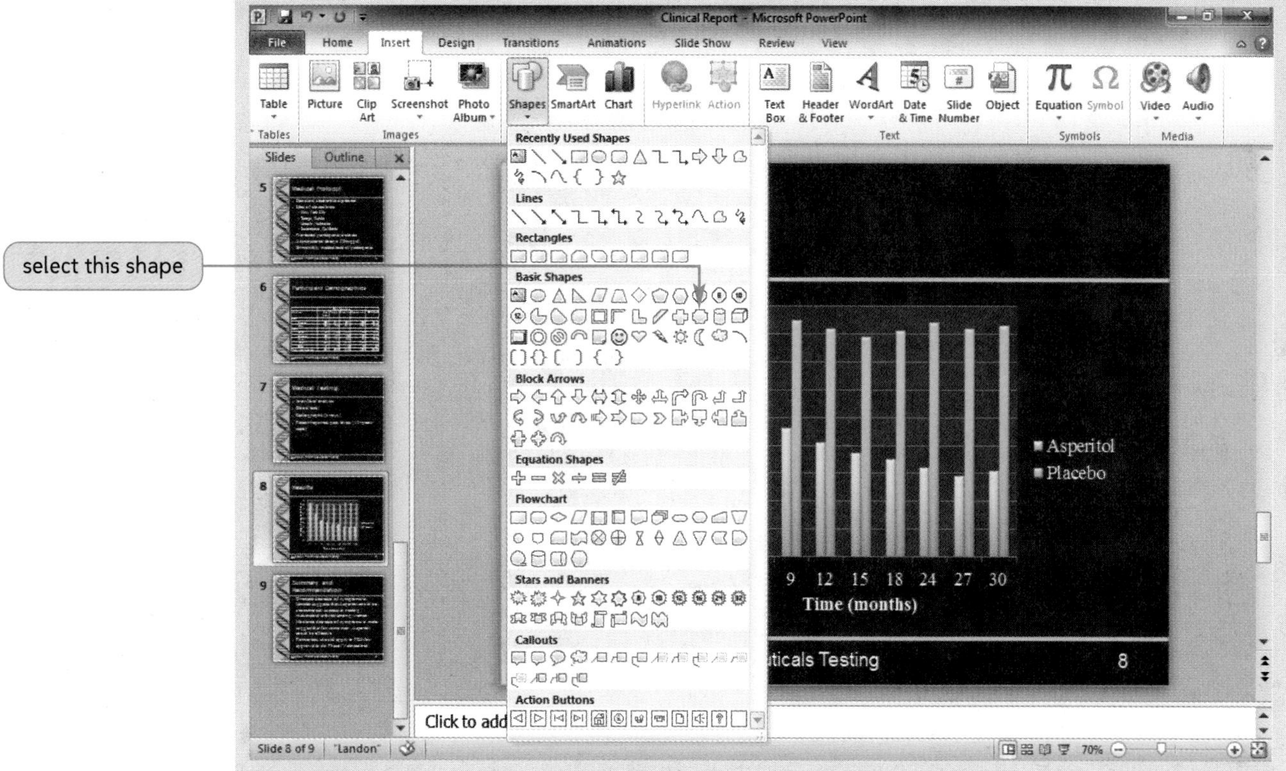

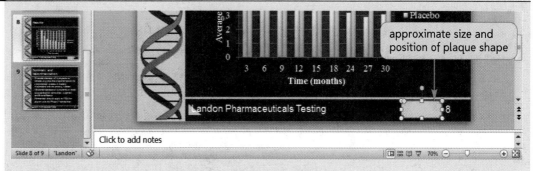

4. Position the pointer between the footer and the slide number near the bottom of the slide, and then drag down and to the right to make the shape shown in Figure 4-20. Don't worry about the exact location and size of the shape; you can fix it later.

Figure 4-20 | **Slide 8 after the plaque shape is inserted**

5. Click the **Drawing Tools Format** tab on the Ribbon.

6. In the Shape Styles group, click the **More** button, and then in the Shape Styles gallery, click the **Intense Effect – Orange, Accent 6** style (last column and the last row). Alyssa wants you to add text to the shape to remind her that clicking this shape will display the Contents slide.

7. With the shape still selected, type **Contents**.

8. If necessary, drag the middle sizing handle on the left or right edge of the shape until the shape is big enough to fit the word "Contents" on one line, and then deselect the shape. See Figure 4-21.

Figure 4-21 **Slide 8 with formatted shape**

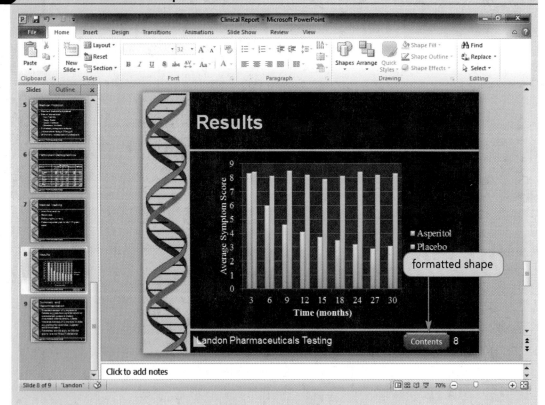

Trouble? If the size and position of the shape in your slide doesn't look like Figure 4-21, make any adjustments now.

You're now ready to make the Contents shape a hyperlink.

To format the plaque shape as a hyperlink to Slide 2:

1. Click the edge of the plaque shape to select it.

   Trouble? If the insertion point is blinking in the text "Contents" you clicked inside the shape. Click the border of the shape to select the entire shape.

2. Click the **Insert** tab, and then click the **Hyperlink** button in the Links group. The Insert Hyperlink dialog box opens.

3. In the Link to panel on the left side of the dialog box, make sure **Place in This Document** is selected, and then click **2. Contents**. This is the target of the hyperlink.

4. Click the **OK** button. The dialog box closes and the shape is formatted as a hyperlink to Slide 2. Because you selected the shape, the entire shape is the hyperlink, not just the text inside the shape, and therefore, the text doesn't change to the green hyperlink color. Shapes and other non-text objects don't change color when they are converted to a hyperlink.

   Trouble? If the text "Contents" changed so that it is green and underlined, you did not select the entire shape. On the Quick Access Toolbar, click the Undo button, and then repeat Steps 1 through 4.

Now you're ready to test the results. You need to test the hyperlinks in Slide Show view because they aren't active in Normal view.

To test the hyperlinks:

1. Display **Slide 2** ("Contents") in the Slide pane, and then on the status bar, click the **Slide Show** button 🖵.

2. Click the **Results** hyperlink. PowerPoint displays Slide 8 ("Results").

3. Click the **Contents** hyperlink on Slide 8. PowerPoint again displays Slide 2. See Figure 4-22. The Results link text is now yellow, indicating that the hyperlink was followed.

Figure 4-22 **Slide 2 in Slide Show view with followed hyperlink**

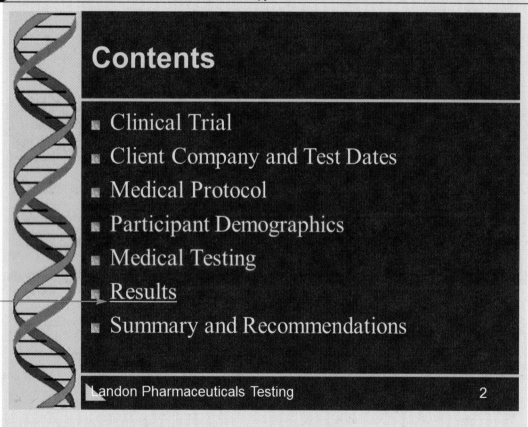

4. End the slide show to return to Slide 2 in Normal view.

In addition to creating hyperlinks on slides, you can add action buttons that have essentially the same effect. Alyssa wants you to insert an action button that will add a link to another presentation.

Viewing a Slide Show with Linked Objects

When you present a slide show using a presentation that contains a linked file, a copy of the linked file is not included within the PowerPoint file itself; only the path and filename for accessing the linked file are there. Any linked files in a presentation must be available on a disk so that PowerPoint can access them, so you should view the presentation on the system that will be used for running the slide show to make sure it has the necessary files and that the hyperlinks are set up properly. The links include the original path and filename to the files on the hard drive of the computer where you created the links. If linked objects don't work when you run the slide show, you'll have to edit the path so that PowerPoint can find the objects on your disk. To update the link path to a linked object in a presentation, click the File tab, click the Info tab in the navigation bar, and then under Related Documents in the right pane, click Edit Links to Files. In the Links dialog box that opens, click the Change Source button. If a hyperlink or an action button opens another file, you should check that path as well by right-clicking the hyperlink or action button, and then clicking Edit Hyperlink.

Adding Action Buttons

An **action button** is a ready-made shape intended to be a hyperlink to other slides or documents. You can use one of the 12 action buttons available in the Shapes gallery, such as Action Button: Home or Action Button: Sound. Each action button can link to any slide or presentation; the various shapes simply offer variety in the way the buttons look.

Adding an Action Button as a Link to Another Presentation

- Click the Insert tab, and then click the Shapes button in the Illustrations group to open the Shapes gallery.
- Click an action button in the Action Buttons section at the bottom of the gallery.
- Position the pointer at the location in the slide where you want the action button to appear.
- In the Action Settings dialog box, click the Hyperlink to option button, click the Hyperlink to arrow, and then click Other PowerPoint Presentation to open the Hyperlink to Other PowerPoint Presentation dialog box.
- Select the presentation to which you want to link, and then click the OK button.
- Click the OK button in the Action Settings dialog box.
- Resize and reposition the action button icon as desired.

Alyssa wants you to add a hyperlink between her presentation and the Landon presentation, which gives the mission statement and contact information of Landon Pharmaceuticals Testing. You'll create a hyperlink to that presentation by adding an action button.

To add an action button to link to the Landon presentation:

1. In the Illustrations group on the Insert tab, click the **Shapes** button. The gallery of shapes appears with the action buttons at the bottom.

2. Click the **Action Button: Document** button located fourth from the right in the bottom row of the gallery. The gallery closes and the pointer changes to $+$.

3. Click to the left of the slide number near the bottom of Slide 2, at about the same location where you placed the plaque shape on Slide 8. A large button with a document icon appears on the slide, and the Action Settings dialog box opens. See Figure 4-23.

Figure 4-23	Action Settings dialog box

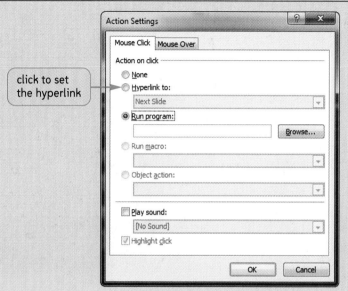

click to set
the hyperlink

4. In the dialog box, click the **Hyperlink to** option button, click the **Hyperlink to** arrow, scroll down, and then click **Other PowerPoint Presentation**. The Hyperlink to Other PowerPoint Presentation dialog box opens.

5. Navigate to the PowerPoint4\Tutorial folder, if necessary, click **Landon**, and then click the **OK** button. The Hyperlink to Slide dialog box opens listing the four slides in the Landon presentation. See Figure 4-24. Alyssa wants to display Slide 2 of this presentation, which contains the company mission statement, when she clicks the Action Button.

Figure 4-24	Hyperlink to Slide dialog box

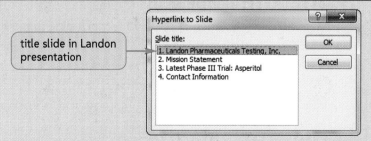

title slide in Landon
presentation

6. Click **2. Mission Statement**, click the **OK** button, and then click **OK** in the Actions Settings dialog box.

7. Adjust the size and position of the action button, as shown in Figure 4-25.

Figure 4-25   Slide 2 with resized Action Button

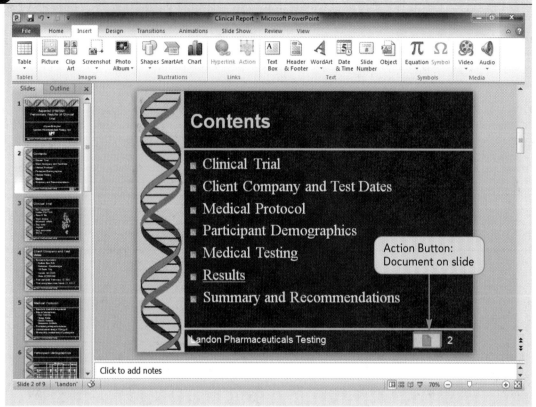

Now you need to test the action button.

To test the action button:

TIP

To return to the original presentation from a linked presentation, press the Esc key or right-click any slide, and then click End Show on the shortcut menu.

1. Switch to Slide Show view with Slide 2 ("Contents"), on the screen, and then click the **action button**. Slide 2 of the Landon presentation appears on the screen. Alyssa wants to jump to Slide 4, which contains contact information.

2. Right-click anywhere on the slide, point to **Go to Slide** on the shortcut menu, and then click **4 Contact Information**.

3. Advance the presentation to display the black slide that indicates the end of the slide show, and then advance the slide show once more. Slide 2 of the Clinical Report presentation appears again.

4. End the slide show, switch to Slide Sorter view, and then change the zoom level to **90%**. Compare your final presentation to Figure 4-26.

| Figure 4-26 | Presentation in Slide Sorter view |

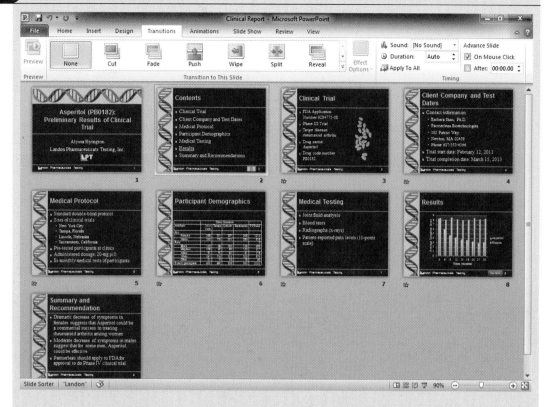

5. Save your changes.

Alyssa is pleased with the completed content of the presentation, which now includes an imported table from Word, an Excel chart, hyperlinks to other slides in the presentation, and an action button with a link to another presentation. In the next session you will get the presentation ready for delivery by checking and adjusting the slide transitions. You will customize handout masters and mark slides during a slide show, collaborate with others, and save the presentation in formats for distribution.

REVIEW

Session 4.1 Quick Check

1. Describe how you use a Word outline to create slides in PowerPoint.
2. What does it mean to embed an object in a presentation?
3. If you modify the source file of a linked object, such as an Excel chart linked to a PowerPoint slide, what happens to the linked object in the PowerPoint slide?
4. Why would you link an object rather than embed it?
5. True or False. You can create a hyperlink to any other slide in a presentation.
6. What is a hyperlink?
7. What is an action button?

SESSION 4.2 VISUAL OVERVIEW

Click the Show Markup button to hide or display comment thumbnails.

Comments are indicated by **comment thumbnails**, which contain the initials of the person who made the comment. Each person's comments appear in a different color in a comment thumbnail, which are numbered to indicate the order in which the comments were inserted by each person.

The **comment box** displays the comment, the name of the person who made the comment, and the date the comment was inserted.

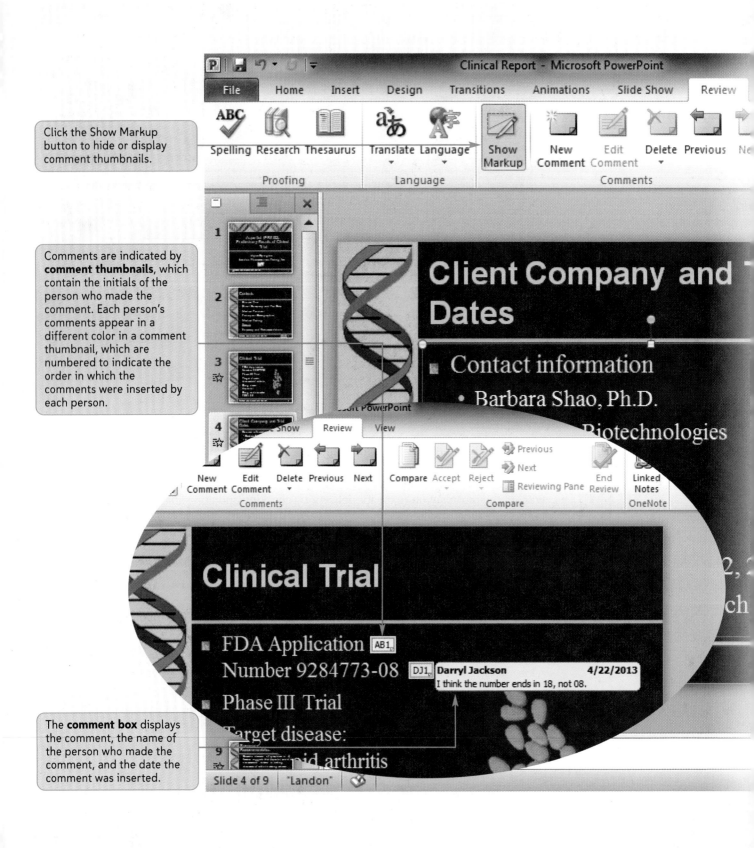

COMPARING AND COMMENTING

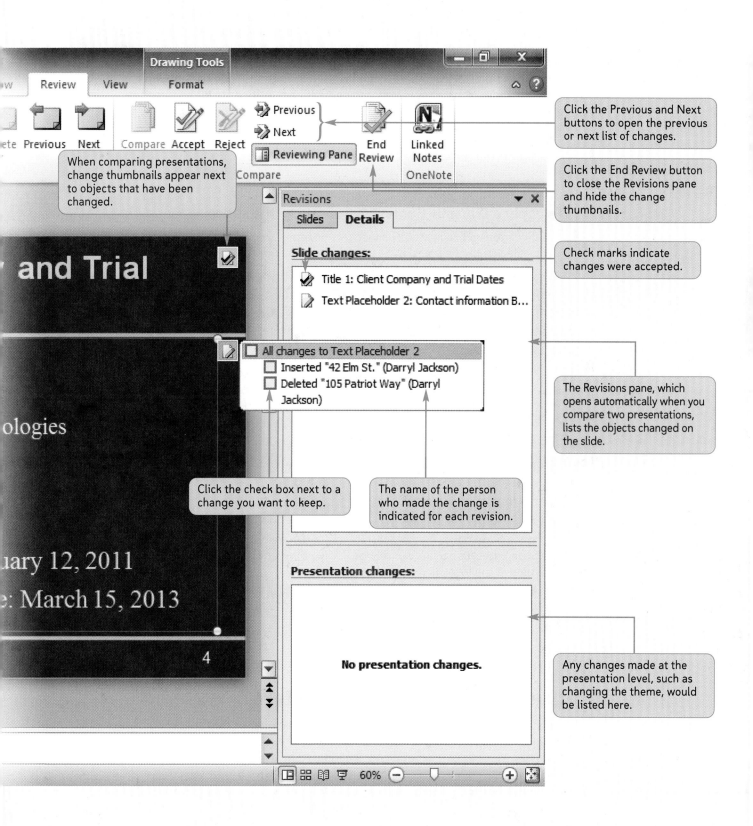

Click the Previous and Next buttons to open the previous or next list of changes.

When comparing presentations, change thumbnails appear next to objects that have been changed.

Click the End Review button to close the Revisions pane and hide the change thumbnails.

Check marks indicate changes were accepted.

Revisions

Slides   **Details**

Slide changes:

Title 1: Client Company and Trial Dates

Text Placeholder 2: Contact information B...

All changes to Text Placeholder 2
Inserted "42 Elm St." (Darryl Jackson)
Deleted "105 Patriot Way" (Darryl Jackson)

The Revisions pane, which opens automatically when you compare two presentations, lists the objects changed on the slide.

Click the check box next to a change you want to keep.

The name of the person who made the change is indicated for each revision.

Presentation changes:

No presentation changes.

Any changes made at the presentation level, such as changing the theme, would be listed here.

Applying a Dynamic Content Transition

Most transitions make the slides appear as if they were in motion as they display during the slide show. To make only the slide content appear as if it were in motion, you can apply one of the transitions in the Dynamic Content section of the Transitions gallery. When an ordinary transition is applied to slides, the entire slide moves onto the screen with the selected transition. When a dynamic content transition is applied to slides, the content on the current slide transitions off the screen using the effect you chose, and at the same time, the slide background fades out. Then the slide background for the next slide fades in as the content for the next slide transitions onto the screen using the selected transition effect you chose. When slides have the same background, it appears as if the content transitions, but the slide background does not change.

Alyssa reviews the presentation and decides she wants you to add a dynamic transition effect to the slides in her presentation.

To apply a Dynamic Content transition to the slides:

1. If you took a break after the last session, open the **Clinical Report** presentation located in the PowerPoint4\Tutorial folder included with your Data Files.

2. Switch to Normal view, if necessary, select **Slides 2-9** in the Slides tab, and then click the **Transitions** tab on the Ribbon.

3. In the Transition to This Slide group, click the **More** button. The Dynamic Content section is at the bottom of the Transitions gallery.

4. In the Dynamic Content section, click the **Rotate** transition. The transition previews by briefly displaying Slide 1 in the Slide pane, and then fading in the slide background of Slide 2 before rotating the content of Slide 2 onto the screen.

5. Click the **Slide Show** tab on the Ribbon, and then click the **From Beginning** button in the Start Slide Show group. Slide 1 appears in Slide Show view.

6. Advance the slide show. You see the same effect you saw in the preview.

7. Advance the slide show to display Slide 3 ("Clinical Trial") on the screen. Because Slide 3 has the same background as Slide 2, it appeared as if only the text were moving onto the screen.

8. Press the **Esc** key to end the slide show, and then display **Slide 2** ("Contents") in the Slide pane. Alyssa doesn't want a dynamic content transition applied to Slide 2 because Slide 2 and Slide 1 have different backgrounds, so she asks you to remove the transition from that slide.

9. Click the **Transitions** tab, click the **More** button in the Transition to This Slide group, and then click the **None** transition.

Next, you'll customize the handout masters.

Customizing Handout Masters

You can customize handouts and notes pages to include specific header and footer information. You can also format handout masters with background styles and color.

Alyssa wants to give her audience handouts. She asks you to customize the Handout Masters.

To customize the Handout Masters:

▶ **1.** Click the **Insert** tab on the Ribbon.

▶ **2.** In the Text group, click the **Header & Footer** button, and then click the **Notes and Handouts** tab in the Header and Footer dialog box. The Page number check box is selected by default.

▶ **3.** Click the **Footer** check box to select it, and then in the Footer box, type **Clinical Report of Asperitol**.

▶ **4.** Click the **Apply to All** button, and then click the **View** tab on the Ribbon.

▶ **5.** In the Master Views group, click the **Handout Master** button. The Handouts Master tab appears and becomes the active tab on the Ribbon, and the handout master appears in the window. Notice that the four options in the Placeholders group are selected, and in the handout master, placeholders appear in each corner of the master. The Footer placeholder contains the text you typed in the Header and Footer dialog box. See Figure 4-27.

Figure 4-27	Handout master

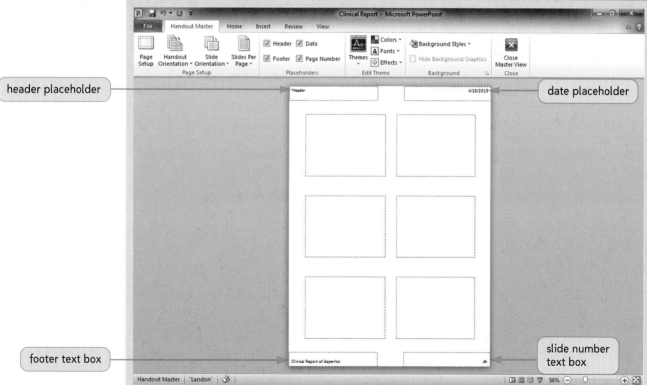

header placeholder

date placeholder

footer text box

slide number text box

▶ **6.** In the Placeholders group, click the **Header** check box to deselect it, and then click the **Date** check box to deselect it. The Header placeholder in the upper-left corner and the Date placeholder in the upper-right corner are removed from the master. The Footer and Page Number check boxes are still selected, and the corresponding text boxes still appear at the bottom of the master.

> **7.** In the Background group, click the **Background Styles** button, and then click **Style 2** in the gallery. The gallery closes and the page background changes from white to light gray.

> **8.** In the Close group, click the **Close Master View** button, and then save your changes.

Alyssa likes the customized handouts and makes printed color copies of them with nine slides per page so that all the presentation slides fit on one page.

Alyssa wants to be able to mark important information on a slide during the slide show. She can do this using the pointer as a pen.

Marking Slides During a Slide Show

During a slide show, you can mark the slides to emphasize a point. The **pen** is a pointer that allows you to draw lines on the screen during a slide show. For example, you might use it to underline a word or phrase that you want to emphasize, or to circle a graphic that you want to point out. PowerPoint gives you the option of three pen types: Ballpoint Pen (draws thin, usually blue lines), Felt Tip Pen (draws thicker, usually red lines), and Highlighter (draws thick, usually yellow, transparent lines). You can change the ink color of any of the pens you select. You can also select the Eraser tool to remove pen lines that you've already drawn. After you go through a presentation and mark it, you have the choice of keeping the markings or discarding them.

To use the pen to mark slides during the slide show:

> **1.** Display **Slide 8** ("Results") in the Slide pane, and then on the status bar, click the **Slide Show** button ⬚. Slide 8 appears in Slide Show view.

> **2.** Move the mouse until you see the mouse pointer. The pointer appears on the screen, but it will disappear again if you don't move the mouse for a couple seconds.

> **3.** Right-click anywhere on the screen, point to **Pointer Options** on the shortcut menu, and then click **Pen**. You can use the Pointer Options shortcut menu to select the type of pen, ink color, and other options. After you have selected the Pen, the mouse pointer becomes a small, red dot. By clicking and dragging the pen on the screen, you can draw lines.

> **4.** Click and drag to draw a circle around the last set of columns to draw attention to it. See Figure 4-28.

Figure 4-28   **Slide 8 in Slide Show view with Pen mark**

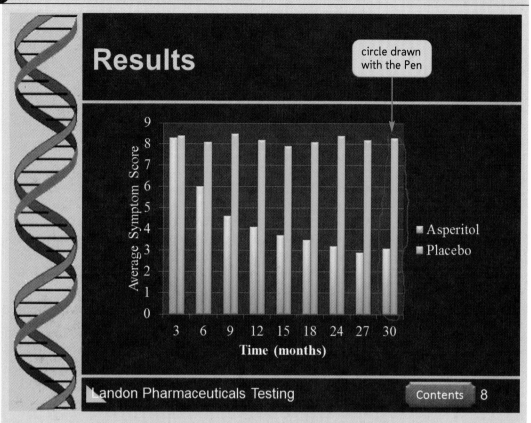

5. Press the **spacebar** to move to Slide 9. Note that you can't click the mouse button to proceed through the slide show while a pointer pen is selected.

6. Repeat Step 3 to select the Pen again, and then starting in the yellow panel on the left, draw an arrow pointing to the first bulleted item.

7. Right-click anywhere on the slide, point to **Pointer Options** on the shortcut menu, and then click **Arrow**. The mouse pointer changes back to the arrow pointer. Now you can click the mouse button to advance the slide show.

8. Click the mouse button to end the slide show and display the black screen, and then click again to return to Normal view. A dialog box opens asking if you want to keep your ink annotations.

9. Click the **Keep** button. Slide 8 ("Results") appears in Normal view. Because you chose to keep the annotations, the red circle you drew around the last set of columns is on the slide. The marks you drew in Slide Show view can be deleted just like any object on a slide.

10. Click the red circle you drew to select it, and then press the **Delete** key. The circle is deleted.

11. Display **Slide 9** ("Summary and Recommendation") in the Slide pane. Notice that the arrow that you drew is on the slide. You'll keep this annotation in the presentation for now.

12. Save your changes.

TIP

If you want to skip a slide during a slide show, in Normal view, click the Slide Show tab, and then click the Hide Slide button in the Set Up group.

Sharing and Collaborating with Others

You can send a presentation to colleagues for review. They can make changes and add comments that you can then review. You can also examine a presentation to make sure it doesn't contain private information or to see if it contains features that are supported by previous versions of PowerPoint. Finally, if you want to send a presentation for review but do not want to allow anyone to make any changes, you can mark the presentation as final.

Adding Comments to a Presentation

It can be helpful to have colleagues review your presentation and give you suggestions on how to improve it or to check it for accuracy. If a colleague notices something, he or she can insert a comment describing the issue.

Alyssa asks you to review her presentation and comment if you see any problems. When you insert a comment in a presentation, it is labeled with the name and initials of the person listed in the User Name and in the Initials box on the General tab in the PowerPoint Options dialog box. You can change this to your own name. You'll do this now.

Note: If you are working in a lab or on a public computer, get permission from your instructor before completing the following steps.

To change the user name in the PowerPoint Options dialog box:

▶ 1. Click the **File** tab, and then click the **Options** command in the navigation bar. The PowerPoint Options dialog box opens with General selected in the left panel.

▶ 2. Note the name currently in the User name box and the initials in the Initials box. If the name and initials in these boxes are not yours, make a note of them as you will need to restore these later.

▶ 3. If necessary, click in the **User name** box, delete the current name, and then type your name.

▶ 4. If necessary, click in the **Initials** box, delete the current initials, and then type your initials.

▶ 5. Click the **OK** button to close the dialog box.

Now that your name and initials are listed in the PowerPoint Options dialog box, you can insert a comment.

To insert a comment in Slide 3:

▶ 1. Display **Slide 3** ("Clinical Trial") in the Slide pane, and then click the **Review** tab on the Ribbon.

▶ 2. In the Comments group, click the **New Comment** button. A blank comment box is inserted in the document with the insertion point inside it. See Figure 4-29. The current date appears in the upper-right of the comment box. The name in the User name box in the General tab in the PowerPoint Options dialog box appears in the upper-left of the comment box. (If you performed the previous set of steps, then this should be your name.) Also, a comment thumbnail to the left of the comment box contains your initials. The number 1 in the comment thumbnail indicates that this is the first comment inserted in this presentation.

Figure 4-29   New blank comment inserted in Slide 3

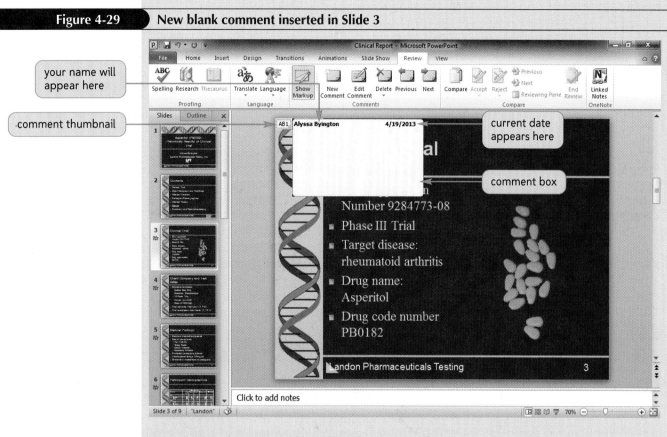

> **3.** Type **Is the number correct?**

> **4.** Click outside the comment box. The comment box closes and you see only the comment thumbnail.

You realize that there are two numbers on Slide 3—the FDA Application Number and the drug code number. Alyssa suggests you edit the comment to make it clearer, and then position it next to the bulleted item it references. You'll edit the comment and then reposition the comment thumbnail.

TIP

You can also right-click a comment thumbnail, and then click Edit Comment on the shortcut menu.

To edit and position the comment in Slide 3:

> **1.** Click the comment thumbnail. A comment balloon opens displaying the comment you typed.

> **2.** In the Comments group, click the **Edit Comment** button. The comment box appears with the insertion point in it.

> **3.** Position the insertion point immediately before the word "number," type **FDA Application**, and then press the **spacebar**.

> **4.** Click outside the comment box to close it.

> **5.** Drag the **comment** thumbnail to position it to the right of "FDA Application" in the first bulleted item.

> **6.** Save your changes.

The Compare process (in the next set of steps) can be unpredictable so save before proceeding.

Comparing Presentations

After a colleague reviews a presentation, you can compare it to your original presentation using the Compare button on the Review tab. After you select the revised presentation, a Revisions pane appears on the right listing the changes. You can select each insertion and deletion and decide whether to accept it.

Alyssa sent the presentation to Darryl Jackson, the lead researcher at Landon. He reviewed it and sent it back. Alyssa asks you to compare your original presentation with his revised presentation.

To compare two presentations:

▶ **1.** In the Compare group, click the **Compare** button. The Choose File to Merge with Current Presentation dialog box opens.

▶ **2.** Navigate to the PowerPoint4\Tutorial folder, if necessary, click **DJ Review**, and then click the **Merge** button. The dialog box closes and the first slide that contains a difference between the two presentations, Slide 4 ("Client Company and Test Dates"), appears in the Slide pane. Two change thumbnails appear on the slide, one next to each object that was changed by Darryl. The changes associated with the first thumbnail are listed in a changes box next to the thumbnail. Darryl's name—the person who made the change—appears in parentheses after each change. The Revisions pane opens on the right. See Figure 4-30. Alyssa agrees with the change Darryl made to the title text.

Trouble? If the change thumbnails do not appear on the slide in the Slide pane, but appear instead on all the slides in the Slides tab, close the presentation without saving changes, open the presentation DJ Review, located in the PowerPoint4\Tutorial folder, and then save it as DJ Review Copy to the same folder. Re-open the Clinical Report presentation, and then repeat Steps 1 and 2, but this time in Step 2, click DJ Review Copy. You might need to do this any time you compare files so that both files were saved on the same machine.

Trouble? If the change icons don't appear on your screen, click the Show Markup button in the Comments group to select it.

Trouble? If Slide 3 appears in the Slide pane listing the comments in the Revisions pane, click the Slide 4 thumbnail in the Slides tab, and then, if necessary, click the top change thumbnail to display the list of changes.

Figure 4-30   **Changes listed on Slide 4**

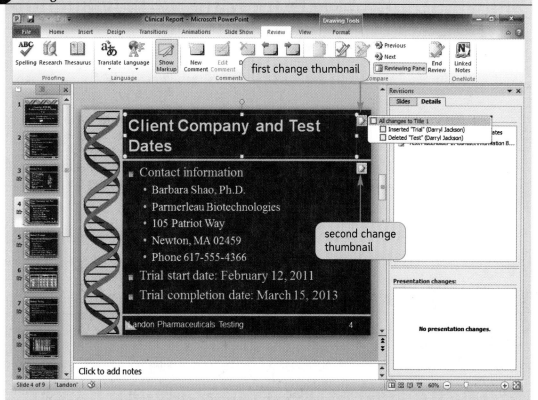

3. In the change box, click the **Inserted "Trial" (Darryl Jackson)** check box to select it. The word "Trial" appears in the title text box.

4. In the change box, click the **Deleted "Test" (Darryl Jackson)** check box. The word "Test" in the title text box is deleted. Notice that the check box next to All changes to Title 1 is also selected, and the change thumbnail now has a check mark on it. Now you'll examine the next change on the slide.

5. In the Compare group, click the **Next** button. The change box next to the title text box closes. The next change box, in this case adjacent to the content text box, opens. Now you can see the changes listed in the Revision pane.

   Trouble? If Slide 3 appears in the Slide pane listing comments in the Revisions pane, you clicked the Next button in the Comments group instead of clicking the Next comment in the Compare group. Repeat Step 5 two or three times as needed to display Slide 4 in the Slide pane with the list of changes associated with the second change thumbnail displayed, and then continue with Step 6.

6. Click the **All changes to Text Placeholder 2** check box. In the slide, "105 Patriot Way" changes to "42 Elm St." In this case, Darryl is mistaken; Parmerleau Technologies recently moved to Patriot Way.

7. Click the **All changes to Text Placeholder 2** check box to deselect it and undo the change on the slide.

8. In the Compare group, click the **Next** button. A dialog box opens stating that there are no more changes and asking if you want to continue from the beginning of the change list. You don't need to review the changes again.

9. Click the **Cancel** button. You are finished reviewing the changes in the presentation.

▶ **10.** In the Compare group, click the **End Review** button. A dialog box opens confirming that you want to end the review and warning that any unapplied changes will be discarded.

▶ **11.** Click the **Yes** button. The dialog box closes, the Revisions pane closes, and the change icons disappear. The change to the title that you accepted appears in the title text object, and the street address remains unchanged.

The Compare command does not list comments that are in the revised presentation, so after you compare two presentations, you should always check to see if the person who reviewed the presentation inserted any comments. You can decide what to do based on the comments, and then you can delete the comments when you are finished. Alyssa asks you to review the comments in the presentation next.

To review and delete a comment in the presentation:

▶ **1.** Display **Slide 1** (the title slide) in the Slide pane. You'll start your search for comments from the beginning of the presentation.

▶ **2.** In the Comments group, click the **Next** button. Slide 3 ("Clinical Trial") appears in the Slide pane, and the first comment in the presentation, the comment you inserted next to "FDA Application," is open in a comment balloon. Notice that another comment appears on this slide as well. The comment contains Darryl's initials and is a different color than the comment you inserted.

▶ **3.** Click the **DJ1** comment thumbnail. The comment balloon for your comment closes and the comment balloon for Darryl's comment opens. Alyssa double-checked the number and tells you that it is correct.

▶ **4.** In the Comments group, click the **Delete** button. The selected comment is deleted.

▶ **5.** In the Comments group, click the **Next** button. The comment balloon associated with your comment opens again.

▶ **6.** In the Comments group, click the **Next** button. A dialog box opens asking if you want to continue from the beginning of the change list.

▶ **7.** Click the **Cancel** button. The dialog box closes.

Now you need to change the user name and initials back to their original values.

To change the user name in the PowerPoint Options dialog box back to its original value:

▶ **1.** Click the **File** tab, and then click the **Options** command in the navigation bar.

▶ **2.** If necessary, click in the **User name** box, delete the current name, and then type the name that was originally in this box.

▶ **3.** If necessary, click in the **Initials** box, delete the current initials, and then type the initials originally in this box.

▶ **4.** Click the **OK** button to close the dialog box.

Using the Document Inspector

The **Document Inspector** is a tool you can use to check a presentation for hidden data, such as the author's name and other personal information, as well as comments, objects that are in the presentation but don't appear on a slide, hidden objects on slides, speaker notes, and custom data used for labeling objects and text in the presentation. Alyssa wants you to check the Clinical Report presentation for hidden data.

To check the document using the Document Inspector:

1. Click the **File** tab. Backstage view appears with the Info tab selected in the navigation bar. Backstage view displays information about the presentation. In the right pane, you see the file properties, including the number of slides and the author name. In the left pane, under Information about Clinical Report, in the Prepare for Sharing section, a bulleted list identifies hidden information and potential problems for people with vision disabilities. The types of hidden data found in the presentation are listed in the Prepare for Sharing section. See Figure 4-31.

Figure 4-31   Info tab in Backstage view

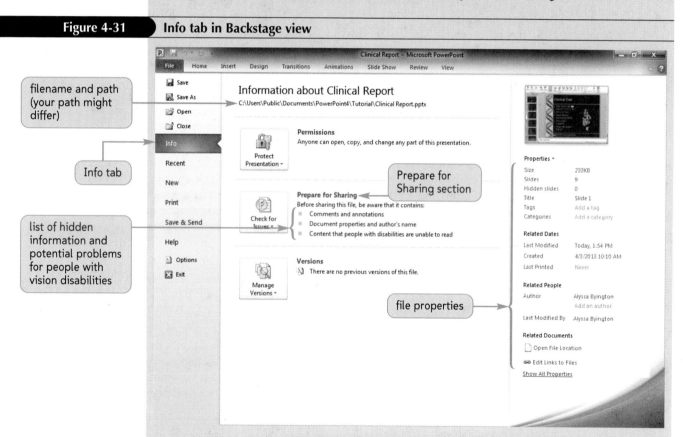

2. In the Prepare for Sharing section, click the **Check for Issues** button, and then click **Inspect Document**. The Document Inspector dialog box opens.

3. Click any of the check boxes in this dialog box that are not checked. See Figure 4-32.

Figure 4-32 Document Inspector dialog box

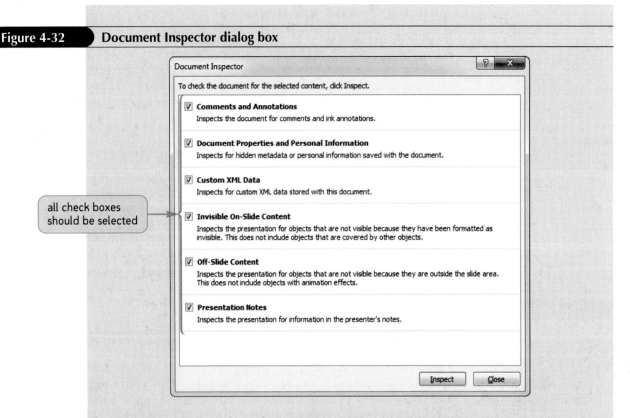

all check boxes
should be selected

▶ **4.** Click the **Inspect** button at the bottom of the dialog box. After a moment, the Document Inspector displays the results. The same items that were listed in the Prepare for Sharing section on the Info tab in Backstage view have a red exclamation point next to them in the Document Inspector dialog box. These items have a Remove All button next to them. Look over the other types of items that the Document Inspector checks. For example, if you happen to import, embed, or link an object that extends beyond the edges of a slide, the Off-Slide Content feature would have detected the problem. The annotation found is the arrow you drew on Slide 9 when you used the pen in Slide Show view, and the comment is the comment you inserted on Slide 3. Alyssa would like you to get rid of both of these items.

▶ **5.** Next to Comments and Annotations, click the **Remove All** button. The button disappears, a blue check mark replaces the red exclamation point next to Comments and Annotations, and a message appears in that section telling you that all items were successfully removed. Alyssa doesn't mind that she is identified as the author of the presentation or that other document properties are saved with the file, so you will not remove the document properties and personal information.

▶ **6.** Click the **Close** button in the dialog box. The dialog box closes and the Info tab in Backstage view is visible again.

▶ **7.** Click the **File** tab to exit Backstage view. Slide 3 ("Clinical Trial") appears again. The comment you made no longer appears on this slide.

8. Display **Slide 9** ("Summary and Recommendation") in the Slide pane. The arrow that you drew using the Pen in Slide Show view is no longer on the slide.

9. Save your changes.

Making a Presentation Accessible to People with Vision Disabilities

The Accessibility Checker allows you to check a presentation for content that someone with a vision disability would have trouble seeing or reading. It lists each error and offers suggestions on how to fix it. To check the presentation for content that is difficult for people with a vision disability to read, display the Info tab in Backstage view. In the Prepare for Sharing section, click the Check for Issues button, and then click Check Accessibility. Backstage view will close, and the presentation appears in Normal view with the Accessibility Checker pane open on the right displaying a list of the errors found. Click each error to see an explanation of the problem in the bottom part of the pane, along with instructions on how to fix it.

Identifying Features Not Supported by Previous Versions

Alyssa realizes that some of her clients and colleagues haven't yet upgraded to PowerPoint 2010, so she asks you to check the Clinical Report presentation for features not supported by previous versions. For this purpose, you'll use the Microsoft PowerPoint Compatibility Checker.

To check for features not supported by previous versions of PowerPoint:

1. Click the **File** tab on the Ribbon to display the Info tab in Backstage view.

2. In the Prepare for Sharing section, click the **Check for Issues** button, and then click **Check Compatibility**. Backstage view closes, and after a moment, the Microsoft PowerPoint Compatibility Checker dialog box opens listing features that aren't supported by earlier versions of PowerPoint. See Figure 4-33. Look over the features in the dialog box. Most of the incompatible features would probably show up properly; you just wouldn't be able to edit them. The last issue listed warns you that the transition effect you selected will not appear in earlier versions of PowerPoint. You inform Alyssa of these incompatibilities so she can decide later if she wants to save the presentation in an earlier format. Notice also that the Check compatibility when saving in PowerPoint 97-2003 formats check box is selected. This means that if you save the presentation in the format compatible with PowerPoint versions 97 through 2003, the Compatibility Checker will run automatically.

| Figure 4-33 | Microsoft PowerPoint Compatibility Checker dialog box |

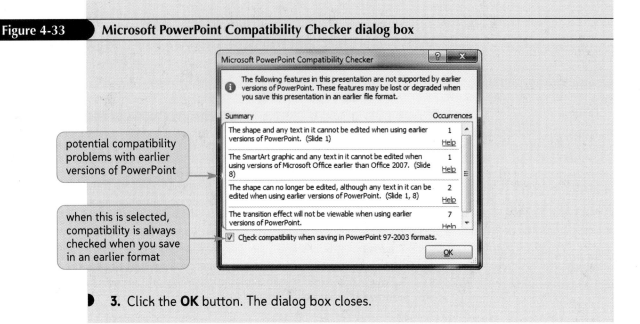

3. Click the **OK** button. The dialog box closes.

Marking the Presentation as Final

Alyssa wants to send a preview of the presentation to her colleagues at Landon, but she does not want them to make changes. One way to prevent people from making changes to a presentation is to mark it as final. This makes the presentation "read-only," which means that others can read but not modify it. After you mark a presentation as final, you can turn off this status, and then edit the presentation, but this will remove the Marked as Final status. You'll mark Clinical Report as final for Alyssa. First, you'll change the name in the subtitle text box to your own name.

To mark the presentation as final:

1. Display **Slide 1** (the title slide) in the Slide pane, and then replace "Alyssa Byington" with your name.

2. Click the **File** tab. Backstage view appears again with the Info tab selected. In the Permissions section, the message tells you that anyone can open, copy, and change the presentation.

3. In the Permissions section, click the **Protect Presentation** button, and then click **Mark as Final**. A dialog box opens stating that the presentation will be marked as final and then saved.

4. Click the **OK** button. The dialog box closes and another dialog box opens telling you that the document has been marked as final.

Trouble? If the dialog box stating that the document has been marked as final does not appear, someone clicked the Don't show this message again check box in that dialog box. Skip Step 5.

5. Click the **OK** button. The Permissions section now indicates that the presentation has been marked as final. See Figure 4-34.

| Figure 4-34 | Info tab after presentation is marked as final |

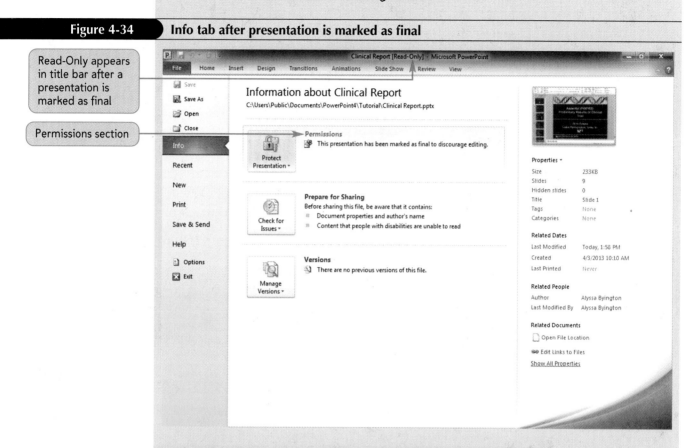

Read-Only appears in title bar after a presentation is marked as final

Permissions section

6. Click the **File** tab on the Ribbon. Backstage view closes and the presentation appears in Normal view. A yellow Marked as Final bar appears in place of the Ribbon, the Marked as Final icon 👹 appears in the status bar, and "Read-Only" appears in the title bar. See Figure 4-35.

Figure 4-35	Presentation in Normal view after it is marked as final

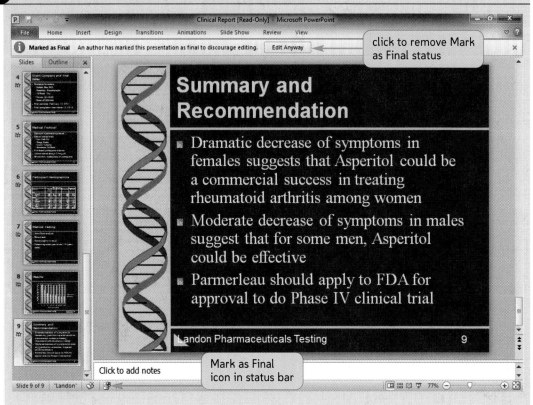

Next, you'll save the presentation using various methods so that others can easily view it.

PROSKILLS

Teamwork: Virtual Teams and Technology

A virtual team is one whose members rarely, if ever, meet in person to work on team tasks or build a corporate culture or team camaraderie. Instead, technology makes it possible for members to be geographically distant yet work as if everyone was in the same room. Virtual team members use technologies such as email and voice mail, file transfer protocol (FTP) sites, telephone, Web conferencing software, and groupware and collaboration software tools, such as those found in Office 2010.

Virtual teams often must work rapidly and cohesively to accomplish tasks, so knowing how best to use these technologies is critical. To make virtual teams function well, team leaders must spend extra time ensuring that each member is equipped to work together in a virtual environment. This means leaders need to build trust early and quickly figure out the best way to communicate with team members. The leader must also find a way to let individuals get to know one another. Since the team can't all gather at a local restaurant after work on Thursdays, for example, using technology to help socialize, share photos, and build community can make a difference in team productivity. Effectively using digital communication tools also can increase team member connection and the ability to get work done efficiently.

Saving the Presentation for Distribution

PowerPoint lets you save presentations in several formats that allow others to view the presentation, but does not allow them to make any changes to it. You can save the presentation as a picture presentation, create a video from a presentation, and save the presentation in PDF format. Each method produces a different type of file for you to distribute. First, you'll save the presentation as a picture presentation.

Saving the Presentation as a Picture Presentation

If you want to distribute your presentation to others so they can see it but prevent them from modifying it or copying complex animations, backgrounds, or other features, you can save the presentation as a picture presentation. When you save a presentation as a picture presentation, each slide is saved as an image file in the JPEG format, and then that image is placed on a slide in a new presentation so that it fills the entire slide.

Alyssa wants to give her presentation to the management team at Pamerleau Biotechnologies so that they can make it available to their employees. However, she doesn't want them to be able to modify it or copy the slide background. She asks you to save the presentation as a picture.

To save the presentation as a picture:

1. Click the **File** tab, and then click the **Save & Send** tab in the navigation bar.

2. In the File Types section in the left pane, click **Change File Type**. The right pane of the Save & Send tab changes to list various file type options that you can save the presentation as. See Figure 4-36.

Figure 4-36   **Change File Type selected on Save & Send tab in Backstage view**

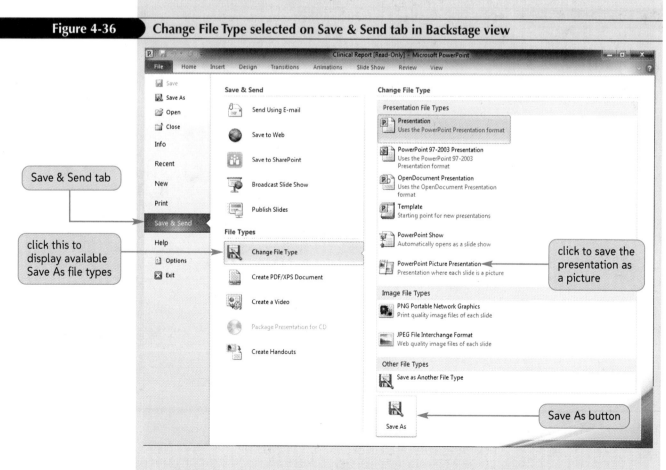

TIP

You can also save the slides as individual image files by selecting one of the file types under Image File Types on the Save & Send tab or by selecting GIF, JPEG, PNG, or TIFF as the file type in the Save As dialog box.

3. In the Presentation File Types section in the right pane, click **PowerPoint Picture Presentation**, and then click the **Save As** button. Backstage view closes and the Save As dialog box opens with PowerPoint Picture Presentation in the Save as type box. The name in the File name box is the same as the presentation filename.

4. If necessary, navigate to the PowerPoint4\Tutorial folder, change the filename to **Landon Report**, and then click the **Save** button. The Save As dialog box closes and, after a moment, another dialog box opens telling you that a copy of the presentation has been saved.

5. Click the **OK** button. The dialog box closes.

You can open the picture presentation in the same way you normally open a presentation. You'll do this now.

To open the picture presentation:

1. Click the **File** tab, and then click the **Open** command in the navigation bar. The Open dialog box opens.

2. Navigate to the PowerPoint4\Tutorial folder, if necessary, and then double-click **Landon Report**. The Landon Report opens in Normal view.

3. In the Slide pane, click anywhere on the slide. Notice that sizing handles appear around the edges of the Slide pane. This is because the objects in the original slide were converted to a single JPEG file. See Figure 4-37.

Figure 4-37   **JPEG image on Slide 1 selected in the picture presentation**

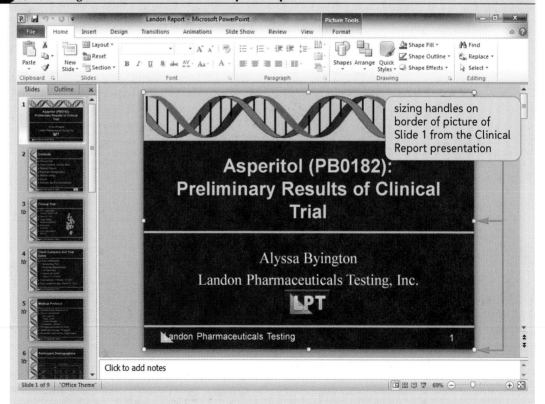

4. Display **Slide 2** ("Contents") in the Slide pane, and then click the action button. The whole image of Slide 2 is selected, not the action button.

▶ **5.** On the status bar, click the **Slide Show** button 🖵. Slide 2 appears in Slide Show view.

▶ **6.** Click the **Results** link. The slide show transitions to Slide 3 instead of jumping to Slide 8 ("Results"). The Results link does not function because this is just a picture of the original Slide 2.

▶ **7.** Advance the slide show. Slide 4 transitions onto the screen with the Rotate transition. Recall that in the original presentation, the Rotate transition rotated the text and objects onto the screen while keeping the slide background static. In this presentation, the Rotate transition was retained, but it appears as if the entire slide rotates because the picture of each slide is the content on the slide that rotates.

▶ **8.** Press the **Esc** key to end the slide show, and then close the **Landon Report** presentation. The Clinical Report presentation appears again.

Saving a Presentation as a Video

You can also save a presentation as a Windows Media Video file (with a .wmv filename extension). When you save it, you can choose the resolution of the video and how long each slide will appear on the screen. After you have created the video, you can play it in Windows Media Player or any other video player.

Alyssa wants you to save a presentation as a video so she can distribute it to Landon shareholders who do not know how to use PowerPoint.

To save the presentation as a video:

▶ **1.** Click the **File** tab, and then in the navigation bar, click the **Save & Send** tab. The Save & Send tab appears in Backstage view.

▶ **2.** In the File Types section, click **Create a Video**. The right pane of Backstage view changes to show options for creating a video. See Figure 4-38. First, you need to select the quality of the video you want to create. Alyssa wants people to be able to play this presentation on their MP3 players, cell phones, or other portable devices.

Figure 4-38 Save & Send tab in Backstage view with Create a Video selected

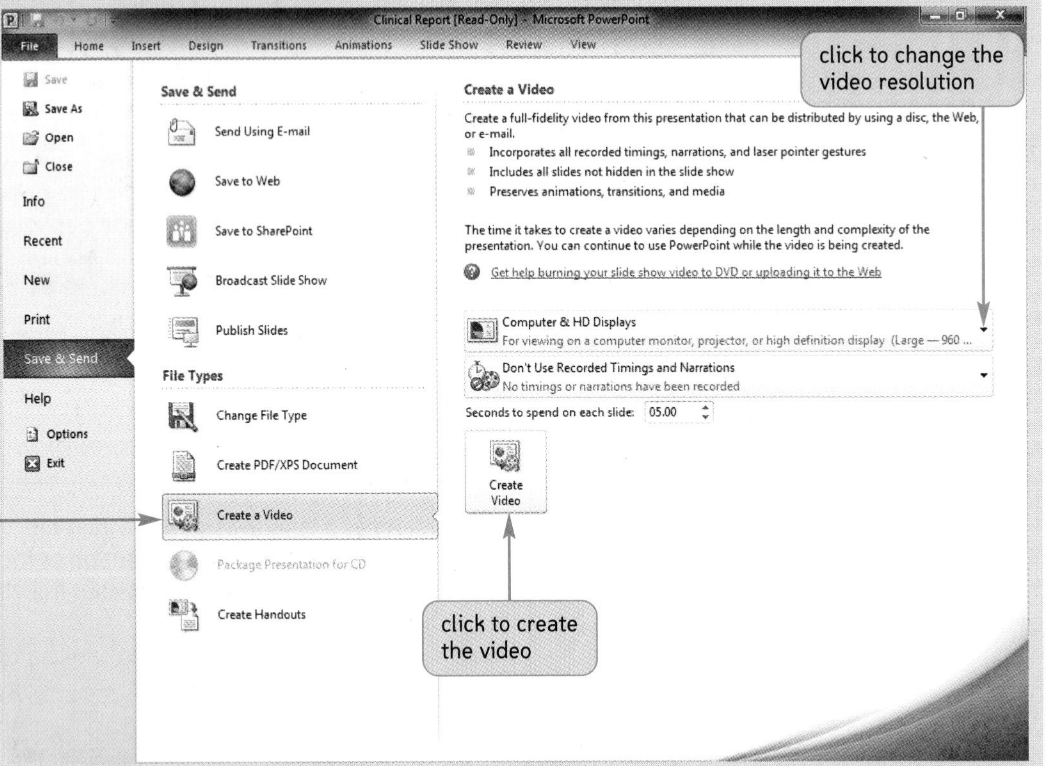

click to display options for creating a video

click to change the video resolution

click to create the video

3. Click the **Computer & HD Displays** button, and then click **Portable Devices**. Next, you need to choose the number of seconds for each slide to be displayed.

4. In the Seconds to spend on each slide box, click the **down arrow** twice. The number of seconds to spend on each slide is changed to 3.

5. Click the **Create Video** button. Backstage view closes and the Save As dialog box opens with Windows Media Video selected in the Save as type box.

6. Change the name in the File name box to **Clinical Report video**, and then click the **Save** button. The dialog box closes and a progress bar labeled Creating video Clinical Report video.wmv appears in the status bar. After a moment, the progress bar disappears.

Now that you've created the video, you can use Windows Media Player to watch it.

To watch the movie:

1. On the taskbar, click the **Start** button, and then on the right side of the Start menu, click **Documents**.

2. Navigate to the PowerPoint4\Tutorial folder. The Clinical Report video file is included in the file list.

3. Double-click **Clinical Report video**. Windows Media Player starts and the video you created starts playing. Figure 4-39 shows the title slide in the maximized Media Player window. Each slide displays for three seconds. Notice that the video retained the transitions you applied. After the last slide appears, the video ends, and options to restart the video and other Media Player commands appear in the Media Player window.

Trouble? If a Welcome screen appears, click the Recommended settings option button, click the Finish button, and then repeat Step 3.

Trouble? If your Media Player window is not maximized, you can click the Maximize button in the title bar.

Figure 4-39   Video in maximized Media Player window

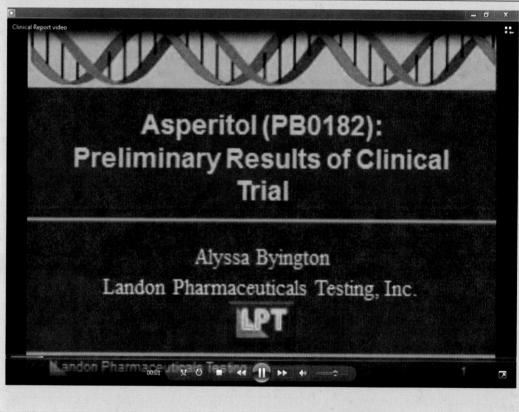

4. On the Media Player title bar, click the **Close** button ▮ X ▮.

5. In the Windows Explorer title bar, click the **Close** button ▮ X ▮. The PowerPoint window is displayed again.

Saving a Presentation as a PDF

Portable Document File (PDF) format is a file format that can be opened on any make or model of computer, as long as the computer has installed the free, downloadable program Adobe Reader. Because most computers have Adobe Reader installed, and any computer connected to the Internet can easily get it installed at no cost, a PDF is an important file format for sharing documents.

INSIGHT

Saving a Presentation as an XPS Document

You can also publish a presentation as an **XPS document**, which is a Microsoft electronic paper format that you can view in a Web browser. When you double-click the filename of an XPS document in Windows Explorer, the document opens and shows the slides as a list that you can scroll through. You can publish to an XPS document using essentially the same method you use to publish in PDF format; the only exception is that you need to click the Save as type arrow and then click XPS Document in the Publish as PDF or XPS dialog box.

The executives at Pamerleau asked Alyssa to email the presentation to several of their sales representatives so that they would have the latest information about the clinical trial. Alyssa knows that anyone can download and install Adobe Reader, so she asks you to save the presentation as a PDF file.

To publish the presentation in PDF format:

1. Click the **File** tab, and then click the **Save & Send** tab in the navigation bar.

2. In the File Types section, click **Create PDF/XPS Document**. The right pane of the Save & Send tab changes to describe the PDF and XPS file types.

3. Click the **Create PDF/XPS** button. Backstage view closes, and the Publish as PDF or XPS dialog box opens with PDF listed in the Save as type box. See Figure 4-40.

   Trouble? If XPS appears in the Save as type box instead of PDF, click the Save as type arrow, and then click PDF.

Figure 4-40 Publish as PDF or XPS dialog box

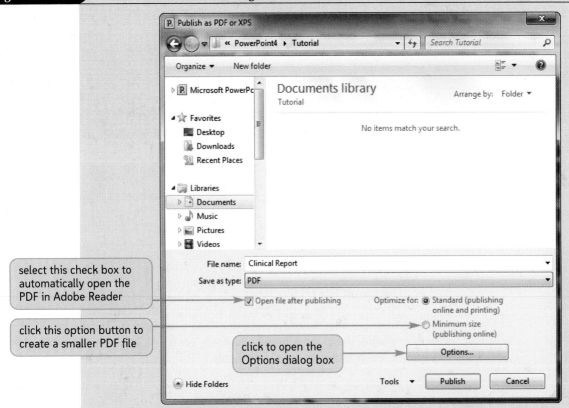

▶ **4.** Navigate to the PowerPoint4\Tutorial folder, if necessary, and then change the filename to **Clinical Report PDF**. You want to create a smaller file size suitable for attaching to an email message.

▶ **5.** Click the **Minimum size** (publishing online) option button. You can change the options for the PDF file.

▶ **6.** Click the **Options** button. The Options dialog box opens. See Figure 4-41. Alyssa doesn't want the document properties to be included, as she expects this file to be widely distributed.

| Figure 4-41 | Options dialog box for saving a presentation as a PDF file |

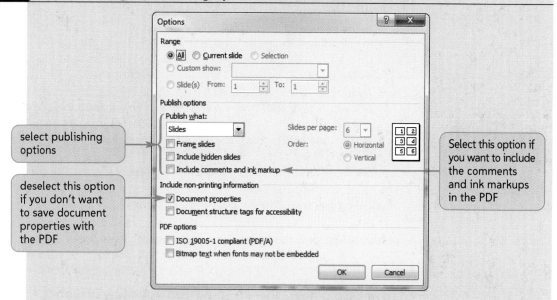

select publishing options

deselect this option if you don't want to save document properties with the PDF

Select this option if you want to include the comments and ink markups in the PDF

▶ **7.** In the Include non-printing information section, click the **Document properties** check box to deselect it.

▶ **8.** Click the **OK** button. You want to review the PDF file after saving it.

▶ **9.** In the Publish as PDF or XPS dialog box, click the **Open file after publishing** check box to select it, if necessary, and then click the **Publish** button. Your presentation is saved in PDF format, and Adobe Reader automatically opens displaying Clinical Report PDF file in the Adobe Reader window.

Trouble? If the Open file after publishing check box and label are dimmed, Adobe Reader is not installed on your computer. Click the Publish button to save the file as a PDF document, and then skip Steps 10 through 12.

▶ **10.** In the vertical scroll bar, click the down scroll arrow to view each slide as a page in the PDF file.

▶ **11.** In the title bar, click the **Close** button   ✕   to exit the Adobe Reader program.

▶ **12.** In the PowerPoint window, close the Clinical Report presentation.

TIP

If Adobe Reader is not installed on your computer, start your Web browser, and then go to Adobe's Web site at www.adobe.com. Look for a link to get the free Adobe Reader.

Saving a Presentation to SkyDrive

TIP

Cloud computing refers to data, applications, and even resources that are stored on servers that you access over the Internet rather than on your own computer.

Another way to make a presentation available to others is to save it to SkyDrive. **SkyDrive** is an online storage and file sharing service. When you create a Windows Live ID, you are also given a SkyDrive account. You can upload files to folders on your SkyDrive and then give others permission to access your folders to view or edit your files.

REFERENCE

Creating a New folder on SkyDrive and Granting Permission for Access

- Click the File tab, and then click Save & Send in the navigation bar.
- Under Save & Send, click Save to Web.
- In the pane on the right, click the Sign In button, and then sign in to your Windows Live account.
- In the pane on the right, click the New button.
- In your browser window, sign in to your Windows Live account.
- On the Create a folder page on your SkyDrive, in the Folder name box, type the new folder name.
- Next to Share with Just me, click the Change link, and then drag the slider to the appropriate option; or click in the Enter a name or an e-mail address box, type the email address of the person with whom you want to share the folder, press the Enter key, and then click the Can add, edit details, and delete files arrow and click Can view files, if desired.
- Click the Next button.

Alyssa wants her assistant, John Cho, to review her presentation. She asks you to post it to a new folder on your SkyDrive, and then give John access to the file by granting him permission to view the folder. First, you need to create the new folder.

To create a new, shared folder on your SkyDrive:

1. Click the **File** tab, click **Save & Send** in the navigation bar, and then click **Save to Web** under Save & Send.

   The right pane changes to display a Sign In button that you can use to sign in to your Windows Live account. See Figure 4-42.

| Figure 4-42 | Save & Send tab in Backstage view after clicking Save to Web |

click this to display Sign In button to sign in to SkyDrive

Save & Send tab

Trouble? If you are already signed into Windows Live, you will see the folders in your SkyDrive account listed instead, as shown in Figure 4-43. Skip Steps 3-6 and continue with Step 7.

3. Click the **Sign In** button. The Connecting to docs.live.net dialog box opens.

4. In the E-mail address box, type the email address associated with your Windows Live ID account.

5. Press the **Tab** key, and then type the password associated with your Windows Live account in the Password box.

6. Click the **OK** button. The dialog box closes, and another dialog box appears briefly while you connect to the Windows Live server. After you connect, the right pane in Backstage view changes to list the folders on your SkyDrive account. See Figure 4-43. You want to create a new folder on your SkyDrive.

| Figure 4-43 | Save & Send tab after connecting to Windows Live |

your Windows Live account name appears here

▶ **7.** In the right pane, click the **New** button. Your browser starts, or if your browser is already open, a new tab opens, and the page to sign in to your Windows Live account appears.

▶ **8.** In the Windows Live ID box, type the email address associated with your Windows Live ID account, click in the **Password** box, type your password, and then click the **Sign in** button. The Create a folder page on your SkyDrive appears. The temporary name New folder is selected in the Name box.

Trouble? If there is an email address listed under sign in and it is not your email address, click the Sign in with a different Windows Live ID link, and then complete Step 8. If there is an email address listed under sign in and it is your email address, point to it, click the Sign in button, type your password in the box below your email address, click the Sign in button again, and then continue with Step 9.

▶ **9.** In the Name box, type **Landon**. This is the name of your new folder. Under the Name box, Just me appears next to Share with.

▶ **10.** Next to Just me, click the **Change** link. A list with a slider bar next to it opens and the Add specific people section appears at the bottom of the window. You can use the slider bar to make the contents of the new folder public by sharing it with everyone, your friends as listed on your Windows Live ID account and their friends, just your friends, or only some friends. You can also share it only with specific people that you list. Alyssa wants to share this folder with her assistant, John.

▶ **11.** Under Add specific people, click in the **Enter a name or an e-mail address** box, and then type **cho_john@live.com**. This is the email address associated with John's Windows Live account.

▶ **12.** Press the **Enter** key. John's email address appears below the Enter a name or an e-mail address box next to a check box with a check mark in it, and a list box to the right identifies the level of access. Alyssa wants John to have more limited access, where he can view files in this folder, but not change the folder's contents. See Figure 4-44.

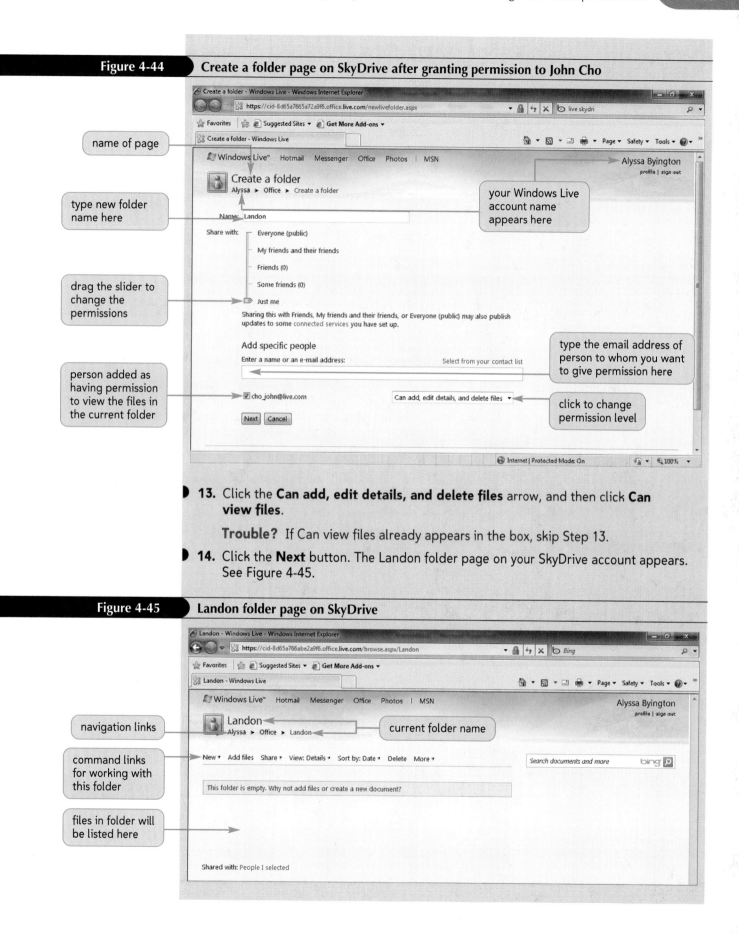

Figure 4-44   Create a folder page on SkyDrive after granting permission to John Cho

name of page

type new folder name here

drag the slider to change the permissions

person added as having permission to view the files in the current folder

your Windows Live account name appears here

type the email address of person to whom you want to give permission here

click to change permission level

13. Click the **Can add, edit details, and delete files** arrow, and then click **Can view files**.

   Trouble? If Can view files already appears in the box, skip Step 13.

14. Click the **Next** button. The Landon folder page on your SkyDrive account appears. See Figure 4-45.

Figure 4-45   Landon folder page on SkyDrive

navigation links

command links for working with this folder

files in folder will be listed here

current folder name

Now that the new folder is created, Alyssa needs you to upload the file to it. You can do this from the SkyDrive folder in the browser window or you can do this from Backstage view in the PowerPoint window.

REFERENCE

Saving a File to a Folder on SkyDrive

- Click the File tab, and then click Save & Send in the navigation bar.
- Under Save & Send, click Save to Web, and then sign into your Windows Live ID account if necessary.
- In the pane on the right, click the folder to which you want to save the file, and then click the Save As button.
- In the Save As dialog box, click the Save button.

To upload a presentation from PowerPoint to a folder on your SkyDrive:

1. On the taskbar, click the **PowerPoint** button [Ps]. The PowerPoint program window with Backstage view displayed is the active window. The new Landon folder does not appear in the list.

2. Click the **Refresh Folder List** button [⟳] to the right of the folder list. You now see the Landon folder in the list. This is the folder to which you want to save the file.

   Trouble? If you do not see the folder list on your SkyDrive, your connection to your SkyDrive timed out. Click the large Refresh button, and then continue with Step 3.

3. In the folder list, click the **Landon** folder.

4. Click the **Save As** button. Backstage view closes, and then after a few moments, the Save As dialog box opens.

5. Click the **Save** button. The Clinical Report file is saved to the Landon folder on your SkyDrive.

When you grant permission for other people to access a folder on your SkyDrive, you need to send them the link to the folder so that they can find it. Alyssa asks you to do this now.

To send the link of a shared folder:

1. On the taskbar, click the button corresponding to your browser. The Landon folder on your SkyDrive appears with the Clinical Report file listed.

   Trouble? If you don't see the Clinical Report file, click the Refresh button [↻] on the Address bar in the browser window.

2. Position the pointer on the filename. A ScreenTip appears listing details about the file, and commands for working with the file replace your name to the right of the file. See Figure 4-46.

Figure 4-46   **Clinical Report file in the Landon folder on SkyDrive**

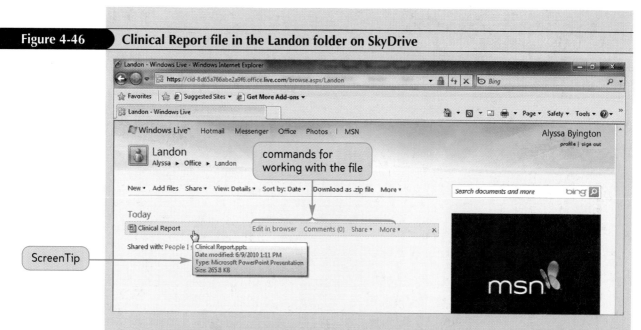

3. In the list of commands that appear, click the **Share** link, and then click **Send a link**. The Permissions for Clinical Report.pptx page appears with a message that tells you that permission for the Clinical Report file comes from the Landon folder. See Figure 4-47. Permission is not granted to individual files on SkyDrive; it is granted to folders at the same level as the My Documents and the Public folder.

Figure 4-47   **Permissions for Clinical Report.pptx page on SkyDrive**

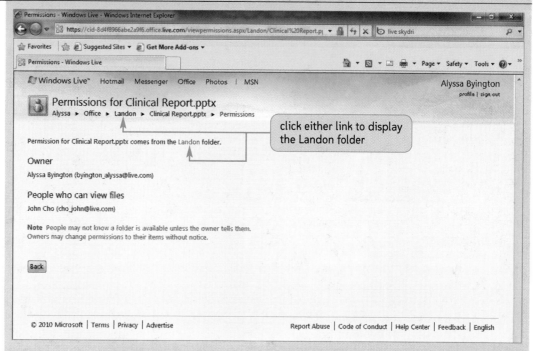

4. Click the **Landon** link. The Landon folder page appears. See Figure 4-48.

Figure 4-48 Landon folder page on SkyDrive

5. In the list of command links, click the **Share** link, and then click **Send a link**. The Send a link page appears. See Figure 4-49. Because you already granted John permission to access the folder, his email address appears in the To box. Alyssa wants you to send a copy of the message to yourself so that you have a record of it.

Figure 4-49 Send a link page on SkyDrive

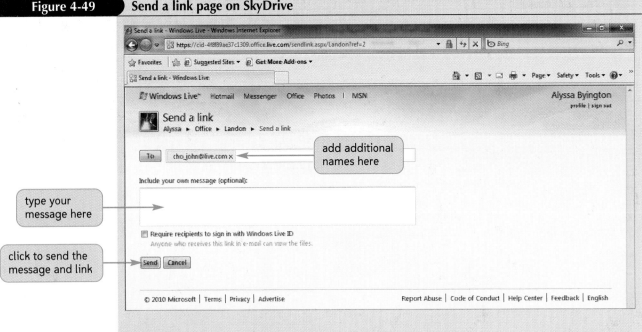

6. In the To box, type your email address.

7. Click in the **Include your own message (optional)** box, and then type **Here is the link to the Landon folder on my SkyDrive**.

8. Click the **Send** button. The Send a link page closes and the Landon folder page appears again.

If you had added additional names in the To box on the Send a link page, those people would have automatically been granted permission to access the Landon folder.

You will receive an email message in your Inbox with the subject "*<Your Name>* has shared documents with you." In the message, there is a View folder button that you can click to go directly to the Landon folder on your SkyDrive.

Once a file is stored on SkyDrive, you can download it to your hard drive if you need to by pointing to the filename to display the links for working with the file, clicking the More link, and then clicking Download.

Alyssa is pleased to have several options for distributing the presentation file to others without allowing them to modify the presentation.

REVIEW

Session 4.2 Quick Check

1. How is a dynamic content transition different from an ordinary transition?
2. True or False. When you mark a slide with the Pen during a slide show, you cannot save your annotations.
3. What appears in the comment thumbnail when you insert a comment?
4. What does the Document Inspector reveal?
5. In Normal view, how do you know if a presentation is marked as final?
6. What happens when a presentation is saved as a picture presentation?
7. What is the file type of a presentation that you save as a video?

Review Assignments

Data Files needed for the Review Assignments: Company.pptx, Hospitals.docx, Landon2.pptx, LPTChart.xlsx, LPTInfo.docx, LT Review.pptx

Alyssa not only gives reports on clinical trials to clients of Landon Pharmaceuticals Testing, she also gives presentations to prospective clients. She now asks you to help prepare an information presentation on Landon Pharmaceuticals Testing. Complete the following steps:

1. Open the file **Company**, located in the PowerPoint4\Review folder included with your Data Files, and then save the presentation to the same folder as **Landon Info**.

2. Import the Word outline **LPTInfo**, located in the PowerPoint4\Review folder, after Slide 2.

3. Apply the Title and Content layout to all of the new slides except Slides 5 and 9. Apply the Two Content layout to Slide 5 and the Title Only layout to Slide 9.

4. Reset the slides, and then turn on slide numbering and apply the footer in the Header and Footer dialog box to all the slides, including the title slide.

5. Export the outline to a Rich Text file named **Landon Info Outline** in the PowerPoint4\Review folder.

6. Start Word, open the **Landon Info Outline** file you just exported, and then change all the text to 11-point, black Calibri. Save the document as a Word document to the same folder using the same filename. Exit Word.

7. Open the **Landon2** presentation located in the PowerPoint4\Review folder, and then copy the picture of the pill bottles on Slide 4 ("Previous Trials") to the Clipboard.

8. Switch back to the Landon Info presentation. Paste the picture of the pill bottles in Slide 5 ("What Our Subcontractors Do"), and then delete the content placeholder on Slide 5. Position the picture approximately centered in the blank area on the right side of the slide. Close the Landon2 presentation.

9. Remove the background from the picture of the pill bottles. Make sure all parts of the pill bottles are marked to keep and all of the gray background is marked for removal.

10. In Slide 8, use the Object command to embed the Word table from the Word file **Hospitals**, located in the PowerPoint4\Review folder.

11. Make the Word program active, change the font size for all the text in the table to 16 points, change the style of all the text in the first row to bold, change the font color for all the text in the table to white, and then change the border color to Orange, Accent 6. Click a blank area of the slide and return to PowerPoint, and then drag the table to position it in the center of the area below the title on the slide.

12. Start Excel, open the Excel file **LPTChart**, located in the PowerPoint4\Review folder, and then save it as **Landon Cost Chart** in the same folder.

13. Copy the chart, and then return to the Landon Info presentation (but do not close the Landon Cost Chart workbook). Use the Paste command to paste the chart as a link on Slide 9 ("Costs per Phase III Patient 2007 to 2013") using the theme from the presentation. Resize the chart so it fits in the blank area of the slide.

14. Use the Edit Data command to display the PowerPoint and the Excel windows side by side, go to Sheet1 in the Excel window, edit the cost per patient in 2009 to $3417, and then save the file and exit Excel.

15. In Slide 3 ("What We Will Cover"), create a hyperlink to Slide 5 ("What Our Subcontractors Do") from the second bulleted item.

16. In Slide 3 ("What We Will Cover"), create a Plaque shape in the lower-right corner of the slide. Add the text **Mission Statement** to the shape, and then resize and reposition the shape so that it fits to the left of the slide number and below the yellow horizontal line, and so the text fits inside the shape on one line. Make the shape a hyperlink to Slide 2.

17. In Slide 5, insert the Action Button: Home at the bottom of the slide, between the footer and slide number. Use the Hyperlink to list in the Action Settings dialog box to link to Slide 3 in the presentation. (*Hint*: Click Slide in the Hyperlink to list.)

18. Adjust the size of the action button so that it fits between the yellow line at the bottom of the slide just to the left of the slide number, and then change the shape style of the action button to Intense Effect – Orange, Accent 6.

19. Apply the Conveyor transition in the Dynamic Content section of the Transitions gallery to Slides 3 through 10.

20. Customize the Handout Master so that it displays only the date and the page number. Change the background style of the Handout Master to Style 6.

21. Run the slide show. Verify that the links on Slide 3 and the action button on Slide 5 work. On Slide 5, circle the third bulleted item ("Prepare matching placebos"), and then underline the slide title. When the slide show is finished, save the annotations.

22. Change the name and initials on the General tab in the PowerPoint Options dialog box to your name and initials, if necessary. On Slide 8 ("Associated Hospitals and Clinics"), insert the following as a new comment: **Please verify that the contact names are up-to-date.**

23. Edit the comment you just inserted by inserting **and email addresses** after "names," and then position the comment thumbnail above the third column in the table.

24. Compare your presentation to the presentation **LT Review**, located in the PowerPoint4\Review folder. Accept all the changes to the title text box on Slide 8, do not accept the second change on Slide 8, and then delete the LT1 comment.

25. Change the name and initials on the General tab in the PowerPoint Options dialog box back to their original values, if necessary, and then add your name as the subtitle on Slide 1.

26. Save your changes, and then, if necessary, change the user name and initials on the General tab in the PowerPoint Options dialog box back to their original values.

27. Inspect the document for hidden and private data. Remove the document properties and personal information. Do not remove the comments and annotations. Save the file again.

28. Check the file to see if there are any features not supported by earlier versions of PowerPoint.

29. Mark the presentation as final.

30. Post the file to a new folder named Landon Info on your SkyDrive, giving permission to Alyssa's assistant John Cho using the email address cho_john@live.com.

31. Save the presentation as a picture presentation named **Info Pictures** in the PowerPoint4\Review folder.

32. Save the presentation as a video named **Landon Info video** in the PowerPoint4\Review folder. Set the resolution for Portable Devices, and change the seconds to spend on each slide to four.

33. Save the presentation as a PDF file named **Landon Info PDF** in the PowerPoint4\Review folder using Standard optimization. Do not change any of the options.

34. Submit the completed presentation and other files in printed or electronic form, as requested by your instructor, and then close all open files.

Apply your skills to create a presentation to recruit new customers for a credit union.

APPLY

Case Problem 1

Data Files needed for this Case Problem: Branches.docx, DH Review.pptx, FLCU.pptx, FLCUChart.xlsx, FLCUOutline.docx, FLCUPhotos.pptx

Flat Lake Credit Union   Dwayne Harris is the manager of the Flat Lake Credit Union in Safford, Arizona. One of his responsibilities is to give presentations to potential customers about the services and benefits of membership in the credit union. Complete the following steps:

1. Open the presentation **FLCU**, located in the PowerPoint4\Case1 folder included with your Data Files, and then save the presentation to the same folder with the file-name **FLCU Services**.

2. Replace "Flat Lake Credit Union" in the title in the title slide with **Services and Benefits of Credit Union Membership** (leave "Safford Arizona" as part of the title), and then type your name as the subtitle.

3. Import the Word outline **FLCUOutline**, located in the PowerPoint4\Case1 folder after Slide 1.

4. Apply the Title and Content layout to all of the new slides except Slides 3, 7, and 9, apply the Two Content layout to Slides 3 and 7, apply the Title Only layout to Slide 9, and then reset the new slides.

5. Display the footer and slide numbers on all the slides except the title slide.

6. Open the presentation **FLCUPhotos**, and then copy the photo of money in Slide 2. Paste this photo in Slide 3 ("Loans") of the FLCU Services presentation. Remove the background of the photo.

7. In FLCUPhotos, copy the photo of the building on Slide 3. In Slide 7 ("Special Member Discounts") of the FLCU Services presentation, resize the text placeholder that contains the bulleted list so it is double its current width, and then delete the content placeholder. Paste the photo of the building you copied to Slide 7, and then position it below the bulleted list.

8. In Slide 8 ("Credit Union Branches"), embed a Word table from the file **Branches**, located in the PowerPoint4\Case1 folder. Resize the table so it appears as large as possible.

9. Edit the table so that the text is yellow and the borders are white.

10. In Slide 9 ("Credit Union Earnings"), link the chart in the Excel worksheet **FLCUChart** (located in the PowerPoint4\Case1 folder), and then resize the chart so it fits in the blank area of the slide. Exit Excel when you are finished.

11. In Slide 10, insert the Action Button: Home, and make it a hyperlink to the first slide in the presentation. (*Hint:* Change the "Hyperlink to" value to First Slide.)

12. Resize the action button to 0.75 by 0.75 inches. (*Hint:* With the action button selected, click the Drawing Tools Format tab, and then use the Shape Height and Shape Width boxes in the Size group.)

13. Move the action button to the lower-left corner of the slide, so it's near the bottom of the picture panel of Flat Lake, and then change the shape style to Intense Effect – Green, Accent 1.

14. View the slide show in Slide Show view. On Slide 2, use the Pen to circle each instance of the word "Free." Test the action button that you inserted on Slide 10. Keep the annotations.

15. Compare the presentation with the presentation **DH Review**, located in the PowerPoint4\Case1 folder. Locate and accept the suggested change (reject the change to the subtitle text on the title slide), and then locate and delete both comments. Do not delete the annotations. (*Hint:* When you accept the change, the check mark might not appear in the change thumbnail.)

16. Inspect the document for private or hidden data. Remove all of the annotations and document properties and personal information.

17. Save your changes, and then mark the presentation as final.

18. Post the presentation to a new folder named FLCU on your SkyDrive. Do not grant permission to anyone to view or edit the files in this folder.

19. Save the presentation as a video named **FLCU video** in the PowerPoint4\Case1 folder. Set the resolution to Portable Devices and set the time to spend on each slide to three seconds.

20. Submit the completed presentation and video in printed or electronic form as instructed, and then close the presentation.

Expand your skills to create a presentation for a wildlife management company.

CHALLENGE

Case Problem 2

Data Files needed for this Case Problem: Bird.jpg, Flower.jpg, WMCchart.xlsx, WMCDesign.pptx, WMCOutline.docx

Wildlife Management Consultants Hillary Trejo of DeForest, Wisconsin, is president of Wildlife Management Consultants (WMC), a small company that contracts with the Wisconsin Division of Natural Resources and the Bureau of Wildlife Management to manage wildlife (plants and animals) in refuges and state forests. Hillary asks you to help her prepare and publish a presentation on the services offered by WMC. She wants you to modify this file so you can use it in other presentations as a design theme. Complete the following steps:

1. Open the presentation file **WMCDesign** located in the PowerPoint4\Case2 folder included with your Data Files. Replace the name in the subtitle with your name, and then save the presentation as **WMC Services** in the same folder.

2. Switch to Slide Master view, and then click the Office Theme Slide Master at the top of the pane on the left side of the window.

⊕ **EXPLORE**
3. Click the placeholder text of the level-1 (top) bullet, and change the bullet to the picture **Bird**, located in the PowerPoint4\Case2 folder. (*Hint:* Open the Picture Bullet dialog box, and then click the Import button.) Make the second-level bullet the picture **Flower**, located in the PowerPoint4\Case2 folder.

4. After Slide 1, import the Word outline in the file **WMCOutline**, located in the PowerPoint4\Case2 folder. Apply the Title and Content layout to all of the inserted slides, and then reset the slides to follow the default design theme.

5. Make each of the bulleted items in Slide 2 ("Services") a link to the corresponding slide in the presentation.

⊕ **EXPLORE**
6. Format the background image Wilderness (text with overlaid plants and animals) as a hyperlink to Slide 2. (*Hint:* Switch to Slide Master view.)

7. In Slide 8, change the layout to Title Only, and then link the Excel chart **WMCchart**, located in the PowerPoint4\Case2 folder. Resize the chart so it fits in the blank area in the slide.

⊕ **EXPLORE**
8. Change the chart design to Style 45. (*Hint:* Click the Chart Tools Design tab, click the Chart Styles More button, and then use the ScreenTips to locate the correct style.)

⊕ **EXPLORE**
9. Customize the Handout Master in the following ways:

   a. Change the font size of the header, date, footer, and page number to 20 points.

   b. Add the header text **WMC Services**.

   c. Add the footer text **Wildlife Management Consultants**, and then increase the width of the footer so the text fits all on one line.

d. Set the background to the lightest Olive Green color in the theme colors. (*Hint*: Click Format Background located at the bottom of the Background Style gallery, set the Fill to Solid fill, and then click the Color button. Click the Close button in the dialog box, not the Apply to All button, or you will apply the background style to all the slides, not just to the Handout Master.)

10. Apply the Dynamic Content Fly Through transition to every slide in the presentation.

✦ EXPLORE   11. Add the Wind sound to the transitions. (*Hint*: Click the Sound arrow in the Timing group on the Transitions tab.)

✦ EXPLORE   12. Separate the presentation into sections. Put Slides 1 and 2 in the first section, Slides 3 and 4 in the second section, Slides 5, 6, and 7 in the third section, and Slides 8, 9, and 10 in the fourth section. (*Hint*: Click Slide 1 in the Slides tab, and then click the Section command in the Slides group. Then click the first slide in the next section, and repeat.)

✦ EXPLORE   13. Name the first section **Introduction**, name the second section **Management**, name the third section **Monitoring**, and name the fourth section **Programs**. (*Hint*: Right-click the Untitled Section bar, and then click Rename Section.)

14. Run the slide show, making sure you test all the hyperlinks.

15. Check the presentation for features not supported by earlier versions of PowerPoint. Make a note of these features.

16. Export the outline to an RTF file named **WMC Outline New**. Start Word, and then open the file you created. Reformat the text so that it is 10-point, black Calibri. Go to the end of the document, and then add text describing the features of the presentation that are not supported in earlier versions of PowerPoint. Save your changes, and then exit Word.

17. Save your changes to the presentation, mark the presentation as final, and then save it as a PDF file named **WMC Services PDF** in the PowerPoint4\Case2 folder. Use the Standard optimization, and do not change any of the default options.

18. Submit the completed presentation and PDF file in printed or electronic form, as requested by your instructor, and then close all open files.

Create a presentation for a company that sells emergency preparedness products.

CREATE

Case Problem 3

Data Files needed for this Case Problem: 72HrKit.jpg, EPR.pptx, EPRChart.xlsx, EPROutline.docx, Flood.jpg, Phone Table.docx, Wheat.jpg

Emergency Preparedness Resources   Emergency Preparedness Resources (EPR) is a growing business in West Wendover, Nevada. The owner and president of EPR, Parker Salvatore, gives presentations on his company's products at emergency preparedness seminars, conferences, and trade shows. Parker asks you to set up a PowerPoint presentation on his company's products. Create the finished presentation, as shown in Figure 4-50, and then create a Web page of the presentation. Read all the steps before you start creating your presentation.

1. The presentation is created from the **EPR** presentation, located in the PowerPoint4\Case3 folder included with your Data Files. Change the name "Parker Salvatore" on Slide 1 to your name, and save it as **EPR Products**.

2. The text for the subsequent slides in the presentation comes from the Word outline file **EPROutline**, located in the PowerPoint4\Case3 folder. Don't forget to apply slide layouts and reset the slides. Make sure the current date, footer, and slide number appear on all the slides.

3. Images that appear in Slides 2 through 4 are **Flood**, **72HrKit**, and **Wheat**, respectively, located in the PowerPoint4\Case3 folder. Remove the background from the Wheat photo on Slide 4.

4. In Slide 5, because the double-columned bulleted list appears as a single list when you first import the outline, change the slide layout to Two Content and use a cut-and-paste operation to move the last seven bulleted items to the second content placeholder.

5. The table of contact numbers on Slide 7 comes from the file **Phone Table**, located in the PowerPoint4\Case3 folder. Format the table by applying the Colorful List – Accent 2 table style.

6. The linked pie chart in Slide 8 comes from the Excel file **EPRChart**, located in the PowerPoint4\Case3 folder.

7. The Action Button: Home buttons shown in the upper-right corner of Slide 2 through 9 are hyperlinked to Slide 1 and are formatted with a shape style. (*Hint*: Insert and format the action button on Slide 2, and then copy it to the other slides.)

8. Apply the Dynamic Content Orbit transition to all the slides except Slides 1 and 2.

9. Add a comment to Slide 8 suggesting that the slide might not be appropriate for this presentation. Position the comment above the slide title.

10. Save your changes, and then save the presentation as a picture presentation named **EPR Pictures** to the PowerPoint4\Case3 folder.

11. Post the presentation to a new folder on your SkyDrive named EPR, granting permission to a friend or colleague to view and edit the files in the folder.

12. Submit the completed presentations in printed or electronic form, as requested by your instructor, and then close the file.

| Figure 4-50 | **Final EPR Products presentation** |

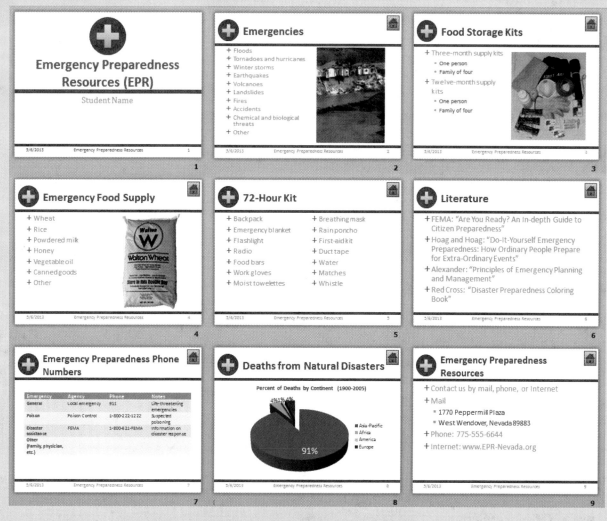

Apply your skills to create a presentation about wetlands.

CREATE

Case Problem 4

Data Files needed for this Case Problem: Wetland1.jpg, Wetland2.jpg, Wetland3.jpg, Wetland4.jpg, Wetland5.jpg

Campus Conservation Consortium   The Campus Conservation Consortium (CCC) is an organization of college students that gives presentations to other students on conserving America's wetlands. Prepare a presentation to your classmates on information about wetlands. You might choose a topic such as grants and scholarships on wetland conservation, analysis and information about wetlands in a particular state, legislation on wetland conservation, description of wetland types (saltwater habitats, freshwater habitats, and upland habitat), use of wetlands by migratory birds or other animals, information about an organization involved in wetland conservation, conservation plans for private owners of wetlands, or other related topics. Complete the following steps:

⊕ **EXPLORE**

1. Using Microsoft Word, create an outline of your presentation on wetland conservation. Include at least six titles, which will become slide titles. (Remember to switch to Outline view in Word to type your slide titles, which will be formatted with the Heading 1 style.) Under each title, add information (content) items (formatted in the Heading 2 style), which will become the bulleted lists on each slide. Use books and magazines from your college library, encyclopedia, the Internet, or other sources of information to get the necessary information on wetland conservation. If you haven't covered Microsoft Word in your courses and don't know how to create an outline with heading styles, use the Help feature in Word.

2. Save the Word file using the filename **Wetlands Outline** to the PowerPoint4\Case4 folder included with your Data Files.

3. In another Word document, create a table. Your table might list various wetland preserves, their total area, examples of major wildlife in the area, or other information. You might be able to find a table on the Internet from which you can extract the data.

4. Save the Word file with the table using the filename **Wetlands Table** to the PowerPoint4\Case4 folder.

5. Open a new, blank presentation, and enter an appropriate title of your choosing and a subtitle with your name as the presenter. Save the presentation as **Wetlands** in the PowerPoint4\Case4 folder.

6. Import the Word outline into PowerPoint.

7. Apply the built-in theme Flow.

8. Apply appropriate slide layouts to the new slides, and reset the slides, as needed, so they have the proper format.

9. Embed your table into one of the slides in your presentation. Resize, reposition, and reformat it as needed to maximize its readability.

10. Include a text box either on the first slide or the last slide acknowledging the sources of your information.

11. Insert at least one action button into your presentation with a link to another slide within your presentation.

12. Include at least two text hyperlinks in your presentation, with links to other slides. The text of the hyperlinks can be bulleted items, text in a table cell, or text boxes.

13. Add graphics to the slide show, as desired. If you want, you can use any of the pictures **Wetland1** through **Wetland5** located in the PowerPoint4\Case4 folder.

14. Apply a Dynamic Content transition to all the slides except Slides 1 and 2.

15. Save your changes, and then save the presentation as a picture presentation named **Wetlands Picture** to the PowerPoint4\Case4 folder.

16. Submit the completed presentations in printed or electronic form, as requested by your instructor, and then close the file.

SAM: Skills Assessment Manager

ASSESS

For current SAM information, including versions and content details, visit SAM Central (http://samcentral.course.com). If you have a SAM user profile, you may have access to hands-on instruction, practice, and assessment of the skills covered in this tutorial. Since various versions of SAM are supported throughout the life of this text, check with your instructor for the correct instructions and URL/Web site for accessing assignments.

ENDING DATA FILES

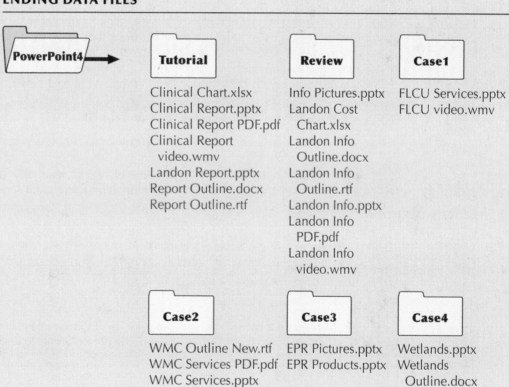

PowerPoint4 →

Tutorial
Clinical Chart.xlsx
Clinical Report.pptx
Clinical Report PDF.pdf
Clinical Report
  video.wmv
Landon Report.pptx
Report Outline.docx
Report Outline.rtf

Review
Info Pictures.pptx
Landon Cost
  Chart.xlsx
Landon Info
  Outline.docx
Landon Info
  Outline.rtf
Landon Info.pptx
Landon Info
  PDF.pdf
Landon Info
  video.wmv

Case1
FLCU Services.pptx
FLCU video.wmv

Case2
WMC Outline New.rtf
WMC Services PDF.pdf
WMC Services.pptx

Case3
EPR Pictures.pptx
EPR Products.pptx

Case4
Wetlands.pptx
Wetlands
  Outline.docx
Wetlands
  Picture.pptx
Wetlands Table.docx

Teamwork

What Is a Team?

The American Heritage Dictionary describes a team as a "group organized to work together." More than just people thrown together, teams consist of individuals who have skills, talents, and abilities that complement each other and, when joined, produce synergy—results greater than those a single individual could achieve. It is this sense of shared mission and responsibility for results that makes a team successful in its efforts to reach organizational goals.

Characteristics of Teams

Have you ever heard someone described as a "team player"? Members on a team get to know how the others work, so they can make contributions where they'll count most. On a football team, not everyone plays the role of quarterback; the team needs other positions working with the quarterback if touchdowns are to be scored. However, before the first play is ever made, the members bring their skills to the team and spend time learning each others' moves so they can catch the pass, block, or run toward the goal line together. Similarly, in a professional environment, the best teams have members whose background, skills, and abilities complement each other.

Managing Workflow on a Team

When team members collaborate on a project, someone needs to manage the workflow. This is especially important if team members are all contributing to a shared file stored on a server or a shared folder on the Internet. Some businesses have the capability to allow team members to co-author a presentation stored on a server. If this capability is not available, however, the team will need to create a strategy for managing the file to make sure that one person's changes do not get overwritten.

One way to manage workflow is to create an ordered list of team members assigned to work on a presentation file, and have team members access and edit the file only after the person preceding them on the list is finished with it. Another way is to allow anyone to access the presentation, but to have each team member save their version of the presentation with a different name—for example, they can add their initials to the end of the filename—and then each person can make their version available for the team member who has been designated to compare all the presentations to create one final version.

Create a Collaborative Presentation

Many people volunteer for a program that requires them to work collaboratively. For example, you might be a coach of a youth sports program, a Boy Scout leader, or a member of a local historical society. Often, volunteer groups require their members to meet occasionally to share ideas and information. PowerPoint is a useful tool for collecting notes, data, and images that you can then show everyone all at once. One way to do this could be to create a presentation for the group, post it to a shared folder on the World Wide Web, such as a Windows Live SkyDrive folder, and each person in the group can add slides containing the information they want to share. Additionally, other group members can add comments to slides if something is unclear or if they have a question. In this exercise, you'll use PowerPoint to create a presentation for an upcoming meeting for a group of which you are a member, using the skills and features presented in Tutorials 3 and 4.

Note: Please be sure *not* to include any personal information of a sensitive nature in the documents you create to be submitted to your instructor for this exercise. Later on, you can update the documents with such information for your own personal use.

1. Start a new, blank PowerPoint presentation, and apply a theme appropriate for the group. It is probably best to apply a theme that does not have a busy background design.
2. Modify the theme colors to match the colors used by your group or association. Add the group's logo or a photo appropriate to the group to the slide master. Consider modifying the background style and using picture bullets for the bulleted lists to add interest. Save the file as an Office Theme so that you can use it for future presentations.
3. Start a new presentation using the theme that you created. Save it with an appropriate name.
4. On Slide 1, type an informative title for your presentation, and add the name of the group as a subtitle.
5. Create a slide that lists the group members who will contribute to the presentation. As group members add to the presentation, they can add their names to the list on this slide.
6. Create at least six slides for the presentation. Consider the purpose of the group as well as the purpose of the upcoming meeting. If you know others have information to share, add slides with titles to help guide them.
7. Add video clips from past group events and recorded sounds to your presentation if you have any.
8. Add interesting slide transitions and custom animations to your presentation. Customize the start timing and the speed of the animations. If appropriate, add a second animation to items.
9. If you have any data to share, consider adding a table or chart that you create in PowerPoint, or consider embedding a Word table or linking to a chart that already exists in an Excel workbook.
10. Decide how you want to manage the workflow, and communicate this process to the group.

ProSkills

11. Save the presentation to your Windows Live SkyDrive folder, and give group members permission to view the file. Send them the link, and ask them to download the file to their own computers. (*Hint*: To do this, point to the file, and then click the Download link.)

12. After group members have made their modifications and added comments to the presentation, compare the presentations or review the single presentation that members took turns modifying. Accept any changes you wish to accept, and decide whether to delete comments.

13. Consider saving the presentation as a picture presentation, a video, or a PDF file if that will make it easier for the entire group to access. Save this file to the group folder on your SkyDrive account.

14. Submit the completed presentation in printed or electronic form, as requested by your instructor, and then close the file.

GLOSSARY/INDEX

TASK REFERENCE

TASK	PAGE #	RECOMMENDED METHOD
Action button, add	PPT 218	*See* Reference box: Adding an Action Button as a Link to Another Presentation
Animation, add a second one to an object	PPT 151	Click Animations tab, click Add Animation button in Advanced Animation group, click desired animation
Animation, change direction or sequence	PPT 100–101	Click animated object, click Effect Options in Animation group on Animations tab, click direction or sequence option
Animation, change speed of	PPT 152	Click Animations tab, click in Duration box in Timing group, type new time for animation, press Enter
Animation, modify start timing	PPT 38	*See* Reference box, Modifying the Start Timing of the Animation of Subbullets
Background, add a texture to	PPT 168	*See* Reference box: Applying a Textured Background
Background, add picture to	PPT 164	*See* Reference box: Adding a Picture to a Background
Bullet, change to picture bullet	PPT 169	Click Home tab, click Bullets button arrow in Paragraph group, click Bullets and Numbering, click Picture, click desired picture, click OK
Bulleted item, demote	PPT 22	Click bullet symbol, press Tab
Bulleted item, move	PPT 24	Click bullet symbol, drag to new location
Bulleted item, promote	PPT 23	Click bullet symbol, press Shift+Tab
Chart, create on a slide	PPT 144	*See* Reference box: Creating a Chart
Clip art, insert	PPT 69	*See* Reference box: Inserting Clip Art on a Slide
Comment, insert on a slide	PPT 228	Click Review tab, click New Comment button in Comments group, type comment in balloon
Date, insert on slides	PPT 43	In Text group on Insert tab, click Header & Footer, click Date and time check box, click desired option button, click Apply to All
Excel chart, link to a slide using copy and paste	PPT 209	*See* Reference box: Linking an Excel Chart to a Slide Using Copy and Paste
File shared on SkyDrive, send link	PPT 250	In SkyDrive in browser, display folder page, click Share, click Send a link, click folder name, click Share, click Send a link, type email addresses in To box, type message, click Send
Folder, create on SkyDrive and grant permission for access	PPT 246	*See* Reference box: Creating a New Folder on SkyDrive and Granting Permission for Access
Footer, insert on slides	PPT 43	In Text group on Insert tab, click Header & Footer, click Footer check box, type footer text, click Apply to All
Graphic, move or resize	PPT 71	Click graphic, drag to new position or drag sizing handle to resize
Handout Master, customize	PPT 225	Click View tab, click Handout Master in Master Views group, customize master, click Close Master View button in Close group
Hyperlink, create to another slide	PPT 212	*See* Reference box: Creating a Hyperlink to Another Slide in a Presentation
Layout, switch	PPT 9	In Slides group on Home tab, click Layout button, click layout
Notes, create	PPT 44	Click in Notes pane, type
Objects, align	PPT 72	Click object, press and hold Shift, click second object, click Align in Arrange group on Picture Tools or Drawing Tools Format tab, click align option
Object, animate	PPT 100	Click text box, click animation in Animation group on Animations tab

TASK	PAGE #	RECOMMENDED METHOD
Object, flip or rotate	PPT 81	Click object, click Rotate in Arrange group on Drawing Tools or Picture Tools, Format tab, click command; or drag rotate handle
Outline, export to Word	PPT 197	Click File tab, click Save As, click Save as type arrow, click Outline/RTF, type filename, click Save
Outline, import from Word	PPT 194	Click Home tab, click New Slide button arrow in Slides group, click Slides from Outline, click outline file, click Insert
Photograph, remove background from	PPT 200	*See* Reference box: Removing the Background of a Photograph
Picture, adjust color	PPT 73	Click picture, click Color in Adjust group on Picture Tools Format tab, click desired option
Picture, change effect	PPT 74	Click picture, click Picture Effects button in Picture Styles group on Picture Tools Format tab, point to desired effect, click desired option
Picture, crop to a shape	PPT 74	Click picture, click Crop button arrow in Size group on Picture Tools Format tab, point to Crop to Shape, click shape
Picture, insert	PPT 67	In content placeholder, click ▨ or click Picture button in Images group on Insert tab
PowerPoint, start	PPT 4	Click 🔵, point to All Programs, click Microsoft Office, click Microsoft PowerPoint 2010
Presentation, broadcast	PPT 105	*See* Reference box: Broadcasting a Presentation
Presentation, create from existing	PPT 34	*See* Reference box: Creating a New Presentation from an Existing Presentation
Presentation, open	PPT 14	Click the File tab, click Open, navigate to folder, click Open
Presentation, print	PPT 50	Click File tab, click Print, select options, click Print
Presentation, save to SkyDrive	PPT 250	*See* Reference box: Saving a File to a Folder on SkyDrive
Presentations, compare	PPT 230	Click Review tab, click Compare button in Compare group, click presentation to compare to, click Merge, click check boxes to accept changes, click End Review button in Compare group, click Yes
Shape, add text to	PPT 79	Click shape, type
Shape, change border color	PPT 65	Click graphic, click Shape Outline button arrow in Shape Styles group on Drawing Tools Format tab, click color in palette
Shape, change fill color	PPT 78	Click graphic, click Shape Fill button in Shape Styles group on Drawing Tools Format tab, click color in palette
Shape, insert	PPT 76	Click Shapes button in Illustrations group on Insert tab, click desired shape, click or drag pointer in slide to create shape
Slide, add new	PPT 7–8	In Slides group on Home tab, click New Slide button arrow, click desired layout
Slide, delete	PPT 27	*See* Reference box: Deleting Slides
Slide, duplicate	PPT 9	Right-click thumbnail in Slides tab, click Duplicate Slide
Slide master view, switch to	PPT 86	Click Slide Master in Master Views group on View tab
Slide numbers, insert on slides	PPT 43	In Text group on Insert tab, click Header & Footer, click Slide number check box, click Apply to All
Slide show, advance	PPT 29	Click mouse button or press Enter or spacebar
Slide show, run from Slide 1	PPT 28	In Start Slide Show group on the Slide Show tab, click From Beginning
Slide show, run from current slide	PPT 28	On status bar, click 🖵

TASK	PAGE #	RECOMMENDED METHOD
Slide sorter view, switch to	PPT 49	On status bar, click ⊞
Slides, insert from another presentation	PPT 125	*See* Reference box: Inserting Slides from Another Presentation
Slides, mark during slide show	PPT 226	Start slide show, right-click, point to Pointer Options, click Pen, write on slide
Slides, reset	PPT 161	Click Home tab, click Reset button in Slides group
SmartArt, add a shape to	PPT 98	*See* Reference box: Adding a Shape to a SmartArt Diagram
SmartArt, animate	PPT 100	Click SmartArt, click animation, in Animation group on Animations tab
SmartArt, create from bulleted list	PPT 96	*See* Reference box: Converting a Bulleted List into a SmartArt Diagram
SmartArt, delete a shape from	PPT 98	Click shape border in SmartArt diagram, press Delete
SmartArt, insert	PPT 93	*See* Reference box: Creating a SmartArt Diagram
Sound clip, insert	PPT 134	*See* Reference box: Inserting a Sound into a Presentation
Spelling, check entire presentation	PPT 47	In Proofing group on Review tab, click Spelling
Table, align text in cells	PPT 142	Click Table Tools Layout tab, click an alignment button in Alignment group
Table, insert on slide	PPT 138	*See* Reference box: Inserting a Table
Table, merge cells	PPT 141	Click Table Tools Layout tab, select cells to merge, click Merge Cells button in Merge group
Table, resize column	PPT 142	Drag column divider line, or double-click column divider line to autofit contents
Text, copy	PPT 18	Select text, click Copy button in Clipboard group on Home tab
Text, cut	PPT 18	Select text, click Cut button in Clipboard group on Home tab
Text, paste	PPT 18	Position insertion point, click Paste button in Clipboard group on Home tab, click Paste Options button, click desired option
Text box, add	PPT 79	Click Text Box in Text group on Insert tab, click slide
Text placeholder, delete	PPT 89	Click text placeholder, click border of placeholder, press Delete
Text placeholder, reposition	PPT 89	Click text placeholder, drag placeholder
Theme, change	PPT 12	In Themes group on Design tab, click desired theme
Theme, create custom	PPT 173	*See* Reference box: Saving a Custom Theme
Theme colors, change	PPT 159	Click Design tab, click Colors button in Themes group, click desired color set
Transitions, add	PPT 40	*See* Reference box: Adding Transitions
Video, adjust volume	PPT 130	Click Video Tools Playback tab, click Volume button in Video Options group, click desired volume
Video, insert in a presentation	PPT 127	*See* Reference box: Inserting a Video into a Presentation
Video, set poster frame	PPT 131	Play video to desired frame, click Video Tools Format tab, click Poster Frame button in Adjust group, click Current Frame
Video, set to play automatically	PPT 129	Click Video Tools Playback tab, click Start arrow in Video Options group, click Automatically
Video, trim	PPT 130	Click Video Tools Playback tab, click Trim Video button in Editing group, drag Start and End sliders, click OK
Word table, embed using Object command	PPT 204	*See* Reference box: Embedding a Word Table in a Slide Using the Object Command